CONCERTOS AND
CHORAL WORKS

Essays in Musical Analysis

CONCERTOS AND CHORAL WORKS

DONALD FRANCIS TOVEY

Oxford   New York
OXFORD UNIVERSITY PRESS
1989

Oxford University Press, Walton Street, Oxford OX2 6DP

Oxford New York Toronto
Delhi Bombay Calcutta Madras Karachi
Petaling Jaya Singapore Hong Kong Tokyo
Nairobi Dar es Salaam Cape Town
Melbourne Auckland

and associated companies in
Berlin Ibadan

Oxford is a trade mark of Oxford University Press

© Donald Francis Tovey

First published 1935–9
This edition first issued as an Oxford University Press paperback 1981
Reprinted, with an index, 1989 (twice)

Library of Congress Cataloging in Publication data

Tovey, Donald Francis, Sir, 1875–1940.
Essays in musical analysis / Donald Francis Tovey.
p. cm.
"Great majority of the essays in the original edition—have been
printed complete, unedited and unabridged, in two volumes"—
Publisher's note.   Includes index.
Contents:—[2] Concertos and choral works.
I. Musical analysis.   I. Title.
MT90.T6 1989b 780'.1'5—dc19 88-225584
ISBN 0-19-315149-9 (pbk. :v. 2)

Printed and bound in Great Britain by
J. W. Arrowsmith Ltd., Bristol

CONTENTS

Concertos

The classical tradition   3

J. S. BACH

Concerto in D minor for clavier   27
Concerto in D minor for two violins   32
Concerto in C minor for violin and oboe   35
Brandenburg concerto in G major, No. 3   37
Brandenburg concerto in G major, No. 4   40
Concerto in A major for oboe d'amore   43
Concerto in A minor for clavier, flute, and violin   45

BEETHOVEN

Pianoforte concerto No. 1 in C major, Op. 15, with
   Beethoven's cadenza   47
Pianoforte concerto No. 3 in C minor, Op. 37   52
Pianoforte concerto No. 4 in G major, Op. 58   58
Pianoforte concerto No. 5 in E flat, Op. 73   67
Violin concerto in D major, Op. 61   70
Triple concerto for pianoforte, violin, and violoncello, Op. 56   79

BRAHMS

Pianoforte concerto No. 1 in D minor, Op. 15   86
Pianoforte concerto No. 2 in B flat major, Op. 83   92
Violin concerto in D major, Op. 77   98
Concerto for violin and violoncello, Op. 102   111

BRUCH

Violin concerto in G minor, Op. 26   120

CHOPIN

Pianoforte concerto in F minor, Op. 21   123

DELIUS

Violin Concerto   127

DOHNANYI
Variations on a nursery song for orchestra with pianoforte,
Op. 23   130

DVOŘÁK
Violoncello concerto in B minor, Op. 104   133

ELGAR
Violin concerto in B minor, Op. 61   137
Violoncello concerto in E minor, Op. 85   143

FRANCK
Variations Symphoniques for pianoforte with orchestra   146

HANDEL
Organ concerto No. 7, Op. 7, No. 1   150

HAYDN
Violoncello concerto in D major   152
    Addendum   153

GUSTAV HOLST
A fugal concerto, Op. 40, No. 2   154

MENDELSSOHN
Violin concerto in E minor, Op. 64   156

MOZART
Pianoforte concerto in A major (K. 414)   160
Pianoforte concerto in B flat major (K. 450)   163
Pianoforte concerto in G major (K. 453)   166
Pianoforte concerto in A major (K. 488)   170
Pianoforte concerto in C minor (K. 491)   175
Flute concerto in G major (K. 313)   180
Flute concerto in D major (K. 314)   181
Andante for flute with orchestra (K. 315)   184
Clarinet concerto in A major (K. 622)   185
Violin concerto in D major (K. 218)   187
Violin concerto in A major (K. 219)   189
Adagio in E for violin with orchestra (K. 261)   192
Concerto for flute and harp (K. 299)   193

SAINT-SAËNS
Violoncello concerto No. 1 in A minor, Op. 33   195

SCHUMANN
Pianoforte concerto in A minor, Op. 54   198
Violoncello concerto in A minor, Op. 129   200
Introduction and allegro appassionato for pianoforte with
   orchestra, Op. 92   204

SIBELIUS
Violin concerto, Op. 47   206

VAUGHAN WILLIAMS
Concerto Accademico in D minor for violin   211

WALTON
Viola concerto in A minor   214

WEBER
Conzertstück in F minor for pianoforte with orchestra, Op. 79 221

Choral Works

J. S. BACH
Mass in B minor   227
Magnificat   257

BEETHOVEN
Choral fantasia, Op. 80   267
Missa Solemnis, Op. 123   270

BRAHMS
Requiem, Op. 45   294
Rhapsodie for alto voice, male chorus, and orchestra, Op. 53 308
Song of Destiny (Schicksalslied), Op. 54   310

DEBUSSY
The Blessed Damozel (La Damoiselle élue)   312

HANDEL
Israel in Egypt 317

HAYDN
The Creation 349
The Seasons 381

GUSTAV HOLST
The Hymn of Jesus, Op. 37 396

PARRY
At a Solemn Music (Blest pair of sirens) 403

VERDI
Requiem in memory of Manzoni 406
Stabat Mater 420

Index 423

PUBLISHER'S NOTE

Tovey's *Essays in Musical Analysis* were originally published in six volumes: I Symphonies (1); II Symphonies (2), Variations, and Orchestral Polyphony; III Concertos; IV Illustrative Music; V Vocal Music; VI Supplementary Essays, Glossary, and Index. (An additional volume was later published devoted to chamber music.) This has always made it difficult to refer quickly to particular essays. Beethoven's orchestral works are scattered through three volumes, as are Elgar's (not the same three), and essays are arranged within a volume mainly, but not entirely, in order of the composers' birth.

The original edition included a certain number of works whose reputation has not lasted. It also contained some essays on solo or chamber works which should strictly have appeared in a separate volume, as well as some concert extracts from operas of a type which are not found in programmes today.

In this new edition all works have been grouped into only three categories: orchestral music, concertos, and choral works. Within each category composers are arranged in alphabetical order and all their works gathered together. The works referred to in the second paragraph have been omitted (a list is appended below). The rest—the great majority of the essays in the original edition—have been printed complete, unedited and unabridged, in two Oxford paperback volumes, one entitled *Symphonies and Other Orchestral Works* and the other *Concertos and Choral Works*. *Chamber Music* is also available as an Oxford paperback.

Essays Omitted from the New Edition

Bach: Cantatas, 'Hold in Affection', 'Vergnügte Ruh', 'Now is the Grace'
Linear harmony
Motet, 'Jesu, priceless Treasure'

Bantock: 'Dante and Beatrice' 'Sappho'

Beethoven: Dungeon scene from 'Fidelio'

Grosse Fuge
'Becalmed sea and prosperous voyage' (Op. 112)
15 variations and fugue, 'Prometheus' (Op. 35)
Précis of the 9th symphony

Berlioz: Scène d'amour from 'Roméo et Juliette'

Brian: Fantastic variations

Busch: Capriccio

Dittersdorf: 'The fall of Phaëton'

Dvořák: Slavonic rhapsodies in D and A flat

Glazunov: Piano concerto

Gluck: Overture to 'Iphigénie en Aulide' leading to 'Orpheus' Act II

Hindemith: Chamber Music No. 1

Joachim: Hungarian concerto
Marfa's soliloquy
Overture to a comedy by Gozzi
Variations for violin with orchestra

McEwen: 'Grey Galloway'

Méhul: Overture 'Le jeune sage et le vieux fou'

Mozart: Piano sonata for four hands
'Martern aller Artern' from 'Die Entführung aus dem Serail'
'Non più di fiori' from 'La clemenza di Tito'

Palestrina: Three motets

Parry: Symphonic Variations
Overture to an unwritten tragedy

Reger: Four tone-poems after Böcklin
Serenade in G for orchestra

Rimsky-Korsakov: 'Conte féerique'

Röntgen: Symphony in F minor

Triple concerto
Old Netherlands suite

Saint-Saëns: 4th piano concerto
Symphonic poem 'Phaëton'

Schubert: Grand duo orchestrated by Joachim
Overture 'Die Weiberverschwörung'
Polonaise in F major
Overture 'The faithful sentinel'
'Wanderer' fantasia arranged for piano and orchestra by Liszt
'Erlkönig'

Schumann: 'Carnaval'

Schmidt: Variations on a theme of Beethoven

Smyth: Mass in D

Somervell: 'Normandy', symphonic variations for piano with orchestra

Spohr: 'Scena cantante'

Stanford: Clarinet concerto

Strauss: Parergon to the 'Sinfonia Domestica'

Verdi: Scena from 'Otello'

Voormolen: Overture, 'Baron Hop'

Wagner: 'Parsifal', Act III
Kaisermarsch

Wagner in the concert room

Walker: Fantasia-variations on a Norfolk folk-song

Weelkes: Four madrigals

Wilbye: Motet, 'O God, the rock of my whole strength'

Zador: Rondo for orchestra

CONCERTOS

THE CLASSICAL CONCERTO
(1903)

INTRODUCTION

Without a sound appreciation of those peculiarities of form which distinguish the classical concerto from the classical symphony the concerto can only be very imperfectly understood, whether by performers or by listeners; for the rational enthusiasm for great classics is the outcome not only of natural taste, but also of long familiarity with all that is purest in art; and so far as the opportunity for such familiarity is wanting, so far will current ideas and current criticism be vague, Philistine, and untrue. Now the number of great works in the true concerto form is surprisingly small; far smaller than the number of true symphonies. And of this small collection a good two-thirds has been contributed by Mozart, whose work has for the last fifty years been treated with neglect and lack of intelligent observation, for which we at the present time are paying dearly with a notable loss both of ear for fine detail and of grasp of musical works as definite wholes.[1] On the other hand, every virtuoso whose imagination is fired with the splendid spectacular effect of a full orchestra as a background for a display of instrumental technique has written concertos that express little else than that effect. Thus the name of concerto is assumed by literally hundreds of works that have not even an academic connexion with the classical idea of concerto form and style; while of the very small collection of true concertos the majority, those of Mozart, are ignored, and the remainder not nearly so well understood as any classical symphony. No composer attempts a symphony without a strong sense of responsibility, and some appreciation of the greatness of the classics of symphonic art, and so neither the number of spurious symphonies nor their tendency is such as to set an entirely false standard of criticism for the art. But that current criteria of the concerto are false, no one who seriously studies that form can doubt. The idea that the professed purpose of the form is technical display has been actually maintained by musicians who yield to none in their reverence and love for the great concertos of Beethoven and Mozart. Yet that idea is in flat violation of almost every fact in the early history of the form; and those who hold it seem to let it

[1] I do not know how many people in 1903 foresaw the vindication of Mozart, of which on the Continent the main impulse was given by Richard Strauss, and which dates in England from the memorable performance of the *Zauberflöte* at Cambridge some eight years after this essay appeared. That performance marked the first stages of Professor E. J. Dent's work upon Mozart's operas.

remain comfortably in their minds side by side with the opposite, and scarcely less untrue notion, that in the works of Bach and his contemporaries the solo part of a concerto is no more than *primus inter pares*. The first idea springs from the assumption (difficult to avoid, where bad works so overcrowd good ones) that art-forms are invented by bad artists to be disgustedly improved off the face of the earth by the great men; and the second springs from the difficulty of recognizing in ancient art anything that does not happen to take much the same shape in modern art.

The only way to avoid these pitfalls is to seek out the typical artistic idea that is to be found in the concertos of the greatest composers. To avoid repeating what I have written elsewhere, I propose to follow out this train of thought in an historical, or at all events chronological, sketch, instead of applying it merely to any particular concerto. Opinions differ so much as to the way in which musical history should be written that I hesitate to call this sketch historical. Its object is to trace the successive forms in which what I shall call the concerto-idea has been realized. Those forms in which it has been falsified by vanity, or obscured by imperfect skill or vague thought, will not come under discussion at all, though to many historians that which is transitional and immature is often more interesting, and always more easy to discuss than that which is permanent and self-consistent.

To avoid a frequent source of misunderstanding, I must point out that neither here nor in any other of my analytical essays is the basis of analysis technical. It is frequently urged as an objection to all musical analysis that to investigate 'how it is done' distracts the mind from the poetic enjoyment of a work of art. So it does; you cannot, for instance, enjoy the first movement of Beethoven's Eroica Symphony if you insist on thinking the while of Beethoven's seven or eight different sketches of its exposition. They are among the most wonderful documents recording the profound workings of a creative mind; but the only way in which they can help you to enjoy the symphony is by directing your attention to what it is. Follow up the sketches, then, as they approach the final version from something now more monotonous, now more violent, now smaller, now dangerously large, always changing with the surprising purpose and power of a creator who ruthlessly rejects all that will not remain as an inspiring force for all time, when what common admirers of genius call 'the inspiration of the moment' has gone the way of dreams and moods. Follow this up until it leads you to the ideal, the realized Eroica Symphony; and you will no longer think that there is anything prosaic in investigating 'how it was done'. But you will see this only if, as you listen to the symphony, you forget the sketches utterly, as Beethoven himself forgot them. They have helped you, not because they showed you 'how it was done', but because they drew your attention to *what* was done; and on that, and that alone, your attention must remain fixed, or the whole object of all that loving and laborious sketching is lost.

Musical analysis then is concerned with *what* is done. Unless the composer has left sketches, any attempt to speak of '*how* it is done' is downright charlatanry, a pretence of solving a problem that is beyond the human intellect. Beethoven himself must have found his old sketch-books a series of perpetual surprises if he ever looked at them a year or two after finishing a work.

An analysis that gives a faithful account of what is done in a work of art cannot but be a help, so long as it is not one-sided and is used in a practical way. Hence in my early essays I have aimed at quoting or at least mentioning every theme in the works analysed, so that the material may lie conveniently before the eye. On the other hand, I have from the outset abandoned any attempt to confine the letterpress to what can be read in the concert-room. Quotations in musical type can be seen while they are heard; but the kind of prose explanation that can be read while the music is going on is as useless in the concert-room as it is at home.

Lastly, as this is an essay on a musical subject I have tried to treat it from a musical point of view. This again is not a limitation to technical matters; music is music, and does not become technical as soon as it is not discussed as if it were a nondescript mixture of intellect and emotion and poetry. As a plain musician I believe music to be music; poetry, a form of literature; painting, one of the plastic arts; and *all* to be poetry. But when I discuss music I shall speak of things musical, as beautiful harmony, breadth, firmness and depth of modulation, nobility of form, variety and contrast of tone, clear and well-motived contrast and harmonious fullness in those simultaneous combinations of melodies which we call counterpoint, for it is these things and others equally musical that make a concerto or a symphony what it is. And if it is objected that these things, as they occur in classical music, are non-poetical, or mere technical means of expressing some poetic idea that lies behind them, I can only reply that, so long as music remains music, this poetic idea will only be attainable through these musical phenomena. Certainly a criticism or an admiration that scorns the musical phenomena does not thereby become poetical; on the contrary, the man who expects music to give him poetical ideas while he refuses to listen to it as music, will infallibly, if he looks at other things as he looks at music, value poetry for the information it conveys when paraphrased in prose, architecture for the problems it solves in engineering, science for its practical use, and in short, everything for its lower and more accidental qualities, and this is the very type and essence of the prosaic mind.

To sum up : I believe the classical concerto to be a highly dramatic and poetic art-form, having nothing in common with the popular and pseudo-academic idea of the form except a few misleading superficial resemblances. I therefore propose to illustrate the poetic and dramatic expression of this form by an analysis that has nothing to do with technique, though it will use any good technical term that may substitute a word for a paragraph; nor anything to do with *a priori* theories of absolute music which will apply equally well to absolute nonsense, though it declines to talk of poetry when its business is to describe musical facts. I merely attempt to describe what may be *observed* by any one really fond of music, who takes pains to study the works of great composers in a spirit that endeavours to understand the ways of minds other than one's own.

THE CONCERTO PRINCIPLE

The primary fact that distinguishes all works that have in them the character of the concerto style, is that their form is adapted to make the best effect expressible by opposed and unequal masses of instruments or voices. Whenever in classical or indeed in any really artistic music, you find that an art-form is to be expressed by a mass of instruments (under which head we may for present purposes include voices), and that this mass inevitably divides itself into two parts that cannot without some embarrassing limitation or *tour de force* be made to balance each other : then you will assuredly find that the form has been modified so as not merely to fit these conditions but to make them a special means of expression.

Hence arises at least half of the prejudice which many fairly experienced lovers of music, and nearly all inexperienced students of composition, feel against the concerto forms. When our experience is no more than enough to give us a keen pleasure in following the normal outlines of an art-form, and in seeing how they give reality and inevitableness to the contrasts and crises of the music, then we are prone to resent any influence that modifies the form, and we do not stop to see whether the new form may not be as grand as the old.

That the conditions of concerto form are in themselves unnatural or inartistic can certainly not be maintained in face of the facts. Nothing in human life and history is much more thrilling or of more ancient and universal experience than the antithesis of the individual and the crowd; an antithesis which is familiar in every degree, from flat opposition to harmonious reconciliation, and with every contrast and blending of emotion, and which has been of no less universal prominence in works of art than in life. Now the concerto forms express this antithesis with all possible force and delicacy. If there are devotees of 'absolute music' who believe that this is the very reason why these forms are objectionable, as appealing to something outside music, we may first answer that, if this were so, then neither Brahms, Beethoven, Bach, Mozart, Haydn, nor any person of so much calibre as Clementi, ever was an 'absolute musician', or had anything to do with such a mysterious abstraction. And secondly we may reply that this dramatic or human element is *not* outside the music, but most obviously inherent in the instruments that play the concerto; and that, so far as such a feebly metaphysical term as 'absolute music' has a meaning, it can only mean 'music that owes its form, contrasts, and details solely to its own musical resources'. As long as musical instruments or voices exist, there will always be the obvious possibility of setting one instrument or voice against many; and the fact that this opposition exists also in human affairs is no reason why music should cease to be 'absolute' or self-supporting —unless we are likewise to reason that man ceases to be human in so far as his five senses are shared by lower animals.

We must now see how the classical composers, to whom music was music no matter how profoundly it reflected humanity, adapted their art-forms to this condition of the antithesis between one and many, or between greater and less. I hope to show that the distinctive mark of the classical work is that it delights in this opposition and makes it expressive, while the pseudo-classics and the easy-going, thoughtless innovators, though they continually try to use it, miss the point with a curious uniformity amid diversity of error, and find every special condition of a concerto embarrassing and uninteresting.

Let us take these conditions in their earliest and, in some ways, simplest form. It is no use going farther back than the aria of Alessandro Scarlatti, or, to keep to familiar examples, Handel, in whom the conditions are not appreciably more developed. The Handelian aria is a clear and mature, yet an early and simple art-form. It owes almost its whole vitality to the opposition and relation between the voice and the accompaniment. When Handel was at work it was already dying of conventionality. And on this point I must beg leave to digress.

Conventionality is generally understood to mean something vaguely to the following effect: that a device may occur a very large number of times, say five hundred, in as many different works of art, and yet be in every instance the right thing in the right place, and therefore good and not conventional; but that the moment it occurs a five-hundred-and-first time, it becomes conventional and bad for all future occasions; so that we are entirely at the mercy of custom and history in the matter, and must know whether we are listening to No. 500 or to No. 501 before we can tell if either is beautiful or conventional. Now, though this is the real basis of more than half the current uses of the term, no one will believe it to be true when it is put before them in this form. The real meaning of 'conventionality' is either an almost technical, quite blameless, and profoundly interesting aesthetic fact, more often met with where art aspires beyond the bounds of human expression than elsewhere; or else the meaning is that a device has been used unintelligently and without definite purpose. And it makes not an atom of difference whether this use is early or late: thus the device of the canon is, more often than not, vilely conventional in the late fifteenth and early sixteenth centuries, and extremely beautiful wherever it occurs in Schumann and Brahms. So long as a thing remains the right thing in the right place, custom has simply nothing to do with it. Custom may help us to understand what might otherwise be distressing in its remoteness from our humdrum ideas; and custom frequently is an unmitigated nuisance, making us feel towards classical works as an overgrown choir-boy whose voice is cracking must sometimes feel towards the forms of worship which have become too familiar to impress him—but custom never makes good criticism or in any way ministers to the enjoyment of art, so long as it is allowed to dictate to us.

This digression was necessary here, because all the concerto forms show an unusual number of constantly recurring features, and it is of great importance that we should never be misled into estimating these features as conventional merely because they are frequent. Indeed, the really conventional composer abolished them long ago. After using them in a hopelessly unintelligent way for some centuries, he naturally concluded that what he could not understand was of no use to any one, and so he avoided them in the very same conventional spirit in which he had at first used them. The original composer is nowhere more triumphantly unconventional than when he chooses an old device because he knows its meaning, and applies it rightly, in the teeth of all popular criticism and current notions as to originality and genius. Let us see how far Handel and Bach bear this out.

The arias of Scarlatti and Handel (and, of course, all opera and oratorio writers between archaic periods and Gluck) obviously depend on the antithesis between a voice and an instrumental accompaniment. This accompaniment is generally conceived as orchestral; and accordingly (though the orchestra is not often very formidable except in warlike scenes where trumpets and drums are treated vigorously), there is almost always the contrast between

the single voice and the chorus of instruments. In fact, wherever
Handel is not either employing some special instrumental effect,
itself of a solo character, or else writing merely for voice and figured
bass, his usual direction for the top part of the accompaniment
is 'tutti unisoni'. But in any case the relation between voices
and instruments is such that, as Gevaert teaches in his works on
instrumentation, as soon as the living utterance of the voice strikes
upon the ear, the orchestra falls into the background. This natural
phenomenon is too powerful to be obscured by any perversions
of modern taste. The callous and stupid use of it ought to have
no influence on us. It has no influence on great artists, though
they often shock contemporary critics, who have no better criterion
of vulgarity than that it is what vulgar people do. As long as we
know too much of what vulgar people do, we shall be worried and
misled by the fact that, among other things, they ape their betters.
Let us study their betters.

In great music, then, we may expect that such a contrast as that
between a voice and an orchestra will always have its original value,
and will be more, instead of less, impressive as the range of the art
increases. Now it so happens that there is in a lesser degree just
that kind of contrast between the quality of tone (not merely the
volume) of a solo instrument and that of an orchestra. The solo
player stands out from the orchestra as a living personality no less
clearly, though somewhat less impressively, than the singer. Hence
there was, in the period from Alessandro Scarlatti to Handel, the
closest affinity, amounting in some cases to identity, between certain
vocal and concerto forms. If we could understand a beautiful
Handel aria so as to have some idea, however incomplete, of that
wherein it differs from his hack-work, then we may hope to understand a Beethoven concerto.

When a voice or instrument is accompanied by something
which it either thrusts into the background as soon as it is heard,
or else fails to penetrate at all, a moment's reflection will convince
us that the easiest way to give both elements their best effect is to
let the accompaniment begin with a statement of the material, and
then to bring in the voice or solo with a counter-statement. This
arrangement brings out the force of the solo in thrusting the
orchestra into the background, while at the same time the orchestra
has had its say and need not seem unnaturally repressed as it
probably would seem (supposing it to be at all powerful) if it were
employed only to support the solo. Again, this ritornello of the
orchestra will, as its name implies, return effectively at the end
of the piece when the solo has reached its climax. The solo is
probably more active, as well as more personal and eloquent, than
the orchestra, and can therefore make a brilliant climax if it

chooses; but it cannot make its climax very powerful in sound as compared with what the orchestra can obviously do with ease; and so this one missing element may be supplied, and the design rounded off, by bringing in the ritornello forte on the last note of the solo, thus ending the piece. Here we have the beginning and end of an enormous number of typical concerto forms. A single unbroken melody might be arranged in this way as a complete piece for a voice and orchestra, with no further elaboration and no other appearances of the orchestra except the opening ritornello and its recapitulation at the close; but generally the voice or solo goes farther afield and attains more than one climax in foreign keys, so that the orchestra introduces parts of its ritornello perhaps three or four times in such a movement.

Obviously much depends on the skill and sensibility of the composer in choosing different parts of this ritornello, bringing the solo into fresh relationship with it at each entry. Very early in the history of the operatic aria an important device was discovered, which is usually associated with the name of Alessandro Scarlatti. Its essential point is that the voice does not complete its first strain at once but allows the orchestra to finish it instead, and then begins again from the beginning, this time to continue. The device obviously has great value in establishing a more subtle relation between voice and accompaniment than is possible when they persist in alternating only in large and complete sections. It soon became 'conventional', that is to say a mere formula in the hands of composers who knew and cared nothing about the contrast and harmony of voice and accompaniment; and Mr. Fuller-Maitland, who describes it fully and accurately in the fourth volume of the *Oxford History of Music*, gives many instances of it in various stages of true feeling and decadence from Bach, in whose hands no device is more conventional than the very laws of nature, to Greene, who, in one of his anthems, shows its last trace in a futile piece of mechanism lazily indicated by a da capo sign.

And yet the device has never died, aesthetically speaking, though we may not be conscious of its ancestry. Wherever a solo depends for its effect on entering after an orchestral ritornello, there we shall find the trace of Alessandro Scarlatti's principle— that the solo should first be inclined to enter into dialogue with the orchestra—the speaker should conciliate the crowd before he breaks into monologue.

I do not propose here to trace how Bach was influenced by his predecessors in this matter. Bach is an original composer, and no conventional ideas about originality will prevent him from using the most hackneyed device in its fullest and oldest meaning. His chief concerto form is in every particular derived from the typical vocal aria form, at least as regards the first movement.

A little consideration of the new conditions involved will help us to arrange the facts clearly. The opposition of solo and orchestra began early to take a greater variety of forms than was possible in the vocal music of the same periods. The main type of early concerto was the *concerto grosso*, in which the opposition was between such a number of solo players as could produce quite a complete mass of harmony to oppose against the orchestra proper. This opposition of the concertino against the orchestra or *concerto grosso* (from which the form takes its name) could even be reduced to a state of things in which all played together and split into whatever groups they pleased; as in Bach's magnificent Third Brandenburg Concerto, which is for a string orchestra which plays in three parts in the ritornello, and divides itself into nine by way of representing solo passages—no further indication of a distinction between solo and tutti being given. Still, apart from the likelihood that Bach was writing for only nine players, and that in performance by a larger band the nine-part passages should be played by the leaders alone, this dividing of the orchestra at once produces a fairly strong impression of that entry of individual tone which we know to be the most expressive feature of the concerto style; and this first movement of the only concerto throughout which Bach does not write for a detached solo-group or single solo, differs in no other way from the rest of his concertos.

We need only think of an aria enormously enlarged, with its square-cut melody turned into a concentrated group of pregnant, sequential figures, such as befit a serious and monumental movement that will not for a moment be confined within the limits of lyric melody. We shall find all the other features of the aria here: the ritornello, of course, states the main figures of the movement in their most forcible shape; then the quasi-solo of the orchestra divided into nine parts begins its version of the theme, but, just as in Scarlatti's arias, bursts into a tutti before the phrase is finished, though the greater scale of the movement (and a higher organization in every respect) is indicated by the fact that this interruption is in a new key. Another interruption occurs before the resumed nine-part passages can deliver a longer sentence; and we have to go some way into the movement before these quasi-solos have any long uninterrupted discourse. Throughout the work the principles of alternation between quasi-solo and tutti are most subtle and delicate in their adaptation to the peculiar conditions of this band. Sometimes the three basses coalesce into tutti while the six upper parts remain individual; in one most impressive place, the basses do this in order to bring out a difficult passage, thus retaining their value as solo parts. Sometimes basses and violins will each coalesce while the three viola parts flourish separately. In short, the combinations are endless, and are all in the highest degree expressive of the peculiar concerto opposition of forces. This is what Bach does under conditions in which the possibilities of concerto style are least obvious.

The Second Brandenburg Concerto is for four solo instruments and orchestra. Here the principles of the form are far more obvious. Yet they cannot be so strongly marked in a concerto for four instruments as in a concerto for one; and if Bach's extant concertos be studied as glorified arias, the vital aesthetic principles will reveal themselves in endless variety. (Incidentally these principles will help us to restore by conjecture the original forms of works extant only in arrangement.) Bach, far more than Handel, likes to organize both his larger arias and his concertos by making the solo enter with a different theme from that of the ritornello, so that when the orchestra breaks in on the first solo with Scarlatti's interruption (or something to that effect) the bit of ritornello so introduced has a new meaning. Sometimes he translates into these larger instrumental forms the things that happen in an aria where a solo instrument as well as a voice is opposed to the orchestra. Further details must be left to other analyses of Bach's vocal and instrumental works. Here we can only add that Bach, like the masters of later concerto forms, makes the relation of solo and tutti more intimate and less contrasted in middle and final than in first movements.

In short, Bach's concerto forms are completely identical with his vocal forms, except those that are dramatic, like some of Handel's, and those that employ the orchestra merely as a support, such as fugues and the severer forms of figured choral.

In the case of festive choruses, where form and brilliance are more important than fugue and solemnity, this identity is such that actual concerto movements have been arranged by Bach as choruses. And the arrangements are so amazingly successful that there is nothing but external evidence to prove that the chorus is not the original. The best illustration of this is the first chorus of a delightful cantata, *Vereinigte Zwietracht der wechselnde Saiten*, written to celebrate the election of one Dr. Kortte to a professorship. The very title of the cantata throws light on the concerto idea; for *Vereinigte Zwietracht* is a singularly accurate and forcible rendering of the root meaning of *concertare*; and Bach generally calls the solo part (*Cembalo, Violino*, or whatever the case may be) *certato*.[1]

---

[1] The true interpretation of this significant point is among my earliest recollections of that great musical scholar, A. J. Hipkins, whose kindness to me began in my childhood.

When we compare Bach's rendering of this 'united contest of turn-about strings' with the third movement of the First Brandenburg Concerto, we find that the framework, themes, and counterpoint are bar for bar the same, with the exception of an occasional expansion (two bars inserted here, half a bar there), to make the approaches to climaxes longer and more suitable to the grander massiveness of choral writing. But what will strike us most forcibly is that the chorus parts are derived, not from the horns and other wind-parts of the original, but entirely from the single solo part, a struggling violino piccolo (Quart-Geige, or kit), that has more difficulty in getting the upper hand of the orchestra than any other solo in the whole classical repertoire. The transformation of this thinnest of solo threads into massive and stirring four-part choral writing is one of Bach's most astonishing feats of easy and unerring mastery. Any ordinary man would have reasoned as follows: 'This movement is the only one in the concerto with a true solo, all the rest of the work being on the lines of the concerto grosso, and depending on the opposition of masses of strings, wood-winds, and horns. And this solo part is not very brilliant, nor does it give me any material I cannot get more easily from the winds. Therefore I will either neglect it, or absorb it into the arrangement I propose to make of the wind-parts, which shall become the chorus. And now that I look at the structure of the movement, I see that there is much repetition caused by this tiresome little solo part, the motive of which will vanish when my chorus carries all before it. So I will cut out all these conventional repetitions, and make the form of my chorus free and terse.' And so our *a priori* theorist achieves a breathless chorus in a jerry-built form. Thus the easy-going innovator (for all conventional minds are bursting with innovation) has arrived at the forms of many popular concertos of modern times. Bach's ways have nothing to do with *a priori* theorizing. In the true sense of the word he is the greatest of theorists, for he *sees*, he *understands*, and his vision is perfected in action.

Bach, or rather his chorus, seems to reply to our reasoner: 'You complain that the violin part is overshadowed, and you point out that the rest of the work is a concerto grosso. But this first movement is not; and your complaint only proves that the violin arrested your attention from the moment it appeared, and made you wish that the orchestra allowed you to hear it better. The violin spoke to you like a voice, and you found it too weak; it shall become a chorus, and you shall learn that the whole orchestra always was its loyal bodyguard. The repetitions you think conventional shall continue to mean here exactly what they always meant —the transformation of a formal statement into the living and moving utterances of a personality; with this new splendour that the personality is that of a happy multitude inspired by one joy. The form of such a movement as this need no more change with a reversal of its balance of tone than the forms of the mountains change as the light falls at morning and evening. Let the horns become trumpets, let us hear the thunder-clap and roll of drums where the chorus sings of "der rollende Pauken durchdringender Knall"; let the voices have more room here and there; but do not dream of losing the vital beauty that not only gives the movement its form, but is its very cause, the opposition of a *personality* to the impersonal orchestra. It is no matter whether that personality be an instrument, personal because isolated, or a chorus, personal because having human speech. The moment it appears it rivets our attention, and the orchestra itself becomes an eager listener expressing its sympathy in harmonious assent.'

As if to demonstrate that the affinity between choral and concerto forms is no accident of an insensitive age, Handel once adapted some non-ritornello choruses (such as 'Lift up your heads') into a huge concerto. The results are absurd enough to make the difference between right and wrong in this matter self-evident.

THE SONATA-FORM CONCERTO

We have seen how the early aria form was adapted to the conditions of a concerto; though we did not enter into many particulars about the aria itself. We must be more careful with the forms that underlie the concertos that are now to be discussed. The best way to avoid a tiresome abstract of ordinary sonata form will be for us to base our analysis on the difference between the sonata forms and those of Bach. The cardinal difference between sonata-style movements and those of the time of Bach is that the sonata movement changes on dramatic principles as it unfolds itself, whereas the older forms grow from one central idea and change only in becoming more effective as they proceed. Bach's grandest movements will show this no less than his smallest. You cannot, indeed, displace a bar without upsetting the whole; but the most experienced critic could not tell from looking at a portion out of its context whether it came from the beginning, middle, or end of the work. Yet almost any sufficiently long extract from the first movement of a sonata by Mozart or Beethoven would give a competent musician abundant indications of its place in the scheme.

It would be convenient if we could say that the polyphonic idea of form is the development of a single theme, while the sonata idea is the development and contrast of several; but it would not be at all true. The first movement of Bach's B minor Sonata for cembalo and flute has fifteen distinct figures—which is more than can be found in the extremely rich first movement of Brahms's G major Violin Sonata—and yet it is a perfect example of the true spirit of polyphonic form; while Haydn often gives us quite mature sonata movements in which it is impossible to find more than one theme. Still, the great thing to bear in mind is that the themes of the old polyphonic movement, if there are more than one, flow one into the other. The movement grows without ever showing impressive preparation for the advent of something new; and its surprises, many though they may be to a sympathetic listener, are never much connected with new themes or indeed with anything we do not seem to have known from the first. But a Haydn movement sets out in search of adventures; and if there is only one theme, that theme will somehow contrive to enter in another place disguised as its own twin brother. There will always be a vivid impression of *opposition* of ideas, and of change as well as development. And Haydn's frequent use of one theme where orthodoxy expects two is a result of amazing invention working on a deceptively small scale and seizing every conceivable means of making the dimensions of his work seem spacious, and its outlines free.

Hence the early instrumental forms were such that a short pregnant ritornello could sum up the principal material of a movement in a single line, while the solo was under no need to introduce more fresh matter than suited its disposition. But the material of sonata forms cannot be so briefly summed up; the ritornello, if it is used at all, must be larger and must contain more than one paragraph.

The great masters of sonata form were not to be persuaded to abandon the ritornello. The larger range of sonata movements, the treatment of the orchestra on lines as dramatic as those of the new forms, and the rise of a corresponding style of solo playing—all these facts conspire to make the ritornello more instead of less necessary than before. Bach's concerto orchestra was almost always merely a string band; when he adds wind instruments to it, these show a strong tendency to detach themselves as subordinate solo parts; and so completely does he falsify the current idea about the parity of his orchestral and solo parts, that his great Double Concerto in C major for two cembalos reduces the string-band to a mere support, necessary and effective, but in no way opposed to the cembalos, who wrestle only with each other. Under these conditions Bach even abandons the ritornello. Not so the masters of sonata form: their orchestra uses wind instruments in every possible combination with the strings, sometimes opposed in groups, as in the old concerto grosso, sometimes in solos, and constantly in perfect blending of tone with the strings as part of the compact chorus. Such an orchestra cannot be allowed to remain permanently in the background. On the other hand, the solo will need to be more brilliant than ever before, if it is to stand out against this orchestra which has already so much contrast of its own. The modern concerto form must rest more than ever on the old and natural concerto idea, the entry of a personal voice instantly arresting attention, and by mere force of its individuality thrusting even the most elaborate orchestra into the background. And the more rich the orchestra, and the greater the number and range of themes, the longer and more effectively may the appearance of this individual voice be delayed by an orchestral ritornello, if only this remains truly a ritornello and does not merge into pure symphonic writing. Here we have the key to the true method of conveying sonata form in terms of a concerto. The ordinary account of the matter, as given in standard treatises, is that the orchestra gives out the first and second subject with most of their accessories, more or less as in a symphony, but all in one key, instead of the first being in the tonic and the second in the dominant; that the solo then appears and restates these subjects somewhat more at leisure and in their proper complementary keys; after which there is a shorter recapitulation of part of the tutti in the new key, whereupon the solo again enters and works out an ordinary sonata development and recapitulation more or less in combination with the orchestra; after which the movement ends with a final tutti, interrupted by an extempore cadenza from the solo player. Now this scheme is, no doubt, rather like a concerto as it sounds to us when we are not listening; but it is falsified in all its most important particulars by nearly every concerto in the classical repertoire except Beethoven's in C minor; and the whole subsequent history of Beethoven's treatment of the form indicates that he learnt to regard the structure of the first tutti of his C minor concerto as a mistake.

Let us try to discover the true concerto form by analysing a great work of Mozart, the Pianoforte Concerto in C major (Köchel 503), referring to parallel cases wherever they may help us.

Mozart begins with a majestic assertion of his key, C major, by the whole orchestra, with mysterious soft shadows, that give a solemn depth to the tone (Ex. 1).

Ex. 1.

Allegro maestoso.

The second of these sombre changes passes into C minor with extraordinary grandeur and breadth, and a new rhythmic figure (Ex. 2) rises quietly in the violins.

Ex. 2.
C minor.

(a)

This new figure bursts out forte in the bass with a counterpoint on the violins (Ex. 3), in the major again, and with the full orchestra.

Ex. 3.

Bass 8ve. *lower.*   (a) *inverted.*

It modulates broadly and firmly to the dominant, which key it explores triumphantly, and finally annexes by trumpeting the rhythmic figure three times on G. Now this is not quite in the manner of a symphony. True, many of Mozart's earlier symphonic first themes consist, like Ex. 1, of little more than a vigorous assertion of the tonic and dominant chords; but they continue in a style that only slowly becomes more epigrammatic and melodious, and hardly rises to any surprising harmonic effect throughout the whole movement; whereas this concerto opening is mysterious and profound in its very first line. It shows at once a boldness and richness of style which is only to be found in Mozart's most advanced work. A symphony in this style would certainly begin with something more like an articulated regular theme, however openly it might be designed to emphasize the tonic and dominant of the key. (Compare the opening of the Jupiter Symphony. The Jupiter Symphony is the *locus classicus* for an architectural opening, but it takes no such risks as the opening of this concerto.) These solemn procedures have much the effect of an *introduction*. That impression is somewhat modified as the music carries us out with its tide, and we realize that we have indeed begun a grand voyage of discovery. This cannot be an introduction that leads to something with a beginning of its own, but it must be a preparation for some advent; and we can best realize how grand it is if we try to imagine the effect with which a chorus might enter at this close on the dominant (end of the passage beginning at Ex. 3). The entry of a chorus, singing the psalm *Dixit Dominus*, would be almost perfectly appropriate; indeed Mozart's church music, which is mostly of an earlier period, rarely attains to such power and solemnity as this opening. If we turn to Brahms's *Triumphlied*, we shall find that the orchestral introduction, though not nearly so long as these first fifty bars, is not unlike them in the way in which it covers its ground and seems to be leading up to something. But of course a chorus thrusts the orchestra far more into the background than a solo instrument can. Our opening tutti must develop further, for the orchestra will not sound relevant if repressed by the feeble tone of a single instrument before it has stated several contrasted themes.

We have, then, paused on the dominant. Observe again that the modulation to the dominant is not like the normal early modulations of symphonies. Though, if taken out of its context, the close of this passage would seem to be clearly in G, yet it here sounds only like very strong emphasis on the dominant of C. True, in symphonies of an earlier period Mozart would have followed his close by a second subject in G; but the effect of doing so is always a little epigrammatic—the taking advantage of a natural emphasis on the dominant so as to turn it into a new tonic; and I believe that Mozart differs, even in his earliest works, from ordinary composers in seeing that the device *is* epigrammatic, whereas they only saw that it was convenient and obvious. But it certainly would not tell in a work in the advanced style of this concerto. The only way to prepare the mind for G major after this grand opening would be to go to *its* dominant and pause on that. But the present close in G (in spite of the F sharp and all the firmness and emphasis) has not taken our minds out of C at all. We feel that we are *on* the dominant, not *in* it. Again, if this were a symphony and Mozart wished to begin his second subject, or preparations for it, at this point he would be almost certain to plunge into a remote and quiet key, most probably E flat, rather than use the old colourless device described above. And it is interesting to note that this is exactly what Beethoven did in the same circumstances in his C major concerto, when he had not yet realized the difference between symphonic form and the form of the concerto-ritornello. (Another reason for making particular note of this possibility of E flat will appear later.)

What does Mozart do? He remains in C; and this fixity of key stamps the introductory ritornello character of the music more and more firmly the longer it continues. Out of that Beethovenish rhythmic figure ♪ ♫ | ♩ arises a quiet march in C minor, half solemn, half gay, and wonderfully orchestrated (Ex. 4).

Ex. 4.

(a)

&c.

This is repeated by the wind, with soft trumpets and drums, in the major. 'Here', explains the believer in standard accounts of concerto form, 'we evidently have the second subject, which the solo will eventually restate in the dominant.' Wait and see.

After this counter-statement there is a delightful kind of Hallelujah Chorus (Ex. 5), which settles with majestic grace into a quiet cadence-figure (Ex. 6);

Ex. 5.

Ex. 6.

Light semiquaver accompaniment.

and the grand pageant of themes closes in triumph. Then the strings seem to *listen*, for one moment of happy anticipation. As they listen the pianoforte enters, at first with scattered phrases (Ex. 7).

Ex. 7.
Strings.   Pfte.

These quickly settle into a stream of florid melody, which grows to a brilliant climax in accordance with the artistic necessity that the solo should hold its own by doing that which most distinguishes it from the orchestra, and should therefore be florid just in proportion to the amount of orchestral impressiveness.[1]

On the top of this climax the full orchestra re-enters with Ex. 1, on the same principle as the bursting in of the ritornello upon

[1] Hence the source of all our delusions as to the relation between the concerto and the bravura styles. A modern concerto *must* be technically difficult, because all the easy ways in which a solo can stand out against an

the first utterances of the voice or solo in the polyphonic arias and concertos. The impressive soft shadows of this theme are now beautifully illuminated by running passages in the pianoforte, which continues the theme in close dialogue with the wind-band. Ex. 2 follows, yet more impressive, thrilled with the rise and fall of pianoforte scales. Instead of leading to a triumphant outburst in the major, it is continued in the minor with very dark colouring and great breadth of rhythm, and culminates on the dominant of C minor, which the full orchestra sternly emphasizes with the rhythmic figure (a) ♩ ♫ ♩. . Here, then, we have another pause on the dominant, not unlike that which we had shortly after Ex. 3. What does the pianoforte do now? It quietly modulates to E flat, exactly as we saw that Beethoven was tempted to do in the opening tutti of his first concerto. And that modulation, which is a mistake in a ritornello[2] because of its symphonic character, is for the same reason beautiful when the solo has entered and established its relation to the orchestra. Here Mozart gives the pianoforte a new theme (Ex. 8) pervaded by that omnipresent rhythmic figure (a).

Ex. 8.

Transition Theme.

(a)   &c.

This modulates to the dominant of G in a broadly symphonic style, thoroughly expressive of the intention to establish the new key with firmness. Contrast what we felt about the passage following Ex. 3. After dwelling on this new dominant with sufficient breadth, the pianoforte settles down into the second subject. This will come as a surprise to orthodox believers in text-books, for it has nothing whatever to do with Ex. 4, which seemed so like

orchestra are harmonically and technically obvious, being the elementary things for which the instrument must be constructed if it is to be practicable at all; and as the orchestra becomes more varied and powerful, the soloist must dive deeper into the resources of his instrument. Hence the concertos of Mozart are in general far more difficult than any earlier ones; those of Beethoven the most difficult of all except those of Brahms; while the concertos of the virtuoso-composers, which exist mainly for technique, are easier than any others, since whatever types of passage they employ are written on progressions schematic at best, so that they can in time be mastered once for all like the knack of spinning a peg-top; whereas the great composer's passages never take your hand where it expects to go, and can be mastered by the muscle only in obedience to the continual dictation of the mind. Mozart's passages are in this respect among the most treacherous in existence.

[2] I continue to apply this term to the whole opening tutti of the largest concertos. The longest opening tutti does not, if rightly designed, lose the unity that characterizes the true ritornello, even if it contains many important changes of key.

a possible second subject. Indeed the only part of it that has anything to do with the ritornello is a variation of Ex. 3, which obviously belonged originally to the first subject, though we may remember that the pianoforte had avoided it when it fell due after the solo statement of Ex. 2.

I need not describe the second subject in detail. Its new and main theme (Ex. 9) is first stated by the pianoforte—

Ex. 9.

and then counterstated and expanded by the wind instruments. The derivative of Ex. 3 follows (see Ex. 10) and leads brilliantly to a climax,

Ex. 10.
(*cf.* 3.)

(*a*) *inverted.*

with all that variety of colour and rhythm and continual increase of breadth which is one of the most unapproachable powers of the true classics, distinguishing them no less from the classicists, who do not know that they lack it, than from the romantic composers, the greatest of whom contrive to make their work depend on renouncing it in favour of epigram and antithesis.

On the top of this climax the orchestra, long pent-up, bursts in with Ex. 3 of the ritornello. And here Mozart contrives one of his most subtle and brilliant strokes. We saw that Ex. 3 originally led to G and closed emphatically in that key, but yet under circumstances that made us feel that we were all the time only on the dominant of C. But now, of course, it begins in G, and Mozart so contrives that it remains there, instead of going on to the present dominant, D, as it would if transposed exactly; and it ends with the *very same notes* for no less than ten bars, *as in its original occurrence*, but now, of course, with the strongest possible feeling of being *in* G, not merely *on* the dominant. Thus Mozart cannot even do a mere repetition without shedding a new light that could not possibly be given by any variation. There is no describing the peculiar and subtle pleasure this device gives. It depends on a delicate sense of key, but has nothing to do with the technical knowledge which enables us to name it; indeed, it is certain to be keenly enjoyed by any attentive listener whose knowledge of music is the result of relish for classical works, stimulated by frequent opportunities for hearing them under good conditions. On the other hand, it is quite possible that many persons skilled in the mechanics of what passes for counterpoint, and having at least a concert-goer's retrospective view of musical history, simply do not hear these effects at all.

The sense of key-perspective can never be made obsolete by new harmonic developments. In otiose styles, whether early or recent, it is in abeyance; but a genuinely revolutionary style is more likely to stimulate than obliterate it. Strauss's opening of *Also sprach Zarathustra* might almost pass for a paraphrase of the opening of Mozart's C major Concerto.

The orchestra ends, trumpeting the rhythmic figure (*a*) on G as a finally established key. The pianoforte re-enters, repeating the figure on the dominant of E. And now it goes straight on with the march theme (Ex. 4) in E minor, which is to furnish our development section. The concerto has been grand and surprising, leaving us continually mystified as to what is to happen, and now it takes shape.

This theme that so happily pulls the whole design together all the way back from its single previous appearance in the ritornello, now moves calmly through a long series of very straightforward sequences through various keys. But though the sequences are simple in their steps, they are infinitely varied in colouring, and they rapidly increase in complexity until, to the surprise of any one who still believes that Mozart is a childishly simple composer, they move in eight real parts.

These eight parts are in triple, or, if we count added thirds, quadruple canon, two in the strings, four in the wind with the added thirds, and two of light antiphonal scales in the pianoforte. No such polyphony has occurred since in any concerto, except one passage in the middle of the finale of Brahms's D minor.

Then there follows a majestic dominant pedal for the next eight bars, not at all polyphonic; the wind rises in a scale which the pianoforte crosses in descent, and just at the most satisfactory moment the full orchestra enters with the opening theme, Ex. 1; and we find ourselves in the recapitulation. The pianoforte shares the continuation, as in its first solo, and proceeds without alteration through the expanded version of Ex. 2 to the E flat theme, Ex. 8. This takes a new direction of very beautiful harmony and leads to the second subject. From this point the recapitulation bids fair to continue to follow its original exactly; but we find that the counter-statement of Ex. 9 is expanded in a new sequence of modulations in minor harmonies, and suddenly we find ourselves again in the broad daylight of the major key, listening to Ex. 4 as it was given in counter-statement in the ritornello! The pianoforte has a brilliant part of its own in this incident. Then the rest of the recapitulation follows, with Ex. 9 as if nothing had happened. And, of course, at the end the orchestra enters with Ex. 3, and comes to a pause on a 6/4 chord, whereon the pianoforte extemporizes a cadenza. After this the orchestra crowns the work with its final triumph of formal balance by repeating, what we have not heard since the first entry of the solo, the closing themes, Ex. 5 and 6.

It will be seen that this whole wonderful scheme entirely fails to fit the orthodox account of concerto form. Evidently the opening tutti has no connexion with the notion of a sonata exposition in one key; it is a true ritornello, differing from that of an aria only in its gigantic size. If further proof were wanted, Constance's great bravura aria 'Martern aller Arten' in the *Entführung* would furnish it, besides showing the use of auxiliary solos in the ritornello, a device revived by Brahms in the slow movement of his B flat Concerto. Of course there are plenty of cases where the second subject is represented in the ritornello, especially where the work is not on the largest scale; but there is no foreseeing what the solo will select from the ritornello. All that we can be sure of is that nothing will be without its function, and that everything will be unexpected and inevitable. I doubt whether three important concertos of Mozart (at least fifteen are important) could be found that agreed as closely in form as Beethoven's three greatest concertos (G, E flat, and the Violin Concerto). In one point they almost all agree, even down to the smallest works; and that is the splendid device of inserting in the recapitulation of the second subject a theme from the ritornello that was not represented in the original solo statement. In Beethoven's hands the concerto grew so large that this device would no longer be weighty enough to pull the design together, and so it has remained peculiar to Mozart.[1]

It is unnecessary to give a full account of the other movements; concertos, as they proceed, naturally use, like all sonata-works, more sectional forms, in which solo and orchestra alternate more simply than in the first movement. This is further necessitated by the fact that it can no longer be effective to lay such tremendous emphasis on the entries of the solo, now that it has so gloriously won its way into friendship with the orchestral crowd. Hence the

---

[1] Further investigation will show that this device is the result of a larger principle which I had not grasped in 1903. The recapitulation in the tonic is a recapitulation of the opening tutti as well as of the first solo. It does not omit the features peculiar to the solo, but it adds to them those features of the ritornello which the solo had not at first adopted. In particular, it is likely to follow the course of the opening much more closely than in the first solo; and the subsequent appearance of a previously neglected theme is the most conspicuous result of this tendency. In Beethoven and Brahms the main principle is quite as clear, though it may not be marked by a special theme.

ritornello idea does not find such full expression in these later movements, though Mozart is very fond of using a simple kind of ritornello at the beginning of his larger slow movements, as in the present work. I give the three main themes of this ritornello in Ex. 11, 12 and 13.

The pianoforte turns Ex. 12 into a second subject and adds more themes to it; returning then by a really colossal passage on a dominant pedal to the main theme in the tonic, and a regular recapitulation of both subjects. Ex. 13 is reserved to round off the movement.[1]

Concerto finales are practically certain to be some kind of rondo. Mozart soon found out how to make the rondo form bring out the solo in the most appropriate way. He gives to the main theme (which is usually announced by the solo) a large number of orchestral accessories, which do not recur with the returns of the theme, until the very end where the solo shares in them as they round off the movement with fine effect.[2]

[1] In some of Mozart's andantes, notably that of the G major Concerto, the themes of the ritornello are so closely welded together that it is a great surprise to hear what we thought was part of one melody blossom out in a new key as a well-contrasted second subject. (See page 108.)

[2] Mozart found this use of accessory themes in the tonic valuable outside concertos. The finales of the two pianoforte quartets and of the great A major Violin Sonata are excellent examples.

Ex. 15.

&c., digressing to C minor.

Ex. 16.

In the present instance, Mozart announces the main theme by the orchestra, and uses the accessories more extensively, making Ex. 15 modulate to A minor for the middle episode. But Ex. 16 appears only at the end of all, after a very big coda. In this finale the free-rhythmed connecting links between the main sections attain a breadth that was never approached until surpassed by Beethoven. Here are the remaining themes:

Ex. 17.
Entry of Pianoforte.

Ex. 18. Transition.

Ex. 19. First Episode.

Ex. 20. Middle Episode (*a*).
(Allied to No. 17.)

Ex. 21. Middle Episode (*b*).

Is alluded to by diminution in the Coda.

CONCLUSION

Only the analysis of individual works can adequately show the later developments of the true concerto form. These chiefly concern the first movement; for the other movements are not much prevented by the special conditions of concerto form from growing on ordinary lines. But the following generalizations may be useful.

1. Beethoven ceased making the ritornello come to a full stop before the solo entered. In his three greatest concertos the end of the ritornello is dramatic and expectant, so that the solo enters on a dominant chord and ruminates in broad passages of immense dignity and beauty before taking up the themes. These passages correspond to the new theme with which Mozart so often begins the solos of his larger concertos; but, with their entry on the dominant and their non-thematic character, they produce a far more thrilling effect. Mozart's nearest approaches to this are in the concerto just analysed, in the much earlier A major Violin Concerto, where the solo begins with a short, florid adagio, in the brilliant and witty Pianoforte Concerto in B flat (Köchel 450), see Essay LXXXVII, and in another big Concerto in C major (Köchel 467), where the solo enters on the dominant.

2. Beethoven did *not* 'emancipate the orchestra' as is commonly held: he could not possibly have made it more prominent and elaborate than Mozart makes it in such works as that described here. On the contrary, he treated the pianoforte much more constantly in full harmony, and this inspired him with the possibility of accompanying it by very incomplete harmony in the orchestra and so producing numberless wonderful effects that can be heard under no other conditions.

3. Beethoven had the art of inventing themes which pass continually through several keys. This enabled him to give the opening tutti of his G major Concerto great variety of tonality without becoming symphonic or losing its unity as a ritornello.

4. In the same work he secures the novel effect of letting the pianoforte begin, and making the orchestra enter *in a foreign key* with the next phrase, after which the ritornello proceeds on the orchestra alone.

5. In his E flat Concerto he discovered the possibility of a rhapsodical solo introduction before the ritornello.

6. In the same work he found out how to construct a gigantic coda out of a new recapitulation of the later themes of the ritornello, including even the entry of the solo. This removes the one real defect of the classical form, that it entrusts the organization of the coda to the player's extempore powers in the cadenza.

Brahms further developed the concerto form in the following ways.

7. He found a way of modulation that gives the ritornello more than one key, and this, not by a series of transitions (like Beethoven's in the G major Concerto), but by a real contrast of fixed keys, all without loss of the necessary unity and flow.

8. He enlarged the notion of a solo introduction and made it both thematic and rhapsodic, thus saving space in the ensuing ritornello.

9. He did not, as used to be said, score too heavily for the solo; on the contrary he is demonstrably lighter than Mozart; but he uses the modern pianoforte in order to add greatly to the volume of a big tutti.

10. He discovered that if the solo takes most of its material from the orchestra, the orchestra may take some fresh material from the solo; and thus he obtained many new contrasts.

11. He found out how to write a symphonic scherzo for pianoforte and orchestra.

Such innovations do not make a formidable catalogue, but they are the outward signs of spiritual forces that are not concerned in the gyrations of the up-to-date weathercock. In the classical concerto forms the orchestra and solo are so organized that both are at their highest development. The conditions of such a problem do not admit many obviously different solutions; and the concertos that abandon the classical form obtain their unlimited variety by being structures of a much looser and less ambitious order. They stand on their own merits, and can be defined only by individual analysis. Beethoven had no reason, for example, to despise Weber's *Conzertstück*; and later composers, from Mendelssohn onwards, would have seen no reason why it should not have been called a concerto. It is manifestly better than Weber's regular concertos; and composers may as well write the best music they can, without being worried by a terminology that would confine the word 'concerto' to a form which exists in hardly thirty perfect examples.

BACH

CONCERTO IN D MINOR FOR CLAVIER AND STRINGS

1 *Allegro.* 2 *Adagio.* 3 *Allegro.*

The making of many of Bach's works is a wonderful history; but the making of this D minor concerto is perhaps the most wonderful of all. Unfortunately the original composition is lost, and this clavier version is one of Bach's adaptations of it. Evidently he was very fond of it (and no wonder), for he adapted it to many occasions. A single glance at the solo passages will show that, like most of Bach's clavier concertos, the work was originally a violin concerto: in this case the greatest and most difficult violin concerto before the time of Beethoven. With the aid of Bach's two earlier extant keyboard versions it is easy to restore the original text with complete certainty, even in the very bold and difficult unaccompanied passage at the climax of the first movement. A restored text of the work as a violin concerto is published, but unfortunately it was done in the Dark Ages as regards Bach-scholarship, and it is demonstrably wrong in every possible way besides several impossible ways. Meanwhile Bach's own wonderful arrangement for clavier is full of magnificent features which the original could not possess; and these may well outweigh the undeniable fact that the solo passages, though much easier to play on the keyboard than on a violin, have none of the points which passages really imagined for the keyboard would have, while they would vividly bring out all the qualities of a violin. This is especially the case with those passages in which one hand is kept repeating a single note, A, E, or D, while the other hand dovetails neighbouring notes around it. On the violin the notes A, E, and D are open strings with more resonance than the other notes, and a special effect is thus produced spontaneously. A pianist can produce something analogous, but he needs to know these facts before he can see the point of the passage. On a harpsichord with two manuals, or an organ, this type of passage can produce a special effect more automatically, and can of course produce it around any note—not only around A, D, and E. (The magnificent harpsichords which Mr. Dolmetsch now makes might even reveal the effects Bach had in mind to a large audience in a large hall: it is unlikely that the best-preserved ancient harpsichord, delightful though it still can be, is quite what it was in its youth; and Mr. Dolmetsch's new harpsichords are probably finer than any instrument of Bach's time. I have seen one of his spinets which has fully the sustaining power of a large pianoforte.) Against the disadvantage, such as it is, of these violin idioms, we may set the wonderful new material Bach has given to the left hand of the clavier player. In the three extant versions of the work we can see this new part (for it is nothing less) in all stages of its growth, beginning with a mere adaptation of the orchestral bass and ending in a rich contrapuntal fabric which it is impossible to conceive as other than an integral part of the whole conception.

So far, however, we are on comparatively technical ground; though I cannot admit that the imaginative treatment of instruments is a merely academic matter. But there is a more significant history to this work than its origin in a violin concerto. One day Bach had occasion to write a church cantata beginning with the text, 'We must pass through much tribulation into the kingdom of God'. Here was an opportunity for doing justice to his favourite and greatest concerto. He arranged the violin part of the first movement for the organ *an octave lower*. This gave it an unusual and impressive darkness of tone, which he threw into relief by adding to the orchestra three new parts for two oboes and a taille (or cor anglais). The cantata, then, begins thus with a great instrumental overture, chosen and arranged as a fit representation of the

heroic progress of the souls of the faithful through the valley of
tribulation. Then comes one of the most stupendous *tours de force*
in all musical history. The slow movement is arranged in the same
way, with the same transposing of the solo part an octave lower and
the same additional wind-parts; but all this is the mere accompaniment to a totally independent four-part chorus! If the result were
confused or unnatural there would be little more to be said for it
than for Raimondi's four complete simultaneous fugues in four
different keys, or for his three simultaneous oratorios, or for many
other scholastic tomfooleries which may be played backwards and
upside down without sounding noticeably more sensible than when
played right-end foremost. But Bach's result is of the same Greek
simplicity, for all its ornamentation, as his original: in fact, it is
just as much an original inspiration as if no earlier or simpler version had existed. The chief interest of comparing these versions
is aesthetic. With works of a transition period, it might be mainly
historical; but here we are dealing with maturity. The composition
and its arrangements can teach us how different elements of the
art are on different planes; and how the great artist, by keeping
these planes distinct, preserves clearness and simplicity in his
whole results, where lesser artists would produce confusion and
pedantry.

Bach's concerto form is easy to follow, so long as we are not
misled by the popular fallacy which supposes that an artistic
contrast becomes less real when it is made less violent. In the
concerto styles from Mozart onwards the contrast between the
solo and the orchestra is greater than that between any other
members of any musical combination; but the more level texture
of Bach's music should not delude us into thinking that he knows
of no contrast between solo and tutti at all. On the contrary, his
whole concerto style depends on it, just as the almost identical
style of the vocal arias of the period depends on the power of the
voice to arrest attention and to thrust the most elaborate instrumental accompaniment into the background. Hence the concerto,
like the aria, naturally begins with a paragraph for the orchestra,
giving the main themes on which the solo is to be developed. And
perhaps the solo will take up these themes at once, or perhaps (as
in the first movement of this concerto and in many other cases) it
will begin with something quite new. My first quotation gives the
opening paragraph (the shortest and most powerful of all Bach's
ritornellos) together with the first notes of the solo. In the solo
theme the demisemiquavers are a detail Bach has added to what we
know to be his original version—an addition typical of the way in
which he transforms violin-figures into a keyboard style (Ex. 1).
The plan of the movement is that of all such concertos: the solo

passages become richer and bigger as the work proceeds, and
from time to time the orchestra crowns a climax by breaking in
with the ritornello, each time appearing in some different related
key, as buttresses appear at suitable points as you walk round a
cathedral.

The slow movement is in a form which only Bach has brought to
perfection, though many an earlier composer used it in a less concentrated way. We may call it the modulating ground bass. The
orchestral ritornello consists of the bass of Ex. 2. Upon the last bar
of this enters the dialogue between the solo and the upper strings,
which I give in the other staves of the quotation.

The ritornello becomes a ground bass to this dialogue throughout the movement, but it differs from an ordinary ground bass in this, that its final cadence shifts to a different key each time, and that before each recurrence a connecting link of three bars (modelled on bars 3-6 of Ex. 2) establishes yet another key for it to start from. At last, of course, it comes round to the tonic; the final cadence is expanded (in the church cantata there is a crowning stroke of genius in the chorus here), and the movement closes, as it began, with the bare ground bass. Part of the unique grandeur and solemnity of this concerto lies in the fact that the slow movement is in the minor mode, and still darker than the other movements. In all Bach's other concertos and sonatas in the minor mode the slow movement is in a major key.

The finale, though in no obvious outward contrast to the rest of this powerful work, is distinctly brighter in tone. Bach has proved that he meant it to be so, by arranging it for organ as a prelude to a cantata on the text 'In the Lord have I put my trust' (*Ich habe meine Zuversicht*). Unfortunately, though we possess the cantata itself, only one page of this arrangement is extant. It shows that Bach has added the same extra instruments, but has not, so far as we can see, transposed the solo part to a lower octave.

I give the ritornello, numbering with roman figures those clauses which the orchestra sometimes brings in separately. It is also necessary to quote the bass of clause 1, because it is in 'double counterpoint' with the treble; that is to say, in some of the later returns of the theme the treble becomes bass and the bass treble.

Ex. 3.

The solo is as full of remarkable violin passages as in the first movement, and the extant fragment of its arrangement as a church cantata prelude throws valuable light on the original form of the final cadenza. The design is on almost the same vast scale as the first movement, so that this movement, though not the longest movement in this concerto, is the most important of all Bach's instrumental finales; a fitting climax to this monumental work.

The preface to the miniature score of this concerto asserts, on the authority of recent musicologists, that the composition is not only arranged from a lost violin work, but that its style shows it to be one of Bach's transcriptions from Vivaldi or some obscurer writer. If any predecessor of Bach could have designed the whole of a single paragraph of this concerto, Bach's position would not have been unique. He has the same kind of scholarship as Milton, and the same power to assimilate his material, no matter where it comes from. But when he arranges Vivaldi, Telemann, or even the best work of his own uncles, every patch added by him annihilates the rest. My disrespect is unparliamentary for a musicology that has no sense of composition. The only composer who could have planned this concerto is John Sebastian Bach.

CONCERTO IN D MINOR FOR TWO VIOLINS AND STRINGS

1 *Allegro.* 2 *Largo ma non tanto.* 3 *Allegro.*

Bach is known to have written two double concertos on similar lines. The well-known one we possess in its original form, and also in one of Bach's own wonderful arrangements for two harpsichords. The arrangement is lowered a tone, as in most similar cases; and, though it loses much with the loss of the violin qualities, it gains some fine detail for the left-hand parts of the two claviers. The slow movement, however, is obviously only a makeshift in this clavier version. The other concerto exists only in the clavier version. It was originally (as technical details prove) in C minor, and has not been transposed. As a concerto for two claviers it is very well known; but it is obviously twin-brother to the famous work now before us, and loses very nearly as much in its arrangement for claviers. Seiffert has shown that it is for violin and oboe.

Nearly all Bach's concertos are exceptionally highly finished; that is to say, we possess them in forms which record a large proportion of what Bach usually left unwritten because he was at the keyboard himself and needed no guidance. An astonishing amount of fine detail in phrasing is given by Bach himself; so that it is no mere purist prejudice to say that performances from modernized editions are more remarkable for what they leave out than for what they put in. Who, for instance, could pick out from a crowd of fussy editorial details the authentic fact that in Ex. 4 it is Bach himself who wishes one violin to play the figures detached while the other plays them slurred? But the main and most misleading omission of modernized productions of Bach comes in the ignoring or the wrongly conceived execution of the continuo, or filling out of the figured bass on a keyed instrument. This device was the eighteenth-century composer's standardized method for settling all that most troublesome class of problems in modern orchestra: the problems of securing that all necessary harmonic filling-out should be at once present and unobtrusive. The details of a really fully figured bass by Bach are almost a complete system of what may be called interior instrumentation—though they concern only a scarcely audible keyed instrument and are written in a kind of musical shorthand. Without their careful execution nobody, for instance, will ever hear the consummate final effect at the end of the slow movement of this concerto when Ex. 4, which has hitherto always been filled out, is left *tasto solo*, that is to say, with the bare bass.

For analysis it will suffice to give the main themes. There are always, in the first and last movements of a Bach concerto, two themes or groups of themes; a tutti ritornello—

Ex. 1.

and a solo theme—

Ex. 2.

which, if independent, as here, is destined to be combined in counterpoint with the tutti. These groups of material are built up into an architectural design, in which portions of the ritornello intervene in different keys like buttresses at the corners of a building. The designs throughout this concerto and its lost twin-brother are remarkably terse without any loss of breadth. For instance, the end of the first movement with no more than four bars of final ritornello ought theoretically to sound abrupt: but it does not.

The slow movements of Bach's concertos leave more to the solo players; and this slow movement has no tuttis at all. Nevertheless its main theme—

Ex. 3.

stands out like a ritornello, alternating with short and more conversational themes, such as—

Ex. 4.

Nowhere has Bach written music with a more irresistible appeal to personal affection.

In the finale Bach takes advantage of the transparency of his string orchestra and of his rhythms, and gives his unmistakable tutti theme to the solo violins, leaving the orchestra to supply merely the accented figures. Hence a special liveliness in the opening, which is entirely lost when the work is played merely with pianoforte accompaniment.

Ex. 5.

The solo themes are in graceful contrast.

Ex. 6.

Twice later on in the movement comes another lyric episode.

Ex. 7.

Everybody will remember with delight the other episode, in which the solo violins give a Handelian mass of four-part harmony in slashing chords.

CONCERTO IN C MINOR FOR VIOLIN AND OBOE
(RESTORED FROM THE CLAVIER VERSION)

1 *Allegro.* 2 *Adagio, leading to* 3 *Allegro.*

Bach's extant works include eight clavier concertos, three concertos for two claviers, and two for three claviers, besides a transcription for four claviers of a concerto by Vivaldi. On the other hand, only three violin concertos and one concerto for two violins have been preserved. Yet the study of all these concertos in connexion with each other and with the rest of Bach's work reveals that as a matter of fact only three of the clavier concertos (the C major Double Concerto, the D major Brandenburg Concerto, and the A minor Concerto) are originally clavier music at all, that all the rest are wonderful arrangements of other works, and that at least one double concerto and the equivalents of three violin concertos are lost. Their restoration from the clavier versions is possible with a very small margin of error.

The C minor Concerto is twin-brother to the well-known D minor Concerto for two violins: indeed, the slow movement of the C minor contains a figure (marked *a* in Ex. 3) which might easily drift into the other slow movement. But there are notable individual features: e.g. the solo echoes in the opening tutti of the first movement.

Ex. 1 *a.*

I.

Ex. 1 b.

After the tutti paragraph with its two ideas, the solo players enter
with a cantabile of their own.

Ex. 2.

Although I have conducted this concerto in a performance with
two violins, I ought to have been able to infer from this theme alone
what Dr. Max Seiffert has demonstrated: that the work is for oboe
and violin, and not for two violins. The instrument that has the
cantabile never has the accompaniment figure; and vice versa. I
had always noticed this as an unaccountable feature in the clavier
version. Its reason is self-evident, if the instrument of the cantabile theme is an oboe. The tone of the oboe is exquisite with the
cantabile theme, above a violin as the vehicle of the accompanying
figure; but that figure would be detestable on the oboe. Therefore
the parts cannot interchange.

The rest of the movement is built up with Bach's usual architecture of solo paragraphs culminating in entries of the tutti in the
various related keys until the harmonic ground has been surveyed
on all sides. The movement is terse, and the solos remain in close
touch with the tuttis throughout.

The adagio (like the well-known largo of the D minor Double
Concerto) begins with a broad melody—

Ex. 3.

stated by the violin and answered in the dominant by the oboe. The
accompaniment is in rich pizzicato chords, until late in the movement where a deep poetic touch appears in the entry of solemn
holding-notes while the solo players develop a wistful new theme.

Ex. 4.

The staccato marks and slurs are Bach's own.

Unlike its famous twin brother, this movement does not complete itself, but leads to the dominant of C minor so as to break into the finale. Of this we need quote only the spirited main theme.

Ex. 5.

In the slow movement a glance at the bass of the extant clavier version will convince any reasonable person that it is a positive duty to restore this work from a condition in which it can be played only on instruments incapable of representing it without make-shifts; while the brilliant passages of the finale, though quite easy to play on keyed instruments, have no particular meaning thereon, but are in the finest style of the violin and oboe in beautiful contrast with each other. If we ask why Bach arranged these works for less effective instruments, the answer is indicated by the survival of the arrangements: he could get them more often played (and probably better played) on the harpsichord.

BRANDENBURG CONCERTO IN G MAJOR, NO. 3, FOR NINE-PART STRING ORCHESTRA

1 Allegro. 2 Solo Interlude, leading to 3 Vivace.

This work is a concerto grosso, a term that does not always imply the same thing, but does here very fitly describe a concerto in which there is no actual solo, but nevertheless a clear contrast between the style of a tutti ritornello and the style of solo passages. This is effected by the grouping of the instruments. In the present instance the tutti ritornello, a long single sentence (the melody of which I here give in full), is scored in three-part harmony, which soon coalesces into two parts and finally into octaves, thus attaining a climax of resonance.

Ex. 1.

The orchestra then breaks up into nine parts, plus the bass and continuo (or unwritten harmonic filling-out by a keyed instrument).
These nine parts, three violins, three violas, and three violoncellos,
discuss the figures of the ritornello (I have lettered these figures in
my quotation) and allow themselves at increasingly long intervals
to coalesce again into tutti outbreaks of this or that clause, thereby
marking climaxes in various related keys. There is plenty of
clearly-marked variety in their possible groupings, more indeed
than in any polyphonic concerto with a single solo, or even such a
quartet of solos as the Second Brandenburg Concerto with its flute,
oboe, violin, and sopranino trumpet. For you may have the violins
coalesced into tutti while the violas and 'cellos are divided; and in
one very impressive, Leviathan-like passage the 'cellos are disport-
ing themselves in a vigorous solo style, though, for the sake of
clearness, they are playing in unison. The work was probably
intended for one instrument to each part, on which condition the
contrasts assert themselves automatically. In performances by
larger bands the nine-part passages should certainly be played as
solos. The work then appears in its full vividness as Bach meant it.

To judge by what passes for orthodoxy on the subject of Bach's
scoring you would believe that he never considered how to make
things clear, but only how to keep his contrapuntal schemes complete and methodical. This is not so: often it is only the theorists
who think that a passage is unintelligible unless they can hear 'the
subject', whereas all that really matters is the mass of harmony
and the balance of the musical sentence as a rhythmic whole; and
hardly less often Bach's method of scoring is as carefully balanced
as Mozart's or Wagner's. But you must not be guided by modern
editorial marks of expression, which take no account of the axioms
of Bach's art-forms (e.g. this distinction between solo and tutti), or
the instruments for which he wrote, or the acoustics of the places
where the music was to be played.

From the many episodes which diversify this very large first
movement I quote the surprising fresh start which is made, about
in the middle, by the first theme treated in a new combination
suggestive of the opening of a triple fugue.

Ex. 2.

Surprises are still in store up to what seems the final ritornello, which is expanded in its last phrase by the interruption of just one more dispersal of the strings into their thrice-threefold division.

Some time after Bach had produced the Brandenburg Concertos, he used this movement as the introduction to a church cantata (*Ich liebe den Höchsten*), and turned the nine parts into fourteen, by adding two horns, two oboes, and a taille or alto oboe. He also greatly lightened and cleared the bass, and gave very complete figuring for the guidance of the continuo player. This figuring should be used without reservation; and, speaking generally, performances of Bach's concerted music without a filled-out continuo are a mistake excusable only on the ground that most of the published fillings-out are worse than nothing at all. The improvements in the bass should also be adopted, but with careful rejection of those particular alterations that result only from the additional wind-parts. It is unfortunately impossible to use these magnificent wind-parts in performances of the concerto as such, for Bach did not arrange the finale for them.

After the first movement there are two queer-looking adagio chords forming a half-close on the dominant of E minor. Handel has familiarized everybody with the effect of a half-close in such a key by way of prelude to a quick movement in the relative major: but the chords as they stand here seem to mean nothing, and are therefore generally omitted. It is as certain as any human inference can be that Bach here extemporized a slow movement or instrumental recitative on the harpsichord, and that these two chords represent its close, as joined in by the orchestra. By great good fortune Bach happens to have written a derelict slow movement in his maturest style which exactly fits this place, except that its last chords are on the dominant of G, a trivial discrepancy which can be easily remedied by altering the orchestral chords to suit it. The last of his six great sonatas for cembalo and violin went through extraordinary vicissitudes in three successive versions, borrowing an aria from a church cantata and a gavotte and courante from a clavier partita. During these changes it shed a beautiful little adagio which had never had any other home and which is undoubtedly wanted here.

Ex. 3.

&c.

It has just the ruminating character which an idealized extemporization should have, though it conceals a close-knit form something like a three-part round that should change its key at each entry, or like a ground bass that every now and then goes to a new key and sometimes rises to the surface. I give its three principal themes in the combination to which they attain in the course of their exposition. Other counter-subjects arise later.

The finale is a kind of gigue in binary form with a second part just three times as long as the first. For the sake of clearness, in all its wheeling dance the basses are never divided; but the upper strings, without sharply marking the line between tutti and solo, bring out every variety of combination, division, and unison.

Bach certainly intended the work to be played by eleven players, the nine concertantists, a double-bass, and the harpsichord. With this combination the distinction between nine-part solo and three-part tutti is very clear. With large string-bands it becomes a mere orchestra *divisi*; and I am sure of the vital importance of my plan of entrusting the nine-part passages to solo players and confining the full string-band to the three-part tuttis.

BRANDENBURG CONCERTO IN G MAJOR, NO. 4, FOR VIOLIN

1 *Allegro*. 2 *Andante, leading to* 3 *Presto*.

Bach evidently aimed at making the six concertos dedicated to the Markgraf of Brandenburg as different as possible in their combinations of instruments, while maintaining throughout the most cheerful of spirits. Lyric sentiment is allowed to luxuriate in the slow movements, but the first movements and finales are among Bach's most brilliant and joyous creations. Each of the six concertos represents not only a different group of instruments, but also a different view of their relation to each other and to the orchestra. The third and sixth are specimens of the concerto grosso, in which there are no solo instruments, but the contrast between solo and tutti is represented by that between the whole mass and smaller groups. The first is also largely a concerto grosso; but a shrill kit-violin gradually emerges from the ensemble, and joins with a solo oboe in the slow movement, while the finale is a minuet for the full orchestra with three trios for three contrasted groups. The second concerto is a quadruple concerto for flute, oboe, violin, and trumpet; and the fifth is a triple concerto for clavier, violin, and flute.

The fourth concerto is often described as a triple concerto for violin and two flutes, but this is not quite correct. It is essentially

a violin concerto, and the prominence of the flutes results from the
singular fact that the themes of the tutti are delivered by them
together with the solo violin in an opening paragraph, throughout
which the orchestra is confined to a staccato emphasis on the main
points. In other words, the solo violin and the flutes dominate the
opening ritornello, which is nevertheless still conceived as a tutti.
The gulf between tutti and solo is thus bridged, but the distinction
remains perfectly clear, just as in the Italian Concerto, where Bach,
writing for harpsichord alone, preserves every possible feature of
concerto form and style. And there, as here, the opening tutti is
exceptionally long. Bars of 3/8 allegro are indeed short, but 83 of
them is a large order. When the whole ritornello recurs at the end
of the first movement, it has more the effect of the da capo of the
whole first part of an aria than that of a mere final symphony. But
the middle episodes show clearly that we are listening to a violin
concerto, and not to a triple concerto. The material of the flutes
remains that of the ritornello, and if in some passages they are
heard with solo matter apart from the violin, this is only because
there is no reason to lose the opportunity of so hearing them. They
should be *flûtes-à-bec*—something between the flageolet and the
recorder.

The following quotations give the themes of the great ritornello:—

and here is the entry of the first genuine solo passage—

The six-bar rhythm of Ex. 1 is unusual with Bach, and the listener is likely to apprehend it as 4+2 rather than as the twice three that the eye at once perceives in the groups of notes. And the listener is probably right: for the sequel proceeds in pairs of bars, and, in any case, when Ex. 1 returns, it will take more than one pair to assert its own rhythm. Theorists are apt to vex themselves with vain efforts to remove uncertainty just where it has a high aesthetic value.

The slow movement is unique in Bach's later works for a Handelian massiveness and an abstinence not only from ornamentation but even from anything that might give the violinist opportunity for adding ornament. Indeed, the violin is for the most part a simple bass to the flutes. In the later version of this work as a clavier concerto in F the slow movement has been entirely re-scored, but without any change of its severity. It leads, with a Handelian half-close, to the finale. The following two bars give almost the whole substance of the slow movement.

' The finale is, if we use terms reasonably broadly, a fugue on the following majestic subject—

The exposition of this makes a grand opening ritornello, and the free episodes, while giving scope to the solo violin, do not neglect the fugue-subject for long. Indeed, in the very first solo the flutes accompany the violin with the subject in stretto at two bars. When the ritornello recurs, as it does at the usual intervals and in the usual variety of keys, it is treated with some freedom, and at the end a new climax is provided, thus—

CONCERTO IN A MAJOR FOR OBOE D'AMORE
WITH STRINGS AND CONTINUO

1 *Allegro.* 2 *Larghetto.* 3 *Allegro ma non tanto.*

The A major cembalo concerto leaves no doubt in my mind that it was originally intended for the oboe d'amore, an instrument mid-way between the oboe and the English horn: being in fact an oboe in A with an English-horn bulb-shaped bell. The opening of the concerto in the clavier version, which is all that has reached us, shows, in the clavier arpeggios of its first two bars, that Bach is trying to give the harpsichord player something characteristic to do.

But he abandons the effort except where this part of the theme appears: and it is perfectly obvious that throughout the work he has no other harpsichord style in his mind except in scattered details for the left hand. At first the scholar is puzzled by an equally conspicuous lack of anything like the violin style which is so conspicuous in the other cembalo arrangements; but as soon as we recall Bach's usual treatment of the oboe d'amore the whole thing becomes intensely characteristic, from the sonorous first solo entry—

to the last note.

In the autograph the slow movement is a veritable palimpsest as to the solo part: and the skill of Wilhelm Rust, the editor of vol. xvii of the Bach-Gesellschaft edition, has enabled us to see Bach's mind at work transforming the original solo, with its irreducible minimum of breathing-places, to the more ornate and uninterrupted flow of rhetoric which fingers can command on keyed instruments. From the version thus extracted and given by Rust in an appendix we can get very close to the original oboe d'amore part.

A second theme in a major key, with the ostinato figure of the strings inverted—

is recapitulated some time afterwards in a lower key, and here it is interesting to observe that Bach, in copying it out, already fills up its breathing-spaces, so that the latter part of the movement is not a palimpsest like the rest. Clearly then, in restoring the work for oboe d'amore, we must follow the first statement of the theme.

Bach never wrote a more radiant melody than the opening tutti of the finale—

nor a more typically angelic one than the entry of the solo.

Ex. 6.

Every point in this concerto demands a wind instrument, and that the oboe d'amore, to express it convincingly. No other instrument of Bach's time had the exact compass and the exact style. Nowadays a clarinet could do it very pleasantly, and could effectively use the clavier arpeggios of Ex. 1. But it would be dull and cold just where the oboe d'amore is deep and thrilling in Ex. 2.

CONCERTO IN A MINOR FOR CLAVIER, FLUTE, AND VIOLIN

1 *Allegro.* 2 *Adagio ma non tanto, e dolce; leading to* 3 *Alla breve.*

This is one of Bach's greatest and richest instrumental works: nor has he ever achieved a scoring fuller and more minutely thought out in every bar. Yet it is from first to last an arrangement of older works that were never intended to be in concerto form at all. The astounding result is an arrangement only in an historical sense, for, had the originals been lost, no sensible person would have wished to restore them or would even have suspected their existence.

The loss of the originals of Bach's other cembalo concertos is disastrous, and their restoration a duty, because they were not keyboard music at all, but violin or wind music. But the first movement and finale of this concerto were originally a big prelude and fugue for cembalo alone; every bar of which has been either retained, improved, or expanded in the concerto. The perpetual flow of the original pieces, which, though energetic, verged on monotony, is gloriously diversified by the noble orchestral ritornellos which Bach builds into opening paragraphs, and which recur at the important cadences, expanding the original movements to half as long again. The solo violin and solo flute are additional parts which it is almost impossible to imagine omitted; thus they are freshly invented and are in no sense 'arranged' from anything else, though they are *derived* from the main themes.

Of the first movement I quote, not the whole ritornello, but the transformations of its first figure.

Ex. 1.

The slow movement, in C major, is arranged from that of the organ sonata (or cembalo trio) in D minor. It is transposed from F, and, while the cembalo left hand plays the original pedal part, the right hand plays that of the upper manual, and the flute that of the lower. To this trio the violin adds a new fourth part in pizzicato arpeggios. But the original movement was in two portions with repeats. Now the repeats are written in full, for the upper parts are turned round, the violin taking the clavier melody an octave lower, the clavier taking the flute part *in situ*, and the flute taking the pizzicato arpeggios an octave higher. Ex. 2 *a* and *b* give the two positions.

A couple of extra bars lead into the finale. Here the orchestra makes a ritornello out of a marvellously ingenious transformation of the original fugue theme which the cembalo gives unaltered. Ex. 3 shows the relation between the two versions.

The ritornello version here relieves the tarantella-like perpetual motion of the original composition, but introduces a very much grander idea. A fine cadenza is inserted before the end, and there is a Mozart-like richness and symphonic quality in the accompaniments throughout. And so this work, historically an arrangement, first and finally achieves originality in its present form.

BEETHOVEN

PIANOFORTE CONCERTO IN C MAJOR, OP. 15, WITH BEETHOVEN'S CADENZA

1 *Allegro con brio.* 2 *Largo.* 3 RONDO: *Allegro.*

The first three pianoforte concertos of Beethoven show, in the opening tuttis of their first movements, a phenomenon almost unique in his works. In other branches of music we may find signs of a struggle with stubborn material, and Beethoven himself sometimes admitted that for this or that problem of vocal and dramatic music he had 'not studied enough'. But in the first two pianoforte concertos all is facile and spacious, while in the third, in C minor, which he declared, before he wrote it, 'will be the best of the three', he not only made a great stride in the direction of his 'second style', but set the model for the orthodox concerto form of his younger contemporaries and later theorists. Yet in all three concertos the nature of the opening tutti is radically misconceived; and that of the C minor Concerto (as is pointed out in my analysis of it) is an advance upon the other two only inasmuch as Beethoven seems to discover the error at the moment of committing it, with the result that its tutti executes a charmingly dramatic *volte-face* in mid-career, as if to say 'But no!—I must not be the beginning of a symphony'. In his later concertos Beethoven realized and carried out the purpose of Mozart's opening tutti, one of the subtlest and grandest art-forms ever devised; but no sooner was he able to do this than he was able to transcend Mozart in every line of instrumental and harmonic form, so that contemporary and later orthodoxy blundered far more grossly about his concerto form than any early failure of his to see the purport of Mozart's.

The composer or theorist may imagine that because Mozart's tutti is voluminous and flowing it is also discursive and can indulge in passages of development. Or he may imagine that it can be throughout like the exposition of a symphony, and that it should accordingly display its first subject, transition, and second subject, so that the listener knows beforehand exactly what the solo instrument is going to do. The first misapprehension is shown by Beethoven in his first two concertos; the second appears in the C minor Concerto and is instantly corrected, but not until its impression has been made with such force that, until Brahms came to the rescue, the opening tutti of the classical concerto remained a mystery to composers and theorists alike.

Now the C major Concerto (which is later than the B flat Concerto published second to it as opus 19) seems to have been an

object of more interest to Beethoven than he admitted. At all
events he wrote no less than three cadenzas to its first movement,
and the third of these cadenzas is one of his most splendid successes
in recording the style of an extemporization. It is fully in his
'second manner', and the compass given to the pianoforte shows
that it must have been written at least as late as the published score
of the C minor Concerto; that is to say, later than the Kreutzer
Sonata, and not much earlier than the Waldstein Sonata, which
it closely resembles in pianoforte technique. It is a wonderful
exception to the general style of the cadenzas Beethoven wrote for
his own concertos (he also wrote two for Mozart's D minor Concerto); and indeed I have not a word in favour of what he called
a *cadenza per non cadere* for the Concerto in G, or of the curious
pianoforte version he made of his Violin Concerto. I remember that a
distinguished English pianist played the G major Concerto in Berlin,
in 1900 or 1901, with Beethoven's cadenzas, not having announced
the fact. The critics really hardly deserved their fate; but it was
unfortunate that they went so far as to call these cadenzas *geradezu
unmusikalisch*, though they might well think them hopelessly inadequate and frivolous. There is another set which is not bad.

But the case of this third cadenza to the C major Concerto is
utterly different: it affords a noble pretext for reviving a neglected
early masterpiece which it harmoniously lifts to a higher plane of
musical thought. I cannot help wondering whether Beethoven
could not have made something almost as great out of his first
cadenza, which he left unfinished just after it had developed on
lines calculated to bring certain discursive passages of the tutti
into closer organic connexion with the whole. The speculation is
interesting, because the point, if achieved, would have anticipated
what he does in the coda of his last concerto (the great E flat, called,
to his profound if posthumous disgust, 'The Emperor').

The C major Concerto begins with quiet and martial energy.

Ex. 1.
(a)

A *forte* counterstatement leads to a grand pause on the dominant, upon which a fragment of the second subject appears in a
remote key, and is carried through other keys in rising sequence.

Ex. 2.

This is very beautiful; but processions (or concerto tuttis) will get into difficulties if they often thus digress in search of the picturesque; and it is this passage which Beethoven worked up bodily into his, unfortunately incomplete, first cadenza. The next passage, founded on Ex. 1, is also discursive—

Ex. 3.

and forms the opening text for all the three cadenzas.

At last the orchestra settles down to a cadence theme in Beethoven's most British-Grenadiers style—

Ex. 4.

and with a final paragraph on figure (a) of Ex. 1 the orchestra comes to a formal close. Not until the G major Concerto did Beethoven follow the example, twice set by Mozart, of letting the solo enter on the dominant chord with an introductory passage. On the other hand he follows several examples of Mozart in beginning with an entirely new theme—

Ex. 5.

though, unlike Mozart, he omits to develop it later, not even finding room for it in any of his cadenzas. The orchestra intervenes with figure (a) of Ex. 1, and the dialogue now follows the orthodox course of a concerto, the pianoforte working out a broad transition to G major, where Ex. 2 appears as a regular and complete melody by way of second subject. After a short digression, Ex. 4 follows, and brilliant passages then run an easy course, though some energetic staccatos markedly anticipate a prominent feature of the E flat Concerto. The anticipation becomes still more noticeable at the end, and amounts to more than coincidence, formal as the

passage is in both cases, and deeply rooted in the organization as
it is in the later work.

The development is, as usual in concertos, largely episodic, the
pianoforte beginning grandly with another entirely new theme
which I need not quote. Perhaps one reason why Beethoven
abandoned his first cadenza was a feeling that if he once began to
pick up loose threads there would be no end to the task; and that
the true course was to accept the pleasure that the Mozartean Angel
of All Art-Forms allows to those who Really Can Extemporize.

The return to the recapitulation is gravely dramatic in Beethoven's best 'first style'; the pianoforte taking its final plunge there-
into by an octave-glissando; at which the modern pianoforte jibs.
The recapitulation itself is adroitly curtailed as to the first subject
and unaltered as to the second.

And now comes the pause for the cadenza. Beethoven's third
cadenza storms away in magnificent Waldstein-sonata style, at first
apropos of Ex. 3, then apropos of figure (a), which starts on a voyage
round the solar system. The second subject (Ex. 2) appears at last
in vastly remote keys, and drifts sublimely from the style of *La
Clemenza di Tito* to the style of *Fidelio*. Thunderous further
developments of figure (a) burst forth, and at last the usual final
shake is heard; but surely rather too much on the dominant of G?
Quite so; we have something to say in G major about Ex. 4; please
don't interrupt! This being said, the shake arrives again and
develops with great excitement—while the orchestra waits for the
final turn. Instead of which the shake trails off into runs. And at
last the cadenza ends without any shake at all.

The difficulties of the classical concerto form are almost entirely confined to the first movement, and especially to its ritornello. In slow movements and rondos Beethoven was from the outset as great a master in concertos as in other instrumental forms; and a quotation of themes is all the commentary required for the rest of this unjustly neglected work. The largo begins with a three-strain melody (A, B, A), of which Ex. 8 is the first clause.

Ex. 8.

A broadly designed transition to the dominant gives an impression that the whole may be developed into full sonata form with Ex. 9 as second subject.

Ex. 9.

But Beethoven prefers to keep space for a less crowded scheme, and he brings back his whole first melody with rich ornamentation and new scoring (in all his early orchestral works there is no other example showing such appreciation of the clarinet), and, without any allusion to the middle portion, concludes with a long-drawn coda full of solemn new ideas.

Beethoven never wrote a wittier paragraph with more Haydnesque irregularity of rhythm than the main theme of the rondo of this concerto.

Ex. 10.

The various transition themes need not be quoted. The first

episode, which is treated (as in all full-sized concerto-rondos) like a second subject—

Ex. 11.

gives rise to a romantic digression in E flat and G minor, such as has made the second subject of the first movement of Beethoven's First Symphony famous; and it is remarkable in how many points the First Symphony follows cautiously the steps this rondo had already taken firmly and boldly.

The returns to the main theme are effected by the following Schubertesque transformation:

Ex. 12.

&c.

The middle episode alternates two superb themes in contrast, the one spirited (compare the corresponding theme in the Triple Concerto)—

Ex. 13.

&c.

and the other quiet, chromatic, and polyphonic.

Ex. 14.

The rest of the movement arises naturally out of these materials, and the coda is full of Haydn-Beethoven surprises, being (with the addition of several small undeveloped cadenzas) a glorified version of the later and less elaborate comic wind-up of the First Symphony.

PIANOFORTE CONCERTO IN C MINOR, OP. 37

1 *Allegro con brio.* 2 *Largo.* 3 RONDO: *Allegro vivace, Presto.*

Beethoven's third concerto was projected at the same time as his first and second; neither of which, as he openly avowed, was so important as this, for which he was reserving his best efforts. It is one of the works in which we most clearly see the style of his first period preparing to develop into that of his second. The main theme—

Ex. 1.

is a group of pregnant figures which nobody but Beethoven could have invented. They would rank as important themes in his latest works; but he here states them, quite successfully and unselfconsciously, in the tonic-and-dominant symmetries that still interested him for their own sake in his first period. With the transition theme—

Ex. 2.

he emphasizes the barest harmonic formulas with a youthful sententiousness peculiar to an artist who has grown conscious that these formulas are still necessary but no longer interesting, and that until some totally new light can be shed on them they are best left undecorated. (Two other works in the same key, the C minor Quartet, op. 18, No. 4, and the C minor Violin Sonata, show the same drastic simplicity at this juncture.)

Now comes a turning-point in the history of the classical concerto. The opening orchestral ritornello of the first movement in the concerto form had been developed by Mozart on a scale that has not to this day been surpassed; with the result that the entry of the solo instrument must, if it means anything at all, mean an event impressive because long delayed. If, then, long delayed, it must be long expected; and the expectation must be roused by the music and not merely by the title of the item on the programme. Mozart's opening tuttis are among the highest triumphs of art in their command of expectant exposition; no two examples are identical in their own plan, or in relation to the solo. Nor can Mozart's forms be correctly said to have a restraining influence on Beethoven's early work. To him these forms were no more orthodox than the forms of Richard Strauss were to the young composers of 1900. Nor indeed have Mozart's concerto forms been codified even yet with any greater accuracy than that of a child's hieroglyph of the human form as a disk supported on a triangle with two five-pronged forks attached as hands.

At all events Beethoven had something better to do than to consult text-books on the subject of concerto form. He did not immediately achieve Mozart's solution of the problem of the opening tutti; indeed it is arguable that he did not at first grasp what the problem really was. In his first two concertos the orchestra enjoys itself in ruminating developments which, like so many of the happy thoughts in Schubert's large instrumental works, stray away from the purpose of exposition. In the C minor Concerto, Ex. 2 takes direct dramatic action and leads to a long passage of preparation for the second subject in its destined new key. This is sheer symphonic exposition; it rouses no expectation of the entry of a solo instrument, and, as we shall find, leaves nothing essential for the pianoforte to add when its time comes. The second subject enters—

Ex. 3.

a cantabile midway between a Mozart heroine and the heroine of Beethoven's *Coriolanus* overture. Suddenly the orchestra seems to realize that it has no right to take the drama into its own hands; that its function is not drama but chorus-like narrative; and with a modulation in itself dramatic, the melody calmly turns round to C major and is followed by a series of cadence-phrases in the tonic minor (including derivatives of Ex. 1) which bring this, the longest of all Beethoven's concerto tuttis, to a massive formal close.

The works of Beethoven that have had the most influence on later composers are rather such transitional compositions than the compositions which Beethoven himself based on the experience he gained therein. It is the C minor Concerto that has ever since been taken as the normal classical example, and not the G major and E flat Concertos, which are supposed to introduce bold innovations. Yet it is only in these later works, and in the violin concerto, with the voluminous preparatory exercise of the Triple Concerto, op. 56, that Beethoven achieves Mozart's methods of handling the opening tutti, plus his own methods of setting the solo free. Spohr, Hummel, Chopin (in his F minor Concerto), and even Joachim in his Hungarian Concerto, all took Beethoven's C minor Concerto as their model for concerto form; and they all regarded as an inimitable and individual stroke of genius the one feature (the sudden shift back to the tonic during the announcement of the second subject) by which Beethoven rectifies something that dangerously resembled a mistake. This stroke being thus regarded as unorthodox, the 'classical' opening tutti henceforth became accepted as an ordinary symphonic exposition, prefixed, for reasons impious to inquire, to a sonata for a solo instrument with orchestral accompaniment. No wonder the easy common sense of Mendelssohn abolished this convention; but the possibilities of concertos with no scope for orchestral organization became fascinating to the virtuoso jerry-builder; and until Brahms tackled the true problem again, the vitality of concerto forms was becoming the vitality of undesirable things.

Beethoven, then, has in this C minor opening tutti recognized and saved a dangerous situation in the nick of time. The pianoforte can now enter and restate the exposition that the orchestra has given. Beyond two introductory bars of scales, dramatically useful in later entries, and a slight expansion of the passage of preparation for the second subject, the pianoforte follows the opening tutti, bar for bar, until the second subject (Ex. 3) has arrived. Here there is of course no need for the *volte-face* made in the original tutti: the pianoforte is now at last free to expand the material into a brilliant group of new phrases. These consist mainly of developments of figure (*b*) in Ex. 1 with running accompaniments, culminating in a long shake, below which clarinets and horns enter with a triumphant version of the whole theme. Then the full orchestra bursts out with its cadence phrases, and soon proceeds to shed new light on the long passage of preparation for the second subject (between Ex. 2 and Ex. 3) by giving it in G minor.

This is a genuine and important innovation, which Beethoven uses with powerful effect in the E flat Concerto, and in the Violin Concerto. Mozart never lets his second tutti modulate, and always brings it to a full close. Beethoven's new experiment goes far to set his form free. The pianoforte enters with its introductory scales, not as a formula on a tonic, but as a dramatic intervention on a dominant. It then settles down to a pathetic cantabile development of Ex. 1, the figure (*b*) unifying the whole design by persisting as an accompaniment. In broad and distinct steps the threshold of C minor is reached, and, after suitable preparation, the first subject begins the recapitulation fortissimo. After the close of the second subject (the triumphant clarinets beneath the final shake now becoming trumpets), the orchestra enters in the minor and soon leads to the usual pause for a cadenza, which Beethoven leaves to the player to compose or extemporize. After the cadenza it was usual for the orchestra to conclude the movement formally with the last few bars of the opening tutti: but Mozart had already found ways of using the solo instrument in the coda, notably in his C minor Concerto, a work which influenced Beethoven profoundly and conspicuously both as a

whole and in detail. And so here the final trill of the cadenza leads
to an unexpected turn of harmony which, together with the quiet
entry of the drums with figure (*b*), is one of Beethoven's most
typical strokes of genius. The pianoforte retains the whole conduct of the coda, and ends the movement with scales recalling
its first entry.

   The largo is the most highly developed slow movement in all
Beethoven's concertos, and *a fortiori* in any concerto. In his later
concertos the slow movements lead into the finales; gaining thereby
various dramatic subtleties and depths by release from the necessity
of completing their own design. But in the C minor Concerto we
have one of the great independent symphonic slow movements,
reaching the climax of Beethoven's powers of solemn expression
in his first period, and indeed quite in keeping with all that he
found to say in his second. The shock of the first chord, in its
remoteness from the C minor of the rest of the work—

Ex. 4.

is in itself a feature of Beethoven's second period, though his
earlier works show some preoccupation with things of the kind.
The impulse came from Haydn, whose later works contain
examples of every possible key-relation. The example of the slow
movement of Beethoven's C minor Concerto has had a direct and
obvious influence on later composers, e.g. Brahms's First Symphony
and Third Pianoforte Quartet.

   An ornate transition theme leads to a well-defined second subject
in the dominant.

Ex. 5.

   This is followed in due course by a sombre episode in dark keys,
with cloudy pianoforte arpeggios accompanying a slow dialogue
in the winds. The episode, which has the function of a development, drifts steadily towards the tonic, E major, and so returns
in its own good time to the first subject. Instead of recapitulating
the transition and the second subject, Beethoven makes a broad
coda out of the orchestral pendants to the first subject, having
already redistributed the dialogue as between solo and orchestra.

   The shock of E major after C minor is chiefly concentrated in
one note, G sharp, the major third of E. This is so near in pitch to
A flat that on keyed instruments the same note has to serve for

both. Haydn, in the last and greatest of his pianoforte sonatas, had ventured upon this shock in a still more paradoxical form, as between the keys of E flat and E natural (equivalent in this case to F flat); he accordingly began his finale with a theme which first taps rhythmically at G natural, and, having duly explained this as third of E flat, proceeds to show that the next step is A flat.

The first two notes of Beethoven's finale are a more immediate and drastic summary of a similar process. Like Haydn, Beethoven has taken care that the last chord of the slow movement shall display his Berkeleyan G sharp. Which Dr. Johnson refutes *thus*—

Ex. 6.

This great rondo is an admirable study in temper, worthy of the wisdom that inspired the tragic style of the other movements. Among the works with which this concerto is always provoking comparison by reason of its singularly direct influence on later composers, three finales are conspicuous—those of Joachim's Hungarian Concerto, Brahms's First Pianoforte Concerto, and Mendelssohn's C minor Trio. It is astonishing how closely both Brahms and Joachim have followed the scheme of this finale, even in such details as the structure of the transition passages and the fugue passage of development after the second episode. The interest in comparing Mendelssohn's C minor Trio finale is different; it is a warning against giving tragic weight to emotions which in real life relieve themselves in a gust of temper. Mendelssohn's first theme is in much the same temper as Beethoven's, and promises a not less spirited career. His second theme is in an enthusiastic mood which would be rather shocked by an apparent lack of moral indignation in Beethoven's energetic second theme.

Ex. 7.

And for the consolatory middle episode and triumphant end of his finale Mendelssohn unfortunately bursts into tears and a chorale. Beethoven's way of sounding the depths is more religiously consistent with his opening.

Ex. 8.

This comfortable and leisurely tune is followed by a little fugue on the main theme (Ex. 6), beginning in F minor. The pianoforte intervenes dramatically and carries us to a remote key which is the more impressive in that it happens to be that of the slow movement. From this the steps back to C minor are broad and firm, and the anticipation of the return to the rondo theme is duly exciting. The recapitulation of both main theme and second subject (Ex. 7) is complete and regular.

But the coda is utterly unexpected. In the tuttis of the main theme the oboe had already made a splendid point by appearing with the theme in the major, transforming its initial G–A♭ into G♯–A♮. Now the pianoforte, entering after an ornamental cadenza, takes up this idea in the following new tempo and rhythm:

Ex. 9.

The rest of this presto is a brilliant series of fresh cadential phrases, the last of which—

Ex. 10.

is a transformation of Ex. 7.

PIANOFORTE CONCERTO IN G MAJOR, OP. 58

(Meiningen Programmes, 1902, with alterations.)

1 *Allegro moderato.* 2 *Andante con moto; leading to* 3 RONDO: *Vivace.*

The G major Concerto is a work of a particularly prolific time in Beethoven's career. Its opus-number places it between the so-called 'Appassionata' Sonata and the three enormous string quartets dedicated to Count Rasoumovsky; but Beethoven was always at work on so many things at once, and so often allowed one work to wait for years before completing it from sketches, that his opus-numbers give little clue to the chronology of anything but publication. In almost any four consecutive years of Beethoven's life the chronology of his works is inextricable. The first idea for a finale to this concerto was a graceful theme in semiquavers, which, a year later, became the principal figure of the prisoners' chorus in *Fidelio.* The present slow movement of the third Rasoumovsky Quartet supplanted a wonderful idea in the same key which could hardly have been developed properly by a string quartet, and which eventually became the allegretto of the Seventh Symphony. Nottebohm's *Beethoveniana* and *Zweite Beethoveniana,* consisting of

copious extracts from Beethoven's sketch-books, will almost impel
one to believe that Beethoven's whole life's work was as connected
as a single composition. We even find the theme of his last sonata,
op. 111, appearing in connexion with early sketches for the Violin
Sonata in A major, op. 30, no. 3.

So much, then, for the chronology of this concerto. Beethoven
himself took the pianoforte part in its first public performance (on
December 22nd, 1808); and, we are told by eyewitnesses and
critics, played very impulsively and at a tremendous pace. This
seems at first startlingly out of character with the first movement,
but the explanation of Beethoven's 'tremendous pace' is simply
that, the tempo being allegro moderato, the rapid passages are
written in triplet semiquavers and demisemiquavers, and are thus
nearly twice as fast as any that had been written before.

All three movements of Beethoven's G major Concerto demonstrate the aesthetic principles of concerto form with extraordinary
subtlety. In the first movement Beethoven lets the pianoforte state
the first phrase—a quiet cantabile which is immediately taken up
by the orchestra entering softly in a bright, remote key, a wonderful stroke of genius.[1]

Ex. 1.

Here the orchestra (a small one without trumpets and drums)
has the next sixty-eight bars to itself, and gives in rapid succession, with beautiful variety of crescendos and *fortes* and *pianos*,
the following themes—

Ex. 2.

A development of No. 1.

leading through a broad crescendo to another quiet theme belonging (as we afterwards learn) to the second subject, and modulating
through a considerable range of keys—

Ex. 3.

[1] Mozart's interesting early Concerto in E flat (K.V. 291) anticipates
Beethoven in allowing the pianoforte to share the first theme with the
orchestra, but only in a jocular fashion with results no more than formal
and witty.

followed by mysterious rising sequences on (*a*) and other figures

Ex. 4.

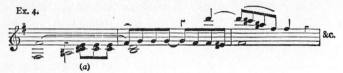

(*a*)

culminating in—

Ex. 5.

a very important theme, which leads to the final figures of the ritornello; viz.—

Ex. 6.

and a new derivative of Ex. 1—

Ex. 7.

on which the solo enters with a meditative, long-drawn development of figure (*a*) which broadens and quickens into brilliant running passages.

Fifteen bars (no less) of this broad expanse lead to the restatement of the material of the opening tutti, with the co-operation of the solo instrument. The restatement begins with Ex. 2, and the pianoforte interpolates a series of brilliant new figures while the orchestra holds the thread with the rhythm ♩ ♫ ♩ | ♩ of (*a*), and the bassoon and other wood-wind take up the theme in dialogue.

Suddenly the pianoforte becomes contemplative in a dark key—

Ex. 8.

and in a few bars of the highest beauty modulates to the dominant, where there is a passage of preparation for the second subject. This soon appears, beginning, to our surprise, with a new melody of which the opening tutti had not uttered a note.

Ex. 9.

Strings.

This is answered by the pianoforte in a playful variation; and another brilliant solo, in which again the orchestra holds the thread with ♩ ♫♫ ♩, leads to Ex. 3, beginning in D minor, and soon enriched with an ornate flow of semiquavers in the pianoforte. This leads through Ex. 4 (as in the tutti) to Ex. 5, all with the most brilliant pianoforte accompaniment. These pianoforte figures seem, as they have already done before, to force their way through the structure till they emerge in a broad open expanse, and we hear the long trill which classical composers have generally found the most convenient way of ending the first solo in the exposition of the first movement of a concerto. Beethoven, however, does not end with the trill; he makes it lead gently to another repetition of Ex. 5 by the pianoforte, beginning this time *piano* (so as to reveal the innate tenderness of this majestic theme), but with a crescendo that brings in the orchestra in triumph with the rest of the ritornello (including Exx. 6 and 7) just as in the opening tutti.

Beethoven has now well and truly laid the foundations of his concerto form and is free to raise his edifice to heights undreamt of in earlier music. As the first essay in this volume shows, the composer's main difficulties in the classical concerto are concentrated in the opening tutti and the solo exposition of the first movement, the rest of the concerto presenting no special problems. Unless appearances have misled me (the chronology of Beethoven's Opp. 53–60 being so inextricable), the voluminous Triple Concerto, Op. 56, is the technical exercise by which Beethoven experimented with dry material in correcting the errors which he recognized in his first three concertos. The obvious stroke of genius by which the pianoforte opens the G major Concerto and gives the orchestra occasion to enter in a foreign key is not more wonderful than the art with which the sequel retains and enhances the processional character of the classical tutti; avoiding alike the dangerous symphonic action which in the C minor Concerto threatens to make the pianoforte an intruder, and the not less dangerous discursiveness which in the C major and B flat Concertos leaves the tutti at a loose end with matter almost more improvisatorial than that of the solo. Contrast those expensive luxuries with the wonderful modulating single theme (Ex. 3) which quietly takes its place in the procession and yet covers a wide range of keys, only to confirm the home tonic more strongly.

Again, note the complete freedom of the solo exposition in expanding in brilliant or ruminating passages and in introducing new matter such as Exx. 8 and 9. Yet the material of the tutti is quite as exhaustively used as in the C minor Concerto, where the pianoforte was rigid in its translation of it. Every allusion to it increases by reflection the cogency of the original orchestral statement.

Imagine the solo version of Ex. 3 as it would sound if we had not heard the opening tutti: brilliant ornamentation for the pianoforte, with a melody on an oboe; beautiful in itself, but no contribution to the balance of forces. But the opening tutti has taught us to associate that theme with the orchestra, and its appearance on a single oboe now gives us the feeling that the orchestra is being properly represented by its most pathetic member; so we listen to the ornamental pianoforte part with worthier feelings than admiration of personal display.

The development begins with the pianoforte interrupting the quiet close of the ritornello (Ex. 7) by striking the rhythmic figure ⁊ ♪♪♪ | ♩ on the minor third, F natural. Then follows a series of mysterious modulations, with an entirely new figure (x) springing out of (a) as if by accident.

Ex. 10.

Suddenly the pianoforte awakens to an energetic mood, which lasts for a considerable time, while the orchestra quietly works out (a) in combination with the new figure (x). At length we come to an impassioned climax in the extremely distant key of C sharp minor, and another mysterious process begins. Figure (a) is worked out again, from its rhythm ⁊ ♪♪♪ ♩ in the basses, to the following extraordinary transformation (the original tonic, G major, having been reached in two steps of a simple sequence)—

Ex. 11.

The new figure (y) will be seen to be a free diminution of the two bars of (a) that preceded it. It is now worked out very quietly as a fugue with a running countersubject. Beethoven does not expect us to recognize that we are in the home tonic, but the fact adds much to the mysterious effect of this very unexpected development. A short crescendo with the rhythm of (a) reasserting itself, first in its usual form, and then diminished (⁊ ♪♪♪ ♩), soon brings us in triumph to the recapitulation of the first subject.

This development is the most complicated passage in all Beethoven's concertos; yet it is perfectly typical of concerto style. Its breadth of sequence and its copious use of episodic matter that has not been heard in the exposition are natural results of the principles we have already seen in operation. The relation between solo and tutti has made the repetition of material in the exposition specially impressive and characteristic, and the recapitulation and coda will make it still more so; and therefore the development needs to be more simple and more contrasted than it would be in a symphony or sonata, apart from the enormous difficulties of balancing solo against tutti in a development on ordinary lines. Accordingly we find that in classical concertos the develement may be based either on the least weighty of the themes of the exposition, or on one that the solo had omitted (a brilliant device of Mozart's), or it may transform the themes almost beyond recognition (as here), or may have much episodic matter (as here also).

Beethoven's recapitulation here follows the opening tutti much more closely than did the first solo; but Ex. 2 is interrupted by a sudden modulation to E flat, where a lofty contemplative passage, corresponding to Ex. 8, leads to the second subject (beginning of course with Ex. 9) exactly recapitulated in the tonic. Where the ritornello bursts in, taking up the thread of Ex. 5, we have a pause on a 6/4 chord, as in all classical concertos; and the whole responsibility for the greater part of the coda is thrown upon the solo player, who is supposed to extemporize the long cadenza that comes at this point. Here we have the only really conventional element in this much-maligned art-form; for obviously a bad cadenza is the very appendicitis of music; and unfortunately Beethoven himself subsequently scribbled some astoundingly bad cadenzas to this most ethereal work. Clara Schumann's cadenzas are better, but feverishly Schumannesque; and a good musician is justified in doing his own best. Fortunately Beethoven has a wonderful way of designing his movement so that a long spell of uninterrupted solo, in a style of development modified by the impulsive manner of an extemporization, shall seem necessary and effective, whether it be actually extempore or not.

Beethoven, knowing that some pages of solo will intervene, repeats Ex. 5, the theme he has just written before. Very quietly it floats upward, and is followed by the final cadence theme Ex. 7 (thus omitting Ex. 6). As this dies away in the upper ether, we are roused by a rapid crescendo, with the rhythm (a) and its diminution (as at the end of the development) surging up till it pervades the whole orchestra, and the movement ends triumphantly.

If I am not mistaken, it was Liszt who compared the slow movement of this concerto to Orpheus taming the wild beasts with his music. This is so apt that it is almost free from the general objection that such comparisons tend at first to substitute their own vividness for that of the music and then to lose their vividness in the necessity for tiresome qualifications of detail. But here the comparison is remarkably spiritual and free from concrete externals. Note, in the first place, that, as in Liszt's own symphonic poem *Orpheus*, it refers to the taming of wild Nature, not to the placating of the Furies, though Liszt tells us that he was inspired by the experience of conducting Gluck's *Orfeo*. But the spiritual, or, if you prefer popular scientific jargon, psychological depth of the analogy is best shown in the one point of resemblance between this unique movement of Beethoven's and a very different one, Orpheus's first sustained address to the Furies in Gluck's opera. The pleadings of Orpheus are met phrase by phrase with a thunderous *No* from the Furies in unison, until the last *No* is a chord which shows that they will at length yield. In this andante the orchestra does not imitate wild beasts or nature, and the pianoforte does not imitate a lyre or a singer. But the orchestra (consisting of the strings alone) is entirely in octaves, without a vestige of harmony, so long as it remains stubborn and rough in its share of the dialogue with the quiet veiled tones of the solo. After its first soft pizzicato note it melts into harmony. In the supreme moment of darkness at the end, the orchestra and solo join in the same material (the chords in this rhythm ♩. ♪ | ♩), whereas they had hitherto been totally contrasted.

The finale breaks in, pianissimo, with an intensely lively theme in that prosaic daylight by which Beethoven loves to test the reality of his sublimest visions. The daylight is the more grey from the strong emphasis the theme gives to the subdominant chord, almost producing the impression of C instead of G major.

Ex. 12.

The treatment of rondo form does not differ much in concertos from its ordinary treatment on a large scale in other works. For the main body of this movement, it will suffice to summarize its form, and devote the rest of the analysis to the enormous coda which (if we take it as beginning after the recapitulation of the second subject) is exactly five-twelfths of the whole movement, not counting the cadenza.

The first theme, after a variation by the pianoforte, has a counter-theme.

Ex. 13.

The orchestra resumes Ex. 12 fortissimo, with trumpets and drums appearing for the first time in the concerto. A transition theme—

Ex. 14.

leads to a very broad passage in triplet quavers on the dominant of D—taking its own time to bring us at last to the second subject.

This begins with a leisurely and serene melody for the pianoforte in extremely wide three-part harmony, of which the bass is a deep tonic pedal. It intends to repeat itself.

Ex. 15.

&c.

The self-repetition impatiently breaks off, saying 'and all that!' The orchestra urbanely gives a completed counterstatement, with intricate polyphony.

Then comes the lightest and simplest possible formula, in brilliant arpeggios. We begin to think it unaccountably simple; when suddenly we wonder to find ourselves on the dominant of C. The orchestra explains, with these rhythms ♫ | ♩ ♪ | ♪♩ ♪♩| ♩ recalling (*a*) and (*d*) of the first theme (Ex. 12); and, after keeping us in suspense an enormous time (nearly forty bars) on this dominant of C, Beethoven brings us back with a long rhythmless run to our first theme. This and all its accessories are repeated unaltered, but Ex. 14 is made to lead to E flat. Here we begin the central episode with a new theme, consisting of nothing but energetic arpeggios of tonic and dominant chords. But this is made to alternate with rich developments of the first three figures (*a*), (*b*), and (*c*). (Note especially the drums as a bass to the wind, with figure (*a*); and the treatment by the pianoforte of figure (*c*) in triplets.)

This leads, through various keys, to the dominant of our tonic G, where a brisk chromatic passage for pianoforte brings us to the broad expanse of dominant preparation that culminates in the second subject, which we thus reach without having again returned to the first. The recapitulation is exact until the end of the humorous arpeggio-theme, which this time lands us on a chord of E flat, where, as before the first return of the main theme, we seem to be dwelling a long time while the orchestra hints ♫ | ♩. But it gradually dawns on us that we are listening to the whole first theme in B flat on the violas.

Ex. 16. (Compare Ex. 12.)

The wood-wind become witty over figure (d); and suddenly the full orchestra enters in a rage on a strange chord, working round to the dominant of C, our old position for a return. The pianoforte turns figure (b) into a slow arpeggio on that chord, taking, as before, an unconscionable time in getting back to our first theme in its original key. This time we have it in a new variation, and the orchestra comes blustering in with yet another, leading to the transition theme (Ex. 14). Now the real business of the enormous coda begins. Figures (a) and (d) seem to be settling down in a leisurely tonic-and-dominant stride, when the dominant chord seems to overstay its time and slowly changes to the vastly distant key of F sharp major. Here we have the placid second subject, Ex. 15, which calmly turns round to C major, and thence back to G, where it is gradually taken up by the whole orchestra with a crescendo, leading to a 6/4 pause for a cadenza. The cadenza (which Beethoven says must be short) is followed by more witticisms on figure (d) (augmented) in the horn; and then we settle down comfortably to another variation (like Ex. 16) of the first theme, which I quote in its still more delightful form as repeated in a remarkably close and persistent canon. It does not defeat its aim by pedantic exactness.

Ex. 17.

The music dies away in that upper ether which it has never left; but all the while we hear more witticisms on figure (d), which suddenly quickens into presto quavers, with a crescendo. On the top of this the full orchestra storms in with the principal theme, more

lively than ever in this quicker tempo. Of course, when it reaches
figure (*d*), the irrepressible wood-wind and pianoforte have a little
more to say before ending this audacious masterpiece of gigantic
and inexhaustibly varied proportions with that astronomical punctuality which gives solemnity to Beethoven's utmost exuberance of
high spirits.

PIANOFORTE CONCERTO IN E FLAT, OP. 73

1 *Allegro.* 2 *Adagio un poco mosso, leading to* 3 RONDO: *Allegro*

From the history of the 'Eroica' we know how Beethoven would
have appreciated the vulgar title by which this concerto is known in
the British Isles. So we will say no more about that, but attend
to the music.

The fifth concerto has a majestic introduction, in which the key
of E flat is asserted by the orchestra and pianoforte in a rhapsodic
outburst. This introduction reappears once at the beginning of the
recapitulation, and plays no further part in the narrative. As in
the first movements of all classical concertos, including Brahms's,
the main threads of the story are set forth very broadly, but with
explicit avoidance of anything like development or combination, in
the opening tutti, which is best called by its primitive title of
ritornello. In this concerto the ritornello is specially formal and
voluminous; but we must be content with two quotations, though
there are at least five distinct themes, and any number of important
derivatives. Most of the derivatives come from the groups here
marked (*a*) and (*b*).

Obviously enough, Ex. 1 is the beginning of the 'first subject';
and it so happens that Ex. 2, which sounds exactly as if it were going
to become the principal theme in the 'second subject', does not
deceive that expectation, as many an equally important theme has

deceived it elsewhere in Mozart, Beethoven, and Brahms. In fact the whole procession of contrasted themes which this great tutti reviews, in severe monotony of key, gives an unusually faithful summary of what the pianoforte is going to discuss. The severe monotony of key provides a firm basis for the marvellous richness of the distant keys of B minor and B major (*alias* C flat), in which the pianoforte is hereafter to present two variations of Ex. 2 before the orchestra turns it into a rousing march in the orthodox key of B flat. The general plan of the whole movement is as follows:

I. Introduction.

II. Opening tutti or ritornello, containing all the themes.

III. First solo, entering quietly with a chromatic scale, and turning the whole opening ritornello into a vast exposition of a 'first' and 'second' subject: with such devices as the modulations just mentioned.

IV. Close of the exposition by resumption of last stages of the ritornello, in the key of the 'second subject'. By a device first introduced by Beethoven in his Violin Concerto, the end of the ritornello is now diverted into a remote new key. Here in due course the pianoforte again enters with its quiet chromatic scale. (No concerto that boasts a modern or Mendelssohnian 'emancipation from the conventional classical ritornello' can achieve such impressive entries of the solo part.)

V. Development, dealing entirely with Ex. 1. The pianoforte part is, for all its beautiful colouring, at first no more than an accompaniment to the whispered dialogue in which the orchestra discusses Ex. 1, chiefly from the point of view of the turn which I have marked with the letter (*a*). By degrees, the rhythmic figure marked (*b*) becomes more insistent, till it arouses the full orchestra, and sets the pianoforte off into a furious passage of octaves, descending in dialogue with the strings, while a solitary bassoon keeps the rhythm (*b*) mysteriously threading its way in the bass. I have called these octaves 'furious', but must take the opportunity of pointing out that the modern pianistic martellato effect is utterly useless here. Not only could Beethoven's pianoforte not produce it, but no first-rate composer has ever wished for anything remotely like it; and I for my part do not believe that Liszt himself, who inculcated it, ever really did it as it is understood nowadays. He may have *looked* as if he were committing all manner of awe-inspiring pianistic crimes, but he had acquired a perfect touch at too early an age for any superb gestures to damage it. (The best evidence is that he sat immobile as a rock, but that his long arms caused him to sit on a high stool and make his chords seem to fall from a great height.) At all events, what Beethoven wants here is the fury of a hail-storm; and you can see daylight through hail-storms, and hear

the bassoon through the right sort of octaves in this passage. On
the other hand there is no fury in the fall of a ton of coals.

The curtain of hail is lifted away into blue sky, and we find ourselves in the very key in which the development started. The calm
closing theme of the ritornello reappears; and in the bass the turn
(*a*) of Ex. 1 moves in slow steps up through distant keys to the
threshold of home; and the quiet excitement becomes breathless
until at last a crescendo leads to—

VI. The introduction, followed by the recapitulation of II. The
modulations at the 'second subject' become still more wonderful, the key being now one of those 'contradictory keys' (C sharp
minor and D flat) of which such subtle dramatic use is made at a
similar point in the Eroica Symphony.

VII. The Coda. The saddest chapter in the story of the concerto
is the classical custom of leaving all but the orchestral wind-
up of the coda blank, and trusting to a display of the solo-player's
powers of improvization to fill up the blank with a cadenza. Here
Beethoven has, for the first time, forbidden extemporization, and
written out in full a coda that begins like a cadenza, but soon
settles down to what turns out to be a final glorified recapitulation of the whole ritornello, from the entry of Ex. 2 onwards.
Gradually the orchestra joins in, beginning with the horns, until
the full band is in dialogue with the pianoforte. At last we hear
a chromatic scale. It was of this passage that Schumann said that
'Beethoven's chromatic scales are not like other people's'. No
wonder! This quiet scale and the following trills have now borne
the Atlas burden of the whole mighty structure for the third time—
first, at the outset of the first solo; then at the outset of the development; and now, leading unswervingly to the glorious close.

The slow movement needs no quotation. It is in B major, the
first remote modulation in the first movement, and it has two
themes—the serene, devout melody of the muted violins (it is a misprint in the band-parts if the lower strings are muted); and the
meditative theme with which the pianoforte enters and moves into
a rather remote key on the shaded side (D major) of the harmony.
Here the pianoforte seems to be settling down in a cadence with a
trill, but the trill rises and rises until it breaks over into the tonic
key again. Thus the pianoforte comes to deliver its ornamental
version of the main theme. As its close fades into a cloud of wavy
light, three wind instruments, led by the flute, give out the whole
theme again, the pianoforte accompanying with the wavy figure
which the admiration of Berlioz has made familiar to all students
of orchestration. At last the waves die down, and nothing is left
but a cold grey octave. This sinks a semitone, and becomes
glowing. As it continues, the pianoforte whispers a strange new

theme with a mysterious rhythm and, finding itself already in
E flat, after a moment's hovering, plunges into the finale.

Ex. 3.

No further quotations are necessary for the enjoyment of this
most spacious and triumphant of concerto rondos. Lovers of
Schumann's *Carnaval* will easily recognize in the second part of
Beethoven's main theme a phrase that enlisted in Schumann's
army of Davidites marching against the Philistines. Equally obvious
is the great part played by the rhythmic figure ♩♪♩ ♫♫ from
its first formal appearance as part of the orchestral group of themes
to its final mysterious domination in the person of the drum.

What gives this rondo its chief impressiveness is the immense
breadth of its middle episode, in which the main theme has three
separate escapades, firstly fortissimo in C major (a bright key in
this connexion), secondly piano in A flat (a sober key), and thirdly
pianissimo (breaking into forte) in E major, a remote key. The
subsequent exciting return, where the violins remind us of what
the pianoforte said at the end of the slow movement, will not escape
notice. The drum passage at the end reveals the sublime depths
from which all these outbursts of hilarity spring.

VIOLIN CONCERTO IN D MAJOR, OP. 61

1 *Allegro ma non troppo.* 2 *Larghetto, leading to* 3 RONDO.

The autograph of Beethoven's Violin Concerto is a lesson in the
correct attitude of a composer towards a player. It was written for
a virtuoso of the name of Clement, and is inscribed to him with a
vile pun on his 'clemency' towards the poor composer. The score
assigns four staves to the violin solo, in order to leave room for
alterations; and in many places all the four staves have been filled.
The violinist whose criticism Beethoven took so much pains to
meet produced (or, as he perhaps called it, 'created') the concerto
under conditions of his own making that were not considered
unusual in those days. The first movement was played in the
first part of the programme, the slow movement and the finale in
the second part. Among the items which took place between these

divisions was a sonata of Clement's own composing, to be played on one string with the violin upside down. Clement survived this performance for many years, and as an old man was seen by a young violinist of very different calibre, who became perhaps as inseparably identified with the Beethoven concerto as any player can be identified with a great work. Joachim's cadenzas earn the right to be treated as integral parts of the composition, instead of as necessary evils. I heard them from him only in an abbreviated form; but he included the full version in one of his last publications, the volume of concertos in his Violin School; and it is interesting to note that in this form the cadenza to the first movement still contains a certain famous chromatic scale in octaves which made a tremendous impression when he played the concerto in London as a boy of twelve, though the cadenza as a whole is very much more important than the already extraordinarily ripe achievement of his boyhood. I believe that in its full form it dates from the same period as his Hungarian Concerto, where, by the way, the same chromatic scale occurs.

Beethoven's Violin Concerto is gigantic, one of the most spacious concertos ever written, but so quiet that when it was a novelty most people complained quite as much of its insignificance as of its length. All its most famous strokes of genius are not only mysteriously quiet, but mysterious in radiantly happy surroundings. The whole gigantic scheme is serene. The only two definitely pathetic passages, the G minor episode in the development of the first movement, and the G minor episode in the finale, are (in spite of the immense solemnity of the horns and the trumpets in the first instance) in a childlike vein, and show how Beethoven in his ripest middle period had far more command of Mozart's special resources than he possessed in those of his early works which imitate Mozart. One might be inclined to say off-hand that the most mysterious stroke of genius in the whole work is the famous opening with five strokes of the drum which introduces the peculiarly radiant first subject on the wood-wind; but in truth there is still more mystery in the astounding D sharp which follows the second strain, for which reason I quote the whole first paragraph.

Ex. 1.

In Beethoven's first sketches he thought of the D sharp as E flat,
a distinction which, unnoticed on tempered instruments, is really
important here. E flat means something harmonically clearer, but
the point about the D sharp is that it indeed is D sharp, though
Beethoven leaves it unharmonized and carefully avoids letting it
move in the direction which would explain it away. We shall see
the explanation in one of the later phrases. The remaining themes
I quote as they occur in the opening tutti. First there is the
important scale theme—

Ex. 2.

which the solo violin is eventually to work out as a transition theme.
The orchestra, however, does not as yet think of it in that light,
but makes it lead quietly to an unexpected crash in a foreign key.

Ex. 3.

This energetic outburst leads more or less in the manner of a
symphonic transition to the second subject, but, as is usual in
classical concertos, leads to it in the tonic, so that there has been
no radical change of key. The second subject, given in the characteristically radiant colouring Beethoven extracts from the wood-
wind throughout this work, is, as given by the orchestra, accompanied by that all-pervading rhythmic figure which the drums
announced at the outset.

Ex. 4.

Broad as this melody is, it becomes still broader as the strings take it up softly with a flowing triplet accompaniment in the minor. This leads eventually to a smiling phrase in the major in which the mysterious D sharp of Ex. 1 is now explained away.

Ex. 5.

Out of this arises a crescendo which brings the full orchestra to the last and in some ways the grandest of this great procession of themes.

Ex. 6.

Suddenly the orchestra dies away in the basses, as if warned of the advent of its master, and the solo violin arises in one of the most spacious introductory passages to be found in any concerto. This entry is quite unforgettable; which is well, because it recurs in a very subtly dramatic way. The solo violin, with the aid of the orchestra, now proceeds to work out the whole procession of themes *seriatim*. Ex. 2 becomes a symphonic passage of transition, leading with great breadth to the dominant of A major, and there preparing for the second subject. (Ex. 3 is held over for another purpose.) The second subject (Ex. 4) enters in the clarinets, while the violin trills on the dominant until it is ready to take up its second phrase. One of the most significant subtleties in the structure of the whole work is that, under the guidance of the solo violin, the second subject is no longer accompanied by the rhythmic figure of the drums.

Mr. Cecil Forsyth, in his book *Orchestration*, remarking on the difference between the tone-colour of a number of orchestral violins in unison and that of a solo violin, says very truly that

in a violin concerto it undoubtedly gives the soloist a somewhat greater chance of 'standing out' from the string ensemble, though, on occasion, the repetition of a simple solo phrase by the orchestral violins has had an almost comic effect, as if they were saying 'this is how it ought really to sound'.

The Beethoven concerto is a sublime object-lesson on this point, inasmuch as that contingency never happens. Here, for instance, the solo violin takes up the theme from the clarinets, and gives it in a region to which the orchestral violins do not happen to mount. (In the recapitulation Beethoven gives it an extreme height and brings it down to normal regions with an impressive swoop essentially the gesture of a solo player.) Now comes the expanded counterstatement in the minor. This is, indeed, entrusted to the orchestral violins, and a wonderful background they make with their melody to the ornamental figures of the solo violin, which does not take up the melody until we reach Ex. 5, where it has the A sharps (as they have now become) and some ornamentations of its own. After this has been expanded to a brilliant conclusion, the orchestral strings have Ex. 6 very quietly; and here again the solo violin, instead of competing with them in sustained melody, soars aloft in vast ramifications of ornament, while the great melody which was originally so short and terse expands in rising sequences. A climax is reached, and the solo violin broadens out on the basis of harmonies forming a cadence, which appears to be ending in the conventional shake that in practically every one of Mozart's concertos ushers in the re-entry of the orchestra. But below this shake the rhythmic drum figure appears with the most mysterious modulations that have yet occurred.

Ex. 7.

Above this profound harmonic cloud the shake rises, and eventually gathers itself into a rush downwards and upwards over a long penultimate chord, leading to the re-entry of the orchestra. And now the orchestra bursts in with the crashing theme (Ex. 3) which, it will be remembered, began in a foreign key, and accordingly now begins in F. With a sublimity which certain lewd fellows of the baser sort would reduce by cuts, the orchestra calmly proceeds with the whole of the original tutti from this point onwards. Hence we have once more the whole second subject, this time with its drum-taps in the violins, followed by its expanded counterstatement in the minor. As if to emphasize the spaciousness of all this repetition, this counterstatement is given fortissimo, and continues unabridged through the appearance of Example 5, still fortissimo. Here, however, there is a sudden twist in the harmony which produces one of those dramatic consequences that are true only when the ground has been thus thoroughly prepared. The rest of the tutti finds itself diverted into the key of C major, a key utterly paradoxical in relation to the D major of the concerto. Accordingly in C major the last theme (Ex. 6) enters, still fortissimo, until, as at the end of the opening tutti, there is a sudden hush; and in this paradoxical key of C major the solo violin mounts upwards with its immense introductory passage. Just when it ought to be closing into the first theme, it pauses on a solitary expectant note. A vast distance below it the basses enter, and suddenly we are in B minor beginning a development of the first subject. The fourth bar of the theme is passed through several keys, always accompanied by the drum figure, until at last both it and the drum figure diminish to quavers, bringing us to a very deliberate settling down in G minor. And here, accompanied by no theme except the drum figure (given in succession by the horns and the bassoons, and lastly by the trumpets and drums), the violin has an entirely new cantabile in a vein of the tenderest pathos. With the entry of the trumpets and drums the key of D minor is reached, and the phrases of the violin become shorter and more and more wistful, while the trumpets and drums turn their rhythmic figure into a solemn steady tread. At last even this ceases; and there is nothing but a holding-note of breathless anticipation as the solo violin mounts upwards in chromatic arpeggios, until the rhythmic figure reasserts itself in different parts of the orchestra, which suddenly bursts out in full and gives the whole first sentence in the tonic, fortissimo. It continues triumphantly with the transition theme (Ex. 2), which the violin takes up and now carries through some new harmonic regions in such a way as finally to settle down upon its preparations for the second subject. From this point the recapitulation is quite regular, until the re-entry of the orchestra with its crashing theme in a foreign key (Ex. 3). This last orchestral tutti leads to the cadenza. Many a clever cadenza occupying the place of a symphonic coda has ruined the work into which its virtuoso perpetrator had introduced it; but Joachim's cadenzas are the work of a classical composer, and they combine the extempore quality, which the cadenza ought to have *ex hypothesi*, with the structural features which its position in a symphonic design demands. Joachim begins his cadenza with the rhythmic drum figure; continues with the transition theme (Ex. 3), and contrives to make a very effective development of the second subject in the triplet rhythm of the accompaniment, which the solo violin had given to it while the orchestra was playing it in the minor. This treatment secures it against any effect of forestalling its quiet appearance after the cadenza, on the third and fourth strings of the instrument when the orchestra re-enters. The sublime calm of the first movement of the concerto reaches its serenest height when the last theme (Ex. 6) is given out quietly by the bassoon, and is answered in its highest regions by the solo violin, bringing the gigantic movement to an end in five bars of a terse crescendo.

In the slow movement we have one of the three cases of sublime inaction achieved by Beethoven, and by no one else except in certain lyrics and masterpieces of choral music. The other two cases are the slow movements of the Sonata Appassionata and the Trio in B flat, op. 97. The form is that of a theme with variations; and in the present instance the theme, in spite of the rich modulations between its third and sixth bars, is practically a single strain, with a characteristic expansion produced by echoing its last two bars.

Ex. 8.

There are other differences between this movement and the two other examples I have mentioned; but the point in all three cases is that a strict set of variations, confined to a melody with none but its own local modulations, and with no change from major to minor and no change of time, constitutes a scheme in which there is no action; or, at all events, which is in so dreamlike a state of repose that it is impossible to bring the movement to any conclusion except that of a dramatic interruption. Wit or humour might explain it away, but the more natural style of such inaction is sublime, and only in songs or choral music can solemn things of this kind be brought to a natural end. Beethoven in his later instrumental works, notably the last quartets, was able to design complete slow movements in this mood by means of certain devices, which are equivalent to just enough action to allow the design to complete itself. In other words, he found that a set of variations on a slow and solemn theme could, without radically or dramatically changing its rhythm, develop the kind of energy that would enable him to construct a coda. At present this was not his intention, and the whole point of this slow movement is that it cannot end. The theme, with its touching broken rhythms and its rich local modulations, is given out by the muted strings. Then the solo violin enters with a dreamlike accompaniment to the theme in the wind instruments. This constitutes a complete variation. In a second variation the solo violin continues the accompaniment with an increasingly florid movement, while the theme is heard in a lower octave. Then the full orchestra (as reduced and muted throughout the slow movement) restates the theme very simply but with the fullest possible tone and harmony. This constitutes the third variation. And now occurs something unique in the history of musical form. The violin re-enters on the last chord with some dreamy arabesques, and without the slightest change of key settles down to an entire new melody, a single broad phrase beginning as follows—

Ex. 9.

which slowly comes to the final trill of a long-drawn cadence. This trill behaves like all the cadential trills in this concerto; that is to say, instead of ending conventionally, it mounts aloft and leaves us awhile in doubt about what is going to happen. And what does happen is true to the nature of dreams, for the main theme re-enters, and we listen in peace to a fourth variation as if nothing had interrupted the normal course of the form. Yet the interruption is not without its results; for with the last bar of this variation another and still calmer new theme appears, connected with the main theme only by the rhythmic figure in the horns.

Ex. 10.

This new theme leads back to the other one (Ex. 9) with still more serene colouring. Then again Ex. 10 sets the rhythm swinging in its own impressively final way, until at last, as the violin slowly mounts aloft, fragments of the main theme (Ex. 8) are heard in the muted horns and strings, while the violin in extreme heights dreams of the figure of the first variation. Nothing can be really final in a movement so ethereal and so static as this larghetto has been from the outset: there is only one way to prove that the vision is true, and that is to awaken in the light of common day and enjoy that light with the utmost vigour and zest. Accordingly the orchestra breaks in with a purposely conventional modulation to the dominant of D. The violin extemporizes a cadenza and plunges into a finale, beginning with one of those drastic rondo themes with which Beethoven loves to shock the superior person (or would if he had time to think of him).

Ex. 11.

With all its light-heartedness and comparative simplicity of form, the finale is the truthful outcome of its sublime antecedents. To

complain that it is not the finest movement in the concerto is
to make the mistake exposed a considerable time ago by Plato,
when he derided the argument that 'since purple is the most
beautiful colour, and the eyes the most beautiful feature, therefore
in every statue the eyes ought to be painted purple'. In no art-form
is it so constantly a mistake to expect the last part to be the 'finest'
as in the concerto form. To find the *right* finale to a scheme so
subtle and delicate as that of a classical concerto is of itself a
crowning stroke of genius. And there is no finale which more boldly
and accurately gives the range, so to speak, of the whole, than this
most naïvely humorous of rondos. Besides its first theme, we
must quote the transition theme with the pendulous introductory
notes from which witticisms are to arise on its later occurrences
(e.g. the only two pizzicato notes for the solo violin in the whole
concerto)—

Ex. 12.

the main theme of the first episode or second subject in dialogue
between the violin and the orchestra—

Ex. 13.

and the pathetic childlike second episode with its fully formed
melody in two parts, each of which is repeated by the bassoon.

Ex. 14.

As in many of Beethoven's finales, the main form of the movement is carried through with a certain economy of development,
in order to throw into relief the full proportions of his coda,
which in some cases is as long as the whole of the rest of the
movement. In the present case the main form, though simple,
takes up a good deal of room; but the coda, even if we did not
allow for the cadenza which Beethoven has left to the player to
extemporize, is considerably larger than any other section of the
movement. It begins by working the most surprising of all the
miracles Beethoven produces from the cadential trill, which in this
case actually modulates to A flat, the most remote of all possible
keys from D. Naturally it is only through a very wide and remark-

able sequence of harmonies that the figures of the first theme can work their way back to the tonic. This done, there is a delightful dialogue on the first theme between the oboe and the violin, and a glorious final climax, in which the violin shows its command of the whole orchestra by being able to silence the fullest and most irrepressible outbursts again and again with its light arpeggios and scales.

TRIPLE CONCERTO FOR PIANOFORTE, VIOLIN, AND VIOLONCELLO, OP. 56

1 *Allegro.* 2 *Largo, leading to* 3 RONDO: *alla Polacca.*

Once or twice in the middle of Beethoven's career we meet with what is usually described as a reversion to an earlier style. This description generally means that certain works make a less powerful and less definite impression on us than others. A close study and a sympathetic hearing of such works is a valuable experience not obtainable from greater things. Without the Triple Concerto Beethoven could not have achieved the Pianoforte Concertos in G and E flat, nor the Violin Concerto. It is in some sense a study for these works; and if it were not by Beethoven, but by some mysterious composer who had written nothing else and who had the romantic good fortune to die before it came to performance, the very people who most blame Beethoven for writing below his full powers would be the first to acclaim it as the work of a still greater composer. Let us take it on its own terms, and see what it can tell us.

None of Beethoven's three previous concertos had satisfied him as to the treatment of the opening orchestral ritornello. In the first two he had allowed the orchestra to develop themes and sequences in a rather discursive way; in the third (in C minor) he had frankly begun like the exposition of a symphony, and had allowed the orchestra to change its mind abruptly just after that impression had been irrevocably conveyed. He is now going to solve the real problem of stating the vast procession of themes on the orchestra in such a way as to prevent any group from seeming to mark a separate development of dramatic action. If the procession can thus be kept, so to speak, on one plane, then the solo instrument or instruments can produce the grandest dramatic effects by spacing all this material out and adding their own material so as to build up a gigantic sonata form, with a second group in a suitable foreign key. But the opening tutti, in maintaining its processional movement, must also have its own dramatic character, and must arouse in more than a negative way some expectation that the orchestral crowd is going to be addressed and dominated by an individual.

The true solution of an art problem is often first achieved on the largest possible scale. Beethoven thoroughly enjoyed spacing out this first solution of his mature form of concerto on the huge scale required by three solo instruments, of which the pianoforte will generally demand its separate statement of each theme, and the violin and 'cello (as a pair) their own statement. The dimensions of nearly everything except the opening tutti in this work are thus at least twice those of any normal concerto, even on Beethoven's scale. Moreover, he is so profoundly interested in the elements of trio-writing against an orchestral background, that his pianoforte part is very light, and his violoncello has, in virtue of its opportunities and position, quite the lion's share of the ensemble. Lastly, the material both of ornaments and themes is severely simple. Players and conductors who are not satisfied with art for art's sake, put all this more shortly and say that the work is dull. Beethoven cannot be thus lightly dismissed, even in a work which is a stepping-stone to greater things. Sometimes, as in the second subject of the finale, its themes descend to dryness. Throughout it is extraordinarily severe; and it demands from performers and listeners the fullest recognition of the grand manner in every detail.

The statement of the opening theme pianissimo in the basses—

Ex. 1.

is one of those mysterious simplicities peculiar to great works. If the composer were Cherubini, every history of music would refer to it as epoch-making; and indeed the continuation is in its severe formality not unlike what Cherubini might have made it. The ensuing crescendo is in Beethoven's grand style, but not beyond lesser powers of invention. I quote its climax for reasons which will appear later.

Ex. 2

Suddenly the unapproachable Beethoven shows himself very quietly in the calm entry of what is afterwards to become the second subject.

Ex. 3.

Formal as this theme appears, it gives us that Greek combination of simplicity and subtlety which is the highest quality in art. It appears here in G major, but under circumstances which make it impossible for the ear to take that key seriously. We simply accept it as the dominant of C, and are not surprised when the theme continues in that key. A beautiful purple patch—

Ex. 4.

asserts for a moment a note of romantic solemnity, but leads to another tonic-and-dominant tributary theme in the same non-chalant marching rhythm as Ex. 3.

Ex. 5.

Then there is a formal and emphatic process of 'presenting arms' in G major, which again cannot possibly be taken as an established key. There is something mysterious in the way in which this passage lets fall an unharmonized cadence figure; but it seems quite natural that, this being so, the cadence figure should go a step farther and end emphatically in C.

Ex. 6.

Evidently we are waiting for something or somebody.

The violoncello enters quietly with Ex. 1 as the main theme; the violin answers it in the dominant; and the two move back to the tonic with great breadth, gracefully ushering in the pianoforte, which, with its third statement, rounds off the theme in trio dialogue with proportionate brilliance and climax. The orchestra then surprises us by bursting in with a new military march.

Ex. 7.

The solo trio takes this up calmly, and proceeds to shed an unexpected light upon the whole past and future of the movement by modulating towards a key of which no hint has been given, the key of A, the submediant. The preparations for this are laid out on a huge scale; and we have the full power of Beethoven revealed in the radiant effect of the entry of Ex. 3 as second subject in A major. The violoncello and the violin have divided its two phrases between them; and the orchestra begins vigorously with a counter-statement, which, however, the solo trio instantly catches up as a variation, carrying it through the purple patch shown in Ex. 4. The variation now develops on a large scale, and comes to a deliberate close in A minor. Or rather, just as it is going to do so, the violin and the 'cello rush in with an energetic new theme.

ex. 8.

f marcato.

The first four bars of this they turn into an expanded variation, and then they join the pianoforte in a vigorous counterstatement, presenting it in yet another variation, and expanding and delaying the close in the grandest style. Indeed, the close is interrupted by a sudden *piano*, and the approach and building up of the character-istic trill is an intense pianissimo unsurpassed even by the closely similar passages in the Violin Concerto. The orchestra bursts in with the new transition theme (Ex. 7), in the unexpected key of F major. From this it passes back to A minor, in which key it con-cludes matters with the passage of 'presenting arms' at the end of the opening tutti. And now is revealed the mystery of the un-harmonized cadence which this otherwise formal passage let fall (Ex. 6). That cadence is made once more to swing round to A major, while the violoncello embroiders a beautiful cantabile upon it and passes straight on to an immense restatement of the opening theme in A major. The solo trio works this out at complete leisure as at the outset, as if there were no such things as modulating develop-ments to trouble about. But when at last the trio chooses, it has no difficulty in starting the development with a sudden plunge into B flat. Indeed the trio seems rather to have been storing energy for this very purpose, and pursues a simple and direct course of dialogue in staccato triplets, while the wood-wind accom-pany with the quaver figure of Ex. 1. Soon the dominant of C is reached; the violoncello and the violin, joined in due course by the pianoforte, call for the recapitulation in an expressive cantabile, followed by provocative references to Ex. 1 in a diminuendo that reaches an exciting pianissimo, until suddenly the anticipatory scales gather up strength and bring back the orchestra with the first theme in full harmony and full scoring.

In the recapitulation Beethoven shows an appreciation of a point established by Mozart, in that he follows this time the course of the original tutti, breaking the fortissimo so that the solo trio can participate in Ex. 2, which is now so developed as to lead to the solo transition material on the dominant of C. This brings the second subject with all its solo accessories into C major; and fresh light is shed upon the vigorous new solo theme, Ex. 8, by the fact that after the first four bars it is continued throughout in the major. In due course the orchestra bursts out again with Ex. 7 in the key of A flat. This is so worked as to lead easily back to C; and we are now surprised by a huge symphonic coda in which the solo trio calmly takes up a phrase which has not been heard since the opening tutti (Ex. 5), and follows it up by making something very brilliant and full of colour out of the passage of 'presenting arms' (Ex. 6). This broadens out and makes, for the last time, one of Beethoven's characteristic pianissimo climaxes, which settles down to a beautiful cantabile for the solo trio, while the orchestra has fragments of the main theme in the bass. Then the orchestra wakes up (*più allegro*) pulling the figure of that theme into a livelier form; and so the huge movement comes to a brilliant end.

It is doubtful whether a large architectural design can be combined with a severe study in pure colour, if the themes are such as to attract attention to themselves. Beethoven's Triple Concerto is rather like Mozart's writings for wind-band, in which Mozart actually goes the length of avoiding any theme which is not purely a formula. In no case of this type will any sensible person suppose that the composer's invention is at fault. It may be significant that the great composer does not often restrict himself to problems of the kind. He leaves it to pedagogues like Reicha to turn out by the hundred perfect solutions of such a problem, for example, as that of writing for five wind instruments that by no human possibility can blend. But when a composer of Beethoven's or Mozart's calibre does give us solutions to an extraordinary art-problem, it is well to listen with some idea of the points at issue.

The indiscretion of Beethoven's Triple Concerto consists in combining a problem that makes for dryness of matter with a problem that makes for exceptional length.

The slow movement foreshadows that of the E flat Concerto in the dark and solemn tone colour of its opening melody with the muted violins.

Ex. 9.

The melody is severely reserved; though here, as elsewhere in the by-ways of Beethoven's art, it would have become famous for its warmth and breadth if it had been ascribed to Cherubini. After the fourth bar the violoncello lifts the whole continuation to a higher octave. As the melody comes to its close the pianoforte enters with a florid accompaniment, and the whole is restated, the first four bars being given by the wood-wind, and the rest continued by the violin and violoncello in the heights. The resulting impression is that of a very large opening indeed; and this impression is strengthened by the broadly dramatic sequel which swings slowly round to the dominant of C, whereupon the solo trio proceeds to make preparations in an intense pianissimo. What it is preparing for turns out to be not a central episode but the finale.

The style of the Polonaise was not uncommon for rondos and finales in Beethoven's time (an example may be found in the slow movement of one of Mozart's pianoforte sonatas); but Beethoven has left us only three polonaises, one in the middle of the Serenade trio, op. 8, one a solitary pianoforte piece, op. 89, dedicated to the Tsarina, and the finale of this concerto. None of these shows any of the formidable temper of Chopin's Polonaises; nor is it over-dressed or in any other way similar to the polonaises of Spohr and Weber, who, when they write a *polacca brillante*—which is the only kind they ever do write—are inclined to make a very smart-society person of it indeed. Otherwise all three of Beethoven's polonaises are eminently aristocratic and charmingly feminine. The genius and romance of the main theme lie in its exquisite modulation to E major and back again, for which reason I quote ten bars.

Ex. 10.

Violoncello.

Violin.

There is a crowd of orchestral and transitional accessories which will turn up at the end of the movement in the coda. They and the very formal second subject do not require quotation; but the listener should look out for the characteristic way in which the second subject lands on its subdominant and thereon seems to

evaporate, until the chord flutters down among the three solo
players as a tonic chord and so leads back to the first theme. The
second episode fills the middle of the movement with two contrasted
themes which no one but Beethoven could have written. Against
the athletic energy of the first—

Ex. 11.

we have a note of reproachful pathos in the second.

Ex. 12.

espressivo.

This leads to a very dramatic passage of preparation on the dominant of C; and when the placid main theme returns it is accompanied by one of the most Beethovenish of thunderous trills in the
pianoforte. A full recapitulation of the first episode ensues, which
in due course evaporates on the subdominant chord. This chord
the solo trio now turns into something rather more mysterious,
which instead of leading to the first theme, delights us by drifting
into Ex. 12. This leads melodiously back to the dominant of C, but
instead of a thunderous trill we have a more matter-of-fact pause of
anticipation. Then the first theme astonishes us by trotting away
at a brisk pace in duple time—

Ex. 13.
Solo variation.

pp

a version which, after due statement and following up, the orchestra
transforms into the following—

Ex. 14.
Orchestral variation.

The orchestra stops abruptly on a 6/4 chord; whereupon the solo
trio executes a written-out cadenza accompanied with occasional
chords on the orchestra, and suddenly dropping into a pianissimo at
its climax. The final trill swells out and fades away; and then the
full beauty of Beethoven's design is revealed in the fact that instead
of ending brilliantly in this double-quick tempo, the polonaise

theme returns in its original rhythm, broken up into dialogue for the solo trio, punctuated by acclaiming chords from the orchestra, and finally settling down in calm triumph to the unquoted accessory themes before the transition. These rise to an end the brilliance of which lies in its formal and ceremonial fitness.

BRAHMS

PIANOFORTE CONCERTO IN D MINOR, OP. 15

1 *Maestoso.* 2 *Adagio.* 3 *Allegro non troppo.*

With this work the genius of Brahms shook itself free alike from formalism and vagueness. Not even Beethoven's Ninth Symphony cost its composer more titanic struggles, and few works of art can have undergone stranger transformations. It began as a sketch for a symphony, written for convenience as an arrangement for two pianofortes to be scored later on for orchestra. Brilliant pianoforte writing, however, had an irrepressible tendency to break in on the one hand, while on the other hand the most important themes were clearly orchestral in conception.

The final result was inevitably a classical concerto, but one of unprecedented tragic power. There is no vestige of immaturity or inconsistency in the style and form. Everything that happens in this gigantic work is as much a *locus classicus* as anything in the last two pianoforte concertos and the Violin Concerto of Beethoven. The storm of disapproval which greeted its first performance at Leipzig had origins of partisan opposition as disgraceful as the row organized by the Jockey Club of Paris when Wagner produced *Tannhäuser* there. But all this tale of storm and stress must be mentioned in order to guard ourselves against letting it at this time of day lead us to think that what is still unfamiliar in the work is immature. Brahms attained maturity in it at every point; and neither in performance nor in listening can we afford to shirk its difficulties as if they were crudities with no artistic justification.

The first danger of misconception rises at the beginning. It is possible and natural to play so powerful an opening with a highly effective and orchestral-sounding fortissimo on the pianoforte; and Brahms undoubtedly at first thought that this fact would represent the real orchestral possibilities. When Joachim (who, at the time, had far more orchestral experience) saw his first attempt to score this opening he burst out laughing; and the scoring as we now know it shows (like many other important works of Brahms at this period) the result of Joachim's advice. What is not always understood by conductors is that the opening now does not represent a fortissimo at all. Nothing could be shallower than the criticism that it is now, what it was at first, an unsuccessful attempt to score pianoforte music for an orchestra. Brahms, whether on Joachim's direct advice or on his own initiative, has abandoned all effort to force the tone and has reduced his orchestra to a sound of distant menace, growing thunderously nearer whenever the harmony changes. All that is needed in performance is to attend to his markings as they stand in the score, instead of deserving the blame, wrongly imputed to the composer, of remaining under the spell of the pianoforte. I do not claim that the scoring is fool-proof.

The first theme of the opening tutti is one of the mightiest utterances since Beethoven's Ninth Symphony.

Ex. 1.

Its climax subsides into a mournful cantabile, accompanied by its ubiquitous main figure (a).

Ex. 2.

In three slow swoops of wheeling flight this rises to a remote key, in which appears a new theme destined later to form part of the second subject.

Ex. 3.

In spite of the foreign key this has not been introduced in an unduly symphonic manner, and we have not lost the sense of introductory style which the opening tutti of a concerto should have. Hence, the abruptly dramatic return to the main key and main theme is well-timed. With tragic irony the tutti rises to a note of triumph.

Ex. 4.

This dies away pathetically, and the pianoforte enters with no bravura display, but with a touching theme worthy of Bach's ariosos in the *Matthew Passion*.

Ex. 5.

From this the pianoforte drifts into a passionate development of Ex. 1 (beginning with the trills at the 8th bar), and passes on to Ex. 2, which it carries into the orthodox 'complementary key' of F, there to give out Ex. 3 as the beginning of the second subject. And now it asserts the function of the solo player in developing dramatically on symphonic lines, and introduces an entirely new cantabile in a vein of noble consolation.

Ex. 6.

This continues with an impassioned development of Ex. 4 into a long flowing paragraph. Brilliant and sonorous as is the pianoforte writing, it has none of the habits or ambitions of virtuoso display, but the paragraph dies away in gentle pathos, and the orchestra concludes the matter with an elegiac epilogue on Ex. 3.

The development starts unexpectedly with a fierce note of triumph (from Ex. 4) on the pianoforte. This turns out to be but a tragic plunge into developments of Ex. 1, which assumes more transformations than can be quoted here. But they will not prove difficult to follow. First, however, Ex. 2 appears in the basses, and modulates grandly into distant keys, as if there to seek Ex. 3. Quite unexpected is the change of mood in Ex. 3, when the pianoforte bursts out with it angrily in 'diminution'.

Ex. 7.

This, combining with figure (a) of Ex. 1, becomes quite light-hearted in a graceful passage which eventually moves to the dominant of D, thereby preparing for the return to the main theme. The recapitulation begins with one of the grandest surprises in music since Beethoven. The orchestra has crashed on to its unison D; the drums are rolling, and this time it is the pianoforte that will deliver the theme. It does so; but instead of taking it on the dark chord of B flat, it blazes out on the chord of E major (dominant of A minor). The rest follows in normal position. Magnificent new harmonic vistas are revealed when the orchestra, after bursting out with the pathetic solo-theme (Ex. 5) in high rage, modulates with it to E minor, and again to F sharp minor, where the pianoforte resumes it, leading to the recapitulation of Ex. 3 in that key with exquisite new ornamentation. A slight change in the following harmonic conduct brings the rest, the recapitulation, from Ex. 6, into the tonic D major; and there is no further change until the final dying away of Ex. 4, which descends to the drums.

From this the pianoforte rouses itself to the tragic issues of the coda. No cry of triumph, such as that which began the development, breaks in here. The pianoforte takes up Ex. 7, beginning quietly and proceeding in a short crescendo till it calls forth the orchestra, with Ex. 1, this time on the chord of D major with an effect of tragic irony. The stormy antecedents of Ex. 4, as at the end of the opening tutti, are worked up to a passionate conclusion of the movement.

It is known that the tragic mood of this first movement was inspired by the catastrophe of Schumann's illness, on the terrible day when he threw himself into the Rhine. The slow movement is a Requiem for Schumann; and that is why in one of the sketches for it Brahms inscribed its quiet devout theme as a *Benedictus*; a fact that gave rise to an erroneous impression that he at first intended it for a choral work.

Ex. 8.

The phrasing throughout the movement is very broad and free. The pianoforte enters with a kind of meditation on the main theme, without binding itself to follow the lines of the whole melody more than allusively. In a quiet dialogue with the orchestra it modulates to B minor, where a spacious middle episode alternates two themes (a long 8-bar paragraph and a short phrase) in binary form.

Ex. 9.

Ex. 10.

The return to the main theme is effected by one of Brahms's master-strokes of harmonic poise (Mendelssohn was the discoverer of the device, which is emphatically not a mannerism). The meditative pianoforte development of the theme now rises to a grand climax, and the ensuing dialogue dies away into a simple but exquisitely poetic cadenza, after which the orchestra concludes with its *Benedictus* in a line of austere beauty. The entry of the drums (silent throughout the rest of the movement) completes the solemnity of the last chords.

The rondo of Beethoven's C minor Concerto has had an extraordinarily strong influence on the form of two concerto finales powerfully independent in their styles. One of these is the finale of Joachim's Hungarian Concerto, a great work which, if it will never be widely popular, will also ever remain one of the major events in the history of the form. The other is the finale of this concerto. There is a superior prejudice to the effect that an orthodox rondo cannot be an adequate finale to a work with so tragic a first movement; but this is not borne out by the immense energy of Brahms's main theme (Ex. 11), with its impassioned second part which arises from its 7th and 8th bars and modulates with romantic depth into C sharp minor, to return in a kind of cadenza evidently modelled on Beethoven's procedure in the C minor Concerto.

Ex. 11.

Nor is there any loss of symphonic power in the immensely broad transition and in the gorgeous paragraphs of the second subject, from which I quote the beginnings of two themes.

Ex. 12.

Ex. 13.

The spacious returns to the main theme are again modelled **on** Beethoven's C minor Concerto; and so, in spite of its greater richness of phrasing and variation, is the middle episode—

Ex. 14.

including its development in a fugue—

Ex. 15.

in which Brahms shows himself a contrapuntist of the calibre **of** Bach and the lightness of Mozart. The main theme (Ex. 11) also enters into combination with this fugue subject, which is moreover treated by augmentation (i.e. given in notes of twice the length) and by diminution.

In due course the rondo theme returns again in D minor, and now the movement strikes out on independent lines. The normal recapitulation is represented by an abridgement of the calm theme of Ex. 12 in a towering passion in D minor, and the coda grows

grandly and slowly into triumph by a development of Ex. 14 in D
major, leading through a pastoral passage on Ex. 11 to a great final
stretto on its first bars, the pianoforte becoming an integral part of
the symphonic orchestra, with complete maintenance of its own
independence.

PIANOFORTE CONCERTO IN B FLAT MAJOR, OP. 83

1 *Allegro non troppo.* 2 *Allegro appassionato.* 3 *Andante.*
4 *Allegretto grazioso.*

Of all existing concertos in the classical form this is the largest. It
is true that the first movement is shorter than either that of Beethoven's E flat Concerto or that of his Violin Concerto; shorter also
than that of Brahms's own first concerto. But in almost every
classical concerto the first movement is as large or larger than the
slow movement and finale taken together, and there is no scherzo.
Here, in his B flat Concerto, Brahms has followed the first movement by a fiery, almost tragic allegro which, though anything but
a joke, more than fills the place of a symphonic scherzo: the slow
movement is the largest in any concerto since Beethoven's C minor,
while the finale, with all its lightness of touch, is a rondo of the
most spacious design. We thus have the three normal movements
of the classical concerto at their fullest and richest, with the
addition of a fourth member on the same scale.

This stormy extra allegro appassionato rather puzzled Brahms's
friends at first. Like Beethoven, he was apt to answer questions
according to the insight shown by the questioner; and so, when he
was asked why he inserted that movement, he said, 'Well, you see,
the first movement is so harmless' (*simpel*).

Perhaps the music itself may give us more light.

The first movement, in spite of appearances, does *not* (with due
respect to the text-books) 'abolish the conventional opening tutti'.
It simply begins with an introductory statement of the first theme
in dialogue between a horn, the pianoforte, and the wood-wind.

Ex. 1.

Then the pianoforte bursts out alone with an energetic figure, and follows it with an impassioned and melodious cadenza preparing the way for the orchestra, which begins the 'conventional opening tutti' or (as it is better called) ritornello with a triumphant version of Ex. 1, passing rapidly on to a review of several themes. One of these—

Ex. 2.

mp espress.

with its vigorous sequels, the pianoforte will later on show to be the principal part of the second subject. Here it is given in D minor, a key not used in the rest of the movement, and concludes with a majestic short cadence-theme fortissimo for full orchestra, derived from the figures (*a*) (*b*) and (*c*) of Ex. 1.

From this foreign key the pianoforte brings us back to the tonic in three powerful chords (figure (*a*) of Ex. 1), and then proceeds to a broad and leisurely discussion of the first theme in dialogue with the orchestra. By degrees the design reveals itself as the real sonata-form exposition of first subject and transition to second subject; that symphonic exposition for which all that we have hitherto had is but an introductory pageant. Several new themes and derivatives appear, and the drift is steadily towards F major or minor, the normal key for the second subject. One important new theme needs quotation—

Ex. 3.

for the quiet rhythmic figure (*d*), here marked with brackets, underlies the whole of the development-section. At present it leads up a long straight avenue to the second subject itself (Ex. 2). It was easy to see that there was passion therein when we heard it in the orchestra; and the usual experience in concertos is that the orchestra can deliver with massive force what the solo-player can make subtle and delicate with eloquence and ornamentation. But here Brahms surprises us: there is ornamentation indeed, but the orchestral version of the second subject was mild compared with the version given by the pianoforte. To the continuation a new theme is added (which clever speculators may, if they choose, derive from figures (*a*) and (*b*)—Brahms will not care), and a furious climax is reached, figure (*a*) booming in the bass beneath cataracts of trills, until at last the pent-up orchestra bursts through with the fortissimo cadence-theme that closed the ritornello. (Yes—'you see, the first movement is so harmless.')

The orchestra continues with an angry allusion to Ex. 2; at last there is a high wail from the clarinets, and, answering from the darkness, the horn gives out the first theme (Ex. 1) sadly in F minor. The pianoforte carries on the dialogue as at the beginning of the work. When it reaches the energetic continuation which it formerly had as an introductory solo, the orchestra takes the lead. (This device, of giving to the orchestra what formerly belonged to the solo, is another of Brahms's new resources; hitherto it had always been the solo that borrowed from the orchestra; and the composers who 'abolish the ritornello' have done less than nothing towards this other side of the balance.)

Soon the key shifts to an immense distance (B minor), and we are in the full swing of the development. This now settles down to a witty dialogue on the rhythmic figure (*d*) from Ex. 3. The smooth melody that binds Ex. 3 together does not appear here, the foreground being occupied by a quite new theme given to the pianoforte. But in the background you will find the steps shown in Ex. 3 systematically carried out in sequence through many rich modulations, all of which, however, group round and revert to B minor, their starting-point. The details crowd closer, and the action, which started in comedy, becomes serious. At last the figure (*a*) of the first subject crashes in, and, while smoky arpeggios rise in the pianoforte, that figure and its continuation (*c*) move grandly from key to key, the bass slowly creeping upward, until a solemn calm is attained on a harmony still very distant from the tonic. Nevertheless this harmony yields easily to the dominant of B flat, our tonic, and in sails the first subject on the horn taken up, as in the introduction, by the pianoforte.

The recapitulation, thus dramatically brought about, represents the first subject only by its first two phrases, and passes thence immediately to Ex. 3 in (or rather, *about*) the tonic. From this point all is exactly reproduced in the tonic, until we reach the furious cascade of shakes which revealed the 'harmless' character of this gigantic movement. Here a momentary deviation into a foreign key gives a point of departure for the coda. The tonic is restored with a sudden plunge into extreme darkness. Out of subdued mutterings the first theme again arises and hovers, while the air seems full of whisperings and the beating of mighty wings. Suddenly the sunlight breaks through, and the movement ends with a triumphant summary, in broad melodious flow, of those topics arising from the main theme that were left unaccounted for in the exposition and recapitulation.

The second movement, a scherzo in form if not in mood, is no less powerful than the first; and if it were a finale instead of being (as it obviously is by nature as well as position) a middle movement, we might be in two minds about calling it tragic, in spite of its jubilant central episode (or trio) and its elemental enjoyment of its own rage. Of its three principal themes the first two—

Ex. 4.

Ex. 5.

are presented like a first and second subject in a terse sonata-form exposition. This exposition is repeated. Then a development ensues; but we are surprised to find it soon veering round to the tonic (D minor), where, after a tremendous orchestral climax, there enters a jubilant new theme in the tonic major—

Ex. 6.

largamente.

which, with an important sequel, has much the effect of a trio. After this trio has thus been grafted on to the development, we naturally have no mere da capo of the scherzo, but a free sonata-like recapitulation of its materials (Exx. 4 and 5) in the tonic. Then there is a tremendous coda. Brahms has blended the solo and the orchestra on quite new principles, with perfect freedom and adequate scope for both, in this unique movement.

If there ever could be any doubt as to the purpose of that stormy second movement, the first notes of the andante should settle it. The key is B flat, the key of the first movement, and its emotion is a reaction after a storm, not after a triumph. Thus both in harmony and mood it would be fatally misplaced immediately after the first movement. After the second its emotional fitness is perfect, and is enhanced by the harmonic value of its being in the tonic of the whole work. It gives this slow movement a strangely poetic feeling of finality, though the slow tempo and lyric style make it obviously unlikely that it can really be the end. The first movement had its storms; the second movement was all storm, and here we are not only enjoying a calm, but safe at home again.

The orchestra begins with a broad melody for a solo violoncello.

Ex. 7.

Later on an oboe joins the violoncello in dialogue; and in the last two bars the pianoforte enters with a new figure (*b*) and delivers a free monologue suggested by the first two bars of the theme (see especially figure (*a*)).

Ex. 8.

(*b*) continued in bass.

No composer has ever surpassed Brahms in the art of making a closely-woven passage seem as if it was extemporized whereas it really carries the communicating threads of a whole vast organization. Compare the slow movement of the Violin Concerto.

The time of storms and anxieties is not yet past: the orchestra breaks in with much agitation, and the pianoforte transforms the calm figures of its first solo (Ex. 8) into matter for a very impassioned dialogue with the orchestra. This is worked out on a large scale and with an energy which goes far to make this slow movement as difficult as the finales of ordinary concertos. At last, however, it comes to a mournful end in the tonic minor; there is sudden modulation, and then, in F sharp major and in slower tempo, an entirely new melody rises. The pianoforte is accompanied by two clarinets. The melody consists of few notes spaced out like the first stars that penetrate the sky at sunset. When the strings join in, the calm is as deep as the ocean that we have witnessed in the storms of this huge piece of music. To crown all, the solo violoncello enters, still in F sharp major, with the main theme. A slight digression at the end of the first phrase brings the

continuation round into the tonic, B flat; and then the rest of the
movement is simply a recapitulation of its orchestral opening with
the addition of an ornamental pianoforte part, until the original
entry of the pianoforte is reached (first two bars of Ex. 8). To this
the pianoforte and violoncello add a close, with a simple chain of
shakes, a slow arpeggio, and soft final chords.

And now we have the finale. What tremendous triumph shall it
express? Brahms's answer is such as only the greatest of artists can
find; there are no adequate words for it (there never are for any art
that is not itself words—and then there are only its own words).
But it is, perhaps, not misleading to say here, as so often of
Beethoven's finales, something like this: 'We have done our work
—let the children play in the world which our work has made safer
and happier for them.'

There are no trumpets and drums in this finale. Neither are
there any storms. There is abundance of young energy and grace,
and there is all that greatness of design which, as Mozart and the
Greeks have proved, is unfailingly sublime, whatever the ostensible
range of the subject. Here the emotional reaction is so convincing
that, with all the 'roaring cataracts of nonsense' that were poured
out on the subject of Brahms's concertos when they were new, it
has, as far as I know, never been suggested that this finale was too
light-hearted for the rest of the work. In the same way it has never
been suggested by even the most sacerdotal Wagnerians that *Die
Meistersinger* is in any way a slighter work than *Tristan*. Such cases
are really well worth noting for the light which they throw on the
relation between the 'subject' of a work of art and the emotions
which the art itself calls forth.

I will leave this great and childlike finale to call forth the right
emotions without further analysis in words; but the listener may
perhaps find some use in a specially full budget of quotations, as
there is a very large number of themes. I therefore subjoin the six
principal ones in the order in which they occur, marking, as usual,
with letters those figures which are used in derivative themes.

Ex. 9.

First Theme.

Ex. 10.

Second strain of First Theme.

Ex. 11.

First Episode or 'Second Subject' I.

Ex. 12.

First Episode continued, II.

Ex. 13.

First Episode continued, III.

Ex. 14.

From middle Episode, or Development.

Ex. 14 alternates with meditations on Ex. 10, which eventually returns in the tonic without waiting for the main theme.

VIOLIN CONCERTO IN D MAJOR, OP. 77

1 *Allegro non troppo*. 2 *Adagio*. 3 *Allegro giocoso, ma non troppo vivace*.

This work is of the same period as Brahms's Second Symphony in the same key. It is his second work in concerto form, the first being the gigantic D minor Pianoforte Concerto, op. 15. Mr. Huberman summarizes a whole essay on the aesthetics of this and of all concertos in the following correction of a famous epigram of Bülow's. Bülow said that Max Bruch had written a concerto *for* the violin and Brahms a concerto *against* the violin. Mr. Huberman says that 'Brahms's concerto is neither *against* the violin, nor *for* violin *with* orchestra; but it is a concerto *for* violin *against* orchestra—and the violin wins'. One of my earliest recollections of a great musical scholar, A. J. Hipkins, is his delight at discovering that the etymology and musical history of the words 'concertanto' and 'concerto' originate in 'certare', to strive.

I give, with slight changes, the analysis I wrote for the London concerts of the Meiningen Orchestra in 1902.

Brahms's opening tutti states all except one of the themes of the first and second subjects, with such terseness that the first three sound like a single theme, being, in fact, absolutely continuous.

Ex. 1.

Energetic as Ex. 3 is, in contrast to the quiet beginning, we are much surprised to find that in three more bars the whole orchestra crashes out in a grand fortissimo, with (a) in the bass, imitated by the treble, and treated in diminution. We may already realize that this is no symphony that we are hearing, but the true headlong single outpouring of manifold material by an orchestra, to be worked out by a solo instrument in classical concerto form. The outburst leads to the themes of the second subject, another series of three themes, all stated in the same continuous style. These are—

Ex. 4.

with its derivative—

Ex. 5.

and a mysterious variation thereof which must rank as an important separate theme, so much is it changed by the division of (f) among the instruments and the conjunction of a new figure (g).

Ex. 6.

This leads to an energetic cadence theme in the minor, beginning thus—

Ex. 7.

and followed by a running figure in semiquavers which may speak for itself. Suddenly the solo violin enters, with rolling drums and a solemn sustained tonic pedal on the deepest notes of the horns. The violin begins with a fiery transformation of the quiet first theme (Ex. 1 (*a*) (*b*)) in the minor—

Ex. 8.

while the string band throws in the strong rhythm ♩ ♩ ♫ ♩. ♩ of Ex. 7 (*h*).

Soon, through the flaming arpeggios of the solo violin, we hear the original form of (*a*) in broad sequences of minor harmonies on the oboe, answered by clarinet, bassoon, and flute, always with the tonic pedal in horns and drum. Gradually the sweeping arpeggios of the violin become more gentle; until in a moment the flame burns softly and steadily, the harmony brightens to major, the tonic pedal gives place to a 6/4 chord, and the rhythm expands, as the orchestral colouring seems to drift away in clouds, leaving the pale tone of the string-band as the background to the solo violin that soars calmly into the quiet heights above, there to begin its song.

The solo restatement of Ex. 1 must be quoted, as the new quaver accompaniment (*i*) of the viola is very important.

Ex. 9.

Between Exx. 1 and 2 the violin interpolates a meditative passage with that sublime calm which only the greatest artists have learnt to call their own. Ex. 2 is made to pass into the dominant. It will be heard in the violoncellos, with a wonderful counterpoint for the solo violin. Ex. 3 appears first in the deep basses and is then repeated in canon by the other strings, the solo violin having another new and independent theme.

The second subject follows Ex. 3 in the orthodox dominant, beginning with Exx. 4 and 5. When we reach figure (*g*) of Ex. 6 the violin turns it into a lovely new theme, beginning thus—

Ex. 10.

(*g*)   New theme.   &c.

This is worked out at some length, before we reach the rest of Ex. 6, which we find at last much enhanced by the new contrast just gained, and still more mysterious from being placed in a firm position on the tonic instead of on a secondary chord as in the tutti. The effect of the double-stops on the solo violin is unique.

Ex. 7 follows, and its continuation is expanded so as to bring the exposition to a stormy close. The orchestra bursts in—with the ritornello, as in all previous examples of concert-form? No; Brahms hits on the grand idea of giving it that stormy transformation of (*a*) Ex. 8, with which the solo made its first sudden entry.

As in Beethoven's Violin Concerto at the same point, the orchestra modulates simply and broadly to C major, the key that is most of all opposed to our tonic D. There it groups the solo violin's additional theme in the second subject, Ex. 10, into eight-bar phrases together with (*f*) as in Ex. 6. This closes in C minor; and the solo violin re-enters with the following intensely plaintive development of (*f*), a landmark in the musical experience of many a Brahms-lover.

Ex. 11.

(*f*)   (*f*)   &c.

True to those principles of balance and variety which have led the great classical concerto-writers to make their developments decidedly episodic in character, Brahms not only dwells long on this without change of key, but enriches it with an entirely new counter-subject (*x*).

Ex. 12.
tranquillo.
(*x*)

(*f*)   &c.

After some time the violin awakens angrily to an energetic mood, and the orchestra takes up the new theme (*x*) and works it out independently in a few stormy sequences, till suddenly there is a bright flash of trumpets. The solo violin re-enters in high rage with an extraordinary new figure on the dominant of D (our main key) as an accompaniment to the gigantic strides of the transition theme, Ex. 3 (*e*), which we hear in the bass. Soon, on a dominant pedal, we find ourselves preparing for the return of the first subject, in a storm of excitement. The solo violin has the powerful variation of (*a*) with which it made its first entry (Ex. 8), and the winds have that figure of accompaniment (*i*) which we saw in Ex. 9. The rhythmic figure (*h*) ♩ ♪ ♩. ♪ also plays a prominent part in this tremendous passage, which at last ends in the appearance of the first subject in grand triumph on the full orchestra. The counter-point (*i*) is given to the violins in their most brilliant register, while the theme is trumpeted forth by all the wind-band.[1]

The violin re-enters with sublime calm, and we have Ex. 2 so placed as to lead to an exact recapitulation, in the tonic, of the whole of the rest of the solo exposition. An amazing new light, however, is thrown on the point at which the violin introduced its own new theme, Ex. 10. The omission of one step in the sequences just before brings it unexpectedly into F sharp major, the brilliant major mediant used by Beethoven in the Waldstein Sonata and the Leonora overtures.

The return to D is easily managed without greatly enlarging the ordinary course of the melody, and the rest of the recapitulation is again quite exact, until the fiery climax which is crowned by the inrush of the orchestra.

And now, will the orchestra enter with Ex. 8 as it did at the beginning of the development? Brahms has something in store which, in this context, is yet more grand. In the unexpected new key of B flat (admirably chosen, as it exactly counterbalances that startling change to F sharp in the middle of the recapitulation) we have that splendid blaze of full orchestra which, in the opening

---

[1] Note how the trumpets themselves alter the first two bars in order to avoid the note B, which is not in their natural scale. Brahms has the modern trumpet, with a complete scale, at his disposal, but he detests any use of the instrument that audibly contradicts its character as a 'natural' instrument whose scale is the harmonic series that exists in the very nature of musical sound itself. Beethoven shows the same fastidious taste in the finale of the Ninth Symphony, where in giving the great choral theme to trumpets he distorts two bars in the second part to avoid a note which, though actually in the natural scale of the instrument, is so harmonized as to sound as if it were not. Such subtleties are among the things which, even more than matters of noise or economy, distinguish the great composer's treatment of brass from the vulgar abuse of it.

tutti, had followed Ex. 3 with the suddenness of a tropical sunrise. This quickly returns to D major, and Brahms actually makes the time-honoured pause on a 6/4 chord, and leaves it to the player to furnish something like half of the coda in an unsupported, quasi-extempore cadenza. Brahms could afford to risk this, since he had dedicated this concerto to the player and composer of the most ideally appropriate cadenzas that have been produced since those grand inspirations that Beethoven extemporized (and so signally failed to write down).[1]

The short conclusion, after the cadenza, begins with a quiet resumption of the first theme with sublime harmonies, and a development of the second figure (*b*) into sequences crowned by some of the tenderest notes ever drawn from a violin. Faint suggestions of the rhythm of Ex. 7, ♩ ♪ ♩, in the horns, are answered by triplets in the solo violin, that recall, in a far-off way, the triplets of Ex. 8, transformed into something infinitely touching and gentle. Then, with astonishing speed, the air becomes full of life and energy; the rhythm ♩ ♪ ♩ ♩ is insisted on sharply by trumpets and drums; the pace quickens; the solo violin has an extremely brilliant version of the counterpoint-figure (*i*), divided between it and the wood-wind—

Ex. 13.

Flutes.

Solo violin.

and the grand movement is ended in triumph before we have regained our breath.

The slow movement is very highly organized on a remarkably broad melody; and the treatment, though thoroughly classical in spirit, is in detail so unlike anything else that a little technical knowledge is apt to be a misleading preparation for its enjoyment.

[1] The hypothesis of the concerto cadenza nevertheless implies that a new cadenza may be produced on each occasion. The problem of cadenza-writing is extremely interesting. In the case of the violin it is complicated by the fact that a composer writing (like Bach) for unaccompanied violin invents themes that require no accompaniment; whereas the cadenza-writer has to make the violin produce an unaccompanied coda-like fantasia on themes that have been conceived as supported by harmonies which they need not have the power of implying in themselves. I append my solution of Brahms's problem at the end of this essay. Two points may be taken as essential to any cadenza for this concerto; namely, the first bar and the final close, where any other plan than Joachim's would be unthinkable. Elsewhere the possibilities, on the right general principles, are incalculable.

The opening theme must be quoted at some length, as the whole subsequent solo is best followed from it.

I number the bars of the melody for reference. The closing strain of this great tune must also be indicated.

The strings make their entry with the initial chords (a), and the solo violin appears with phrases that on a first impression seem to be freely declamatory. If that was all that could be said, they would not have the wonderful and touching effect that we experience in them. As a matter of fact the violin is giving us an exact and systematically expanded variation of the whole opening melody. I quote the three bars that correspond to those numbered 1 and 2 in Ex. 14.

With this hint we can follow the rest by fixing our attention on Ex. 14, making two of its bars correspond with three or four of the violin solo. When we come to figure (e), bars 9 and 10, there is a sudden change to the key a semitone higher; one bar being still systematically expanded into two. The time slackens; (e) is given by 'diminution' (i.e. in semiquavers instead of quavers), and in the extremely distant key of F sharp minor the violin begins an impassioned central episode. This consists of a highly ornate melody, containing two new figures (*g*) and (*h*)—

Ex. 17.

(*e*) diminished.

(*h*), it will be seen, being accompanied by (*e*) diminished. As soon as this has formed a regular eight-bar melody, it is given again in an expanded counterstatement. (*g*) is assigned to the violoncellos in a form which I give here, as it is important that it should not escape notice.

Ex. 18.

(*g*) varied.

The counterstatement follows the lines of Ex. 16 on a larger scale with more and more elaborate ornamentation, especially as regards figure (*h*), while the diminution of (*e*) is treated in splendid rising modulations in the accompaniment. Three bars of these modulations bring us back to our tonic, F; the clouds drift away leaving the violin singing peacefully in the blue vault, and the oboe returns with its world of melody. The violin, which now has a rich accompaniment, interpolates, after the second bar, three bars of its augmentation, Ex. 16, after which the melody proceeds as at first, till we come to the twelfth bar. Here the violin gives us a new development of figure (*b*) in dialogue with the horn, crescendo.

Ex. 19.

Horn.

This comes to a climax, and as it dies away, we are thrilled to hear the lovely codetta, Ex. 15, for the first and last time since its original appearance. The initial chords (*a*) entering again on the bassoons and horns, followed by a beautiful closing change of harmony, round off this wonderful organization so perfectly that even the vast range of key and contrast through which we have been carried cannot dispel the impression that the whole movement

is a single unbroken melody. Thus the reason why some critics
have thought it too slight is the very reason why it is gigantic.

The same inexhaustible variety and resource in unexpected alternations and correspondences in melodic grouping that we find in the
slow movement appear in the extremely spirited and humorous
finale. This is a rondo; like many of Beethoven's finales, rather terse
in its formal body, but with an enormous expansion in the coda.

The first theme is given by the solo violin—

Ex. 20.

Allegro giocoso, ma non troppo vivace.

in alternation with the full orchestra. The last figure (*c*) should be
specially noted. The tune has a second part on the same material,
which must be quoted independently here to facilitate reference
later on.

Ex. 21.

This leads, with a short crescendo (listen to (*a*) in the basses), to
a resumption of Ex. 20 by the full orchestra, with a characteristic
tightening of the sequences of (*a*), bringing the cadence-figure (*c*)
into the tonic.

A transition passage founded on (*c*), first augmented and then
diminished, leads playfully by a devious path to a very stormy and
wayward second subject in the dominant. The scales that precede
it should be noted, but I need only quote the beginning of the
second subject itself.

Ex. 22.

Like many second subjects in Beethoven's finales, this soon shows
a tendency to drift back from its key. It dwells on the chord of
F sharp minor, till it overbalances itself and falls straight back
into the first theme in the tonic as at the beginning. But the
orchestral counterstatement does not continue to recapitulate this
after the third bar. Figure (*b*) is broken up into rising sequences,
and the violin enters with placid arpeggios in the quiet key of the
subdominant, while (*a*) is worked out by the orchestra. The
violin arpeggios merge into a graceful new theme in a totally
unexpected rhythm.

The arpeggios and figure (*a*) intervene for a moment, in their
own 2/4 time in B major. The new 3/4 theme returns in E major,
a key strongly opposed to our tonic, D, and then in C major, the
one key that is still more opposed. Then the orchestra breaks up
these new figures (*f*) and (*g*), giving (*g*) by augmentation, while the
violin has expressive counterpoints, all in the key of G minor (in
the major of which this episode began).

Suddenly the gentle theme is brushed impatiently away. We
hear an expanded version of the scale passages that led to the
second subject, and the second subject itself inevitably follows in
the subdominant. And Brahms gives us a perfectly regular recapitulation of it, as if this were quite a normal position for its
reappearance, instead of being a unique combination of two formal
peculiarities that had hitherto always stood alone; the appearance
in a foreign key, and the omission of the first subject. When he
comes to the point where it overbalanced itself on the chord of
F sharp minor, now of course B minor, we naturally expect the
return of the long-lost first theme. Instead, we are surprised and
delighted to hear its still more long-lost second part, Ex. 21. The
listener will readily appreciate its powerful effect in pulling the
whole structure together. It has not been heard since the opening;
it reminds us of the first part of the theme, which was last heard
before the paradoxical middle section, that so tersely combined
the qualities of a melodious and independent central episode with
those of a solid piece of thematic development. Then we had the
unexpected recapitulation of the second subject in the subdominant. Now we return, not to the tonic, which would not be
bright enough to give relief immediately after so unusual an
expanse of subdominant, but to the key of this second part. And

Brahms now expands it, making it cover other keys, such as the dominant of F. And as he proceeds, we understand yet more. That second part did originally lead to a final restatement of the first theme, which of course now returns with greater force than ever. It takes its fill of expansion and climax; and its closing figure (c), augmented, becomes the text for a great accompanied cadenza by the solo violin.

Ex. 24.

As the violin settles down to a trill that gradually becomes a chain of modulations, we hear (a) in the strings; and when, after the modulations, the tonic is re-established, the whole phrase (a) (b) is heard in the basses (a fine point that should be watched for). Then, on a dominant pedal, the rhythm of (a) ♪ ♫ ♩ is, to borrow Sir George Grove's happy phrase, *blown at the hearer*, in answer to the sequences of the violin. We reach a climax and a pause. Then the time quickens, to a stirring march rhythm, in which we have a new version of the principal theme, with laughing *gruppetti* on the wind instruments, and a lively tread of drums and trumpets.

Ex. 25.

This rapidly rises to a climax, especially through the aid of its new version of (b). No less suddenly does each successive climax (they are several and short) give place to the following transformation of the second subject (Ex. 22).

Ex. 26.

With a running fire of unexpected variations on (*a*) and (*b*), the gigantic work ends in a glory that is intensified by the sudden alternations between *forte* and *piano* which, while they take our breath away, preserve the balance between solo and orchestra up to the last moment.

Cadenza for Brahms's Violin Concerto by D. F. Tovey.

CONCERTO FOR VIOLIN AND VIOLONCELLO, OP. 102

1 *Allegro.* 2 *Andante.* 3 *Vivace non troppo.*

An important work for an unfamiliar combination of instruments
is always at a disadvantage; mainly for the reasons which make the
combination unfamiliar. One *chinoiserie* by Ravel does not make
an art-form of duets for violin and violoncello; and the sound of
this combination of extremes is inherently strange without a
middle part to bridge the gap. But the strangeness is not an
absurdity, such as the combination of a violin and a double-
bass would be. It is, when properly handled, a powerful stimulus to the musical imagination alike of listeners, players, and

composers. When Brahms brought the resources of his ripest experience to the handling of this combination together with an orchestra in the last of his orchestral works, the novelty for many years completely puzzled even those critics who took an official attitude of apostleship towards his music. The explanation of the difficulty is simple enough. Brahms did not make the new work a systematic display of the charms of the new combination, but simply expressed some of his most powerful and dramatic ideas for all the world as if the combination of instruments was perfectly familiar. His critics and his admirers had, in short, to deal with Brahms's most powerful ideas as well as with the unfamiliar combination, and it is pathetic to see the struggles of such a critic as Hanslick with this excursion beyond the lines laid down by him in his apostleship. The most familiar features of Brahms's way of developing themes, as for instance in the middle of the finale, where the phrases of the heroic middle episode are in their restatement dramatically interrupted by echoes through which the solo instruments are heard with their own ornamentation, similar devices in the middle of the slow movement, and the terseness of the slow movement as a whole—these and other equally normal features impressed Brahms's friends as well as his hostile critics just as if they were technical immaturities. There is no other explanation for this than the fact that everybody expected in a modern double concerto to hear as much of the violoncello as if there were no violin, and as much of both as if there were no orchestra. In the meantime Brahms did as Mozart and Beethoven always did—he treated his orchestra symphonically. Accordingly the orthodox complaint became, first, that the solo parts were enormously difficult; secondly, that it was impossible to hear them; and thirdly, that there was not nearly enough of them. As for the pathos and the poetry of the work, all this general disappointment made it out of the question to speculate whether such qualities existed at all.

It is to be hoped that at this distance of time there may be less difficulty in taking the work as it really comes. Any one who has made a study of musical first impressions in general and of concertos in particular, knows at once that the complaints described above are illusions. If the work is of a loosely-knit texture, the composer can thicken his score almost with impunity. For instance, the Dvořák Violoncello Concerto (over which Hausmann on his last visit to Brahms found him boiling with generous admiration) is, on a moderate computation, twice as heavily orchestrated as this, the most difficult of Brahms's concertos; and the truth is that Brahms's thickest accompaniments in this Double Concerto are written with scrupulous economy, whereas Dvořák's are alarmingly reckless. But with a loosely-knit work many points may escape the

listener without much damage to the sequel. In works such as this
of Brahms, every theme and every inner part has its results in later
chapters of the story. Therefore it is as well for us to have a good
number of quotations for our present analysis.

The dominance of the solo violin, the still greater dominance of
the violoncello, and finally, the wonderful solidity of harmony and
wide compass of the united couple, are demonstrated in the introduction. First the orchestra throws out a challenge in the shape
of the figures of the first subject on the dominant (that is to say,
the threshold of the key).

Ex. 1.

The last three notes of the orchestral phrase are instantly taken up
by the violoncello, entirely unaccompanied, in a most impassioned
kind of recitative. Then the wood-wind enter gently in the major
with the first phrase of the second subject, one of Brahms's
tenderest themes.

Ex. 2.

This time the solo violin takes up the last three notes, at first
meditatively. It is soon joined by the violoncello and works up to
a climax of extraordinary fullness of harmony, ending in an uprush
of scales and chords which leads to the entry of the whole orchestra
with the first subject launched full on the tonic into the course of
a mighty concerto ritornello.

Ex. 3.

Brahms proceeds simply and broadly, but in a style which does not
make any confusion between the lines of a concerto and those of
a symphony, though he boldly strikes out into a foreign key in
preparation for his second subject. The passage of preparation

with its fierce syncopations is the most impassioned theme in the whole work.

Ex. 4.

And when the theme of the second subject bursts out in F major (a different key from that for which it is destined in the solo), it continues in a storm of passion. No worse mistake in interpretation could be made than for this orchestral version to be treated in the style of the solo. Again I must quote the theme as it occurs here, on account of its continuation.

Ex. 5.

Very soon it has passed back to A minor with abrupt questionings, and a new theme bursts out which will be heard again in the coda.

Ex. 6.

With this the orchestra comes to its conclusion, and the violoncello impetuously enters with a new development of the first theme—

Ex. 7.

answered after four bars by the violin. (Always it will be found that the original first bar of Ex. 1 (a^1) is answered sooner or later by the second bar (a^2) whatever new developments have happened in between.) The two instruments develop this idea rapidly and passionately to a climax in which they discuss the second phrase of Ex. 3 (those very striking minims in its fifth bar), and after this they settle down to a spacious and entirely new transition theme in dialogue.

Ex. 8.

Starting with the utmost energy and drifting towards the orthodox key of the second subject (C major), this yields to a melting mood; and the preparation of the second subject, with the figures of the first theme tenderly reiterated in the oboe and flute through the interlacing arpeggios of the solo instruments, broken by an impressive silence in the middle, would be the most pathetic passage in the concerto, but for the fact it leads to the still more pathetic expanded version of the second subject announced by the violoncello and eventually taken up by the violin. I know no more powerful instance of the dramatic possibilities of concerto form than the way in which this melody changes its character according as it is stated in the ritornello or expanded in the solo. Suddenly however it breaks into a stormy passage, leading to what in the ritornello appeared to be the transition theme (Ex. 4). The violin and violoncello have but to state the first two bars of this (which they do with extraordinary fullness of sound) for the whole orchestra to burst in at the same height of passion as it had reached in the ritornello; and it comes to an even greater climax, being under the stress of plunging into a somewhat distant key for the development. In the midst of the storm the two solo instruments enter together with the first theme, and proceed to work out the figure of triplet crotchets which characterizes its third bar. This becomes a mysterious figure at twice the pace with a characteristic change of accent in the wood-wind.

Ex. 9.

(I may mention, as a sample of the intelligence which is sometimes brought to bear upon the interpretation of Brahms, that at a performance by a good foreign orchestra, I found that some one had corrected this 'discrepancy' of rhythm in the band-parts!) Soon the syncopated theme reappears in a pathetic calm in the orchestra, while the solo instruments weave round it a network of trills. Before long the calm becomes a stiff breeze, and the breeze a storm, through which the first theme cries out angrily in the wood-wind. Suddenly the storm ceases, and the syncopations of

Ex. 4 soar upwards in the violoncello and violin through remote
modulations in a pathetic passage, which the most disappointed
detractors of this work on its first appearance admitted to be
sublime. We are on the threshold of the tonic, and the violin
and violoncello come back to the uprush of scales and chords
(the chords now alternating with the orchestra) with which they
ended the introduction.

And so the recapitulation now begins in the tonic in the orchestra,
just as the big ritornello did. Its second sentence, however, is delivered by the solo players, and leads straight to the solo transition
theme of Ex. 8. Slight changes in the course of the harmonies
keep the music in the key of A. There is the same pathetic passage
of preparation, with its impressive bar of silence. Then the expanded version of the second subject is given out high up by the
violin, the violoncello having a new flowing accompaniment. In
due course the fatal syncopated theme evokes the stormy orchestra,
which now carries the latter part of the ritornello to its greatest
climax. This owes much of its power to the fact that its last theme
(Ex. 6, which has not been heard since its first appearance) is now
combined with the figures of the first subject (Ex. 1). This brings
the violin and violoncello back upon the scene in tragic passion
with the same statement as that of their first entry after the
ritornello. There is something extraordinarily sonorous in their
appearance here in octaves, and still more in their boldly coalescing
in unison as the passion yields to a tragic calm with a ritardando. From this they rouse themselves with the syncopated figure
(Ex. 4), and the tragedy is consummated by the transformation
of the second subject itself into a final outburst of indignation,
the theme being given in pizzicato chords in the minor, while the
solo instruments emphasize the bass of the harmony by a stormy
figure of their own. With a final allusion to their transition theme
(Ex. 8) the solo instruments bring down the full orchestra upon the
last chords.

The slow movement begins with a signal of two notes on the
horns answered in the upper part of the scale and in a high octave
by the wood-wind. On the four notes thus delivered, the solo
violin and violoncello immediately build one of the broadest and
most swinging melodies ever written.

Ex. 10.

This is worked out as a complete tune in two parts with repeats.
The second part is peculiarly gorgeous in its deep harmonies, and

its climax is heightened on repetition. Then without further development or pause the middle episode enters in the somewhat remote key of F. It begins with a very quiet melody for the wood-wind scored with a highly-seasoned reedy tone.

Ex. 11.

The violin and violoncello answer this with a new theme in rather wistful dialogue which modulates richly.

Ex. 12.

Then the reedy theme (Ex. 11) returns unaccompanied, with semi-quaver movement by the solo instruments, and expanded by very characteristic echoes of the last two notes of each phrase in pizzi-cato chords. A quite short but far-reaching passage moves in a few steps through remote keys, when suddenly the first two notes of the introductory signal are heard in the trumpets. The solo instru-ments respond to them, and in a notoriously difficult but very majestic passage float down again to the whole first melody, which on repetition they expand in a simple but surprising way which will not escape notice. When the great melody has come to an end, there is a short and peaceful coda in which the two middle themes (Exx. 11 and 12) are heard simultaneously. As this reaches an exquisite dying fall, the figures of the first theme come surging back again until the solo instruments rise up on to the answer to the opening signal (that is to say, the second bar of Ex. 10), to which the trumpets reply quietly with the first bar; and so, with the majestic and difficult returning passage on the tonic chord, the slow movement ends in a golden glow.

From the point of view of first impressions, the finale of this double concerto commits the most deadly crime possible to a great work—it shows a sense of humour. Let us admit this, and let us accept the still more serious fact that the first theme is playful, which is not always the same thing as humorous. This does not prevent it from giving rise at the end of the movement to one of the most pathetic passages in the whole work. Apart from the humour and the unusual combination of instruments, the chief difficulty in contemporary appreciation of the finale arose from the fact that, like the slow movement, it is very terse, and therefore failed to impress the listeners of the 'eighties and 'nineties with the true breadth of its proportions. (It is an odd thing that the critics who are loudest in their denunciations of unnecessary length are always the first to grumble that a terse statement is inadequate.) The form of this broadly designed but short finale is the clearest of rondo-types. In Ex. 13 I give the first phrase, calling attention to the figure I have marked (a), for the sake of its extraordinary consequences in the coda.

Ex. 13.

The first episode or second subject is a full-toned aspiring melody—

Ex. 14.

the rhythm of which expands in a remarkable way in its counter-statement, compelling Brahms temporarily to change his time to 3/4 and 4/4, until he abruptly breaks it off and leads back to the first theme. This now gets no farther than its first phrase, after which it is playfully laughed into evanescence until nothing is left but rhythmic fragments amid a silence. Suddenly out of these rhythmic fragments arises a fiercely triumphant new theme in a key compounded of F major and D minor with a preponderance of D minor.

Ex. 15.

With the aid of an angry alternating second part, which I do not quote, this leads to a counterstatement by the orchestra, inter-rupted by characteristic echoes of the last two notes of its phrases. (These echoes form the only discoverable ground for the allegation that the structure of this very spacious middle episode is disjointed. As a matter of fact, the device is one of those bold simplicities which give the scale of design, and secure that it shall continue to surprise by its breadth and flow long after we have known the

whole work by heart.) Then follows a calm swinging tune in
F major given by the wood-wind, with a delicate accompaniment
of rising arpeggios in the solo instruments derived from those
echoes.

Ex. 16.

The solo instruments work it up vigorously on their own account,
till it leads to a gorgeously bright and soft version of Ex. 16 in D
major with the syncopations smoothed away. Then Ex. 15 bursts in
again. Its angry sequel is now used to lead us back to the tonic, and
the rondo theme (Ex. 13) re-enters in due course, followed by all
its accessories. This now goes through a wide range of key before
alighting upon the second subject (Ex. 14) triumphant in the tonic
major. The second subject now leads immediately to the coda,
which is in the major throughout. It begins in a slower tempo
with a calm version of the first theme (Ex. 13), from the third bar
of which arises a most touching stream of melody in dialogue
between voices of different octaves outlined in arpeggios by the solo
instruments.

Ex. 17.

It is the privilege of works in sonata form that they can, without
weakening or falsifying tragic issues, bring their finales to a happy
ending. The tragedy of the first movement has been told without
flinching, but told within the quarter of an hour which contains
symphonic movements on a large scale. Within that quarter of an
hour we have not time to see enough of the world in which such
tragedies take place; and we are allowed to see its glorious melodies,
its humours, and its capacities for happiness, in the other movements. And so the whole concerto leads up to the wonderful
tenderness of this last page which finally breaks into joyful triumph,
and brings the great work to an end.

MAX BRUCH

VIOLIN CONCERTO IN G MINOR, OP. 26

1 PRELUDE: *Allegro moderato, leading to* 2 *Adagio.*
3 FINALE: *Allegro energico.*

When Max Bruch died at the age of 83, the news came to many as a revelation that he had lived so long. Though he never dominated the musical world as Spohr did in his own day, yet he was the type of artist universally accepted as a master, about whose works no controversy could arise because no doubt was possible as to their effectiveness and sincerity. Like Spohr, he achieved this mastery in all art-forms; and, unlike Spohr, he developed no irritating mannerisms. If it were possible to imagine a large work by Spohr in which there were no cloying chromatic harmonies, the idea would closely correspond with that of a masterpiece by Max Bruch. At present it seems the correct thing to say that his G minor Violin Concerto is his only surviving work; but the two other violin concertos (both in D minor) and the Scottish Fantasia need nothing but the attention of violinists to prove quite as grateful to performers as to the public. Moreover, I find myself entirely in agreement with the writer of the article in Grove's *Dictionary* who says that Bruch's greatest mastery lies in the treatment of chorus and orchestra; and I have not the slightest doubt that a revival of Bruch's *Odysseus* (which the writer regards as his most successful work), and perhaps still more of his last choral work, a Kyrie and Sanctus, which I heard in Berlin in 1907, would make a fresh and stirring impression on any audience that will listen naïvely to beautiful music for music's sake. Poorer things have survived from the enormous output of Spohr, simply because players periodically rediscover their effectiveness. Spohr and Mendelssohn were so completely idolized by a masterful majority of musicians in their own day that grave injustice was done to all music in which new and refractory elements were struggling for expression. The result was that kind of so-called classical period which should accurately be called pseudo-classical. The injustice of a pseudo-classical period produces with the swing of the pendulum another kind of injustice in the next generation. No art is then allowed to have any merit that does not consist almost exclusively of new and refractory elements nobly struggling for expression. This does not repair the older injustice, it merely transfers it. Clever people tell us that you can train a poodle to produce pseudo-classical art. If this is true, you have only to shave your poodle hind part foremost and let its hair grow where formerly it was shaven, and the very same poodle will produce art in which refractory new elements are nobly struggling for expression. But after all, in the long run mastery tells.

The lot of a fastidious artist, conscious of mastery as a gift entrusted to him during a period of destruction, is not enviable; nor, perhaps, do the wisest of masters so regard their own personal mastery or their own period. Brahms's mastery was so great that it gave rise to furious controversy, but he knew how to extricate himself from encounters with the shockable; and on the few occasions when he encountered Max Bruch his disposition to tease appeared at its worst. Lovers of music ought, at this time of day, to show more gratitude to those who devote themselves to making beautiful things. It is not easy to write as beautifully as Max Bruch. 'But', you will say, 'that does not go to the root of the matter: perhaps the very reason why this beauty of yours bores us is that we see it is a mere matter of mastery over difficulty.' If you can see that in the case of Max Bruch, I give it up; but I find his case quite different. It is really easy for Bruch to write beautifully, it is in fact instinctive for him; and such instinct is a matter which all modern critics and psychologists will agree to rate very high. Further, it is impossible to find in Max Bruch any lapses from the standard of beauty which he thus instinctively sets himself. I have only to call attention to the second subject of the rondo of this concerto as a touchstone. There are several popular violin concertos which now hold the field, and in all of them the second subject of the rondo is a most regrettable incident, and is also the most popular feature of the work. I forbear to name the instances but it is surely significant that this most successful of Max Bruch's works shows one of its noblest features just where some of its most formidable rivals become vulgar.

The concerto is in three movements, only two of which are complete. Instead of the formidable organization of a first movement in classical concerto-form with a great orchestral exposition of themes afterwards to be fully developed in sonata-form by the solo player, Bruch contents himself with a prelude in which the solo violin enters into a solemn dramatic dialogue with the orchestra. The themes do not require quotation, though soon after the main key G minor has been established, a contrasted melody, quite definite enough for a second subject, appears in the key of B flat. In spite of this, however, the manner of the whole movement is introductory; it is an introduction so broad that it tends to take a

definite shape; and we need not do it the injustice to imagine that it
was merely an abortive first movement. Thus its design is not cut
short but is completed when, after the violin has returned to G
minor, the orchestra comes storming in with a vigorous tutti, in
which the gentle second theme has become an impassioned outburst in the minor. When this has run its course, it subsides into
the opening phrases, and the declamation of the solo violin returns
in greater elaboration. Suddenly the orchestra bursts out in
pathetic enthusiasm on the dominant of E flat, and leads to the
second movement, a fully developed slow movement in sonata-
form. I quote the three main themes; the first subject—

the all-important transition theme—

and the second subject as it appears in the bass below florid
counterpoint (unquoted) of the solo violin.

The exposition of the second subject ends with Ex. 2, which is
always used to effect cardinal action in the piece. By way of
development we have an expanded version of the first subject in
G flat, followed by the transition theme, Ex. 2, in the same key
with a beautiful new melody above on the solo violin. By degrees
this works round to the tonic, E flat, with a crescendo; and now
occurs with the entry of the orchestra, a masterly and dramatic
stroke of form which I summarize in outline.

This shows how the first bar of Ex. 2 is taken up by one orchestral group after the other, until the second subject enters grandly below and so carries us out on the full tide of its recapitulation. The coda is grafted very simply and naturally on to this and brings the movement to a peaceful end.

The finale begins in the key of the slow movement with an excited crescendo anticipating the figure of its main theme and swinging round to G major. It works out a broad and transparent scheme with the aid of its lively first subject—

Ex. 5.

and its bold and noble second subject.

Ex. 6.

There is no lack of rich accessory themes, but they can be appreciated without quotation. Max Bruch's First Violin Concerto thoroughly deserves the great success it has always had. Nobody who can appreciate it will believe for a moment that its composer has written nothing else worthy of the like success.

CHOPIN

PIANOFORTE CONCERTO IN F MINOR, OP. 21

1 Maestoso. 2 Larghetto. 3 Allegro vivace.

Chopin's F minor Concerto, op. 21, is really earlier than that in E minor, which is numbered op. 11. Both works belong to the period of his triumphs as the young Polish pianoforte virtuoso whose opus 2 (Variations for pianoforte with orchestra) was greeted by Schumann with the expression, 'Hats off, gentlemen; a genius!' It was necessary for Chopin to compose works with orchestral accompaniment in order to assert his position as a composer; otherwise the public, which is not easily persuaded that an artist can accomplish anything besides the first object that happens to have attracted attention, might have regarded him as a mere pianist. As it was, excellent pianoforte composers like Moscheles remained to the end of their days convinced that their own musicianship was more solid than Chopin's. To demonstrate the sense in which they were right is a theoretic possibility. But it is not interesting.

There is some interest in the fact that Schumann's enthusiastic recognition of Chopin's genius was elicited by just the works in which he is hampered by forms for which his training had given him no help. Some critics would go farther, and say that he had but little talent for the sonata style; but no judge of composition would say this of Chopin's Violoncello Sonata, nor can any serious critic explain away the masterly and terse first movement and scherzo of the B flat minor Sonata. The concertos need more indulgence. The first movement of the E minor is built on a suicidal plan which Chopin's adored master, Elssner, must have at least approved if not actually taught, since it is to be found in two earlier works and can hardly be conceived to have resulted from natural instinct. The F minor Concerto, though not a powerfully organized work, has no fatal flaw; and its style is the perfection of ornament. The chief subject of orthodox objection has been its orchestration; but nowadays we can take a simpler view of this matter. Klindworth, a very masterly and masterful pianist with an excellent all-round musicianship, could never contemplate a line of standard pianoforte music without showing how much better it might have been arranged. When he had tidied up Chopin's pianoforte technique he turned his attention to Chopin's orchestration. This he found thin, and so it is. We may frankly concede that Chopin knew nothing about the orchestra—at least, not much more than Sir Michael Costa. But Klindworth seems to infer that the only alternative to thin is thick. At all events he reorchestrated the F minor Concerto really very cleverly, in the style of a full-swell organ, with a beautiful balance of tone. In order to penetrate this, even the tidied-up solo part had to be rewritten in a heavier style. Klindworth duly points this out, and remarks that those purists who wish to confine themselves to Chopin's original pianoforte part must accordingly abstain from using the improved orchestration. In other words, Chopin's orchestration, except for a solitary and unnecessary trombone part (not a note of which requires replacing), and a few rectifiable slips, is an unpretentious and correct accompaniment to his pianoforte-writing. We may be grateful to Klindworth for taking so much trouble to demonstrate this.

Chopin begins with an orthodox opening tutti. The quiet first theme—

Ex. 1.

is followed by an accessory used in the development.

Ex. 2.

Bassi 8va.

The second subject, though (as in Beethoven's C minor Concerto) it appears in its destined complementary key instead of in the tonic—

Ex. 3.

- &c.

does not, in the manner of its entry, unduly forestall the broader statement it is to receive later from the pianoforte. Altogether Chopin shows far too fine a gift for design in this opening tutti to justify the prevalent custom of cutting it short. The impatient dramatic entry of the pianoforte needs all the delay Chopin has given before it.

One other theme must be quoted, a passage in C minor, which key Chopin (striking out on unusual lines first found in Beethoven's Coriolanus Overture) adds to the scheme of his second subject.

Ex. 4.

&c.

In the development the orchestra accompanies the pianoforte with figures from Ex. 1 and Ex. 2. After a certain amount of dramatic expectation, the first subject returns in F minor. But the pianoforte promptly changes the topic and brings back the second subject not in the tonic, but in its old complementary key, a singular but not unsuccessful experiment in form. Chopin may have had in mind certain rare procedures in Mozart. The continuation is expanded in a different harmonic direction, which brings Ex. 4 in F minor, so that from this point Chopin is able to work up to a final climax. The short closing tutti alludes to Ex. 2 and the opening theme.

Schumann's enthusiasm for the slow movement, voiced through the persons of his imaginary Florestan and Eusebius, was boundless. I quote the main theme, divested of its ornaments. The listener will thus gain a clearer notion of Chopin's art than can be given by the sight of a mass of detail, which only long practice can bring into shape as intelligible phrases.

Ex. 5.

The unornamented portion stands out in relief as a haunting refrain.

Ex. 6.

The middle episode is a dramatic recitative, accompanied by an orchestral tremolo with pizzicato double-basses. This is as fine a piece of instrumentation as Berlioz could have chosen to quote in his famous treatise. In the final return of the main theme Ex. 5 is more elaborately adorned than ever. Ex. 6 remains in its perfect simplicity, but a bassoon imitates it at the second bar, continuing in counterpoint of an adroit simplicity worthy of Bach or Mozart. The movement ends with the same passage that served as its short orchestral introduction. Like the romance of the E minor Concerto, it is a masterpiece in a form and a mood which neither Chopin nor any other composer reproduced later.

The finale is a delightful example of the long ramble through picturesque musical scenery, first straight up a range of keys and then straight down again, which Chopin, for reasons unknown to history, called a rondo. I quote the main theme—

Ex. 7.

an orchestral accessory—

Ex. 8.

the first item of the surrounding scenery—

Ex. 9.

and the important mazurka-like main second subject, accompanied *col legno* (i.e. with strings played with the wood of the bow), an effect rather in vogue in the concertos of Chopin's young days. The respectable Hummel uses it, and Chopin revered him.

Ex. 10.

This, when Chopin is comfortably home again in F major, is reduced to a horn-call inscribed *Cor de Signal*; upon which invitation the pianoforte perorates with fairy-like brilliancies, for the most part new, alluding only at the last moment to one of the sequels of Ex. 10.

DELIUS

VIOLIN CONCERTO

In the art of to-day, there is no more intimate note than that of the later works of Delius. He was never a sensational composer; and the large orchestra and brilliant technique of his early works never displayed any tendency incompatible with the almost oriental depth of meditation which he has attained in recent works such as the Violin Concerto and the Double Concerto.

It would be a mistake to infer, from the shortness and number of the themes here quoted, that the Violin Concerto is either a disjointed or a complicated work. It is, on the contrary, so continuous a stream of ruminating melody that the shortness of the quotable themes is really, as with Wagner's Leitmotivs, a symptom of the length of the paragraphs; while, on the other hand, the course of Delius's work is subtle only (and a very important 'only') in its emotional reactions, and extremely simple in plan. The themes follow in a natural sequence of discourse, with no more complex link than might be supplied by the clause 'and that reminds me': until a point is reached at which it is agreeable to recapitulate some of them from the opening. The classical key-system is only occasionally alluded to, and most of the harmonic phenomena depend on regarding chords of all degrees of artificiality as direct tone-

sensations, unanalysable as the taste of a peach, with none of the
classical sense of their individual notes as coming from given
directions in order to 'resolve' on explanatory notes.

In Delius's art, even more than in Debussy's and Cyril Scott's,
the instrumental tone-colour of every chord is quite as important
as the actual notes. For the most part the tone-colours are exquisitely soft and mellow; and even when Ex. 3 finds itself forced to
the extreme high notes of the trumpet, there is a technical mastery
in the scoring which ensures that with first-rate playing the effect
is glowing rather than shrill.

The function of the solo violin is to sing and to decorate; chiefly
to decorate. The difficulty of its part arises entirely from the almost
complete absence of familiar harmonies and intervals, and at no
point is the difficulty connected with technical display.

After two introductory bars for the strings, the solo violin pours
out the three following themes in a wayward stream of meditation.

Ex. 1.

Ex. 2.
Slower.

Ex. 3.

To these may be added a majestic outburst of the brass.

Ex. 4.

f Brass.

The middle section (if one may use the term of such unsectional
music) is in a slower time, and comprises two important cantabile
themes.

Ex. 5.

Ex. 6.

A short cadenza leads to a recapitulation of the first four themes with a change in the direction of key. Very unexpectedly a quaint new section, in a naïve dancing rhythm, creates a diversion from the ruminating mood of the whole.

Ex. 7.

Allegretto.

It alternates, however, with a variation of Ex. 5 in the following form.

Ex. 8.

Finally the figures of Ex. 1 conclude the work on a chord once known to theorists as the 'added 6th'—one of the very few names in musical theory that fit the facts.

Ex. 9.

For more reasons than concern theorists we might well regard this music as an example of the Lydian mode, as Milton would describe it—

> And ever against eating cares
> Lap me in soft Lydian airs,
> Such as the melting soul may pierce . . .

DOHNANYI

VARIATIONS ON A NURSERY SONG FOR ORCHESTRA WITH PIANOFORTE, OP. 23

The composer has dedicated this work 'to the enjoyment of lovers of humour and to the annoyance of others'. And we know that the man who can write comedies as well as tragedies makes better and wiser tragedies than the man who is annoyed by comedy. There is nothing unreal or undignified in the artistic organization and emotional range of this work, which must rank high among the modern classics in one of the severest of art-forms.

The work begins very tragically, the brass being specially afflicted.

Ex. 1.

Through this 'symphony in Woe minor', a solemn canto fermo of eight notes—

Ex. 2.

(with sharps and flats that come and go) looms large in the horns. The tragic introduction dies away—

Ex. 3.

—with a bang; and then the pianoforte enters with the theme— which explains the solemn canto fermo. (Nothing will induce me to quote it.) The string orchestra accompanies with delight, in harmonies that become increasingly learned as confidence is gained; until at the last clause a bassoon bursts out with the venerable ecstasy of the parent of the Jabberwock-slayer who 'chortled in his joy'.

The first six variations follow the theme closely in combinations and dialogue with different groups; of which we may mention the

two-flutes-and-piccolo *versus* two-bassoons-and-contra-fagotto of
Var. 4; Var. 5, with its combination of pianoforte, harp, and bells
(the bells giving the theme in its form of canto fermo with
the sharps and flats that come and go); and the astonishingly
ingenious Var. 6, an étude for pianoforte and wind instruments
without parallel in classical or modern orchestration.

Ex. 4.
Wood-wind.

Pianoforte.

With Var. 7, the theme blossoms out into a spirited Viennese
Waltz, developed at leisure.

Ex. 5.

Var. 8 is a March, glum but dogged. Into the guileless tonality of
the underlying theme, the sharps and flats come and go with such
freedom that the foundations of the key settle and heave with
alarming irregularity.

Ex. 6.
Alla marcia.

The next variation is a scherzo full of grim surprises—

Ex. 7.

—such as the unison of the piccolo and contrafagotto with the
canto fermo; and it culminates in a desperate recitative of the
pianoforte which leads to Var. 10, a passacaglia, or solemn dance
on a ground-bass—the ground-bass being our canto fermo in the

minor mode. As the first of the eight notes of this canto fermo is
the same as the last, its recurrences overlap the eight-bar rhythm
by one note. Röntgen hit on the same device in the Waltz in
his *Azzopardi Variations*, a *jeu d'esprit* I hope some day to describe.

Ex. 8.

The pace gradually increases until the whole orchestra finds itself
wailing like the brass in the introduction (see Ex. 1), and at last the
theme bursts out in the major (Var. 11) as a chorale. The harmonies, as usual, become more and more chromatic as the tune
proceeds, drifting into the whole-tone scale of Deomnibussy (which
is a more eclectic affair than that of Debussy). It dies down, and,
after a dispute between the pianoforte and the wind as to what
the key shall be, the finale breaks away in a merry fugue.

Ex. 9.

The subject and counter-subject of this fugue are just as happy
inverted as right side up, and after a brilliant climax the original
theme of childhood returns. It is not surprising that its adventures
have taught it a new and elegant phrasing which it had not
possessed when it first appeared. There is some little argument
over its last notes, but the contrafagotto agrees with the piccolo
as to how that should be settled, and the orchestra gathers itself
up and hastens to reach the end in time with the pianoforte's final
glissando.

DVOŘÁK

VIOLONCELLO CONCERTO IN B MINOR, OP. 104

1 *Allegro.* 2 *Adagio ma non troppo.* 3 FINALE: *Allegro moderato.*

The superstition still survives in some quarters that Brahms, because of his own consciousness of supreme mastery and fastidious taste in form, must have been a pedantic critic of composers whose style was less disciplined. It still passes for orthodox criticism to compare Brahms and Dvořák as composers of opposite schools. The historic facts are that Brahms and Joachim were the two first to recognize and acclaim the genius of Dvořák. This does not mean that either of them pledged himself to regard all Dvořák's output as worthy of him, and still less does it imply that either thought his most popular works his best. Among friends Brahms could be generously indiscreet, and at this time of day there can be no harm in publishing one of his indiscretions, which was told to me by Hausmann. On perhaps the last occasion on which Hausmann called upon Brahms in Vienna he found him reading a score that had just been sent him. Brahms, before he would talk of anything else, must first give vent to his grumble: 'Why on earth didn't I know that one could write a violoncello concerto like this? If I had only known, I would have written one long ago!' This is all the more remarkable as Brahms had in fact given the violoncello the lion's share in one of his most recent and greatest works, the Double Concerto for violin and 'cello, op. 102; a work which, then violently abused by all the critics, is now coming into its own. The Violoncello Concerto of Dvořák is not without its composer's more amiable weaknesses; nor is it possible to say that all the weak points are, as in some other great works by Dvořák and Schubert, suggestive of new types of form. But it is permissible to plead that the weaknesses do not matter. Both the slow movement and the finale relapse into Charles the Second's apologies for being such a unconscionable time in dying; but it is impossible to grudge them their time, and as a matter of fact none of the three movements of the concerto is of unreasonable length. Dvořák developed in his later works a curious habit of planting his harmonies firmly on to the tonic of whatever key he had drifted into, and giving thereon a series of short phrases, each of which comes in the manner of an afterthought suggested by the one before. There are not many forms of instrumental music where this kind of construction is dramatically effective; but it has its claims where the style can inspire affection, and it goes far towards explaining itself when the means of expression is a solo instrument to which a large orchestra appears to be listening with rapt attention.

In the first movement there is no feeling of diffuseness or redundancy, though the construction is by no means close-knit. Dvořák is, as throughout the work, peculiarly full of invention; and, to begin with, he abandons the modern position adopted by him in his comparatively slight and sketchy violin concerto, and states the main themes of the movement in a full-sized classical orchestral tutti. He even goes so far as to put the second subject into its own foreign key; a device which Beethoven in his C minor Concerto contradicted at the very moment of suggesting it, because it makes the opening tutti too like the beginning of a symphony. I quote the two main themes of the first subject and the second subject as they occur in the opening tutti.

The second subject is one of the most beautiful passages ever written for the horn. I purposely quote more than its first phrase, as its highest merit lies in the simple originality of the continuation. In the opening tutti this leads to a naïvely perfunctory new theme for the full orchestra which I do not quote. It gets Dvořák out of the difficulty of concluding a tutti which might otherwise just as well have done for the exposition of a symphony; and we need not trouble ourselves about its unpolished manners, since, having done its duty and declined in a dramatic diminuendo, it is never heard again. Then the violoncello enters, quasi improvisando, and pours out an inexhaustible flow of splendid developments of the first theme, leading (in dialogue with the orchestra, on lines quite different from those of the opening tutti, but equally naturally) to the second subject. The second subject is now followed by a large variety of new accessory themes with some very rich changes of

key, and eventually comes to a climax, upon which the orchestra
re-enters grandioso and begins the development with a dramatic
transformation of the first theme, modulating to the distant key
of A flat minor (= G sharp minor). In this key the violoncello
re-enters and, instead of carrying the development through further
wanderings of key, settles down to a sustained episode in which
the figure of the first theme is worked out in a cantabile. Soon the
violoncello takes to a rippling arpeggio figure, while the cantabile
is carried on by wind instruments. This drifts easily towards B
minor, and thus we feel that we are returning, perhaps unexpectedly soon, to the tonic. The entry of a drum with an impressive
low roll is dramatically ominous, and the violoncello swiftly rushes
to the crisis. The event paradoxically justifies the shortness of its
preparation and the suddenness of its accomplishment, for the
theme which enters in the tonic is not the first subject but the
second subject, triumphant in the full orchestra. Dvořák has, to
put the matter briefly, brought this great loosely-knit first movement within surprisingly moderate dimensions by 'short-circuiting'
its development and recapitulation. The success is brilliant, both
in form and in dramatic expression; and the total impression left
by the movement is unequivocally that of a masterpiece, whatever
theorists may say.

The slow movement has either two themes or five or six, according as you choose to single out any of the numerous afterthoughts
tacked on to each of its sentences. I compromise by indicating its
material in two composite quotations, one from the quiet main theme
and the other from the tragic central episode.

In both groups of material there is the persistent tendency to come time after time to a close on the tonic, as I mentioned at the outset. This is accentuated when the violoncello in the recapitulation turns the first theme into a sort of cadenza in dialogue with the orchestra, where every phrase is so explicitly of the nature of an ending that it is not easy to separate the coda from the rest of the design. The listener will be materially helped in his appreciation of the whole by the following quotation. It shows that the extremely quiet passage which follows the quasi-extempore recapitulation of the theme is really a transformation of the stormy first phrase of the middle episode (Ex. 4).

Ex. 5.

We shall do injustice to such a piece of music if we imagine that its habit of perpetually closing in the tonic is merely a weakness. It is obviously essential to the point of the music; nor is the point really difficult to appreciate when every moment is an outstanding example of euphony.

The finale, a short-circuited rondo, begins with a dramatic marching introduction for the orchestra, foreshadowing the main theme, the gist of which is then given out by the violoncello.

Ex. 6.

From the large number of other themes I quote the transition with its continuation for the violoncello (which continuation elsewhere brings about a return to the tonic)—

Ex. 7.

and later

and (overleaf) the theme of the first episode, which never recurs—

Ex. 8.
Clar.

'Cello.   &c.

with the first theme of the second episode in rather slower time—

Ex. 9.

which eventually surprises us by short-circuiting the whole
structure (compare the similar case in the first movement) and
appearing on a solo violin in the tonic major. Here, then, Dvořák
settles down to another glorious series of epilogues in a steady progression of picturesqueness and calm. Eventually, in quite a slow
tempo, the ghost of the first movement (Ex. 1) appears seraphically
in the clarinets. But at last the orchestra rouses itself. The trombones give out the figure of the rondo theme (Ex. 6) in solemn big
notes; and, after all, the work ends allegro vivo in high spirits.

ELGAR

VIOLIN CONCERTO IN B MINOR, OP. 61

1 *Allegro.* 2 *Andante.* 3 *Allegro molto.*

Elgar's Violin Concerto, like the *Enigma Variations*, and probably
like many other of its composer's finest inspirations, is a character
study. This is attested by its dedication to some one unnamed, in
the words prefaced in the score: '*Aquí está encerrada el alma de
...*(1910).'

Of all external subjects for music the illustration of human
character is the most purely musical; if indeed it can be an external
subject at all. Music either has character, or it is meaningless, and
the character either has human interest or none. We nourish our
interest in the characters of animals by describing them in human
terms; and if there is such a thing as 'cosmic emotion', it is
nourished by contrasting the vastness of the universe with the
insignificance of man, while at the same time we pride ourselves in
the fact that it is the human mind which recognizes the contrast.
The blank space which stands for the name of the person whose soul
is enshrined in this concerto shows that nothing is to be gained by
inquiring into the private affairs of Sir Edward Elgar and his friends.
The soul of the music is musical, and we need no further external
programme. My analysis, therefore, will have nothing but musical

facts to present to the listener. I give as nearly as possible a complete list of the themes, a policy which saves many a difficult paragraph of description. But the quotations, though numerous, are very short; and the listener will be grievously misled if he infers from this that the melodies represented by them are short. There is in fact the same danger here as there is in the orthodox discussion of Wagnerian leitmotiv, and such famous examples of the use of an all-pervading figure as the first movement of Beethoven's C minor Symphony; the danger that the analysis may ignore the flowing paragraph in its fascinated study of the pregnant word. When such one-sided analysis is made a basis for the teaching of composition, the results may be paralysing or destructive; and there are such things as compositions that have no flow and no real coherence, because the composer has been deceived into believing that a composition can be built upwards from single figures, 'logically' connected by a process which has little more logic in it than a series of puns.

The following fifteen quotations are, then, no more than the first words or leading words of the paragraphs and the processes which they initiate. I quote them thus briefly, not because the melodies are short, but because there are so many different long melodies and long processes based on the same figures that it is convenient to quote their common factors. If this work were a Wagnerian opera, nothing would be easier than to label one pair of bars the motive of longing, and another the motive of ambition, and to imagine that the composer and the dramatist were both equally capable of designing a dramatic scene by permutations and combinations of some twenty such motives and titles, each consisting of six or seven such highly significant notes that the initiated listener is miraculously certain of their meaning. Such a doctrine would not be worth refuting, but for the fact that composers themselves have been misled by it. This concerto refutes it triumphantly. I have heard it admired for the shortness of its themes, and I have heard it blamed for its lack of broad melodies. The answer to the equally mistaken admiration and blame is already to be found in the fact that the first paragraph is an entirely straightforward matter containing three distinct and important themes.

Ex. 1.

Ex. 2.

Ex. 3.

Even so it is not quite complete, but closes into the next paragraph, which works out, in broad melodious sequences of urgent character, a new theme announced in a darker key.

Ex. 4.

The next theme is destined, later on, to express a serene calm—

Ex. 5.

but the modulations to which it here gives rise, lead quickly to an excited climax in an extremely remote key, with a new figure closely allied to Ex. 2.

Ex. 6.

This swings round in five bars back to B minor, where we have Ex. 4 in an inner part below new counterpoints, followed by a further development of Exx. 1 and 2. So far we have heard nothing of the solo violin. What we have been listening to is a fine modern example of the classical opening tutti of a concerto. These six themes have been welded together in a continuous flow of melody. The changes of key, though more remote and more frequent than those of any older concerto, have all been changes possible in a flow of melody; they have not been events marked off from each other by dramatic action. The master who is to hold this large orchestra spell-bound, and set all these themes out on their various different planes, has not yet spoken. We have now reached the moment when the orchestra is eagerly awaiting him. The strings speak of him wistfully, as in the two bars represented by Ex. 1. Their sentence is finished for them by the master himself.

This entry of the solo violin realizes in a new way the true relation between the solo and the orchestra in the classical concerto form. After a short but broadly ruminating recitative, the violin, passing through Ex. 2, discusses Ex. 4 with the orchestra. Then Ex. 3 (which, by the way, is obviously closely allied to Ex. 1)

is developed through a wide range of keys as a rich transition
passage, drifting slowly but surely, with the aid of its ally Ex. 6, to
G major. In this key Ex. 5 now blossoms out as a broadly lyric
second subject. After this has been given free expression we are surprised for a moment by the appearance of Ex. 1 in its original key,
a phenomenon which, however, does not mean a return to the tonic,
inasmuch as one of the subtleties of the opening tutti was that its
first chords were ambiguous in key. Thus the oracle proves its
tragic infallibility, for the key turns out to be F sharp minor, the
dominant minor. Ex. 4 is worked up, with various derivatives from
Ex. 1, and a new counterpoint from the solo violin, to a great climax
in which Ex. 3 also plays its part; until at last the full orchestra
crashes in with an impassioned tutti beginning with Ex. 4 and passing through remote keys with a still more impassioned development
of what was once the calm lyric strain of Ex. 5. Ex. 1 joins powerfully in the stormy dialogue and soon brings the development round
to the original key.

Suddenly the storm subsides, and the solo violin re-enters,
completing the half-spoken word of the orchestra as on its first
entry, but with a quite new meaning, while muted horns murmur
the rhythm of the first bar of Ex. 4. The effect is quite clearly
that of a return to a recapitulation; and what now follows has
all the manner thereof. In actual fact it is very free. The main
theme of the second subject (Ex. 5), for instance, appears almost
at once below the meditative florid figures of the solo violin,
and executes some beautiful remote modulations before the violin
resumes the transition themes, Exx. 4, 3, and their accessories.
It then appears again in sequences that recall its tentative appearance in the opening tutti; and when at last it settles down to
a real feeling of recapitulation its key is not the tonic, but D
major. This establishes the same balance of keys that Schubert
has in his Unfinished Symphony; but as the original course of
Elgar's second subject swerved from G major to the dominant
F sharp minor, it now has to take a different direction to swing
round from D major to B minor, the main key. This it effects with
more sombre dramatic force than before; the entry of the brass
being particularly impressive where the violin resumes the discussion of Ex. 4 in B minor. From this point the coda grafts itself on
to the recapitulation, and, with the impetuous intervention of Ex. 2,
brings the movement to its impassioned end with the first theme,
Ex. 1, and its variant, Ex. 3.

The slow movement is in the extremely remote key of B flat.
There is something quaint in the fact that two modern violin concertos which are almost at opposite poles of artistic outlook should
both be in B minor, and both have this exceptional key relationship

in their slow movements. Of Saint-Saëns's third Violin Concerto it may be said without offence that it is all publicity, whereas Elgar's Violin Concerto is one of the most intimate works of this century. In most respects the comparison between the two works sheds little light on either of them, but it is interesting to compare the most obvious single feature in the slow movement of each. Everybody who remembers the slow movement of Saint-Saëns's B minor Violin Concerto instantly thinks of the passage where the violin plays arpeggios in harmonics two octaves above a clarinet. Everybody who remembers the slow movement of the Elgar Violin Concerto thinks of the way in which the orchestra first states eight bars of naïve melody, whereupon the solo violin enters with an equally naïve counterpoint *as an inner part.*

Soon the violin leads the orchestra into remote regions; and new themes appear—

which rise to a climax in D flat.

In this key the first theme (Ex. 7 with its counterpoint) is resumed, and leads through Ex. 8 to a broad new theme in D natural.

This, though it sets out very firmly in D, does not remain there long but fetches a compass quickly back to B flat, where, with the return to the main theme, we also have other themes freely recapitulated in their order. The last words are said by the orchestra with Ex. 10 pianissimo, answered by the violin with Ex. 9.

The finale is very rhapsodical and dramatic. Its outstanding features are an opening in which the solo violin seems to be playing a kind of prelude on a figure of rising turns. This requires no quotation until an inner part of the orchestra interpolates a theme which afterwards becomes important.

Ex. 12.

This appears to be a determining point, inasmuch as it brings the harmony to the crisis of closing in the key of B minor, which all this improvisatorial opening is intended to establish. It is obviously right that after the slow movement in the remote key of B flat, the main key of the work should be specially emphasized. This impression once clearly conveyed, the harmony, after all, swerves boldly aside, and in D major there enters the most prominent theme in the finale.

Ex. 13.

Other themes that are used with a sense of being transitional material are Ex. 12 (soon taken up with majestic passion by the whole orchestra) and a combination of it with new figures—

Ex. 14.

foreshadowing the second subject itself.

Ex. 15.

Out of these materials the scheme of exposition and recapitulation is easy to follow, and soon runs its course. It accordingly lands us in B major; and now, in what is formally speaking the coda of the work, comes the real series of events for which all this is a prelude. The second theme of the slow movement, Ex. 8, enters in B major adapted to the tempo of the finale, and is brought by both the solo violin and the orchestra through a wide range of key to a climax over which the themes proper to the finale (Exx. 13 and 12) return in full vigour.

Suddenly the music dies away into the minor, and the themes of the first movement reappear slowly and mysteriously (Exx. 1, 4, and 5) in the cadenza, which has become famous as one of the most original dialogues between a solo instrument and an orchestra that have ever been imagined. The device of the 'pizzicato tremolo', which Elgar has invented in this passage, ought henceforth to be a matter of common knowledge in orchestral music. There is nothing like it for filmy harmonious transparency and mystery; and it is one of the simplest things in the world. But we wrong this cadenza if we ascribe its aesthetic value to an orchestral effect. The priceless thing is to find such devices invented in the service of music which enshrines a soul. It is not a sensational effect; and those who have heard of it by reputation and expect to be startled by it will be disappointed. It is simply a common-sense solution of the problem of providing an exquisitely faint harmony that will keep entirely in the background on any notes required. After the cadenza, the introduction to the finale is resumed and leads to a brilliant coda in which Exx. 8, 15, and 13 conclude the work in triumph.

VIOLONCELLO CONCERTO IN E MINOR, OP. 85

1 *Adagio, introductory to Moderato, leading to 2 Allegro molto.*
3 *Adagio, leading to 4 a recitative, leading to*
5 *Allegro ma non troppo.*

Although the musical language of this work is unaffectedly classical, its forms are unlike those of any other concerto; conspicuously unlike, for instance, the elaborate classical design of Elgar's Violin Concerto. The Violoncello Concerto is a fairy-tale, full, like all Elgar's larger works, of meditative and intimate passages; full also of humour, which, in the second movement and finale, rises nearer to the surface than Elgar usually permits. Though the work is highly organized, an elaborate analysis is not necessary so long as enough themes are quoted. Lucidity is the aim and the achievement of its form and style; not the thin mundane lucidity of a Saint-Saëns concerto, nor yet the arrogant lucidity of the epigrammatist who has not got over his famous discovery of the stupidity of most people.

Mutatis mutandis, this violoncello concerto well represents its composer's Schumannesque mood. This term will seem grotesque to those numerous musicians to whom orchestration is the *sine qua non* of musical thought; but Schumann's helplessness in that category rather reveals than conceals the shyness that goes with such intimate moods. The shyness is, however, just as compatible with consummate mastery of the orchestra; and indeed Elgar's orchestration is as unworldly as it is masterly. In the Violoncello Concerto the orchestra is throughout concentrated on the special task of throwing into relief a solo instrument which normally lies below the surface of the harmony. Brilliant orchestration is thus out of the question; but there is no lack of subtle and beautiful tone-colour, inexhaustibly varied within narrow limits and by the simplest means.

After a short recitative-like introduction by the violoncello—

Ex. 1.

the first movement begins with an indolent sequential theme, announced unharmonized by the violas—

Ex. 2.

and repeated by the violoncello. The movement is not in sonata form, but is a simple lyric design with a middle section in 12/8 time. This is introduced by the following theme—

Ex. 3.

which then blossoms out into the major mode thus—

Ex. 4.

There is a free recapitulation of the main section (Ex. 2). Then, after a momentary allusion to the introduction (Ex. 1), the second movement, a lively scherzo in G major, begins tentatively with the following figure:

Ex. 5.

Allegro molto.

This soon gathers speed and seems about to work itself out, with a few other themes, as a free sonata-form movement, with a second subject beginning in the remote key of E flat, which, however, it soon abandons.

Ex. 6.

largamente   *a tempo.*

Having produced just enough effect of development to take us beyond lyric forms, the impish little movement scurries back to its G major and vanishes with the detonation of a burst bubble.

The serene slow movement, in B flat (the Ultima Thule from E minor, the key of the concerto), is a single broad melody. For future reference I number its first two phrases separately.

Ex. 7.

Adagio.

Ex. 8.

&c.

The movement ends on the dominant, with its first phrase (as in Ex. 7), and thus leads into the introduction to the finale. This introduction begins in B flat minor, with an adumbration of the future main theme, which is turned by the violoncello into a recitative not unlike that at the beginning of the concerto. The finale then begins, in full swing.

Ex. 9.

It is a free rondo, with a mischievous second subject, slightly suggestive of dignity at the mercy of a banana-skin.

Ex. 10.

The movement is spaciously developed on a large scale, with many and varied episodes. A complete surprise awaits us towards the end in a new slow theme of romantically abstruse harmony and full of pathos.

Ex. 11.

The metre, already new, changes to 3/4, where yet another fresh theme—

Ex. 12.

rises to a climax of passion, thence to subside into the second strain of the slow movement (Ex. 8), and from that to the opening of the concerto (Ex. 1). Then the main theme of the finale works up tersely to a spirited and abrupt end.

CÉSAR FRANCK

VARIATIONS SYMPHONIQUES FOR PIANOFORTE
WITH ORCHESTRA

No two art-forms in instrumental music can be much more unlike each other than the two kinds of variation-work represented by Elgar and César Franck. The Elgar Variations are a series of tone-pictures each asserting its own completeness and its contrast with its neighbours, but, with only three exceptions, all very closely confined to their theme. The Franck Variations are a single flowing series forming little more than an episode placed between an introduction about half as long and a finale more than twice as long. The introduction and finale are on a totally different theme from that of the variations, this variation theme being only hinted at in the introduction and being only brought in as a bass counterpoint in two passages in the finale. Of regular variations there are only six, all flowing without change of tempo out of their theme, which is not a long one. In fact the work is a finely and freely organized fantasia with an important episode in variation-form. All the habits of César Franck's style contribute here to the happiest results. He is before all things a master of the extempore manner. This is a very different thing from being a composer who extemporizes on paper. Except in the hands of a master whose experience is so vast that it has become forgotten in the depths of instinct, the process of extemporizing on paper is disastrous, being too slow for spontaneity and too quick for self-criticism. The memory (on which musical form depends) is in a false position, and drugs itself with mechanical copying of recapitulatory passages in the required keys, instead of developing the healthy imagination which vividly realizes the effect a passage will have when it re-appears in the recapitulation.

The improvisatorial manner of Franck is a very different thing; it is a genuine love of portraying the growth of ideas. His introductions and connecting links are vast and ruminating; but Franck does not fall into the error of making them lead only to each other: they lead very surely to the ideas they aim at. The ideas themselves are epigrammatic, like most good things in the French language; and there is no danger of their being lost in the ruminating profundities which surround them. As for the moods and contrasts, with all their subtlety nothing can be clearer. The manner is always openly dramatic without ever descending to theatrical makeshifts. Franck has been compared to Bruckner, the symphonic composer whom the Wagnerian party of the 'seventies hoisted into the position which they loudly denied to Brahms. It seems a pity that Teutonic patriotism forbade them to discover Franck while they were about it. Franck and Bruckner certainly have in common the completest unworldliness, combined with a style which is dramatic in gesture and range, but constitutionally incapable of adapting itself to the theatre. Otherwise, to compare the two composers is unilluminating: it is difficult to exaggerate the clumsiness of Bruckner and the deftness of Franck.

The introduction to these Symphonic Variations states with dramatic roughness a figure (a) which is dimly suggestive of part of the variation theme. The pianoforte, however, answers with something really much more important, figure (b).

These two themes are worked up in dialogue in Franck's delightful ruminating style, together with another idea which I do not quote. Soon the time changes to 3/4, and the strings (pizzicato, with staccato wind over a roll of kettledrums) give out two phrases of the variation theme as it is going to be. The pianoforte, however, intervenes with a sustained and impassioned speech on the theme of figure (*b*). Then the orchestra re-enters, and the dialogue is resumed in ominously dramatic tones. After a fierce climax it calms down, and at last the pianoforte is free to give out the variation theme in the shape of the following quiet melody, much on the lines of that of the middle movement of Franck's Symphony.

The first variation is in dialogue (figure by figure) between pianoforte and orchestra. In the second variation the violoncellos have the theme. The third is in flowing movement for the pianoforte accompanied by pizzicato chords for strings, the winds gradually joining in melodically. The fourth variation takes the theme fortissimo, passing through various keys, in terms of figure (*a*) in Ex. 1. It expands dramatically and leads to a softer but not less lively fifth variation in the same rhythm in D major, with an easily galloping pianoforte accompaniment. This fifth variation (if it is rightly so counted) dies away into the original key (F sharp minor) before it is complete; and the sixth variation sails in slowly in F sharp major. A beautiful meandering counterpoint ripples throughout the pianoforte part while the theme, in the violoncellos, forms the bass for the first eight bars (you can follow it from Ex. 2). The rest is given by the wind instruments.

Then the mode changes to minor, and slowly, below the flowing arpeggios of the pianoforte, the violoncellos spell out a wonderful dream on the theme of Ex. 1, figure (b). There is no more thought now of variations: the rest of the work is concerned with building up a brilliant finale on this other theme. The dreaming passage which leads to this finale is obviously the most poetic part of this very poetic work. The finale itself is quite reckless in its innocent gaiety. It represents the variation theme only by its first two notes (a); and the other theme (b) is too happy to be shocked at its transformation into a dance-tune.

Ex. 3.

Later on the variation-theme appears to the extent of a clear eight-bar phrase as the bass of one of the episodes in the dance.

Ex. 4.

There is, shortly after this, one hint of dramatic darkness, which gives way to a brief pianoforte passage of peacefully flowing meditation; but soon the lively tempo returns and the work dances cheerfully away to its happy end.

HANDEL

ORGAN CONCERTO, NO. 7 (OP. 7, NO. 1)

Andante (C), *leading to* 2 *Andante* (3/4), *leading to* 3 LARGO, *e piano*
(*D minor*). 4 BOURRÉE: *Allegro.*

Of Handel's fifteen organ concertos this is one which is a little
more completely written down than most. It has only one blank
space marked *ad lib.*, and it actually indicates where the pedals of
the organ are to be used. If we were to attempt to produce Handel's
op. 7, Ex. 3, in accordance with the intentions of the composer, the
margin of conjectural restoration would be so great that we should
be hardly justified in holding Handel responsible for the result.
The direction *Organo ad libitum Adagio e Fuga* leaves a margin for
discretion, or indiscretion, equal to nearly half the work. Handel is
himself to blame if a large portion of what purports to be his organ
music is really the composition of the late W. T. Best. In any case,
if the composer does not condescend to write his music down, somebody else has to complete the record. The finest performances of
Handel's concertos have been those by musicians capable of extemporizing in the composer's style. From childhood I used to hear
Handel from Sir Walter Parratt, and had no idea that anybody
could play this music with any less Handelian elements. But until
Max Seiffert applied methods of scholarship to the editing of
Handel's concertos, no published edition made any advance
towards the de-Bestification of the text.

The present work is unique, like all Handel's works. If uniformity of procedure were a proof of authenticity, a Higher
Criticism could prove each of Handel's concertos spurious on
the evidence of all the others.

After four bars of grandiose dialogue between the organ and the
orchestra (strings and oboes), Handel drifts into a ground bass;
the dialogue partly anticipates that bass, so that you do not notice
that the composition has settled down thereto until its obstinacy
attracts your notice. Here is the bass—

Ex. 1.

All sorts of things happen on it, and it sometimes changes its key.
Once, when it is in G minor, Handel quotes the *Passacaille* of his
eighth clavier suite, reversing the accents.

Ex. 2.

The **fifth** variation after this quotation is to be supplied extempore, presumably with a cadenza. The gap can be filled with authentic Handel from the G minor Suite. Then the introductory dialogue is resumed, leading back to B flat and to a pause. We are to begin a new movement.

The new movement, in triple time, turns out to be on the same ground bass! Among its many fancies is the following Hornpipe, such being the rhythm which Handel, in his half-dozen examples, associates with that dance.

Ex. 3.

The third movement, largo e piano, is a solemn elegy in D minor, with a bass which, though not rigid, has still much of the effect of a ground bass.

Ex. 4.

The finale is a bourrée with a tune such as only Purcell achieved before Handel, and nobody has even attempted to achieve since.

Ex. 5.

The original root of Handel's popularity lies here: such tunes devastated the town like any modern music-hall success, though possibly with a little more spiritual nourishment for their victims. The gavotte in *Ottone* was played on all the musical salt-boxes in the three kingdoms. Sir Hugh Allen once suggested that barrel-organs might be employed to spread a taste for good music wherever they grind. Let us equip the first of these noble pioneers with this bourrée and the gavotte in *Ottone*.

HAYDN

VIOLONCELLO CONCERTO IN D MAJOR

1 Allegro moderato. 2 Adagio. 3 Allegro.

The concertos of Haydn all date from his Esterhazy period, and are on a small scale, like the horn concertos of Mozart. Their forms hardly deviate from those of the vocal aria on a large scale; but, even before the modern editor has enjoyed himself over them, they give remarkable scope for the art of the virtuoso player.

At present the only orchestral parts available for this concerto are those of the venerable and voluminous Gevaert, whose reign over the Brussels Conservatoire and whose treatises on ancient music and modern orchestration sufficed in themselves to make an epoch in musical education.

The worst of such thoroughness is that, where it re-scores the classics, the results are like the leg that was so beautifully suited for a top-boot—'Same size all the way up, sir!'

Haydn's scoring of this concerto was probably primitive, possibly for strings alone, and certainly the better for a pianoforte to exercise the obsolescent function of the continuo. That function being now exercised by Gevaert with a wind-band in the style of a full swell-organ, the orchestra must do its best to play the accompaniments gently.

The first theme surprises us by being based on a *cliché* we would have thought peculiar to Mozart. My knowledge of the lesser contemporaries of Haydn and Mozart is severely limited by my patience, and I have not found this *cliché* elsewhere.

Ex. 1.

But in the slow movement the same *cliché* is followed by one equally peculiar to Haydn.

Ex. 2.

Nobody can tell me the exact notes of the tune of 'Here we go gathering nuts in May'; but everybody agrees that the finale of Haydn's 'cello concerto is suspiciously like it.

Ex. 3.

And perhaps the wicked people who, with the late Mr. Rudyard Kipling among them, persecuted the miso-auto-bureaucrat squire, J.P., and M.P. for Huckley, may have reverted to the Haydn archetype when they turned this innocent tune into *The Village that Voted the Earth was Flat*. At all events, bars 5 and 6 of Ex. 3 irresistibly remind me of

> Flat as my hat,
> Flatter than *that!*

But we digress. And so does Haydn. [But see Addendum, below.]

ADDENDUM

SINCE my analysis of the work known as Haydn's Violoncello Concerto, op. 101, was written, a miniature score has been published giving the work in its original form, with a preface explaining that Dr. Hans Volkmann has proved that this concerto is not by Haydn but by Haydn's pupil, Anton Kraft (1752–1820). The demonstration is admittedly not complete, but I find no difficulty in giving Kraft the credit for a very pretty piece of work in a form in which Haydn never put forward his full powers, and which, if genuine, would have belonged to a period at which his style and forms were imitable enough to tempt many publishers to secure a market for other composers by ascribing their works to a master whose early popularity was so remarkable. My analysis will not, I think, be found to contain anything committing me to uphold this charming concerto as a great work. The average quality of Haydn's output at Esterhaz is such that the greatest scholars have been compelled, when selecting the unquestionably authentic symphonies, to make a longer list of doubtful than of spurious works. A stroke of genius will settle the question, and so will any high power of composition: that is why I see red when musical philologists cast doubts on Bach's tremendous D minor Concerto. But the absence of these qualities will not settle the question with early works ascribable to Haydn. The only thing that puzzled me in the present instance was the prominence of a definitely Mozartean cliché in the opening themes of the first movement and slow movement. The slow movement begins with two bars of pure Mozart followed by two of pure Haydn. In an analytical programme it was no part of my business to disturb the listener by questions which are vexing as long as they raise doubts. Now that I have

no doubt, I shall in future give Anton Kraft the credit of his very
pretty work; and I shall expect my audience not to be snobbish
about it.

GUSTAV HOLST

A FUGAL CONCERTO (OP. 40, NO. 2)

1 *Moderato*. 2 *Adagio*. 3 *Allegro*.

The art-forms of Bach and Handel are gaining influence at the
present day in proportion as the later sonata forms of Mozart and
Beethoven are ceasing to interest the modern composer. Max
Reger's *Conzert im alten Stil* is a somewhat vague imitation of an
eighteenth-century concerto grosso, but it does not achieve much
more of an 'ancient style' than an impression of remoteness, and it
makes no attempt to use the real forms of the old concertos. The
happy and inventive Triple Concerto by Julius Röntgen is a real
example of the polyphonic concerto form and style; and Holst's
Fugal Concerto, for the unusual combination of flute and oboe,
turns the genuine old forms to new purposes of wit and fancy.

In the first movement the string orchestra states a fugue-subject
in octaves, doing duty (in four bars) for the opening tutti that is to
give the gist of the whole movement in one pregnant paragraph.

Ex. 1.

The oboe and flute enter by way of answering this subject in
turn. They then introduce a new figure, which has a way of drifting
into the scale at the end of the main theme.

Ex. 2.

But its further purpose is to combine, all at sixes and sevens,
with the main theme inverted in the bass, coalescing with it at the
third bar.

Ex. 3.

(This inversion is all the happier for not being pedantically exact.) On these materials the little movement works itself and vanishes in a merry pianissimo.

The slow movement sheds strange lights on the key of D major and its environs. It is quite diatonic, and D major is the key. And the colour is not modal; there is nothing Doric or Phrygian about it. But our minds are diverted from the tonic throughout, and when other keys are visited we never get in touch with their tonics.

The time is a slow 3/4, but a mysterious bass moves across it twice as slow, while the flute announces a subject for a canon or fugue.

Ex. 4.

A plaintive middle episode takes a new theme into remoter harmonies.

Ex. 5.

While some very beautiful modulations are dying away, the violas drift into the main theme (Ex. 4), in what will be G if Ex. 4 is in D. The movement is thus brought round to a close which clearly is in D. The tonic being thus asserted at last, the music glides in the direction of the dominant. Whereat the finale bursts in with the following quizzical fugue-subject:

Ex. 6.

Tutti.

After various adventures, including lackadaisical cadenzas, apropos of its last notes, on the oboe and flute, followed by attempts at inversion and a ferocious transformation in square time (2/4), this subject fulfils its destiny. For it is obvious to the meanest capacity that it was destined to be a counterpoint to the Old English Dance Tune, 'If all the world were paper'. Even the double-bass knows that, though he has a severe cold in his head—technically known as a sordine.

Ex. 7.

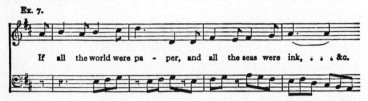

If all the world were pa - per, and all the seas were ink, ♪ ♪ ♪ &c.

After this revelation has been expounded, the little concerto trots peacefully away until, suddenly rearing and scratching itself, it disappears in a trill for the two wind-instruments and a rising pizzicato scale in the absurd rhythm of Ex. 6.

MENDELSSOHN

VIOLIN CONCERTO IN E MINOR, OP. 64

1 *Allegro molto appassionato, leading to* 2 *Andante, leading to* 3 *Allegretto non troppo, leading to* 4 *Allegro molto vivace.*

How often do we hear the most remarkable stroke of genius in this most popular of violin concertos? I had not heard it in 1921, when I wrote this analysis. The manners of British concert-goers have improved since then; and even then my audience was not offended at being told that a burst of applause between the first movement and the andante obliterates a dramatic orchestral effect and reduces the introductory bars of the andante to one of those ugly misconstruings which produce the conviction (ascribed by a Master of Balliol to the British schoolboy) that no nonsense is too enormous to be a possible translation from a classical author. I have never been able to make out why, when disaster overtakes this connecting link, conductors do not adopt the only possible remedy, which is simply to repeat the short final tutti, and so secure that Mendelssohn's intention shall somehow be realized.

Mendelssohn is supposed to be the typical classicist in music; that is to say, he is supposed to be the master of those who after a classical period imitate the classical forms faithfully and skilfully. As a matter of fact, the best works of Mendelssohn have all in their respective ways been the starting-points of some musical revolution. Mendelssohn may truthfully be said to have destroyed the classical concerto form, inasmuch as his perennially beautiful Violin Concerto and his two somewhat faded pianoforte concertos revealed to all contemporary and later composers an easy way of evading a problem which only Mozart and Beethoven could either state or solve in terms of the highest art. In the Violin Concerto Mendelssohn's inspiration is high and vigorous. He is not so much evading a classical problem as producing a new if distinctly lighter art-form. It is not unprofitable to speculate whether the pathetic and tranquil second subject (Ex. 3) would not have gained in depth and dramatic power if some hint of its melody had been given with force and passion in the first energetic orchestral tutti. This could very well have been managed with no notable increase in length of that tutti, and would have instantly brought the first movement into the lines of a genuine development of Beethoven's concerto style, besides anticipating by some forty years Brahms's re-discovery of the true function of the orchestra in a concerto. But the possibility escaped Mendelssohn's notice, and was indeed very unlikely to occur to a man who had twice before deliberately suppressed the orchestral tutti, function and all, in his treatment of the concerto form. His Violin Concerto thus became the original type of the majority of modern concertos; and being, as it is, an original inspiration, it is far greater than any work that has ever followed its tradition. Again and again it turns up as a source of inspiration for later composers, many of whom would be horrified at the notion of confessing a debt to anything so old-fashioned. Yet I rather envy the enjoyment of any one who should hear the Mendelssohn concerto for the first time and find that, like *Hamlet*, it was full of quotations. This being so, I will leave the rest of my description to the most necessary of the quotations, viz. the first theme—

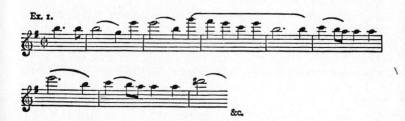

Ex. 1.

&c.

given out in full by the solo violin and worked up to a climax on which the orchestra breaks in; the transition theme—

Ex. 2.

given out by the orchestra and developed by the solo violin; and the second subject—

Ex. 3.

given out by the wood-wind above the famous long holding note which the violin supplies as bass. The usual procedure in concertos is for the brilliant passages of the solo player to culminate in a shake closing into the re-entry of the orchestra. Mendelssohn here makes his brilliant passages an accompaniment to the first theme. They do culminate in a shake; but, by one of Mendelssohn's wittiest inspirations, it is the orchestra that bursts out with the shake, which the violin answers with impassioned dialogue from the first theme. The development begins with the transition theme and comes to its climax in a remote key with one of those intensely quiet passages of slow return to the tonic which Mendelssohn always executes with consummate mastery, and sometimes, as here, with the poetic power of a great composer. On to this passage is grafted the cadenza which, both for its unusual position in the movement and its extraordinary skill and effectiveness, constitutes one of Mendelssohn's most famous strokes of genius. Here, as elsewhere in the concerto, Mendelssohn's example has been imitated with disastrous consequences by less adroit composers, notably in a once well-known and well-meaning violoncello sonata by Rubinstein. You must not transplant Mendelssohn's cadenza *totidem notis* into every place where you find it better than anything of your own invention.

Mendelssohn's cadenza is of extreme simplicity, which conceals an almost Greek subtlety of fitness. It is thoroughly dramatic in the way in which it prepares for the return to the opening theme. The orchestra softly brings the first subject into full swing as the arpeggios of the violin settle to a rapid spin; and the recapitulation follows an easy and effective course, omitting much and expanding nothing, until the coda, which moves in faster tempo to a stormy end. But hush!—what is this that emerges from the last chord?

Ex. 4.

Few things in music are more essentially ugly than a vague and meaningless introduction to a lyric melody, designed with the avowed and sole aim of marking time 'till ready'. Of such introductions this opening of Mendelssohn's andante has most unjustly been made the prototype. It is no such thing, except when untimely applause has made it begin with a nonsensical entry of the bassoon on nothing in particular, followed by a few other fumbling notes which can only drift from the unintelligible to the obvious. What Mendelssohn wrote and meant was one of his most romantic changes of key and mood. And it is perfectly naïve: all the spurious imitations in the world will not rob it of its freshness.

The movement has true breadth and dignity. Its middle episode, which I need not quote, achieves a real expression of agitation and anxiety without the fussiness which Mendelssohn was too often apt to express instead; and the serene coda is of that childlike truth and simplicity which it is an insult to call pretty.

The wistful little allegretto that connects the andante with the finale is also quite an unspoilt child. The finale has perhaps been the cause of some unpleasing perkinesses in ill-bred descendants—but there is no doubt about its own good-breeding. Its first theme I quote in its combination with a sedate new theme that first appears in G major in later developments.

Ex. 5.

The second subject—

Ex. 6.

is undeniably 'cheeky'; but we can stand this from Mendelssohn in this work—just as we can stand it from Rossini. I doubt whether Mendelssohn was particularly tolerant of it in Rossini: 'cheekiness' is an aristocratic schoolboy term of reproach, and no two schools can abide each other's 'cheek'. But all schools unite in the detestation of an outsider's imitation of their own 'cheek'; and we can enjoy these indiscretions of Mendelssohn and Rossini because the delinquents are not imitators, but complete if un- scrupulous masters of the situation. And so this finale spins along in high spirits, in which no one need be ashamed to share. It is not in Schiller's world of Joy as attained by Beethoven—the world where 'all men are brothers'; but if it cannot ignore the superior person it has every right to poke fun at him.

MOZART

PIANOFORTE CONCERTO IN A MAJOR (KÖCHEL'S CATALOGUE, NO. 414)

1 *Allegro.* 2 *Andante.* 3 RONDO, *Allegretto.*

This is one of a group of three small pianoforte concertos which Mozart wrote not long before *Figaro*, during the period of the six string quartets which made Haydn acknowledge him as the greatest composer he had ever heard of. These concertos are small as the wild strawberry is small; they are no stunted growths, nor

are they school-pieces of 'educational' value; they are highly
characteristic and mature masterpieces. The smallest is in F major,
and its character is somewhere between that of an Aberdeen terrier
and a Dandie Dinmont; it does not happen to show fight, but its
quiet sagacity is no sign of weakness. The largest is in C major. To
the little old orchestra of strings, two oboes, and two horns, for
which all three are written, it adds trumpets and drums, with which
it makes dramatic jollifications; the slow movement reacts from
these in a style which is the source of Mendelssohn's Songs without
Words; and the finale is a fairy-tale in which a melancholy adagio
twice introduces the marvellous into the design.

The little A major Concerto is in style midway between these
two; and it would be difficult to find another work of Mozart in
which practically every single theme is so typical of his style. Even
small works of art in these large forms usually assert a composer's
style more in their treatment of themes than in any large proportion
of the themes themselves. Those of the little F major Concerto are
almost all common formulas, and so are more than half of those of
the little C major; but here it almost seems as if Mozart had concentrated the most personal features of a dozen compositions on
this single work. He appears to have been fond of it himself and to
have played it or taught it often to his favourite pupils, for he has
left two complete sets of cadenzas for it, by no means as perfunctory
as his written cadenzas usually are. As a rule it may be taken that
Mozart's written cadenzas do not adequately represent what he
would extemporize in the places where they are required; but this
concerto gives us the exceptions. They are very short, but full of
valuable features in design.

The opening tutti of the first movement gives, as usual, the
principal themes of the first subject—

Ex. 1.

followed by a vigorous transition theme which I do not quote; and
the second subject, a gallant little march, full of Mozart's Tyrolese
raillery.

Ex. 2.

Besides these we have an important feature in Mozart's mature concerto form; a prominent theme which is ignored by the solo instrument when it first gathers up the threads of the opening tutti, but which pulls the whole form together when the recapitulation follows the lines of the tutti more faithfully, and puts this theme in its proper place.

Ex. 3.

Lastly, there is the final cadence-figure which (as in the earlier flute concertos and elsewhere) the solo has a way of neatly turning into a new transition theme. I need not quote it, as this description will suffice to identify it.

There are people who still believe that Mozart's whole idea of pianoforte playing was confined to a pretty tinkle. It may surprise them to hear that Mozart's friends were fond of asking him to 'make the pianoforte sound like an organ', and that he delighted in so obliging them. What they meant thereby is shown by the first theme of the slow movement, which the pianoforte, when its turn comes, gives in very full chords.

Ex. 4.

Another theme, which afterwards constitutes the second subject, is remarkable for its likeness to the first theme of the first movement (see Ex. 1).

Ex. 5.

Such resemblances come too often and too prominently in Mozart's concertos to be accidental. They are sometimes placed where they have exactly the same function in each movement, and are always placed where they must attract attention.

The finale, beginning with a lively little formula-tune—

Ex. 6.

continues with an excellent theme full of sly resource, which brings about most of the action throughout the movement.

Ex. 7.

The pianoforte, which, after stating Ex. 6, gave way to a tutti full of accessory themes, re-enters with a new cantabile transition melody, which I need not quote, though it is the source of some pretty dialogue in the coda. It leads to the first episode (or second subject), in which, among other themes, Ex. 7 is developed. Like nearly all concerto finales this movement is a rondo; and so in due course Ex. 6 returns, and then Ex. 7 leads to the middle episode beginning with a playful tune in D major. Look out for the violas with their mocking imitations.

From this middle episode Mozart returns, not to the first subject, but to the solo cantabile transition theme, and so to the recapitulation of the second subject. Then follows a coda in which Ex. 7, the transition theme, and all the accessories given by the first tutti round off the whole design with delightful freedom. Notice, for example, the whimsical pauses in the transition theme when, after the cadenza, it enters into dialogue with the orchestra.

PIANOFORTE CONCERTO NO. 15, IN B FLAT MAJOR (KÖCHEL'S CATALOGUE, NO. 450)

1 *Allegro.* 2 *Andante.* 3 *Allegro.*

Ludwig Deppe, the originator of the method of pianoforte playing on which I was trained, used to call Mozart's fifteenth concerto 'the most difficult concerto in the world'; as readers of Amy Fay's *Music Study in Germany* may remember. In the days which that book commemorates it was still possible for a responsible critic to remark (as Beethoven himself would have remarked) that we should regard Mozart's cadenzas and passages as child's-play. Amy Fay already thought that 'such a critic ought to go to school again'. Mozart's own opinion is interesting. He produced this concerto as one of three, together with the great Quintet for pianoforte and wind-instruments, in March 1784; having early in February produced the Sonata for two pianofortes. Of this concerto, with its soldierly brother in D major and two others, he writes to his father on 24 May: 'I cannot come to a decision between those two concertos in B flat and D. I consider them both concertos that make one perspire; but in difficulty the one in B flat beats the one in D. Besides, I am very anxious to know which one of the three concertos, in B flat, D, and G, you and my sister like best; for the one in E flat is not at all in the same class, being a concerto of quite a peculiar kind and written rather for a small orchestra than for a big one.'

The Concerto in G is a large work written in April of the same year.[1] From Mozart's letter we learn that the difference between

[1] *Vide* following analysis.

small and large orchestras is not a matter of trumpets and drums. Our Dresden-china Mozart is a fiction which we may remorselessly hand over to the most panclastic of scullery-maids.

Of a symphony smaller than the Linz Symphony Mozart writes that it went '*magnifique*' with forty violins, ten double-basses, six bassoons, and all the wind doubled. This treatment would not suit even a heroic concerto, but the fact puts an end to miniature views of Mozart's style.

The opening theme of this B flat concerto—

Ex. 1.

shows Mozart in his most *schalkhaft* (or naughty) mood, and the change of accent at * shows that his naughtiness is stimulated by his most dangerous wit.

The raillery is continued even more quizzically. But soon Mozart, though refusing to leave the tonic chord, plunges into the usual forte theme which comes to the usual half-close. Then, thinks the usual theorist, we have the usual second subject.

Ex. 2.

But, as we have seen before, it is impossible to tell which, if any, of the themes of a Mozart tutti is going to belong to the second group.

Another tutti theme, beginning with a conspirator's crescendo, leads to the cadence-figure of the whole ritornello. On the stage this would imply a ribald gesture addressed to deluded husbands. See *Figaro*, Act IV, No. 26 '*gia ognuno lo sa*'.

Ex. 3.

While the orchestra is finishing some final chords, the pianoforte enters with a declamatory running figure, which it turns into an introductory cadenza. It then states the main theme, Ex. 1. Having completed this, it proceeds on entirely new lines, and modulates broadly to the dominant, where it gives out a second subject, consisting, with all its accessories, of themes that have never been suggested by the opening tutti at all.

Ex. 4.

At the end of this the orchestra bursts out with a dovetailing of the two forte themes of the tutti; ending, of course, with the cornute gesture of Ex. 3. The latter figure of this theme is turned into a chromatic run by the pianoforte, which thus begins a short but adequate development. This becomes dignified in becoming episodic; and the return to the first subject is, as always in Mozart, delightfully comfortable in the impression it gives of accurate timing.

With the recapitulation we see the full breadth of Mozart's concerto form. It is quite as much a recapitulation of the first tutti as it is of the first solo, and consequently it gathers up threads which the first solo had left unused. Thus it uses the first tutti forte before preparing for the second subject, and in the course of the second subject it inserts Ex. 2. Lastly, it follows the end of the solo not by a forte but by the original conspirator's crescendo. Even after the (presumably extemporized) cadenza, the orchestra turns its last chords to fresh account, no longer overlaid by the pianoforte.

The slow movement is a set of ornamental variations on one of Mozart's most beautiful themes.

Ex. 5.

Two double variations (i.e. variations in which the repeats of the two halves of the theme are themselves varied) suffice with a short coda to make a movement of great breadth and of almost solemn tone.

With the finale Mozart becomes *schalkhaft* again. Says the Fool in *King Lear*—

'This prophecy shall Merlin make, for I live before his time,'

and in the same spirit we may suppose Mozart to have foreseen that one day Schumann would write a pianoforte quartet with a slow movement which takes Mozart's naughtiest theme seriously.

Ex. 6.
Mozart.

Schumann.

No concerto-rondo by Mozart can do with less than seven different themes. Of these I must quote, besides Ex. 6, two themes from the tutti—

Ex. 7.

Ex. 8.

and (omitting the cantabile transition theme, with which the pianoforte re-enters, and the theme of the middle episode) the beginning of the first episode (or second subject) with its more than intelligent anticipation of Liszt's dovetail-hand technique.

Ex. 9.

The returns to the main theme (Ex. 6) are particularly witty. For the first return Mozart wrote an extra cadenza (not given in the score); and the second is reached from the extreme distance of A minor by a dialogue between pianoforte and oboe.

At the end of the movement Ex. 7 and Ex. 8 are combined in an amusingly dramatic way.

PIANOFORTE CONCERTO IN G MAJOR
(KÖCHEL'S CATALOGUE, NO. 453)

1 *Allegro*. 2 *Andante*. 3 *Allegretto*, *with Presto* FINALE.

The Concerto in G, written in 1784, is one of Mozart's richest and wittiest. The slow movement is full of deep and tender feeling, with a certain gravity in its sweetness and light; but the first movement and finale are in the most intellectual vein of high comedy, culminating in an epilogue of pure *opera buffa* on a more expansive plan than almost any other of Mozart's codas. The scoring, for small orchestra without clarinets, trumpets, or drums, is as consummate as that of the three great symphonies; and the pianoforte part is highly polished, without any of the problems Mozart sometimes presents by leaving it in a sketchy state to be filled out extempore by himself as the pianist. He even wrote two separate sets of cadenzas for the first two movements. Both sets are far from perfunctory, and it is difficult to choose between them.

Of the first movement I quote, first, the opening theme—

Ex. 1.

and (passing over its forte sequel) the wistful cantabile which afterwards becomes the second subject.

Ex. 2.

A dramatic incident in a dark key—

Ex. 3.

will show later on that the development is not quite so episodic as it seems. The ritornello ends with three contrasted themes, of which I quote the first, with its *Don Giovanni* sharpened octave.

Ex. 4.

The pianoforte enters with Ex. 1 and follows the course of the ritornello closely until it sees opportunity for modulating broadly to the dominant. Here, however, it introduces the second subject with a quite new theme—

Ex. 5.

after which the cantabile (Ex. 2), with its introductory quaver figure, appears. It is followed by a series of running and arpeggio themes, until the orchestra caps the climax by entering with its first (unquoted) forte theme. The development has an air of being episodic throughout; but its first part is suggested by Ex. 3. At the end of the recapitulation, this intervenes dramatically in its original shape.

The slow movement is one of those profound utterances of Mozart in terms which are almost confined to formulas; the language of the *Zauberflöte*, the last (so-called 'Jupiter') Symphony, and the *Requiem*. Few casualties of criticism are more amusing than the collision between such works of art and the plausible dogma that 'every important musical composition must have strongly original themes'. The truth is that nobody knows exactly what a theme is, or how many themes make an idea, or even how many ideas may go to a theme and whereabouts in the theme they may be situated.

Externally and conventionally the main themes of this wonderful andante are, first, a solemn pleading phrase, which breaks off with a pause (Ex. 6) and is followed by an arioso formula for oboe with a long swelling first note. This my quotations omit, and I give in Ex. 7 the dialogue for three instruments which arises from it.

Ex. 6.

Ex. 7.

Who would have thought that this dialogue is going to become the second subject in a highly developed sonata form?

A majestic forte theme joins the procession, and the tutti concludes with the one obviously 'original' theme of the movement, a profoundly expressive blend of minor and major modes.

Ex. 8.

The modulations throughout the movement are in a grand dramatic vein, the dramatic note having been already indicated by the unusual pause after the opening phrase (Ex. 6).

Classical concertos contain few examples of the variation form: there are only four in Mozart (the present finale, that of the C minor Concerto, the slow movement of a concerto in B flat, and a so-called rondo written as a new finale to an early concerto in D). The variations in the G major Concerto are among the most witty and ingenious achievements in this form before Beethoven. The wit begins with the theme, of which Ex. 9 is the first strain.

Ex. 9.

From Mozart's petty-cash book we learn that this tune attracted not only the notice of the general public but also that of the birds, or at least that of the bird-fanciers, for he spent thirty-four kreutzers on a starling which delighted him by producing his tune in the following Cloud-cuckoo-land version:

Ex. 9a.

The variations, most of which are double (i.e. with varied or totally contrasted repeats), attain to great remoteness from the external melody; the fourth, in the minor mode, being a mysterious piece of counterpoint on a quite new idea strictly following the structure of the theme.

The fifth and last variation (a double variation with violent contrasts) expands into a coda which leads to the presto finale or epilogue, a comic wind-up big enough for *Figaro* and unique in Mozart's instrumental works. Most of its themes are new. Two of them I quote.

Ex. 10.

Ex. 11.

The original theme (Ex. 9; not 9a) romps in among the other conspirators as if it had known them all its life.

PIANOFORTE CONCERTO IN A MAJOR (KÖCHEL'S CATALOGUE, NO. 488)

1 *Allegro.* 2 *Andante.* 3 *Presto.*

The three months of June, July, and August 1788 are famous for the creation of Mozart's three greatest symphonies; but they are not more wonderful than the single month of March 1786, in which the two pianoforte concertos in A major and C minor were written. These works are in no way inferior to the symphonies, nor are they less sharply contrasted with each other. The pathos of the C minor Concerto is even more profound than that of the G minor Symphony, though the texture is less concentrated. The A major Concerto is, with the additional element of pathos in its remarkable slow movement, as eminently a study in euphony as is the E flat Symphony, which it further resembles in revealing the clarinets as Mozart's favourite wind instruments, and omitting the oboes. Before the year was out Mozart had produced another concerto (in C major) which fully equals the Jupiter Symphony in triumphant majesty, and even in contrapuntal display. (See the analysis in the Essay on the Classical Concerto.)

As there is no rule without an exception to prove it, I readily admit that the first eight and a half pages of this A major Concerto completely tally with that orthodox account of classical concerto form which I have taken such pains to refute every time I have discussed a classical concerto. And if a single concerto, and that a work which the text-books have not selected as specially typical, can establish a form as 'normal' in points wherein all the other classical examples differ from it and from each other so radically that these points can hardly be identified at all; then perhaps Mozart did here produce an orthodox first movement—as far as the middle of the ninth of its twenty-two pages. But at that point things begin to happen which cannot be found in any other concerto.

However, it is perfectly true that of the five themes (or more, according as you take broad phrases or single clauses) which the orchestra gives in its opening tutti, the pianoforte takes up the first four quite faithfully in their order, making Ex. 1 the first subject;—

Ex. 1.

continuing the forte orchestral sequel (which I do not quote) as a regular transition leading to the dominant; transposing to that key (with the aid of only two extra bars) the exquisitely graceful and gallant theme which the orchestra had already in the first instance marked off by a formal preparatory half-close---

Ex. 2.

and following it with the next theme. This is a somewhat more dramatic paragraph, in which three bars, with rustling inner movement tinged with minor harmony, are answered by a spirited major close, which in its turn gives way to a plaintively quizzical question and answer in the 'relative minor' (F sharp in the tutti, C sharp when we have it in the solo statement). The continuation of this is the only part of the first tutti which the pianoforte expands into a longer and more brilliant passage so as to prepare for a big re-entry of the orchestra, instead of passing on to the formal little orchestral cadence theme with which the first tutti had closed.

But quickly upon this big re-entry of the orchestra there comes the inevitable shock to orthodoxy. The need for such a shock is more pressing than any matter of terms or technicalities. The objection to the 'orthodox' accounts is that they inculcate spurious forms, and so induce composers to revolt from the study of classical music because it is identified in their minds with what they instinctively feel to be bad. Now in the present instance, if Mozart had not at this point some stroke of genius in preparation—if his only intention were to write a development on the preceding themes and return to a regular recapitulation—his form would be orthodox, but stiff; at all events no better than Spohr's concerto form, and considerably less good than the best of so modest a master as Viotti, who (as Joachim and Brahms agreed) was quite capable of intelligent experiments. By what possible means can Mozart, as far as we have followed him here, manifest the principle governing the recapitulation of all his other concertos, that the solo recapitulates, not its own version of the first and second subject, but a fusion of its version with that of the original tutti? Here the two are as nearly as possible identical. Well, let us see what happens.

The orchestra has hardly got beyond the beginning of its resumption of the first forte of the opening tutti when it breaks off, and after a half-bar's silence softly gives out a quite new theme which brings a deeper and graver mood to add to the grace of the whole work.

Ex. 3.

The pianoforte takes this up in a florid variation, and with the aid of another new episodic theme in semiquaver movement, works out a broad development in dialogue with the orchestra. Thus, when the recapitulation is reached, the old themes return with complete freshness. And, what is perhaps more remarkable though less obvious, the development had none of the looseness of effect that in ordinary sonatas is apt to result from basing it mainly or entirely on 'episodes'. The episode was here a thing of absolute dramatic necessity. And after the now inevitably and rightly regular recapitulation, Mozart paradoxically vindicates his principle of making the solo refer more closely to the orchestra than to its own exposition of the themes. For when he comes to the last climax of pianoforte passages, it is the pianoforte that breaks off and, after a half-bar's silence, gives out Ex. 3 in its original simplicity and gravity. Afterwards the orchestra too has its say. And the poor pianoforte player has the appalling task of making a cadenza that shall not set the Mozart-lover's teeth on edge. (Mozart has written a cadenza for this concerto, but a more than usually perfunctory and inadequate one. It is doubtful whether he would have regarded any of his written cadenzas to first movements as adequately representing his way of extemporizing, and it is quite certain that he could not wish to be represented by this one; though, like all his cadenzas, it conveys at least one useful hint.) Finally the orchestra rounds off the movement with its little cadence theme which has not been heard since the end of the first tutti.

The slow movement (Mozart's only composition in the key of F sharp minor) is of the most touching melancholy. Its first theme—

Ex. 4.

is stated by the pianoforte alone, and shows in its second bar a feature of late eighteenth-century style which we accept as familiar, without curiosity as to its meaning. One of the most superb vocal gestures of the eighteenth-century singer was the display of an unerring aim in skips from one extreme of the voice to the other, especially when the notes were selected as being opposed to each

other in harmony, and so specially difficult to judge accurately.
It was, as it ought still to be, the highest boast of the player of
an instrument that 'he made his instrument sing'; and Mozart
had an unrivalled reputation for that quality in his pianoforte
playing. There is not the slightest difficulty in playing the low
E sharp in Ex. 3 with the left hand and the next B with the
right; and even with one hand the risk of the skip in this slow
tempo would be quite unnoticeable; but the whole point of the
phrase is that the skip is conceived as an enormous change of
vocal register. The pianoforte is a supernatural singer with a
compass of five octaves—not more, in Mozart's time; but five
octaves is more compatible with a vocal style than seven and
a half.

The orchestra introduces another theme—

Ex. 5.

which the pianoforte takes up in a chromatic variation. This leads
to A major, in which key we have a lighter and perhaps happier
episode. I say 'perhaps', because the childlike new themes are full
of prophecy of poor Donna Elvira when her affectionate simplicity
is bringing her back into the power of Don Juan. Here, however,
there is no sardonic or comic background. The main themes soon
return, the pianoforte part being written in a skeletonic way
which Mozart certainly must have filled out with ornamentation. I claim to be an absolute purist in *not* confining myself to
the written text. With Beethoven the case is already different; yet
even Beethoven absent-mindedly sent the score of his C minor
Concerto to the publisher after it had been performed, and the
publisher returned it rather angrily, pointing out that the pianoforte part had never been written at all. This is the extreme case
which decisively shows that the autograph score of a Mozart concerto is not always the best place to look for the pianoforte part as
he would have it played.

The most difficult point comes near the end, where the mood
is almost that of Wordsworth's—

> Roll'd round in earth's diurnal course
> With rocks, and stones, and trees.

Here there is no doubt that Mozart intends to use the effect of a
singer's display of the extreme compass of his voice; and whatever
ornamentation one attempts must show this instead of disguising it.

In concertos Mozart's rondo form contains features which he uses elsewhere; and the finale of the present concerto is remarkably like the finales of the great A major Violin Sonata, the two pianoforte quartets, and that most wonderful neglected masterpiece, the Sonata in F for four hands. The essential feature in the concerto-finale is that the solo player states the theme, and the orchestra gives a counterstatement, to which it appends a long string of other themes, none of which is destined to reappear until the last stages of the work, where they all troop in and make a triumphant end. Mozart was delighted with the effect, in other works than concertos, of this string of themes in the tonic and the resulting delay before any new key is established. He then establishes his new key rather abruptly, and enjoys another luxurious string of themes in it. Richard Strauss, one of the greatest Mozart-lovers of modern times, has produced some of the essence of this effect in the structure of *Till Eulenspiegel*. I cannot quote more than three of the themes of the present finale; but there are no less than ten perfectly definite and important ones, not counting various running passages that could easily be distinguished from each other. The end of the tutti distinctly recalls the quizzical F sharp minor incident at the corresponding point in the first movement.

Here is the first of the four themes in the first subject:

Ex. 6.

I do not quote the two transition themes which the pianoforte gives out after the orchestra has had its say. From the second subject I quote its first theme—

Ex. 7.

which in the recapitulation is given in the major, and its irrepressible third theme which figures largely in the coda.

Ex. 8.

The middle episode contains at least two more themes, one in F sharp minor, the other in D major; and when the time comes for returning to the tonic, it is not the main theme but the transition themes that turn up. The main theme is thus all the more welcome when it reappears, and is followed by its train of accessories, divided between the pianoforte and the orchestra. In addition to this, there is a big coda, towards the end of which Ex. 8 sails in with a grandiose subdominant colouring that adds to its glorious effrontery.

PIANOFORTE CONCERTO IN C MINOR (KÖCHEL'S CATALOGUE, NO. 491)

1 Allegro. 2 Larghetto. 3 Allegretto.

I do not propose to repeat here what I have said elsewhere on classical concertos. But besides quoting certain themes I have three general points to make, one special point, and one anecdote.

My first point concerns Mozart's own special treatment of the form of the first movement of a concerto. In no other form does he show so much variety, and I cannot recall any two cases in which his procedure is the same through the whole movement. But there is one interesting general principle. As every concertgoer knows, the first movement begins with a long orchestral ritornello, and the accepted text-book theory (which is very incorrect) asserts that this ritornello contains the first and second subjects all in the main key, and that when the solo instrument enters, it restates and expands these, distributing them into their proper keys and, in co-operation and alternation with the orchestra, building them up into a more or less normal development and recapitulation, the bulk of the coda being, unfortunately, left to the mercy of the solo-player's gift of extemporizing. Now you cannot possibly tell which of the many later themes of the opening tutti is going to belong to the group of first subject, and which to the second. Most people would confidently guess that in the present case the theme which begins in the middle of Ex. 2 belongs to the second subject.

Ex. 1.

Ex. 2.

But the pianoforte seems to know nothing about it, or indeed about any of the orchestral themes except Ex. 1, and even this it only takes up in continuation (from figure (*b*)) when the orchestra violently forces it on the attention. The first pianoforte theme is a long, slowly-moving cantabile which I do not quote. Then the orchestra, as we have seen, intervenes with Ex. 1, which the pianoforte, disregarding the first four bars, develops into a transition passage. This leads with great deliberation to an immense second subject containing any number of new themes, of which Ex. 3—

Ex. 3.

is the second and most important. Besides this there is a rich passage in which the flute gives Ex. 1 in E flat minor, accompanied brilliantly by the pianoforte. There are several other themes and passages, all of them new, thoroughly in the manner of second-subject material, and all utterly subversive of the doctrine that the function of the opening tutti was to predict what the solo had to say. At last the full orchestra enters with what sounds, in retro-spect, like a free version in E flat of the original last phases of the tutti. As a matter of fact this also, except its touching soft close, is really new as well as free.

The development is begun by the pianoforte with its own (un-quoted) opening cantabile. Then the orchestra intervenes with Ex. 1 in F minor, and a broad and simple development ensues, arising mainly from figure (b^2). The middle stage of this is marked by a passage of fine, severe massiveness, in which the majestic anger of the orchestra is answered by rolling arpeggios from the piano-forte. At last the recapitulation is reached. And now we can see very clearly one of Mozart's peculiar principles of concerto form; a principle far less easily traced in either Beethoven or Brahms, though both these masters use it. With Mozart the principle is definitely this: that the recapitulation recapitulates not so much the first solo as the opening tutti. Here we have the extreme case, in which the first solo (and hence everything that has to do with the second subject) has been entirely new. Hence we are struck with the full force of the fact that now in the recapitulation the orchestral and solo materials are for the first time thoroughly combined. Of course the result is quite impossible to fit in with any ordinary text-book theory of sonata form; the second subject is ruthlessly compressed, the order of its themes altered, and there is nothing to correspond with the flute passage founded on Ex. 1. But Ex. 2 appears in full, and pulls the whole design together as nothing else could do. This device of holding one of the most prominent tutti themes in reserve for the recapitulation is peculiar to Mozart, and is retained by him even where there is no other evidence of the principle we have just seen illustrated.

My second point illustrates some characteristic differences in the emotional ranges covered by Haydn, Mozart, and Beethoven. Neither Haydn nor Mozart produced more than a small proportion of works in minor keys; and while their ways of characterizing the minor mode are by no means conventional, nearly all their works in minor keys have a special character. Tell me that a mature but unknown large work of Mozart is in a minor key, and I will confidently assert that while it may have humorous passages it will certainly have both passion and pathos, and that while the pathos will almost certainly not amount to tragedy, it is very likely that much of the work will border on the sublime. If a large work of Haydn is in the minor mode it is almost sure to conceal pathos beneath a blustering temper in its quick movements. With Beethoven we reach the world of tragedy. Now the recapitulation of a second subject in a minor movement is likely to make these distinctions very clear. For, if the second subject was, as usual, originally in a major key, what is to become of it when it is recapitulated in the tonic? Haydn, in his later works, nearly always indulges in a 'happy ending' by turning the whole thing into the tonic major. Mozart (except in the finale of the D minor Concerto, where he achieves both his own and Haydn's method by adding a happy epilogue) always makes a pathetic transformation of his originally happy second subject into the tonic minor. This is pathetic but not tragic. Beethoven seems, at first sight, to return to Haydn's practice, but really he has transcended Mozart's; his major recapitulation has all the power of tragic irony, and the catastrophe follows in the coda.

Near the end of the first movement of this concerto a curious detail occurs. The cadenza comes in the usual place, after the recapitulation: there is the usual pause of the orchestra, and blank space left for the extempore solo; but the usual concluding shake is not indicated and the orchestra re-enters with a connecting passage of two bars which is not to be found elsewhere in the movement. After much thought I have come to the conclusion that the omission of the shake is not an oversight, and that Mozart had in view a novel way of ending the cadenza in this case. It is a pity that this concerto is not one of those for which he wrote down his own large collection of cadenzas, for these, though perfunctory like all similar attempts to write down what should be extempore, are priceless evidence as to the style and technique of this difficult lost art. As it is, I am reduced to guesswork.

The first theme of the child-like slow movement—

Ex. 4.

raises in its fourth bar my last general point, the most difficult of all the problems that beset the interpreter of Mozart's concertos. At first sight it seems hard to realize that the naivety of that fourth bar can be intentional. Yet Mozart must have thoroughly impressed upon his young pupil Hummel that its whole point was its utter simplicity; for many years afterwards Hummel, having become the most brilliant and authoritative pianist-composer in Europe, published an arrangement of eight of Mozart's greatest concertos, in which he rewrote almost every bar of the pianoforte passages and brought them up to date. Yet he did not dare to touch this bar, until at its fifth and last appearance he added one little turn. But this raises the whole question of extempore ornamentation in Mozart's concertos. I am far from pretending to settle the problem. Hummel's ornamentation will certainly not do; but it should be studied, for he had all the knowledge we have not, though his temperament was inflated rather than inspired. It is quite certain that the plain text of Mozart's pianoforte part is often incomplete; for instance, you find a clarinet and a bassoon varying their repetitions while the pianoforte part at the same moment has always the old bare outline. Clearly the orchestral players could not be left to extemporize variations, and the pianist could. But one is thankful to do as little as possible; for any deviation from Mozart's style, even a deviation into early Beethoven, sets one's teeth on edge. I am inclined to think that the problem set by this slow movement in particular is the reason for the otherwise inexplicable fact that this C minor Concerto, perhaps the most sublime of all Mozart's instrumental works, is less known at the present day than the D minor, which happens to look less incomplete.

In Beethoven's young days these things were not difficulties but opportunities. Players and singers were judged quite as much by their taste in ornamentation as by their capacity for making the best of what the composer wrote down. According to Dannreuther, even the word *semplice* in the recitatives in Beethoven's D minor Sonata is a special warning to the player not to add ornaments; and we actually find Chopin, in an early posthumous set of variations, inscribing the theme *semplice e senza ornamenti*.

Be this as it may, Mozart's C minor Concerto was in Beethoven's time one of his most famous works, and it made a profound impression on Beethoven. The theme of the finale can only be called sublime.

Ex. 5.

In the first stages of sketching for his C minor Symphony, Beethoven was thinking of making a pathetic finale, and he jotted down a theme in 6/8 time that was little more than a variation of this, a variation that would have passed almost unnoticed among the variations Mozart's finale actually consists of. Some of these variations are pathetic, some childlike (e.g. the cheerful episode in A flat, and the graceful one in C major), and some majestic, as the orchestral fortes and the one in flowing four-part polyphony for the solo. But, as with Greek art, the subtle sublimity is a function of the simplicity and clearness of the surface; until at last the whole pathos of Mozart's work is summed up in the last variation, in 6/8 time.

Ex. 6.

It must have been the haunting second phrase of this (bars 5–8) that made Beethoven exclaim to Ries as they listened to it during a rehearsal: 'Oh, my dear fellow, *we* shall never get any idea like this.' Perhaps this was true enough of Ries. But even of Beethoven himself it is true that he did not strike this particular vain of pathos and romance until his art had gone beyond all possible reach of Mozart's direct influence. Then indeed, in the finale of the Quartet op. 95, Beethoven did produce a heart-rending theme of the same incomparable simplicity.

FLUTE CONCERTO IN G MAJOR (KÖCHEL'S CATALOGUE 313)

1 Allegro maestoso. 2 Adagio non troppo. 3 RONDO: *Tempo di Menuetto.*

The two flute concertos of Mozart appear to have been written, together with the Concerto for flute and harp, in 1778. This, in G major, is not less witty and beautiful than the one in D major. In an interesting series of articles in the *Chesterian*, Louis Fleury commented upon the tendency of the flute composers of a hundred years ago to write pretentiously and pompously for this childlike and elfish instrument. The crushing solemnity of the nineteenth-century virtuoso musician certainly did produce depressing developments. Kuhlau wrote magnificent sonatas and duets and concert pieces, which earned him the title of the Beethoven of the flute. We have still to learn that Beethoven was at any time known as the Kuhlau of the orchestra. Mozart had a gentle vein of irony which often goes with a long range of prophetic vision, and we may take it that when he inscribes the first movement of this Concerto in G major *allegro maestoso* he writes the inscription with his tongue in his cheek. He is in fact doing very much what Mendelssohn did in the *Midsummer-Night's Dream* music, when Pease-blossom, Cobweb, and Mustard-seed make their bows to Bottom the Weaver to the accompaniment of a flourish of trumpets on two oboes, while two flutes execute a roll of drums. I quote enough of the first and second subjects of the first movement to show the range of contrast between the majestic attitude of the opening, where you are requested to keep grave—

Ex. 1.

Allegro maestoso.

and the second subject, which begins in an unexpected part of the scale and continues in epigrammatic vein.

Ex. 2.

The slow movement is the richest and most beautiful movement in these flute concertos. Here Mozart has boldly substituted two flutes for the oboes which constitute with the horns the usual wind band in his smallest concertos. Thus the solo flute is now standing out against a background largely of the same colour. But the strings are muted; and the horns, in a lower key than in the first and last movements, provide a darker tone. The solemn opening figure, in which the flute has no share, intervenes with dramatic weight at the turning points of the structure.

Ex. 3.

The movement is in the usual arioso sonata form.

The finale is one of those graceful *tempo di menuetto* rondos which Mozart seems to have given up writing in his later works.

Ex. 4.

In spite of its leisurely tempo it gives the flute more scope for its characteristic fantastic agility than the rest of the work. It is broadly designed without any unusual features, and ends quietly, like almost all Mozart's examples in this tempo.

FLUTE CONCERTO IN D MAJOR (KÖCHEL'S CATALOGUE, NO. 314)

1 *Allegro aperto.* 2 *Andante.* 3 *Rondo. Allegro.*

It is very good for an artist to make the best of a task he dislikes; so long as there is a good best to be discovered for it. It is said that Mozart could not abide either the flute or the harp; yet, as we shall see, when at the command of a Duke in Paris he had to write a double concerto for those instruments, he dissembled his love in a long and charming work, and only on the last page ushered the harp downstairs in an exposed passage which neatly contained the two perfectly simple things which no harpist, ancient or modern, can play.

As for the flute, whatever he may have said about it, he liked it well enough to write two concertos, an andante with orchestra which is conspicuously lovely in tone and feeling, and two quartets for flute and strings which are by no means perfunctory. These five works are all comparatively early, ranging from 1777 to 1778; but Mozart was a mature artist in most art-forms at the age of twelve; and not even an opera can be dismissed as an 'early work' if he was twenty when he wrote it. He took the flute seriously enough in these highly-finished little works: more so than in his supreme masterpiece *The Magic Flute* (which indeed has only two episodes to justify its title).

Of course, he is incapable of such a blunder as to write for a big orchestra with a long and heroic opening tutti, by way of preparing for the entry of his Puck or Ariel. His opening tutti is short, though it summarizes the whole movement from the first subject—

Ex. 1.

to the second, with its warning notes such as usher in a change of key in a Viennese waltz—

Ex. 2.

and its mischievous cadence-theme—

Ex. 3.

the last bar of which (figure (*a*)) the flute has a characteristic way of detaching for purposes of its own. At the end of the movement this figure tricks the Eminent Critic into giving the performers the exquisite pleasure of being blamed for deficient ensemble when they play the last bars accurately. Throughout the movement the second violins behave with an opera-buffa malice which Mozart particularly cultivated at this period: it makes all his early concerto-tuttis crowded with contrapuntal and operatic life; and it almost conjures up an awful vision of an early Rossini whom one could take seriously, much as, according to Professor Saintsbury, the rhymed headings to the pages of *The Rose and the Ring* evoke the ghost of a Milton with a sense of humour.

As for the flute, Mozart may not have been the earliest to understand its fantastic agility—these questions of priority interest nobody who wants to listen to music—but no one before or since has better seen the point of its qualities: the agility that can in the same breath give and deny local habitation to whatever airy nothings it is pleased to name; and the innocence which can seem superhuman rather than cold, so long as the composer does not give it phrases indicating passions of which it is ignorant. None of Mozart's flute-music happens to be pathetic, except the slow movement of the D major Quartet: the exception shows that there was nothing either in the Flute or in Mozart's idea of it to prevent his being as pathetic as Gluck in the Elysian scene of *Orfeo*, or Brahms in the finale of his Fourth Symphony. There is no limit to the beauty and pathos of childhood, so long as it is true to the nature of childhood. It so happens, however, that in this concerto the only serious note is to be found in the serenity with which the flute answers the quasi-heroic gestures of the first theme of the slow movement—

Ex. 4.

and in the second subject in dialogue between flute and orchestra.

Ex. 5.

As for the finale, two quotations from its numerous collection of themes will show its lightness of heart, its flexibility of rhythm—

Ex. 6.

(note in Ex. 6 that the theme, though it foreshadows Blonde's lively air in the *Seraglio*, has none of that young person's squareness of phrasing), and its richness of counterpoint—

Ex. 7.

in a central episode complicated enough to get the copyist of the earliest extant band-parts into a thorough muddle.

It is in some ways a pity that music of this order never gets the kind of vulgar valuation that comes to pictures and beautiful pieces of furniture. This Flute Concerto is supremely artistic in every way; its slightness and smallness are functions of its greatness; and we might expect it to fetch a fabulous price if it were an escritoire, or a porcelain dinner-set, or any other form of art which daily usefulness has caused to be produced anonymously in good periods as well as in bad.

ANDANTE FOR FLUTE WITH ORCHESTRA
(KÖCHEL'S CATALOGUE, NO. 315)

The last and perhaps the most beautiful of Mozart's flute works, this Andante may possibly have been intended as a substitute for the andante of the Concerto in G. The very beautiful and elaborate slow movement of that work requires two flutes in the orchestra besides the solo player, and Mozart may have found that this was inconvenient. The other cases in which there is a single movement, slow or quick, for a solo instrument with orchestra are all known to be cases of reviving an old work and substituting the new movement for the corresponding old one. Be this as it may, the new movements are at their best by themselves, and the original works are best in their early form. The production of a concerto at a public concert in Mozart's, and even as late as Chopin's time, was one of those best of all possible events in which every detail was a necessary evil. The first movement was produced in one part of the concert, the slow movement and finale were produced about an hour afterwards when the audience had been gratified by other items which might now find place in a rather primitive variety entertainment. Nothing more clearly proves the genius of the greatest masters of eighteenth-century music than the undoubted fact that their concertos and symphonies have an inviolable unity, which at the time of their composition was appreciable by the composer alone, or to the few who studied the works in private.

More than anything else in the flute works of Mozart, the style and themes of this andante are prophetic of his yet more magic flute of thirteen years later. The position and melodic type of the first theme is very like that of the tune with which Tamino in *Die Zauberflöte* first tries the power of the magic flute, with the effect of bringing on to the stage a complete menagerie of fascinated birds and beasts.

My quotation indicates the picturesque introductory chords for oboes, horns, and pizzicato strings, which are cunningly developed later on into a second subject. The movement is worked out in the typical arioso sonata form, and is one of the ripest examples of Mozart's style at its comparatively early date of composition, 1778.

CLARINET CONCERTO IN A MAJOR
(KÖCHEL'S CATALOGUE, NO. 622)

1 *Allegro.* 2 *Adagio.* 3 RONDO: *Allegro.*

As far as the art of writing for the instrument is concerned, Mozart may well be considered to have invented or at least discovered the clarinet. His three compositions in which the clarinet is the leading wind instrument, namely the Clarinet Concerto, the Trio for pianoforte, viola and clarinet, and the Quintet for clarinet and strings, belong to the last years of his life and are among his most beautiful works. The concerto is in the full-sized classical form and by no means on a small scale. If it were a pianoforte concerto, it would be among the more important ones, though Mozart has avoided involving his sharply characterized solo instrument in any polyphonic discussions with the orchestra. Mr. Forsyth in his admirable book on orchestration has quoted copiously from both Stanford's concerto and Mozart's by way of showing among other things how the essentials of clarinet-playing remain the same to-day as they were in Mozart's time. It is interesting to compare the orchestra of the two works. It stands to reason that in neither of them will clarinets be present in the background, but Mozart's solo clarinet is in a different relation to its background from Stanford's, for Stanford relies upon oboes as a contrast to his solo instrument in wind tone, whereas Mozart has only flutes, bassoons, and horns. He thus surrounds his clarinet with no strong contrasts of tone at all, and yet there is no lack of relief. The softness of the flutes rather enhances the vitality of the clarinet. I quote three of the many themes of the first movement.

Ex. 1.
1st Subject.

Ex. 2.
Transition.

Clarinet.

8a.

Ex. 3.

The slow movement will be recognized as well known by many listeners who have never before realized where it came from. I have heard it as a horn solo and as a violin solo, and in almost any form except that in which Mozart wrote it.

Ex. 4.

The finale is a full-sized rondo of which the following are the main themes:

Ex. 5.

Ex. 6.

Ex. 7.

A point as fine as any in Mozart's chamber and orchestral music is the freedom with which the second subject (Ex. 6) is treated in its recapitulation before leading to the spacious coda.

VIOLIN CONCERTO IN D MAJOR
(KÖCHEL'S CATALOGUE, NO. 218)

1 *Allegro.* 2 *Andante cantabile.* 3 RONDO. *Andante grazioso, alternating
with Allegro ma non troppo.*

Of Mozart's violin concertos the fourth, in D, and the fifth, in A,
show the style of his adolescence at its wittiest. The fourth is in
higher animal spirits and therefore has less leisure for meditation
than the A major; but it is not less witty, and, like the A major, it
has its surprises in dramatic incident and form.

As the orchestra is without trumpets the opening theme imitates
those heraldic perquisites with great vigour.

Ex. 1.

The main theme of the second group is graceful, with the peculiar
tang of Mozart's style at the age of nineteen.

Ex. 2.

There are as many other themes as there are musical sentences,
so that this opening tutti contains at least four more that would
deserve quotation. And the solo violin has many more of its
own. But the most interesting matter is the question of how it
can deal with Exx. 1 and 2. To those who do not know this concerto
I will not divulge the secret of how the solo violin, like the sonnet
in Milton's hands, becomes a trumpet; but there is no harm in
remarking that it delivers Ex. 2 in a deep bass voice.

The slow movement is serious in manner, but not less inveterately witty in detail. Its main theme is grave.

Ex. 3.

Its second group is heralded by an ornate theme.

Ex. 4.

Mr. Fox Strangways, in an interesting analysis of certain criteria

of melodic beauty, crowned his argument with a gesture of
humorous despair induced by a phrase in the coda of this movement,
where the violin (like the Duke of York with his 20,000 men)
simply walks up a scale and then walks down again. But Mr. Fox
Strangways knew all the time that this phenomenon was the surface
of a harmonic process without which it would have no meaning.
Still wittier is the way in which the movement ends with a phrase
that had hitherto always appeared to be merely medial.

The contredanse of Mozart's time was a dance with abrupt
alternations of tempo; and there were also minuets *mit eingelegten
Contredansen.* From such origins arises a special kind of rondo, to
be found in more than one of Mozart's violin concertos, and also
in his D major Violin Sonata, the rondo of which is twin brother to
that of the present work.

The main theme asks wistful questions in a slow tempo (*Andante
grazioso*).

Ex. 5.

And the questions are answered quizzically in a quick movement
(*Allegro ma non troppo*)—

Ex. 6.

which leads to the dominant, where a second group begins with
the following theme—

Ex. 7.

The two tempi alternate in consequence of the rondo form. But
the second episode, beginning in B minor, leads to another
change of tempo in the shape of a slow gavotte in G major—

Ex. 8.

which is continued with a delicious theme over a drone-bass.

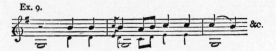
Ex. 9.

When Ex. 5 returns, it is worked out in regular recapitulation with Exx. 6 and 7, and the concerto ends, like its middle movement, with a sudden dying away in mid-phrase.

VIOLIN CONCERTO IN A MAJOR
(KÖCHEL'S CATALOGUE, NO. 219)

1 *Allegro aperto.* 2 *Adagio.* 3 *Tempo di Menuetto.*

Mozart's five authentic violin concertos were all written in Salzburg in 1775 when he was nineteen years of age. The Concerto in E flat, which is the most frequently played, and which purports to be the sixth, may be based on genuine material, but no competent musical scholar believes that it can possibly be genuine in the form in which it is known to us. The seventh concerto was discovered early in the present century, and has been often played with success. It is not in a perfectly satisfactory state of preservation; but, if it is a forgery, it is an exceedingly clever one, and it does not make the mistake of imitating a generalized Mozart of no particular period. No composer has had so many forgeries foisted upon him as Mozart. There are five spurious masses, including the celebrated Twelfth Mass; a concertante for four wind instruments and orchestra, purporting to be the lost work known to have been written in Paris for a rather different combination; a number of spurious songs; several sonatas and smaller pieces; to say nothing of the peculiar disaster of instrumental parts added to genuine works so unskilfully that the authenticity of the whole seems questionable until the additions have been removed. What is known, then, about Mozart's violin concertos is that in 1775 he made a brilliant beginning in this most difficult art-form, and never afterwards followed it up. It is noteworthy that the three greatest violin concertos in existence are all peculiarly happy but solitary efforts of their composers: Beethoven, Mendelssohn, and Brahms. It is not so remarkable that Mozart produced five violin concertos in one year as that he produced them early in his career. It was natural to produce several, since the scale of the form at that period was not large. I have had occasion, in commenting upon the flute concertos which belong to the same period, to call attention to the special vein of epigrammatic comedy which characterizes Mozart's style up to the age of twenty-three. In the A major Violin Concerto it attains its height, and is also combined with a specially fantastic kind of childlike beauty. Mozart's form at this period was almost as full of experimental features as Haydn's, and the work is full of surprises.

The opening theme as given out by the orchestra seems to be merely a formal assertion of the chords of the key in the usual eighteenth-century style, but I quote together with it a totally new idea which the solo violin is eventually going to build upon it.

Ex. 1.

The theme which afterwards becomes the second subject is one that could walk into the House of Lords with the same friendly self-possession as into its own kindergarten.

Ex. 2.

And who would have thought that the formula which ends the orchestral tutti—

Ex. 3.

could so coolly become an important transition theme when the solo violin takes it up?

Ex. 4.

The entry of the solo violin itself is one of the greatest surprises ever perpetrated in a concerto. We expect it to begin either

directly with a statement of the opening theme, or else, if Mozart
is inclined to anticipate Beethoven, with some preliminary running
passages. We certainly did not expect that the violin would begin
with a sustained arioso in a very slow adagio time with a running
accompaniment. There is a childlike grandeur in this gesture,
which almost overawes the sense of humour to which Mozart was
undoubtedly appealing. You may take this as a measure of the
poetic power underlying all the fun. For the rest of the movement our four quotations will suffice. It was surprising enough
when Ex. 3 developed into the solid structure of Ex. 4, but it is
still more surprising when it turns out to be the absolutely abrupt
end of the whole movement.

The slow movement is not less notable for the terse and epigrammatic character of its themes. The essentials of them are all stated
in the opening tutti, the substance of which is expanded by the
solo violin much on the lines of the first movement in sonata form.
I quote the two figures in the stream of melody which become
articulated into first and second subject.

The finale is, like most concerto finales, a rondo. In a moderate
tempo di menuetto it begins as if it was going to pass all its existence
in graceful ease. I quote the first theme with its codetta.

The first episode on the dominant presents just the kind of contrast
one would expect; and the return to the main theme follows in due
course. The second episode, beginning in F sharp minor, with
darker colouring and a somewhat wider range of key, is again just
what the situation seems to require; and in the second return of
the main theme the attentive ear may note that there is a little more

detail in the accompaniments, whereby the design is unobtrusively kept alive. The next thing to expect would be a recapitulation of the first episode in the tonic, with some slight modification of the transition leading to it. But suddenly we have a contredanse in A minor (2/4 time), scored with the grotesque effects characteristic of the real dance-music of the Viennese public ball-rooms in 1778. Mozart gives this full scope to express itself with all manner of repeats and alternating sections. It enlarges the range of the finale as triumphantly as that impressive adagio arioso enlarges the range of the first movement. After this the rondo theme returns and leads to the orthodox recapitulation of the second subject and to a final return, the accompaniments naturally varying in detail each time; and to crown all, this broadly designed movement ends with the simple abruptness of the codetta to the theme (Ex. 8).

It is not surprising that this work was a great favourite with Joachim, who wrote cadenzas for it that are among the most perfect that have been written for any concerto.

ADAGIO IN E FOR VIOLIN WITH ORCHESTRA
(KÖCHEL'S CATALOGUE, NO. 261)

This broad and dignified aria for violin was produced by Mozart as a substitute for the more kittenish slow movement of his A major Violin Concerto, on an occasion when that work was played by a violinist named Brunetti, who, we may infer, wanted an opportunity of displaying his full range of tone. We need not infer that Mozart wished the new adagio to remain permanently as a part of the A major Concerto, the childlike humour of which it would only embarrass. Public performances of concertos, even as late as Chopin's time, were given in conditions that make it a marvel that the great composers showed any sense of unity of mood and style; and Mozart had more to gain than to lose by pleasing Brunetti in a performance where the first movement was to be given in the first part of the concert and the rest in the second part after several other items. On the other hand, we gain a rare addition to the small number of single movements for violin and orchestra; a piece at least as important as the violin romances of Beethoven, and, for all its seemingly automatic handling of forms already highly conventionalized, far more distinguished in style.

The orchestral violins (but not the lower strings) are muted, and the wind-band consists of two flutes and two horns. The A major Concerto has oboes instead of flutes, and thus Mozart seems to be taking special measures to throw the solo violin into higher relief in this movement. With this tiny orchestra he achieves many remarkable tone-colours by a few unexpected holding-notes and by sforzandos in the inner parts.

Ex. 1 shows the main theme; Ex. 2 a characteristically pregnant connecting link; and Ex. 3 is the beginning of the second subject.

Ex. 1.

Ex. 2.

Ex. 3.

CONCERTO FOR FLUTE AND HARP (KÖCHEL'S CATALOGUE, NO. 299)

1 *Allegro.* 2 *Andantino.* 3 RONDO: *Allegro.*

In 1778, during Mozart's visit to Paris, the Duke of Guines commissioned him to write a concerto for flute and harp. Mozart shows no great respect for dukes as such in his family letters, and so we may believe him when he writes that the Duke plays the flute incomparably and the daughter plays the harp '*magnifique*'; the resources of the German language apparently failing him as English avowedly failed Dr. Johnson when he was '*pénétré* with His Majesty's goodness'. Accordingly, though these instruments were precisely the two that he could not abide, he soon began to luxuriate in the fun of writing for them. The possibilities of the single-action harp of the eighteenth century he exhausted in this work. Nothing could be done for it but to proceed on the lines of very sketchy pianoforte music with an anxious avoidance of cantabile; but the flute reconciled him so far that after his Paris visit he produced five by no means uncharacteristic works for it, of which the three with orchestra (two concertos and an andante) are discussed in this volume.

It is not necessary to quote more than four of the sixteen themes which Mozart sends streaming out in festive processions throughout and around this work. Although a developed style for the harp cannot be said to exist within fifty years of Mozart's death, this concerto is no exception to the rule that Mozart's imagination for combinations of instruments and harmonies is infallibly accurate and incomparably vivid. He has here to reckon with the fact that the harpists in 1778 were preoccupied with making their instrument speak a language it could not properly pronounce; and he makes no miscalculations. Even the daughter of a duke could not, in spite of her *magnifique* playing, prevent the mischievous Mozart from twice asking the harp to say 'shibboleth' at the end of the finale. (And, by the way, the will to play practical jokes is distinctly discoverable in Mozart's works. I, for my part, feel absolutely certain of his intention of getting the choir to mock the pronunciation of some friend of his in a certain Mass, once well known, where the word 'Osanna' is set in close stretto to a syncopated rhythm, and a fortissimo mark is placed under the third syllable in all the voices and instruments at every single one of the forty or fifty repetitions of the word.)

The technique of the flute, unlike that of the harp, was not only essentially mature in 1778, but had already reached a second period of development. For Bach and Handel the flute was a cantabile instrument well suited for principal melodies or polyphonic threads played in its lower registers among an ensemble of soft instruments. But already in Mozart's time the habits of the flute had changed in order to enable it to assert itself in the new styles of symphonic and dramatic orchestration, and he never loses an important feature by writing low for the flute in a tutti, as Haydn, who also developed the new technique, continued often to do in his latest works. This being so, it is interesting to find that the Duke of Guines had a flute provided with holes (possibly also keys) for the low D flat and C; which Mozart evidently could not count upon in any of his later flute works, as he never wrote those notes again. This, at all events, indicates that it was not ducal stimulus that induced him to write his remaining five solo works for the flute. (It was 96 ducats.)

Those extra low notes for the flute will be heard by the alert listener about half-way through the first movement, during its development, where they are used as a bass to the harp! For the rest it will suffice to quote the opening themes; of the first movement—

Ex. 1.

and of the luxurious slow movement, in which the style of the harp
is at its best within the possibilities of 1778, and the string orchestra
is throughout enriched by division of the violas into two parts—

Ex. 2.

and the opening and closing themes of the five which are poured
out in the first tutti of the rondo.

Ex. 3.

The viola and second violin of this last theme contain one of the shib-
boleths with which Mozart worries the harp on the last page, a passage
in which the hands and strings are brought into mutual interference.
There is no reasonable doubt that this is malicious; and so is the
other passage, in which Mozart goes out of his way (altering, in
recapitulation, a perfectly safe theme) to introduce some chromatic
steps for which even the modern harp is not conveniently suited. Of
course there is nothing embarrassing in these jokes, which the composer expects to turn against himself in either of two possible events;
for the passages will either be played with success, or something
appropriate and more effective will be substituted for them.

SAINT-SAËNS

VIOLONCELLO CONCERTO IN A MINOR, OP. 33

1 *Allegro non troppo, leading to* 2 *Allegretto con moto, leading to*
3 *Tempo primo, leading to* 4 *Un peu moins vite.*

The worldly wisdom of Saint-Saëns is at its best and kindliest in
this opusculum, which is pure and brilliant without putting on
chastity as a garment, and without calling attention to its jewellery
at a banquet of poor relations.

Here, for once, is a violoncello concerto in which the solo instrument displays every register throughout its compass without the slightest difficulty in penetrating the orchestral accompaniment. All the adroitness of Saint-Saëns is shown herein, and also in the compact form of the work, which, following Mendelssohn in abolishing all orchestral tuttis, except connecting links, goes further than Mendelssohn inasmuch as it relegates to the finale the function of the recapitulation in the first movement, and thus combines the effect of three movements with that of a single design.

The violoncello opens at full speed with a lively subject in cross-rhythms that evidently means business.

The second subject is a Schumannesque epigram, of which the tender mood is soon broken into by the business of Ex. 1.

An orchestral interlude on new material—

leads to a development that, instead of going to remote keys, returns to that of Ex. 2, which it expands, leading peacefully into B flat. (Saint-Saëns has often made effective use of keys a semitone apart, as here, A minor to B flat; the B minor Violin Concerto with its slow movement in B flat; the C-minor-D-flat pair in his Third Symphony; the C minor Violoncello Sonata, &c.)

The middle movement, a slow-movement scherzo, suggests a group of those little dancers supported on a tripod of bristles that move so prettily if you put them on the lid of a pianoforte and play.

The violoncello enters ruminatively—

Ex. 5.

and accompanies the dance with sustained melody, taking up its
figures only at the end, to subside into Ex. 4 in deep bass: whereupon the orchestra brings back the business of Ex. 1 and leads to
the finale.

This begins with a new melancholy tune (compare Ex. 5)—

Ex. 6.

which is followed by a bustling semiquaver theme which I do not
quote.

There is a calm middle episode, giving the lower strings of the
violoncello a welcome opportunity to sing.

Ex. 7.

After Ex. 6 returns, the design of the whole work is completed
by further use of Ex. 1, and by the reappearance of Ex. 3 in A
minor. Whereupon the violoncello triumphantly sings quite a new
tune in A. major. And so they lived happily ever after.

SCHUMANN

PIANOFORTE CONCERTO IN A MINOR, OP. 54

1 *Allegro affetuoso.* 2 *Intermezzo: Andantino grazioso, leading to* 3 *Allegro vivace.*

There is a depth and a breadth in Schumann's lyric vein which already shows that it was no mistaken ambition that led him to turn from it to larger designs. His career was shortened and clouded by illness, but this concerto is one of at least a dozen large works which utterly refute the Wagnerian judgement of Schumann as a might-have-been. A work so eminently beautiful from beginning to end, so free, spacious, and balanced in form, and so rich and various in ideas, is more than proof that Schumann was justified in attempting any and every art-problem. It is a worthy monument to the sanity of art; and while it illuminates the tragic pathos of Schumann's later years, it is itself untouched.

The first movement, composed in 1841, had an independent existence for four years as a fantasia for pianoforte and orchestra. Thus, though it has all the essentials of a very big first movement in sonata form, it never professed to be the first movement of a classical concerto. The orchestra makes no attempt to muster its forces for its own full connected statement of the themes. At the climaxes it bursts out with a short triumphant passage in the manner of a ritornello; but for the most part it behaves very much as the strings behave in Schumann's quintet: though it has far more colour, and is, for all its reticence, much above Schumann's normal achievement in its purity and brightness of tone.

My first quotation gives the energetic introductory figure (*a*), which leads to the first theme, and is used once in the development.

Ex. 1.

After the pianoforte has answered the plaintive cantabile theme, the violins give a transition theme—

Ex. 2.

of which the figure (*c*) becomes very important later. The second subject is made of a broad stream of impulsive melody derived from (*b*) of the first theme—

Ex. 3.
Clarinet.

and using figure (*c*) in the course of its dialogue. Figure (*c*) also forms the text of the triumphant ritornello with which the orchestra bursts in at the climax. Then there is a dramatic change of key to A flat, in which remote region the pianoforte gives out an altogether new version of the first theme (*b*) in slow 6/4 time, in the tenderest of dialogues with the orchestra. When this comes to its natural close, the pianoforte breaks abruptly into the original tempo with figure (*a*), and then proceeds to work up figure (*b*) in an impassioned stream of melody, joined by more and more of the orchestra and driving irresistibly through a wide range of key until at last it resigns itself in a solemn close into the main theme in the home tonic.

From this point the recapitulation follows its normal course, until the point where the orchestra is to break in with its ritornello. But here the pianoforte goes on playing through it, and soon breaks its way into an unaccompanied cadenza. A triumphantly paradoxical feature of this very happy outburst of apparently extempore eloquence is that its themes happen to be entirely new until at last figure (*b*) appears below a long trill. Then the threads, new and old, are gathered together, and the orchestra re-enters with figure (*b*) marching at the double, in 2/4 time. Much passion lies suppressed in the gallant spirit of this march, which approaches, makes its climax, and recedes into romantic distance, until at last it flashes out in an abrupt end.

Whatever Schumann may have felt about this fantasia in 1841, his instinct was true when in 1845 he recognized that it was only the first movement of a larger work. The slow movement is of the very centre of Schumann's most intimate and tender vein; childlike in its gently playful opening—

Ex. 4.

while in its sustained, swinging second theme—

Ex. 5.

it attains a beauty and depth quite transcendent of any mere prettiness, though the whole concerto, like all Schumann's deepest music, is recklessly pretty.

Nothing can be more romantic than the coda, in which figure (*b*) of the first movement reappears and leads dramatically into the finale.

From the six or seven important themes of this glorious movement I select the first subject—

Ex. 6.

the second subject with its famous *deux-temps* rhythm—

Ex. 7.

&c.

the new theme which appears in the course of the rich development—

Ex. 8.

and the delightful surprise of another brilliant new theme which cheerfully begins the coda as soon as the recapitulation is over.

Ex. 9.

Never has a long and voluble peroration been more masterly in its proportions and more perfectly in character with the great whole which it crowns with so light a touch. Every note inspires affection, and only an inattentive critic can suspect the existence of weaknesses to condone. Fashion and musical party-politics have tried to play many games with Schumann's reputation, but works like this remain irresistible.

VIOLONCELLO CONCERTO IN A MINOR, OP. 129

1 *Nicht zu schnell; leading to* 2 *Langsam; leading to* 3 *Sehr lebhaft.*

Schumann's Violoncello Concerto, long regarded as a thankless task, has been brought to light in the present day by consummate musicianship and sense of beauty on the part of a leader among those violoncellists who refuse to confine the possibilities of their instrument to the obvious. The scoring of this concerto is no obstacle to its performance, being remarkably free from the dangerous thickness of Schumann's usual orchestral style. In general his orchestral sense is at its best in his accompanying of solos of all kinds. If the violoncello seems, on a first hearing, to be at any disadvantage, this is not because the accompaniment (*Begleitung des Orchesters* is Schumann's own title) is heavy, but because the form shows little or no disposition to expand. Terse exposition, short ruminating developments, and interludes all gathered up as quickly as possible to the business of schematic recapitulation; every feature indicates Schumann's growing dislike of anything that could be called display. Still, the work was written before this dislike merged into the morbid condition which ended in fatal illness. The qualities of the violoncello are exactly those of the beloved enthusiastic dreamer whom we know as Schumann; and as a flow of intimate melody the first two movements rank high in his art. The finale, too, has its point. In the 'eighties Kensington used to compare Browning with Brahms. The unavowed reason for this profundity was that both begin with Br: the more conscious reason was that both were considered obscure, manly, and rugged. Brahms, who throughout his life spent as much pains in smoothing his style as Browning took in winning and carrying off his bride, would probably have not been flattered by the comparison had he been more conscious of the existence of Kensington or of England. But there is a real analogy between Schumann and Browning. Both are the 'essentially manly' poets of people who innocently wallow in sentiment: and when Schumann is nervous he is apt to develop exactly Browning's habit of digging you in the ribs and illustrating grave realities with some crack-jaw quadruple rhyme. And so we may accept Schumann's finale as Browningesque.

The following list of themes will suffice for all purposes of analysis.

Ex. 1 is a broad melody, announced, after three opening chords, by the violoncello, and developed for thirty bars to a climax.

Ex. 1.

The orchestra enters with an impassioned new theme—

Ex. 2.

built up into a short tutti, into which the violoncello breaks with

ruminating phrases leading into C major. Here they grow into a
regular second group. From this one figure requires quotation, with
its simplification in the wood-wind, which becomes prominent in
many sequels.

Ex. 3.

Ex. 4.

The movement runs its course with all Schumann's quiet antithetic
rhetoric.

The development begins by introducing an agitated triplet
figure, traceable perhaps to a casual ornamental detail in previous
violoncello passages.

Ex. 5.

Later on the violoncello combines with Ex. 4 another figure (which
persons who pay super-tax on brains may derive from Ex. 5 by
'augmentation' without making the slightest difference to its
intelligibility).

Ex. 6.

This develops into one of the most thoughtful passages in the work,
and leads to the first theme (Ex. 1) in F sharp minor, soon broadly
moving to the tonic, A minor, where a full normal recapitulation
follows.

A short tutti (compare Ex. 5) leads to a sudden dramatic change
of key and tempo, and the slow movement which now follows
consists of a single lyrical melody in F major. No quotation
is required, but the listener should mark the exquisite moment
where the violoncello sings in slow double-stops—a triumph of
Schumann's instrumental imagination.

The orchestra alludes to Ex. 1, which the violoncello continues
in agitated recitative, combining it with topics from the slow move-

ment and other themes, until it breaks into the finale, with a bluff reaction against sentiment.

Gentler utterances (especially the main figure of Ex. 1) contrive nevertheless to work their way into the design; and the provocative first theme itself strikes tender notes as a second subject, in spite of gibes from the violas.

An ingenious cadenza, remarkable, like most of this concerto, for its predilection for the lower strings of the violoncello, leads to a rapid coda, in which keen listeners will detect an allusion to Ex. 5. Ingenious as Schumann's cadenza is, there is good classical precedent for letting the violoncellist produce something not quite so gruff. Jacobi has written an excellent one, piously in touch with Schumann's *Innigkeit* and efficacious in conciliating us with the finale as a whole. Jacobi having thus broken the ice, I confess to some hankering to try and write a cadenza myself; but Schumann's shyness is very deterrent.

INTRODUCTION AND ALLEGRO APPASSIONATO
FOR PIANOFORTE WITH ORCHESTRA, OP. 92

I cannot account for the neglect of this work, which has always seemed to me to be one of Schumann's happiest and most inventive pieces. Even its orchestration is unusually successful, with little of the thickness and few of the risks of Schumann's orchestral writing.

The introduction, with its recklessly pretty romantic theme—

Ex. 1.

is really beautifully scored; and both the form and matter of the allegro appassionato are admirably dramatic and in perfect proportion. The Allegro starts in a towering temper in E minor—

Ex. 2.

suddenly yielding to a quieter but energetically rising theme starting in C.

Ex. 3.

This only establishes E minor more firmly, and a new theme sets the action of the drama fully in motion.

Ex. 4.

Another figure arises out of this, which I quote as it occurs later, on the dominant of C.

Ex. 5.

It leads to a second group preceded (as the example shows) by figure (b) from Ex. 1, which figure now becomes an important factor in the development.

The second group contains several more themes and is one of Schumann's finest specimens of the art of making flowing paragraphs. The way in which the aforesaid figure (*b*) insinuates itself into the texture is admirable; and so is the brilliant staccato theme (unquoted) which provokes the trumpets to assert the triplet figure of Ex. 2.

The development begins quietly with Ex. 3 on a chord of F, which promptly leads back to E minor, where Ex. 4 re-enters, soon to modulate further. Ex. 5 is taken up busily, but suddenly the theme of the introduction, Ex. 1, floats in above. With these threads a fine and dramatic development is built up, with none of the stiffness that may be imputed to many of Schumann's longer forms elsewhere. The return comes at the top of a grand climax, and the subtlety of the whole design is revealed by the fact that G major, the key of the introduction, proves to be that chosen for the recapitulation of the second subject, instead of E, the key of Ex. 2. The theme of the introduction again intervenes (in B flat, a soft and dark key in relation to G) at the beginning of the coda, the rest of which is greatly enlivened by a deliciously voluble new theme—

Ex. 7.

such as only the Schumann of the Quintet and the Pianoforte Concerto could invent.

SIBELIUS

VIOLIN CONCERTO, OP. 47

1 Allegro moderato. 2 Adagio di molto. 3 Allegro, ma non tanto.

Perhaps the Violin Concerto of Sibelius has not yet had time to become popular; but I can see no reason why it should not soon take place with the Violin Concerto of Mendelssohn and the G minor Concerto of Max Bruch as one of the three most attractive concertos ever written. Personally I am impelled to place it above those two famous works, nor do I think that my present enjoyment of it will wear out. Of course the great concerto form of Mozart, Beethoven, and Brahms is another story; instead of being lighter than symphonic form, it is perhaps the most subtle and certainly the most misunderstood art-form in all music. But in the easier and looser concerto forms invented by Mendelssohn and Schumann I have not met with a more original, a more masterly, and a more exhilarating work than the Sibelius Violin Concerto. As with all Sibelius's more important works, its outlines are huge and simple; and if a timely glance at an atlas had not reminded me that Finland is mostly flat and water-logged with lakes, I should doubtless have said that 'his forms are hewn out of the rocks of his native and Nordic mountains'. The composer to whose style the word 'lapidary' (*lapidarisch*) was first applied by the orthodoxy of the 'nineties is Bruckner; and if the best work of Sibelius suggests anything else in music, it suggests a Bruckner gifted with an easy mastery and the spirit of a Polar explorer. Strange to say, the results are of no inordinate length. Sibelius, unlike Bruckner, has an instinct which saves him from misapplying the classical sonata forms to a music that moves at quite a different pace; he does not design motor-cars with a box-seat for the driver, nor does he build reinforced concrete skyscrapers in the style of the Parthenon. There is plenty of sonata form in his works; but it is not a nuisance to him as it was to Bruckner; nor, on the other hand, is he, like Bruckner, at a loss when he diverges from it. The real problems of musical form are always, in the last resort, problems of movement; and Sibelius has his own special sense of movement, which delivers him from the need of Bruckner's desperate and dangerous gesture of 'I pause for a reply'. It gives him complete command of the arts of rousing expectation and of slow gradation to a climax. He does not aim at the time-scale of classical sonata forms, and therefore is not liable to the difficulties of those composers who are not conscious that the time-scale has something to do with the effect of the musical events that are to happen in it. One of Sibelius's most famous and successful devices is that of building up a symphonic finale out of broken figures that come together, like the Vision of Dry Bones, into a broad melody only by way of supreme climax at the end. (Very clever critics have been known to discover that this form lacks the eventful variety of the classical symphonic finale.) But the acid test comes when the inventor of so effective a device has to write a finale where it will not work; as, for instance, in a violin concerto, where it is impossible to ask a solo violin to live upon scraps for three-quarters of the finale, and then to dominate the full orchestra by giving its celebrated imitation (on one string) of the three trombones at the end of the Tannhäuser Overture. Hence there is nothing of the kind in the finale of this violin concerto: the characteristic 'lapidary' vastness is achieved by equally drastic simplicities, accurately to the purpose.

The first theme is a ruminating melody given out by the solo violin.

Ex. 1.

Nothing is more characteristic of Sibelius than the austerely diatonic dissonance of the first note, with its rhythmic position just as far off the main beat as its harmonic position is off the chord. I mark with (a) and (b) two figures that are used in other combinations; but a detailed analysis, though interesting to a student, is unnecessary for the enjoyment on a first hearing of a work which is always lucid, and never more so than in its most original features.

The violin works its melody up to an impassioned climax ending in a cadenza; and, without any transition passage, the orchestra announces the second subject, in B flat and 6/4 time.

Ex. 2.

From this arises an allied figure, to which the solo violin adds an important comment in 4/4 time. We shall find that the style of

Sibelius is nowhere more distinguished than in its novel and yet inevitable cross-rhythms.

The violin brings this meditatively to a close in B flat minor, and then the orchestra breaks out grimly with a new theme.

This yields to a gentler strain—

which, however, is punctuated by fierce accents, and ends in a low-pitched crescendo, which leads to a despairing cadence theme.

When this has died slowly away in utter darkness, the violin re-enters and, while the basses continue to hold B flat, changes the key to G minor. An allusion to the main theme (Ex. 1) turns unexpectedly towards A minor, which key is affirmed in an angry gesture from the orchestra. And now the violin plays a highly developed cadenza, modulating widely and working out the main figures of Ex. 1 in an admirable style of extemporization governed by organic life. It returns to G minor, and in that key a recapitulation begins, with the main theme (Ex. 1) in the bassoon. The

violin resumes it with the second phrase. When, at the climax of
this solo, the orchestra intervenes, it is in order to start a new and
impassioned development with rich modulations, the main theme
being welded to a new figure (*x*) which develops a life of its own.

Ex. 7.

At the climax, in B major, trombones thunder out the despairing
notes marked (*f*) in Ex. 6; and then phrases from the middle of the
second subject (Ex. 3) build themselves up, in combination with
the solo violin, reaching a climax of tenderness in the key of D
major, our tonic, which darkens to the minor. The violin solo has
settled into a long trill, beneath which the theme is mournfully
pulsating away. Suddenly there is an uprush of energy, and the
remaining themes (Ex. 4 and 5) enter *in extenso* with a brilliant
counterpoint for the solo violin. The final theme (Ex. 6) gains its
full meaning by the following bold combination with Ex. 1—

Ex. 8.

and thus brings the first movement to an end for which brilliance
is an inadequate term.

The slow movement, after a wistful introduction—

Ex. 9.

settles down to a noble paragraph of melody for the solo violin—

Ex. 10.

When this has come to its close, a dramatic interlude arises from the wistful introductory figure. The following specimen of Eurythmics—

Ex. 11.

shows what Sibelius can make practicable and natural in the way of cross-rhythms.   Both the upper parts are played by the solo violin.

Soon the great main melody returns, this time in the orchestra, the solo violin having fine counterpoint until it resumes the melody in its last phrase; after which a single line of coda suffices.

In less than fifty lines of full score the finale achieves gigantic proportions and brilliant high spirits without banality. The form seems elementary, but the spacing is Handelian; that is to say, there is no means of discovering how it has been achieved.

Only two themes need be quoted; the main or rondo theme— evidently a polonaise for polar bears—

Ex. 12.
Strings.

Drums.

and the second subject, in a rhythm known to Couperin, Bach, and Handel as that of triple-time with the 'hemiole' as in a French courante, but taken by Sibelius at a pace and with a swing alto-gether shocking to the eighteenth-century dancers of courantes. It quibbles upon the distinction between twice three and thrice two; and Sibelius used it steadily throughout the middle movement of his third symphony.

Ex. 13.

With this we can safely leave the finale to dance the listener into Finland, or whatever Fairyland Sibelius will have us attain.

VAUGHAN WILLIAMS

CONCERTO ACCADEMICO, IN D MINOR, FOR VIOLIN AND STRING ORCHESTRA

1 *Allegro pesante.* 2 *Adagio.* 3 *Presto.*

Why *Accademico*? This work is certainly written in no ancient style. Perhaps it is 'academic' in the sense that it is strictly consistent in its own rules; and perhaps the composer wishes to indicate that in his opinion these rules are by this time so well established that they ought to be taught in schools. If such an opinion is correct, I fear that the University of Edinburgh will remain behind the times as long as I am there. It is one thing, and a thing both feasible and necessary, to bring students to understand and enjoy music that would be completely unintelligible to any composer of sixty years ago; it is quite another matter to set about devising exercises in its grammar to students who find the elements of the classical grammar difficult.

If to be academic is to be of crystalline clearness and symmetry, this work is as academic as Mozart or Bach or any classical master, whether he was, like Mozart, abreast of his time, or, like Bach, ninety years behind it and ahead of any assignable future time. Another quality that may be put down to the credit of academic art is consistency of style. Everybody knows that Vaughan Williams is intensely English, that he is an enthusiastic and expert collector of English folk-songs, and that he has learnt much from modern French music in general and from Ravel in particular. But though it may amuse a certain kind of expert to trace these origins in his music, it is quite unnecessary for the intelligent enjoyment of it. He has made a style of his own out of whatever interests him, and no composer is less liable to fall into reminiscences of other music.

So let us listen to this concerto without further prejudice as to what is or is not academic (such as Consecutive Fifths, the Ottava Battuta, the False Relation of the Tritone, and other progressions condemned as licentious by the Great Masters of the Golden Rockstro), and let us also not inquire further into such private affairs as the origins of the composer's ideas. Whatever the origin, the results are true to them, for the results are original. This is no pun, but a statement of fact. The original artist is, as Swift pointed out in *The Battle of the Books*, not the spider whose unpleasant and glutinous web is merely his own unpleasant inside turned outwards, but the bee whose honey is skilfully wrought from its source in the flowers.

The *Concerto Accademico* begins with a spirited ritornello theme—

Ex. 1.

in which the solo violin plays with the orchestra, emerging in a high fifth here and there. Soon the solo makes its official entry with a new theme derived by diminution from the fourth bar (*a*) of the main theme.

Ex. 2.

After a short cadenza Ex. 1 is resumed. With sudden change of key a new theme enters, also derived from (*a*)—

Ex. 3.

and lending itself to decoration by the figure of Ex. 1. An incident in cross-rhythm adds a note of romantic mystery to the Bach-like, imperturbable amble of the whole.

Ex. 4.

Then the figures of Ex. 1 and 2 are developed *seriatim* and combined in new sequences, over which a new theme emerges as a counterpoint in one part after another.

Ex. 5.

This development leads to a recapitulation of the previous themes in the tonic, followed by a coda in which Ex. 4 plays its part.

　　The slow movement is another Bach-like scheme, in which a

solo violoncello joins with the solo violin. The main theme, in a
Dorian G minor—

Ex. 6.

alternates with a 'soft Lydian air' (Ionian or Aeolian, as you may
prefer)—

Ex. 7.

which eventually modulates widely in combination with Ex. 5, and
finally settles in the original Dorian mode.

The finale is a jig, of which the main theme borrows features
from a theme in the opera *Hugh the Drover*.

Ex. 8.

Another tune in triple time combines with this duple jig-measure.

Ex. 9.

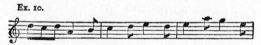

In a kind of Aeolian-Mixolydian dominant key a new jig-theme
forms the second element in a terse binary scheme.

Ex. 10.

Above it a counterpoint is added.

Ex. 11.

The exposition is repeated from the beginning.

The development section adds a new counterpoint—

Ex. 12.

which is afterwards used to weld the recapitulation to the coda, in which three themes are combined (Exs. 9, 11, 12); the Dorian mode giving place to D major, in which key the concerto comes to the quietest and most poetically fantastic and convincing end imaginable.

WALTON

VIOLA CONCERTO IN A MINOR

1 *Andante comodo.* 2 *Vivo, con moto preciso.* 3 *Allegro moderato.*

The style of this work is modern in so far as it could hardly have achieved its present consistency before 1920 (the actual date is 1929); but it does not consist of negatives. Hence it will arouse the anger of many progressive critics and composers in these days of compulsory liberty. Walton's music has tonality, form, melody, themes, and counterpoint. The counterpoint, and hence the harmony, are not always classical. Classical counterpoint is harmony stated in terms of a combination of melodies: classical harmony, when correctly translated from whatever instrumental conditions may have disguised it, is the result of good classical counterpoint where the inner melodic lines are not meant to attract attention. Modern counterpoint tends actually to avoid classical harmony. It prefers that the simultaneous melodies should collide rather than combine; nor does it try to explain away the collisions.

It wishes the simultaneous melodies to be heard; and if they har-
monize classically the combination will not assert itself as such.
Hence modern counterpoint is no longer a technical matter at all;
its new hypothesis has annihilated it as a discipline. But this very
fact has thrown new responsibilities on the composer's imagination.
A technical discipline becomes a set of habits which, like civilization
itself, saves the artist from treating each everyday matter as a new
and separate fundamental problem. The rule-of-thumb contrapuntist need not trouble to imagine the sound of his combination;
his rules and habits assure him that it cannot sound wrong. The
composer who has discarded those rules and habits must use his
imagination for every passage that he writes without their guidance.
It is by no means true that mere haphazard will suit his purpose.
Nor, on the other hand, is it true that any great classical master
used rules as a substitute for his imagination. One of the first
essentials of creative art is the habit of imagining the most familiar
things as vividly as the most surprising. The most revolutionary
art and the most conservative will, if they are both to live, have this
in common, that the artist's imagination shall have penetrated every
part of his work. To an experienced musician every score, primitive, classical, or futurist, will almost at a glance reveal the general
question whether the composer can or cannot use his imagination.
About details I would not be so sure. To the experienced musician
Berlioz has no more business to exist than the giraffe; 'there ain't
no such animal'.

Walton is no Berlioz; a glance at his score will suffice to show an
art that has been learnt as peacefully as any form of scholarship.
And it is possible to read the first twelve bars of this Viola Concerto
carefully without finding anything irreconcilable to an academic
style in the 'nineties. After the twelfth bar the range of style
expands. But let us note that it thereby differs from the many other
modern styles which contract. Walton's style is not sentimental;
but neither is it anti-romantic.

Similarly, it is neither theatrical nor sensational; and its forms
do not at first seem to have more than a slight external resemblance
to sonata forms. Yet it has essential qualities of sonata style in its
ways of getting from one theme to another and in its capacity to
give dramatic meaning to the establishing of a new key. Walton's
dramatic power has asserted itself in oratorio; but its unobtrusive
presence in this thoughtful piece of purely instrumental music is
more significant than any success in an oratorio on the subject of
Belshazzar's feast. The sceptical critic can always argue that an
oratorio, especially on such a subject, can hardly go wrong unless
the librettist's intellect is subnormal. But when a composer can
write an effective concerto for viola (an instrument with a notorious

inferiority complex) and can move in it at something like the pace of a sonata, it is as obvious that he ought to write an opera as that Bruckner, Wagnerian though he was, ought not, and fortunately did not.

The concerto begins with two bars of orchestral introduction which I do not quote, though I shall have to allude to them later. The viola enters with a broad lyric melody in A minor.

Ex. 1.

N.B.

The collision between C sharp in the accompaniment and the C natural in the melody is bold, but it is resolved in the classical way. Nevertheless it is destined to become an unresolved thing in itself and, as such, to be the initial and final motto of the whole work. Accordingly I give this motto here in its tonic position—

Ex. 2.

though its first appearance (during the counterstatement of Ex. 1) is at a high pitch in the course of a sequence that sweeps round a whole enharmonic circle of keys. But the figure soon detaches itself as an individual actor in the drama, and claims derivation from the first two notes of Ex. 1.

What may conveniently be called the second subject (though as my readers know, I have reasons for deprecating the term) first appears in D minor.

Ex. 3.

Its essential feature is the coiling of a sequential figure across the rhythm and across the harmony at every sort of angle. Its transformations are shown in every subsequent cantabile that is not derived from Ex. 1. Another new figure—

Ex. 4.

originates most of the rapid passages in the sequel, and from it, if we wish to use classical terminology, the development may be said to begin. Ex. 1 becomes fierce in an entirely new rhythm—

Ex. 5.

which, sometimes reduced to monotone and ragtime—

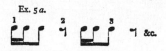

Ex. 5 a.

alternates dramatically with developments of Ex. 3, which steadily grows in beauty and pathos. As the drama unfolds, the motto, Ex. 2, asserts itself. The last phase of the development is introduced when the viola makes its exit with Ex. 4, and the orchestra, entering with Ex. 5 in ominous agitation on the dominant of C sharp minor, rouses itself to tragic passion, and with grand classical breadth works its way round to the home dominant, and so to a pathetic slow decline in which the later figures of the main theme (Ex. 1, the part marked 'N.B.') are heard solemnly augmented.

Over the still reverberating dominant pedal the viola re-enters with a two-part version of the (unquoted) introductory bars, expanded into a short cadenza and leading to the return of Ex. 1. While the viola breaks into a running accompaniment, the melody, softly delivered in a higher octave, makes a single simple statement rounded off with a pathetic cadence, and the viola adds a line of coda alluding to Ex. 3 and ending with the motto, Ex. 2. The whole movement must convince every listener as a masterpiece of form in its freedom and precision, besides showing pathos of a high order.

The middle movement is a lively rondo in E minor with plenty of ragtime rhythms which, unlike those of jazz, are allowed to throw the music out of step, so that the composer has now and then to change the time-signature for one or two bars. The listener need not worry about these changes; an odd bar of 3/4, 3/8, or 5/8 is merely a practical necessity for conductor and players; it happens whenever the composer has found that his groups of 3 or 5 quavers across his 4-quaver bars will land him on a main beat either too soon or too late for his whim. Much has been said in favour of jazz; but jazz, though a composer may be generous in his acknowledge-ment to it, never kept a movement going like this. A list of themes must suffice by way of analysis; letters and figures in the quotations will show a few significant points in the thematic and rhythmic structure. In general scheme the three movements of this concerto agree in the common-sense device of reserving the display of the full orchestra for a penultimate stage in which it can make a big climax, leaving room for a coda in which the solo instrument can deliver its final summary.

Here is the main theme of the scherzo, delivered by the viola, with wood-wind echoes.

Ex. 6.

From its scale-figure (C) many things result; especially a habit of making accompaniments out of bits of scale marching up or down in obstinate little groups of 3, 4, 5, alone, or in 3rds, and always inclined to collide with beat and harmony. The continuation—

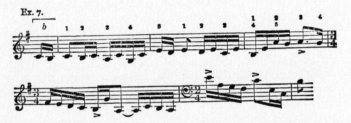

Ex. 7.

arises out of figure (*b*) and shows how the ragtime refuses to explain itself away. Jazz has often lulled me to sleep by its underlying monotony; but Walton's rhythms keep me on the alert.

A transition theme, using a figure akin to (*b*)—

Ex. 8.

leads to the main theme of the first episode.

Ex. 9.

The second episode is the beginning of extensive development, starting in F and modulating widely.

As the 5-note underlying scale and the semiquaver figures show, it lends itself easily to 'conflation' (as the palaeographist would say) with the other themes; and the transition-theme, Ex. 8, appears conspicuously in the sequel. As in the other movements of this concerto, the orchestra eventually arises in its might, bringing the development to its climax, and leading, at its own leisure, to the final return of the main theme in the tonic. The viola resumes its control in the ensuing compound of recapitulation and coda. The movement ends, according to its nature, with Haydnesque abruptness and Bach-like punctuality.

The lyric qualities of the first movement, and its moderate tempo, have already supplied whatever need this work may have for a slow movement. Yet it is a bold stroke to follow so typical a scherzo by a finale which also begins in a manifestly grotesque style which the bassoon and contrafagotto can do nothing to bowdlerize.

But the grotesque is, as Ruskin has defined it, the sublime refracted by terror; and this finale is no joke. In its total effect it is the majestic and pathetic conclusion of a work that is throughout large in all its aspects. The form will explain itself: here is the main figure of the transition theme—

and here is the 'second subject'—

from which an important figure arises.

Later in the movement the viola draws a long line of pathetic cantabile over an ostinato development of the first theme.

This cantabile becomes tragically important before the end of the movement.

Another point that may be quoted is the following combination of Ex. 14 with an augmented version of the main figure of Ex. 11.

When the orchestra, as in the previous movements, gathers up the threads Ex. 11 reveals itself as a purely majestic subject for a fugal stretto, and the listener will soon become convinced that the total import of the work is that of high tragedy. This is wonderfully realized in the coda. What happens at the end is this: the main theme, Ex. 11, has settled into an ostinato in 9/4 time, and over this the viola brings back the lyric melody of the first movement, Ex. 1, with which the concerto ends, not in the same way as the first movement, but with similar Bach-like punctuality.

There are so few concertos for viola that (even if I happened to know any others) it would be a poor compliment to say this was the finest. Any concerto for viola must be a *tour de force*; but this seems to me to be one of the most important modern concertos for any instrument, and I can see no limits to what may be expected of the tone-poet who could create it.

WEBER

CONZERTSTÜCK IN F MINOR FOR PIANOFORTE WITH ORCHESTRA, OP. 79

1 *Larghetto, ma non troppo, leading to* 2 *Allegro passionato, leading to* 3 *Tempo di Marcia, leading to* 4 *Presto assai.*

Weber's *Conzertstück* is the origin of the post-classical concerto form established by Mendelssohn and followed by Saint-Saëns, and by Max Bruch in his best-known violin concerto. No composer since 1850 would deny the full title of concerto to a work of this range. Like Spohr's *Gesangscene* Concerto, it exemplifies the essentially dramatic, not to say operatic, character that underlies, historically and aesthetically, the concerto as an art-form. But Weber is an inveterate illustrator, whose sense of form becomes liveliest when he has a programme to direct it, as in his overtures. And we know, from the testimony of Weber's pupil, Julius Benedict, what the programme of the *Conzertstück* is. It was told to Benedict on the morning of the first performance of *Der Freischütz,* when Weber played to him this newly finished concerto. 'The Châtelaine sits all alone on her balcony gazing far away into the distance.'

Ex. 1.

'Her knight has gone to the Holy Land. Years have passed by: battles have been fought. Is he still alive? Will she ever see him again?

'Her excited imagination—

Ex. 2.

calls up a vision of her husband lying wounded and forsaken on the battle-field. Can she not fly to him and die by his side?

'She falls back unconscious. But hark!

Ex. 3.

'What notes are those in the distance? Over there in the forest something flashes in the moonlight—nearer and nearer. Knights

and squires with the cross of the Crusaders, banners waving,
acclamations of the people! And there—it is he!'

Octave glissando from deep bass G to top C of pianoforte.
'She sinks into his arms' (*con molto fuoco e con leggierezza*).

Ex. 4.

'Love is triumphant. Happiness without end. The very woods
and waves sing the song of love; a thousand voices proclaim his
victory.'

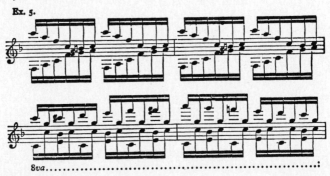

Ex. 5.

Hollywood needs Weber to teach it its business. We cannot do
these things nowadays; the *Conzertstück* puts all later and more
ambitious efforts to shame. Once upon a time it was thought to
be great music. When that delusion was dispelled, we proceeded
to mistake it for bad music. This was a worse, because a snobbish,
delusion. Weber, in all his innocence, has far more kinship with
Beethoven than with his fellow-pupil Meyerbeer; and the nearest
classical parallel to the mood, as well as the 'programme', of his
finale is the finale of Beethoven's *Lebewohl* Sonata. The art of
'registering' emotions is no mean accomplishment, whether it be
achieved at Hollywood in 1931 or at Dresden in 1821. And in that
art Weber never fumbles. He may move awkwardly from one
situation to the next; the stage carpenter may even appear in
shirt-sleeves during the transformation-scenes; but the emotions
are unmistakable and commanding of respect. One exception must

be admitted, though it is not evident in the *Conzertstück*. Weber died young, and his style had not yet become always equal to expressing joy; in moments of jubilation his characters sometimes seem to borrow their rhythms from the poultry-yard. But the finale of the *Conzertstück* does not deserve any such charge. We must go to Beethoven for any deeper glow of joy; and Weber does not here expose himself to any damaging comparison, for he attempts no form on a scale that he cannot perfectly master. The four movements are astonishingly successful in covering the exact ground of their own ideas at such length as leaves each ready to lead to the next. The way in which the end (or rather the debouching) of the Larghetto anticipates the theme of the Allegro (Ex. 2) is as ingenious as any device of Liszt. A few weeping notes of a solitary bassoon indicate the Châtelaine's return to consciousness before the march is heard. These notes are a *locus classicus* for the perfect dramatic use of a special quality of tone. The march itself has a sentimental touch in all its phrases (see the cadence into the fourth bar) that exactly fits the romantic situation. A real march would never do: we want a tapestry march for our tapestry châtelaine. On the modern pianoforte, octave glissandos, especially when upward, are rasping to the finger-nails. But they make admirable screams. As to the finale, I frankly confess that it thrills me. Weber's range of harmony is hardly wider than Gluck's; and when he gets beyond tonic and dominant his changes are really as grand in effect as in intention. As for the pianoforte writing, it conclusively proves Weber to have deserved his reputation as one of the greatest players ever known on any instrument. Every detail of it must have been discovered during extemporization at full speed: there is no other means of guessing that such passages lie well for the hand at all. And yet there are people who try to modernize Weber's pianoforte style! We might as well psycho-analyse his Châtelaine.

CHORAL WORKS

J. S. BACH

MASS IN B MINOR

TEXT

As arranged by Bach (hence slight deviations from the English Prayer Book version). With references to the musical examples.

1. KYRIE

1.

Exx. 1–2. *Chorus.* Kyrie eleison.
Exx. 3–4. *Duet.* Christe eleison.
Exx. 5–8. *Chorus.* Kyrie eleison.

Lord, have mercy upon us.
Christ, have mercy upon us.
Lord, have mercy upon us.

2. GLORIA

2.

Ex. 9. *Chorus.* Gloria in excelsis Deo.

Glory be to God on high,

Ex. 10. *Chorus.* Et in terra pax hominibus bonae voluntatis.

and on earth peace to men of good will.

Ex. 11. *Aria.* Laudamus Te; benedicimus Te; adoramus Te; glorificamus Te:

We praise Thee; we bless Thee; we worship Thee; we glorify Thee:

Exx. 12–14. *Chorus.* Gratias agimus Tibi propter magnam gloriam tuam.

we give thanks to Thee for Thy great glory.

Exx. 15–16. *Duet.* Domine Deus, Rex coelestis, Deus Pater omnipotens; Domine Fili unigenite Jesu Christe altissime! Domine Deus, agnus Dei, Filius Patris!

O Lord God, heavenly King, God the Father Almighty; O Lord the only begotten Son, Jesu Christ, most high; O Lord God, Lamb of God, Son of the Father.

Ex. 17. *Chorus.* Qui tollis peccata mundi, miserere nobis: Qui tollis peccata mundi, suscipe deprecationem nostram:

Thou who takest away the sins of the world, have mercy upon us: Thou who takest away the sins of the world, receive our prayer:

Ex. 18. *Aria.* Qui sedes ad dexteram Patris, miserere nobis:

Thou who sittest at the right hand of the Father, have mercy upon us.

Exx. 19–21. *Aria.* Quoniam Tu solus sanctus, Tu solus Dominus, Tu solus altissimus.

For Thou only art holy; Thou only art Lord; Thou only art most high—

Exx. 22–4. *Chorus.* Cum Sancto Spiritu in gloria Dei Patris. Amen.

with the Holy Spirit in the glory of God the Father. Amen.

3. CREDO

3.

Exx. 25–7. *Chorus.* Credo in unum Deum.

I believe in one God,

Exx. 28–9 *Chorus.* Patrem omnipotentem, factorem coeli et terrae, visibilium omnium et invisibilium:

Exx. 30–1. *Duet.* Et in unum Dominum, Jesum Christum, Filium Dei unigenitum, et ex Patre natum ante omnia saecula: Deum de Deo, lumen de lumine, Deum verum de Deo vero genitum, non factum, consubstantialem Patri, per quem omnia facta sunt;

Qui propter nos homines et propter nostram salutem descendit de coelis:

Ex. 32. *Chorus.* Et incarnatus est de Spiritu Sancto ex Maria Virgine, et homo factus est;

Exx. 33–4. *Chorus.* Crucifixus etiam pro nobis sub Pontio Pilato, passus et sepultus est:

Ex. 35. *Chorus.* Et resurrexit tertia die secundum Scripturas; et ascendit in coelum; sedet ad dexteram Patris, et iterum venturus est cum gloria judicare vivos et mortuos, cujus regni non erit finis;

Ex. 36. *Aria.* Et in Spiritum Sanctum, Dominum et vivificantem, qui ex Patre et Filio procedit, qui cum Patre et Filio simul adoratur et conglorificatur; qui locutus est per Prophetas: Et in unam sanctam catholicam et apostolicam ecclesiam.

Exx. 37–9. *Chorus.* Confiteor unum baptisma in remissionem peccatorum, et exspecto—

Exx. 40–2. *Chorus.* resurrectionem mortuorum, et vitam venturi saeculi. Amen.

The Father omnipotent, Maker of heaven and earth, and of all things visible and invisible:

And in one Lord Jesus Christ, the only begotten Son of God, born of the Father before all worlds: God of God, Light of Light, Very God begotten of Very God,* not created, being of one substance with the Father, by Whom all things were made: Who for us men and for our salvation descended from heaven;

And was incarnate by the Holy Ghost of the Virgin Mary, And was made man,

And was crucified also for us under Pontius Pilate. He suffered and was buried.

And the third day He rose again according to the Scriptures, And ascended into heaven, And sitteth on the right hand of God the Father. And He shall come again with glory to judge both the quick and the dead: Whose kingdom shall have no end.

And I believe in the Holy Ghost, the Lord and Giver of life, Who proceedeth from the Father and the Son, Who with the Father and the Son together is worshipped and glorified, Who spoke by the Prophets: And I believe one Catholic and Apostolic Church.

I acknowledge one Baptism for the remission of sins. And I look for—

the Resurrection of the dead, And the life of the world to come. Amen.

4. SANCTUS

Ex. 43. *Chorus.* Sanctus, sanctus, sanctus, Dominus Deus Sabaoth.

4.

Holy, holy, holy, Lord God of hosts.

* This is according to Bach's punctuation.

Exx. 44–5. *Chorus.* Pleni sunt coeli et terrae gloria ejus.[1]	Heaven and earth are full of His glory.
Exx. 46–9. *Chorus.* Hosanna in excelsis.	Hosanna in the highest.
Aria. Benedictus qui venit in nomine Domini.	Blessed is he that cometh in the name of the Lord.
Hosanna in excelsis, *da capo.*	

5. AGNUS DEI	5
Exx. 50–1. *Aria.* Agnus Dei qui tollis peccata mundi, miserere nobis.	O Lamb of God, Who takest away the sins of the world, have mercy upon us.
Exx. 52–4. *Chorus.* Dona nobis pacem.	Grant us peace.

The Kyrie and Gloria of this enormous work were sent by Bach to the Kurfürst of Saxony in 1733, with a request to be appointed to his court. The request was not granted until 1736. By 1738 Bach had finished the Mass, but he did not send the rest of it to the Kurfürst, though that prince was a Roman Catholic. According to Lutheran usage a Kyrie and Gloria comprised all the music required for a Mass; and Bach's four short Masses contain nothing else. He accordingly had already given the title of Mass to the portion sent to his prince in 1733. He was evidently not encouraged by its reception, and the four short Masses afterwards written for Dresden contain between them only five movements not known to be arrangements, sometimes very perfunctory and sometimes absurdly inappropriate, from Church Cantatas.

In the B minor Mass itself the adaptations from earlier work begin at the *Gratias*, and become more and more frequent as the Mass proceeds. But it would be a hasty inference from this that Bach lost interest in the work. The Agnus Dei is no mere adaptation of the beautiful aria 'Ach bleibe doch' that has the same ritornello in the Cantata *Lobet Gott in seinen Reichen*. The aria in the cantata is longer by three-eighths, and for two-thirds of its entirety different in material. A new composition could not have cost Bach more trouble than the Agnus Dei. And the changes imply no dissatisfaction with the original aria: they are dictated by the altogether different structure of the new text. The theme common to both compositions remains, because it is the right thing in both places.

The case of the *Dona nobis pacem* is less clear. No doctrinal or symbolical reason can be plausibly given for its being set to the same music as the *Gratias*, and there is a manifest artificiality in singing to a single clause a double fugue whose two subjects were originally made for two clauses. Yet even here there is a certain

[1] sic: instead of the liturgical reading *tua*.

fitness in ending with this particular movement. Only in the pure vocal polyphony of the sixteenth century does a Mass end with a natural musical finality. As soon as orchestral ideas heighten the values, the text of this last section of the Mass forms an anti-climax which only Beethoven, with his living memories of the bombardment of Vienna, could turn into something vivid. In the *Gratias* Bach had something at once monumental and quiet, the recurrence of which would round off his Mass without violence to the words, but rather with an expression of confidence that the peace prayed for would be given to those who seek it. And the fact that the music had been heard more than an hour ago serves to perfect its finality.

The other known adaptations in the B minor Mass will be dis-cussed as we come to them. Schweitzer points out that though Bach writes habitually as a Lutheran, there is a vital sense in which he conceives this Mass as Catholic. But it ought not to be necessary to point out that if we criticized it from the point of view of the Roman liturgy we should soon prove that it was wrong from beginning to end. In some respects it is almost drastically Protes-tant; most notably in the Sanctus where Bach is himself beating time to the angels swinging their censers before the Throne, and has entirely forgotten the awe-struck mortals kneeling in silence before the miracle which gives them immortality. But surely the mere scale of the whole work should have sufficed to prevent any-body from imagining that it was part of a church service. Beethoven could have designed his Mass in D for the successive installation of two Royal Archbishops instead of one, if he had been allowed to work on Bach's scale.[1]

Still, we need not add to Bach's inveterate Protestantism the mere errors of a performance that ignores the divisions of the text. Nobody need be a liturgiologist to understand musical settings of the Mass. But what can anybody be expected to under-stand, who, being brought up in a civilization at least officially Christian, does not know where the Nicene Creed ends? Bach

[1] I should have thought this paragraph comprehensive enough to satisfy most people. But it has provoked a surprising amount of protest from critics and private persons who contrast my 'view that Bach shows Protestant tendencies' with the view of Schweitzer and Terry that he is illustrating the Church Universal. The objection seems to be based on two assumptions: first, that 'the ability would warrant' startling supposi-tions as to Bach's church and Shakespeare's race; secondly, that Protes-tants, as such, believe themselves to be cut off from the Church Universal. No such belief is implied in the historic protest that the practices and doctrines of the Roman Church needed reform. Hence the terms Protes-tant and Reformation. It is as indisputable that Bach intended to illustrate the Church Universal as that he also prayed to be 'preserved from the murderous cruelty, cunning, and arrogance of the Pope and the Turk'.

has taken special pains to show that the *Resurrexit* is not the end: yet his final ritornello, which so carefully takes the edge off the climax of that chorus and leaves us calm enough to resume the doctrinal thread, is often omitted. The omission is a sign that the performance has been undertaken without the faintest idea of what Bach meant by the great group which he entitles *Symbolum Nicenum*. Accordingly we must put in the forefront of our conception of the B minor Mass the fact of its division into the five sections (sometimes called Hymns) of all normal Masses: viz. Kyrie, Gloria, Credo, Sanctus, and Agnus Dei. The Gloria usually follows the Kyrie with little or no pause. A considerable pause should, in this huge work, separate the Gloria from the Credo. An even longer pause is convenient between the Credo and the Sanctus; for the chorus has to regroup itself for the six-part Sanctus and the antiphonal double-choir Hosanna.

With these two intervals the work falls into its natural divisions, none of which is inordinately long or devoid of refreshing contrasts.

A word is needed as to the art-forms prevalent in Bach's choral music. Fugue is, of course, prominent. But it is not in itself so much a form as a texture, like blank verse, hexameters, heroic couplets, *terza rima*, &c. A piece written entirely in fugue is, then, properly called 'a fugue'. But parts of other pieces may be written *in* fugue of a strictness equal to that of the fugues that are nothing else. The main formal element of Bach's choruses is not fugue, for that has little power to determine a form, but the ritornello, such as constitutes the opening of nearly all concerto movements and the instrumental openings of arias. Most of these choruses of Bach which are not entirely in fugue will be found to be concerto-like amplifications of an opening ritornello; and in several cases where no such ritornello appears, its existence in an earlier version of the composition can be either verified or inferred.

Now the naïve listener, if endowed with a quick and retentive memory, is more likely to appreciate the way in which Bach uses ritornello than the listener who knows something about fugue. My own experience is that I discovered many relatively unimportant points in the structure of the B minor Mass before I realized the folly of regarding the ritornellos as merely introductory. This error the naïve listener does not commit; for him the music begins at the beginning, and so he has the better chance of recognizing the beginning when it recurs in a higher light. For this reason my musical examples outline some of the ritornellos, actual and conjectural, in full.

The ritornello gives the form of a concerto to the whole, and recurs, entire or in sections, at each important close, in various keys, until it has buttressed all sides of the edifice; while the

fugue-passage corresponds to the special material which the solo
player contributes to the concerto. And in most cases we shall find
that in the first fugue-passage the voices are unsupported by the
orchestra, which either leaves everything to the continuo or has an
independent accompaniment, while in the second fugue-passage
the orchestra doubles the voices. The same principle is seen in the
fugues in the motets for double-chorus; at first one choir sings the
fugue against an independent second choir; afterwards the two
choirs unite, voice by voice, as the subject enters in each part.
Thus with Bach's small choirs the volume of sound regulated
itself. With our large choral societies we have to take care lest this
natural scheme should be obliterated. And our orchestras are in
one sense too small for big choirs; we do not need larger orchestras
on the whole, but we need a dozen oboes and a dozen flutes
instead of twenty-four players of ten different kinds of instrument.
However, there is no harm in throwing clarinets into unison with
the oboes in Bach's tuttis. Not even Berlioz or Mahler knew (as
Handel knew) what twelve oboes would sound like; but we do know
that their tone becomes darker and actually less pungent by multi-
plication; and we also know that the precise colour is not so much
Bach's object as the power of penetrating so that all parts of the
polyphony are heard.

1. KYRIE

The first Kyrie of the B minor Mass is so vast that it seems as
if nothing could control its bulk; yet the listener needs no analysis
to confirm his instinctive impression that it reaches its last note
with an astronomical punctuality. The foundation of this impression is that the form is such as will seem ridiculously simple
when it is correctly described. Helmholtz has prettily illustrated
the capacity of the ear to analyse into component sounds the
inextricable complexities of the waves that reach it. All depends
on the point of view. If you are bathing in the sea you will not
have much success in analysing the corrugations of the wave-
fronts that break over your eyes. But if you are looking down
on Brodick Bay from the shoulder of Goatfell you will be able
to see all the interlockings of waves from wind, tide, steamers,
down to the circles radiating from the diving-bird. Bach's ritornello gives us just such a hill-side view of the wave-system of his
Kyrie. After setting the standard for scale and style in four mighty
introductory bars for full chorus and orchestra, the ritornello
begins. Its theme is a fugue-subject, confined at first to the upper
voices. The whole matter of the ritornello is entrusted to the
wood-wind, oboes d'amore in two parts doubled by flutes, until,
towards the end, the basses enter with the subject. Meanwhile

the strings have accompanied the whole with a beautiful harmonic halo.

Here is the ritornello—

Ex. I.

The voices enter in the next bar. What will they do with this
material? Well, the theme is a fugue-subject; so the five-part
chorus begins with a five-part fugue exposition, which necessarily
coincides with the ritornello for the first five bars. After this, however, it must diverge, so as to lead to the entries of other voices. The
accompaniment is reduced to the two oboes d'amore and the continuo. The last voice to enter is the bass, after an anomalous entry
of the first figures in the second soprano. As the bass finishes, the
second soprano makes a true entry of the whole subject in the
dominant. The orchestra supports this and henceforth the other
entries voice by voice until it is supporting the whole chorus. This
sixth entry proves to be the beginning of a choral recapitulation of
the whole ritornello in the dominant, so that the F sharp minor
cadence in bars 9–10 becomes a close in C sharp minor. In the
episode the voices add entirely new counterpoints to bars 11–14; a
fact which shows the danger of supporting large choirs by small
orchestras; for unless the orchestra can assert itself here, the form
is lost. At the bar corresponding to 15 the voices reunite with
the orchestra and remain reunited until the end of the ritornello.

Now the orchestra has an interlude in which portions of the
theme drift in short sequences through various keys, including
A major, the only major harmonies in the whole movement. Within
eight bars there are four changes of instrumentation. Then the
bass enters in the tonic at extreme depth as the beginning of a
second exposition of the fugue. The orchestral bass necessarily
supports the voice, but the rest of the orchestra is independent,
the strings being also independent of the wind. The fugue rises
from voice to voice, the tenor being unsupported by the orchestra.
But violas support the alto, and violins the first soprano. The last
voice to enter is the second soprano; and by entering in the
subdominant it inclines the harmonic balance of the whole
towards firmly establishing the tonic. The joints of this second
fugue are larger than those of the first, and their rhetorical point
consists in the advancement of the step marked * in Ex. 1. In the
first fugue that step has been pathetically flattened as in Ex. 2 (i).
Now it is heightened as in Ex. 2 (ii) and (iii).

Ex. 2.

The natural result of bringing the fifth entry into the subdominant
is that the sixth entry follows in the tonic. It thereupon initiates
a final choral recapitulation of the whole ritornello. No wonder
this huge movement seems after all to end punctually. Notice
that though this form is so absurdly simple, it is so poised that no
human ear can detect the moments when recapitulation begins.
One fugue entry is exactly like another, and, even when marked
by the support of the orchestra, the sixth entry does not immediately give away its secret. Furthermore, there is all the fine
detail, of which Ex. 2 shows the more obvious points.

The *Christe eleison* is a duet for two sopranos, or soprano and
mezzo. The ritornello, given by all the violins of the orchestra—

is on material in which the singers do not share except for one
passage where they use the figure here marked (*a*). For the rest
they are either warbling in thirds with whole-hearted Italian delight
in physical beauty, inspired by Bach's joy in divine glory—

or else pleading in canon—

The second Kyrie is a strict fugue in F sharp minor, in which
the orchestra supports the voices without any independent part
except in the bass. The subject, with its flat supertonic and
diminished third, has a gravity akin to that of the first Kyrie, but
confidence seems to have become stronger.

The small notes indicate the close stretto (or overlap of subject
and answer) in later stages of this fugue. The voices often cross,

producing contrasts of tone which recall certain subtleties in the
styles of Palestrina and Orlando di Lasso.

Ex. 7.

An important imitative episode—

Ex. 8.

&c.

adds greatly to the energy of the whole, especially as it is never
brought into combination with the main theme.

And so the first division of the Mass ends in F sharp minor
instead of B minor. From this point onwards neither B minor nor
any other minor key is the fundamental key of the Mass. Everything henceforth is grouped about D major.

2. GLORIA

CHORUS.   *Gloria in excelsis Deo.*

Trumpets announce a jubilant ritornello theme beginning
thus—

Ex. 9.

The structure is clear and four-square; nor do the voices obscure
it when they enter and begin it in the tonic in order to lead to
the dominant and, after a short interlude, restate it there. The
completion of a symmetrical design follows, and the movement
closes into something very different but not less joyful. In solemn
sequences the massed voices enter into dialogue with divers
sections of the orchestra in modulations that range over the

darker keys beyond the subdominant, closing into the supertonic
minor. Then the orchestra alone carries the sequences into higher
regions over a deep pedal and eventually closes in B minor. The
figure of these sequences now takes shape as a glorious fugue-
subject announced by the first soprano.

Ex. 10.

et . . in ter - ra pax ho-mi - ni-bus bonae vo-lun-ta - tis

Before the alto enters with the answer the soprano has begun a
florid countersubject, as shown in the quotation. The five voices
enter in an exposition which is quite regular until the fifth entry.
This, in the second soprano, is a note too high, which lands us in
E minor. Thence the initial figure of the first countersubject
(*b*) modulates in dialogue with the orchestra, which had hitherto
been accompanying the fugue with staccato chords. The former
introductory sequences on figure (*a*) of the main theme are now
resumed, while the trumpets watch like the kings who

> sate still with awful eye,
> As if they surely knew their sovran Lord was by.

The sequences drift into the whole theme in the tonic. Soprano
and alto, disengaging themselves from the full chorus, resume
the fugue which is now supported by the orchestra. This time the
fifth entry is in its proper tonic position. The episodic sequences
follow, in stronger and more tonic positions, until two final entries
of the whole subject (alto in dominant, second soprano, and
trumpet in tonic) conclude the movement.

ARIA. *Laudamus te*, for Mezzo-Soprano with Violin Solo.

What Schweitzer calls Bach's joy-motives, both rhythmic and
melodic, abound in this florid air, which almost anticipates Haydn
in its conviction that God will not be angry at being praised
cheerfully.

Ex. 11.

The solo movements in the B minor Mass are particularly varied
in the relation between the voices and the ritornello. Whereas in

the *Christe* the voices were almost entirely independent, here the
singer combines new matter most deftly and unexpectedly with
that of the solo violin. And as there are no middle sections and
da capos in the B minor Mass (unless you count the ritual repetition
of the Hosanna), so there are no miscalculations as to the length of
these things which Bach has to write out in full. The solos end as
punctually as the choruses.

The *Gratias* is a transcription of the first chorus of the cantata
Wir danken dir, Gott written for the Sunday preceding the muni-
cipal elections (Rathswahl) in 1731. As the German text means
precisely the same as the Latin, no doubt can exist as to the fitness
of the music for its present position. The chorus is a strict fugue
in stretto throughout. The orchestra supports the voices (written
in four parts), but the trumpets add a fifth and sometimes a sixth
part. The fugue-subject is one of the oldest in all music.

Ex. 12.

The asterisks mark the points at which answers can overlap. The
second clause, *propter magnam gloriam tuam*, has a theme of its
own—

Ex. 13.

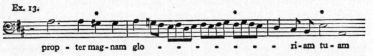

which enters as soon as the bass has taken breath after announcing
the first subject. It is likewise in close stretto. The first subject
is then resumed, with a new rhetorical point in the widening of
its main leap.

Ex. 14.

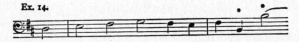

Then the second, or notes to that effect, is combined with it. But
such a combination is not the main business of this fugue, and the
subjects continue to prefer to develop alternately. So, after an
effective counterdevelopment of *propter magnam gloriam* led by
the soprano, the real business begins when no less than thirteen
entries of the first subject, all on tonic and dominant are piled
up without intermission, the trumpets providing the 8th and 9th
entries in extra parts. This I believe to be Bach's record in such
edifices. The nearest approach to this that I can recollect is
a pile of eight overlaps in the first fugue of the Forty-eight.

The second subject reasserts itself after the 13th entry has boomed in the bass, and then a shortened stretto ends the fugue. Small wonder that it should prove a fitting and majestic prayer for peace (why not say peace with honour?) at the end of the Mass.

DUET, for Soprano and Tenor. *Domine Deus.*

The ritornello is for flute in dialogue with muted strings. A later version, in a Latin church cantata (known as Church Cantata No. 191) comprising three numbers of the Gloria (*Gloria in excelsis,* the present movement, and the *Cum Sancto Spiritu*), shows that all the flutes should play. So does the autograph of the Mass.

The voices stand in a novel relation to the ritornello, giving a kind of free augmentation of its theme.

By a happy device each voice sings a different clause; thus already emphasizing the unity of the Father and Son, which is to be more precisely illustrated in the Credo. They interchange parts, so that no word fails to rise to the surface. A middle section in E minor and B minor deals with the clauses *Domine Deus, Agnus Dei, Filius Patris,* and, by its minor tonality and more supplicating tone, prepares for the *Qui tollis.* Bach is undisturbed by the conscientious scruple which in many other works compels him to complete the design by a da capo, sometimes (as in the Cantata *Es erhub sich ein Streit*) even to the detriment of the sense. Whether a movement closes in its own tonic or leads elsewhere, all the single sections of the B minor Mass are subordinate parts of the five great groups. In the Latin cantata this movement is set to the words *Gloria Patri et Filio et Spiritu Sancto* and has no middle section. In the Mass the *Qui tollis* enters on the fourth beat of the last oar of the middle section; a point very inadequately displayed in the Bachgesellschaft edition, but conspicuous in the autograph.

CHORUS. *Qui tollis.*

The *Qui tollis* is a four-part chorus in B minor, in almost strict canon, with two other florid parts, also freely canonic, for flutes.

Ex. 17.

It is an arrangement of the first movement of the Cantata (46) *Schauet doch und sehet*, transposed from D minor and with its sixteen bars of opening ritornello omitted. In the Cantata it leads to a great fugue in quicker time. The appropriateness of the music to its new environment is obvious. What better expression can be found for the burden of the sins of the world than that which was designed for the words 'Behold and see if there be any sorrow like unto My sorrow'?

ARIA, for Alto, with Oboe d'amore. *Qui sedes.*

The words *qui sedes ad dexteram Patris* elicited from Beethoven a tremendous shout, followed by utter collapse. Bach does not here lift his eyes up to the Throne; his prayer arises from its native humility and needs no reminder of the insignificance of man. Widor has finely commented on the delicious notes of the oboe d'amore, and Schweitzer is characteristically illuminating as to the gestures of submission in the theme.

Ex. 18.

ARIA, for Bass, with Horn and Bassoons. *Quoniam tu solus sanctus.*

This aria presents extraordinary difficulties in the management of the continuo; for all the instrumental parts are low, so that the accompaniment must lie for the most part above them. Nothing can be more delicious than the colour of the opening—

Ex. 19.

Corno da Caccia.

Bassoons.

Continuo.

but in the long run it is apt to become indistinct. To disagree
with Schweitzer is dangerously like disagreeing with Bach. But
I have doubts about Schweitzer's suggestion that violoncellos
should join with and sometimes relieve the bassoons, though I
gladly take advantage of a similar device in the *Et in Spiritum
Sanctum* suggested by a note in a strange hand in the autograph.
The bassoon has peculiar acoustic properties. I find that the
violoncello always sounds as a bass to the bassons, even when,
as in bar 3 of Ex. 1, it goes above them. The wind instrument is
more vocal than the stringed, and no voice can ever make a bass to
an instrument. Mozart wrote a sonata for violoncello and bassoon,
and invariably treated the violoncello as the bass, though the
bassoon can go lower. In this *Quoniam* distinctness can be attained
by two precautions. First, the bassoon theme must always be
brought out as a main theme and not treated as an accompaniment.
Secondly, the double-basses must never play with the violoncellos.
The ritornellos may be supported by double-basses without violoncellos, and the vocal passages by violoncellos without double-
basses. The pianoforte (or harpsichord if available) is better for
filling out the harmony here than any stop of the organ. Otherwise Schweitzer relieves a strain on my conscience by his conclusion that Bach required no other keyed instrument than the
organ for his continuo. Nevertheless it is a great convenience to
have something for the purpose that is not a wind instrument.
The voice only dimly alludes to Ex. 19, and derives most of its
material from the next bars.

Ex. 20.

Its own first theme is new.

Ex. 21.

CHORUS. *Cum Sancto Spiritu*

The *Quoniam* closes into the final chorus of the Gloria. I am
as sure as I can be of anything that this is an arrangement of a

lost work, and that voices have been adapted to its opening
ritornello, which I conceive to have originally taken the following
shape—

Ex. 22.

It is much easier to see how the present result could have been
reached by adding voices to the first and later statements of a formal
ritornello-scheme, than to imagine how the scheme thus modified
could have occurred to Bach at all as a direct setting of the words.
Besides, we see the process in all its stages in the last movement of
the Credo. In the Latin cantata Bach carries the evolution of the
Cum Sancto Spiritu a stage farther. Adapting it to the words,
Sicut erat in principio, &c., he is obliged to add a bar, with a new
figure, at symmetrical distances in his ritornello. In the unknown
original chorus, the vocal theme, represented as follows in the
Mass—

Ex. 23.

Cum Sanc-to Spi - ri - tu

was probably identical with figure (*a*) in Ex. 22. From the ritor-
nello-material emerges a very energetic fugue—

Ex. 24.

Cum Sanc-to Spi - - ri - tu in glo - - - -
- - - - - - - ri - a De - i Pa - tris. A - men.

in the treatment of which a salient feature is the frequent anticipation of its subject in other voices a beat before and a beat behind
the real entries. As usual, the first exposition of this fugue is unsupported by the orchestra. In the Mass the accompaniment is
merely the continuo; but in the Latin cantata Bach afterwards
added a most delightful independent accompaniment mainly
derived from the first notes of the fugue theme. This accompaniment ought unquestionably to be used in performances of the
Mass; it greatly enhances the force of the rhythm, it is full of colour,
and it is quintessentially Bach.

As usual, after the ritornello has intervened in other keys, the
fugue is resumed with the voices doubled by the orchestra, until
everything merges into the framework of Ex. 22 beginning at its
fifth bar.

3. CREDO

CHORUS

Gevaert is unquestionably right in saying that, before the chorus
begins the great Mixolydian fugue with which Bach opens his
setting of the Nicene Creed, a bass voice (or voices) should pronounce its immemorial theme on A, as the priest would intone it
in the service of the Mass. The chorus will thus begin with the
answer. The theme is perhaps the most pregnant of all Gregorian
tones, as it obviously ought to be.

Ex. 25.

Cre - do in u - num De - um.

Bach treats it as a seven-part fugue over a bass that is in perpetual motion of steady crotchets such as students practise in the
'third species of counterpoint'—thus once more showing the truth
of the modern poet's dictum that 'All is not false that 's taught in
public schools'. Of the seven parts in the fugue five are vocal,

and the other two are violin parts differing from the vocal ones only in their higher range. Again I find myself unconvinced by Schweitzer's argument that here and in the *Confiteor* the voices ought to be supported by other instruments besides the organ. Within the ritornello choruses it is self-evident that the structure is actually conditioned by the contrast between unsupported fugue-passages and fugue-passages doubled by orchestra; and I can see no reason, except practical makeshift, why such a contrast should not extend to whole movements in juxtaposition. And a movement like this Mixolydian Credo returns to an old practice of Schütz a century earlier. Schütz would have called each of these violin parts a *Vox Instrumentalis*, and would have written the words under it, not without care as to the division of syllables!

Bach discovers in this Gregorian tone many possibilities of stretto, mostly at strange intervals such as the second. The asterisks in Ex. 25 show where answers overlap the subject, and Ex. 26 shows the archetype of the later stretti.

Ex. 26.

The stretti culminate in a blaze of polyphony over an augmentation of the theme in the vocal bass (the orchestral bass never ceases its march in crotchets). Counting one entry in 6ths as double, and counting also those syncopated entries that have to avoid collisions by clipping a note here and there, the other voices and violins give no less than seven entries of the theme while this augmentation is proceeding. Here is a reduction of the whole stretto, divested of the bar-lines which, in the score, lie across the rhythm and so obscure the reader's view.

Ex. 27.

This Mixolydian fugue serves as introduction to another fugue in plain D major and lively rhythm, freely accompanied by the orchestra. In order to follow the previous Mixolydian close this fugue has to begin with its answer—

Ex. 28.

Pa - trem om - ni - po - ten - tem, fac - to - rem coe - li et ter - rae,

which, led by the bass, is masked by shouts of *Credo in unum Deum* from the other voices. The tenor responds with what is the real subject; and from this point the movement is bar for bar identical with the first chorus of the Church Cantata *Gott, wie dein Name* (171). Here is the theme of the cantata, from which may be seen how subtly and skilfully Bach fits his declamation to the matter in hand. The downward 7th on *omnipotentem* is the very reason why that word coheres and sounds powerful; but it originated in a detached top note which exactly gave the syntactical force of 'so'.

Ex. 29.

Gott, wie dein Na - me so   ist auch dein Ruhm bis an die Welt En - de

The orchestra soon merges into the voice-parts, to which a trumpet adds a fifth part, again happily adapting the theme to its own special needs.

Bach does not check the festive energy in order to express any sense of awe at *et invisibilium*. The *piano*, which many editors insert near the end, is doubtless intended to repair the result of Bach's inattention; but you really cannot ask three trumpets and a kettle-drum to express invisibility by hammering a low D with a lively rub-a-Dub-a-dub-a-DUB!

DUET, for Soprano and Alto. *Et in unum Dominum.*

For Bach to write in free canon is no more remarkable than for Milton to write in blank verse. Hence it would have cost him more effort to avoid illustrating than to illustrate, as he does, the unity of the Father and Son by a canonic theme.

Ex. 30.

This 'neither confounds the Persons nor divides the substance', for the figure that is detached in one voice is slurred in the other!

In a footnote to his delightful essay on Handel the late Lord
Balfour gently twits Bach on the quaintness of his symbolism,
and supposes that if the whole Trinity had had to be represented
Bach would have written a canon three in one in the unison.
I cannot at present remember any such illustration of the Trinity by
Bach; but Palestrina's Mass *Sanctorum meritis* is entirely permeated
by a canon three in one in three tenor parts which are displayed
by themselves at *Pleni sunt coeli et terra.* But the canon is not in
the unison; it illustrates the *Filioque* clause, and is in the second
and third, as *'proceeding* from the Father and the Son'. This is all
very quaint, but it does not prevent *Sanctorum meritis* from being
among Palestrina's finest works.

Bach's *Et in unum Dominum* illustrates yet more points. What
is the meaning of this new feature in the strings after the words
de Deo vero?

Ex. 31.

At present, nothing in particular; nor can we find any reason but
the convenience of a musical pattern why these words, together
with *per quem omnia facta sunt*, should be set in a minor key. But
the words beginning with *qui propter nos homines* remind us of
the Divine Love that endured unspeakable sorrows for our salvation,
and so there is no difficulty in seeing why the music here, returning
to the home tonic, closes in the minor mode, almost abruptly and
with deep pathos. And now we find that Ex. 31 means *descendit
de coelis!* So here we have the not uncommon case of a salient
detail the meaning of which does not appear until it is heard for
the second time. The converse case is equally unobjectionable;
if a detail originally illustrated certain precise words, that is no
reason why it should not recur symmetrically when those words
are no longer present—unless, of course, the ideas are incompatible. Now the *Et in unum* movement originally showed this
converse case. As first written it got through the words more
quickly, and had reached *qui propter nos homines* where we now
have *Deum de Deo*, &c. And so *descendit de coelis* was represented
in situ by Ex. 31. Then the present return to G major and minor
was the *Incarnatus*, the second instrumental descent being now
appropriately reminiscent. There is something to be said for
returning to Bach's original distribution of the words and over-
riding his evident conscientious objection to singing the *Incarnatus*
clause in two different settings. But I confess to feeling the force
of Bach's scruple.

CHORUS. *Et incarnatus est.*

It is not surprising that Bach came to think it a mistake to include the *Incarnatus* as a mere final section of this duet. This mistake he promptly repaired by setting this central doctrine to a chorus which for simplicity, depth, and mystery cannot be surpassed, though different achievements (such as Beethoven's) may have equal claims to reverence. A violin figure hovers like the Spirit of God moving on the face of the waters, while the orchestral bass throbs slowly and the voices work out a symmetrical movement on imitative sequences of a simple chord-theme, the bottom note of which is often quite other than what we expect.

Ex. 32.

Et in - car - na - tus est,

CHORUS. *Crucifixus*

The first known mention of this wonderful movement is in a letter from Beethoven to his publisher Tobias Haslinger, asking him for any choruses by Bach that can be procured, especially a *Crucifixus* which is said to be very remarkable and to be founded on 'a *basso ostinato*—like you!' Here Beethoven gives the bass of Bach's *Crucifixus* in F sharp minor, a tone too high. I do not know whether Haslinger was able to send Beethoven the *Crucifixus*; certainly Beethoven never saw the rest of the Mass, nor any of Bach's choral works.

It is evidently a mistake to suppose that any number of such adaptations as this *Crucifixus* could prove that Bach was losing interest in the composition of the B minor Mass. Not all his adaptations are successful or justifiable; but he spent quite as much pains and often as much original inspiration over adaptations as over new works. The original version of the *Crucifixus* is the first chorus of the Cantata *Weinen, Klagen, Sorgen, Zagen* (12), where it is in F minor, and has a middle section without use of the ground-bass. The ground is in minims, which Bach subdivides into crotchets in the Mass, thus producing a more emotional throb. The chromatic descent is Bach's typical motive of grief: it is older than its well-known appearance in Purcell's lament of

Dido, and it is conspicuous in Bach's early *Capriccio on the departure of a beloved brother*.

Ex. 33.

The instrumentation in the Mass is beautified by the antiphonal use of flutes; and a first instrumental statement of the 4-bar ground-period has been added. The voice-parts are hardly altered more than is necessary for the new rhythm of the words. But instead of the final tonic close, Bach is inspired with one of the greatest of all his strokes of genius in the unexpected modulation to G major with a cadence of immeasurable depth.

Ex. 34.

CHORUS. *Et resurrexit*

The resurrection is proclaimed in a phrase of which Schweitzer specially commends the declamation. Nevertheless I believe he would readily entertain the supposition that there is a lost original work behind this chorus. The ritornello I believe to have run more or less as follows:

Ex. 35.

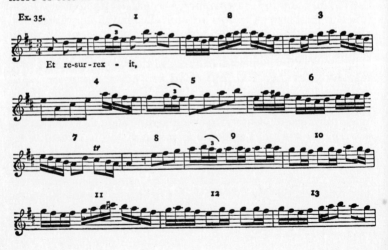

probably longer by 4 bars between 16 and 17

There is no fugue (unless you count a few imitative coloraturas) in this chorus, which perhaps was originally much more formal than it appears now. The passage *et iterum venturus est* I believe to be intended here for a solo voice; and I should expect that the original words would give an excellent reason why this passage was so treated. The autograph is absolutely clear that the accompaniment is *piano*, a nuance which is meaningless here except in relation to a solo voice. As if to give a new musical explanation of the words *non erit finis* Bach concludes with no less than twenty bars of instrumental ritornello, some of it ostentatiously lightly scored. Here again I should expect the original words to show why bars 9–15 of Ex. 35 have hardly any bass. The word *coelum* does not suffice to explain this, for Bach's heaven always rests on a very solid foundation.

I have already given my reasons for considering it a blunder of the first magnitude to omit this ritornello. It is Bach's first step in surmounting the most unmusical part of the Nicene Creed. After we have been stirred to the depths by those miracles of Christianity which all can recognize though none can pretend to understand, we now are asked to find music for the controversial points that were settled at Nicaea by the theologians. For the musician there are several solutions of this really appalling problem. The easiest is to set everything to equally attractive music, as Palestrina set 'Here beginneth the first chapter' and the letters of the Hebrew alphabet, and as Mozart often set all the words of the Mass (including caricatures of the pronunciation of his clerical friends) to equally attractive clichés of opera buffa. The most ingenious method is that by which Beethoven marches to Zion through all these clauses with enthusiastic shouts of 'Credo! Credo!' over the monotone of the lower voices. The most interesting method is that of Ethel Smyth's Mass in D, which is the only Mass I know which might illustrate Manning's aspiration to repair his earlier neglect of the Holy Ghost in his preaching and meditation.

ARIA for Bass. *Et in Spiritum Sanctum*

Bach's method is more definite than Palestrina's, and more decorous than Mozart's; but in essentials it agrees with both these

masters. If doctrine is beyond musical illustration, let us illuminate
it with musical decoration. The ritornello of the *Resurrexit* has
reduced the emotional tension till we are well in the mood to listen
to the most graceful music Bach can give us. Schweitzer regards
the key-word of this aria as *vivificantem*; and his explanation
amply suffices to justify Bach in his ways here. Who could have
thought that the jangle of such Latin as *unam Catholicam et
Apostolicam Ecclesiam* could have produced such music?

Ex. 36.

In the autograph a note in a strange handwriting suggests two solo
violins as an alternative to the two oboes d'amore. I find that great
relief is given to players and listeners by assigning the accompaniment of the vocal passages to the violins and giving the oboes only
the ritornellos, with an occasional overlap.

CHORUS. *Confiteor unum baptisma*

Now we draw towards the real climax of the Creed; that which
concerns our means of salvation. Bach was too severely orthodox
a theologian to dream of concealing the 'acknowledgement of
baptism' perfunctorily beneath shouts of 'credo', as Beethoven
conceals it. The baptism is the means of the remission of sins;
and means and end have each their own theme, first stated separately and afterwards in combination. Here is the combination—

Ex. 37.

Con - fi - te - or, con - fi - - te - or

in re - mis - si - o - - nem pec - ca - to - - rum

Those who are curious in such matters may like to know that this
combination is interchangeable in peculiar ways, viz. at the
11th and 13th, besides the usual inversion at the octave. The
asterisks show the points at which the themes can be answered in

stretto. The orchestral bass is largely independent of the vocal
bass, and moves for the most part in crotchets, but not with the
perpetual movement of the *Credo in unum Deum*. The resources
of the fugue are unfolded steadily. At a certain point the orchestral
bass may be heard to pause on the dominant; without however
interrupting the flow of the fugue, which continues while we
become aware that the text is being declaimed in Gregorian tones
by the vocal bass with the alto in canon. Ex. 37 shows the version
of this in the second Credo as given in the *Liber Usualis* now issued
according to the practice of Solesmes.

Ex. 38.

Con - fi - te - or   u - num bap - tis - ma   in re - mis - si - o - nem pec - ca - to - rum

This differs but slightly from what Bach had before him, which
he represents thus—

Ex. 39.

(*a*) Con - fi - te - or   (*b*) u - num bap - tis - ma

(*c*) in re - mis - si - o - nem   (*d*) pec - ca - to - rum

Then the tenors take it up, not in canon, but with notes of twice
the length. The fugue has not come to the end of its resources
when the tenors have finished. But suddenly a veil of awful
mystery is drawn. Bach's modulations are normally confined to
a narrow range of five very directly related keys. Outside this
there is a large region which Haydn and Beethoven explored
thoroughly, and Beethoven's range extends to a kink in harmonic
space. But when Bach goes outside his narrow range he never
anticipates Beethoven in treating remoter keys as related; he always
heads abruptly to wherever the kink in harmonic space can be
found; in other words, he modulates enharmonically. The veil of
death is not all darkness to the eye of faith; but the light which
shines through it deepens its mystery.

Bach sets the words *Et expecto resurrectionem mortuorum* to slow modulations each one of which comes as a shock to all smaller expectations. In the copy of the Bachgesellschaft score in the Reid Library this page is marked in Oakeley's handwriting with the words 'This might be engraved on Bach's monument'.

The general trend of the modulations follows a more or less continual slow descent of the bass.

CHORUS.   *Et expecto resurrectionem*

Suddenly the expectation rises from awe to rapture, and trumpets proclaim the ascension of ransomed souls. The final chorus of the Credo is another adaptation so ingenious that, although now widely recognized as such, it escaped the notice of several Bachgesellschaft editors, including the one who edited the Cantata *Gott, man lobet Dich in der Stille* (129), of which this chorus was the original number. It was a very formal and festive affair with a square-cut opening ritornello, fully repeated as a closing ritornello, followed by a middle section, and a da capo in full with both ritornellos.

Here is the original ritornello as in the cantata—

Ex. 40.

In the Mass the notation is *alla breve* in bars of half the length. The whole chorus in the Mass takes 105 bars which correspond to 53 of the cantata, or less than twice the ritornello as given in

Ex. 40. Yet Bach has twice inserted 8 new bars, equal, each time, to 4 in the cantata! Clearly then his procedure is extremely terse. Much of the vocal material is new, and the chorus is in five parts instead of four; but the following examples show the two *attacco* themes that have been taken from the cantata and adapted freely to the new words.

And now we learn how to achieve finality. The opening ritornello had been combined with voices and then shortened: the closing ritornello does not exist, though the chorus quotes its last bars (Ex. 40, half-bars 27–28–29). But these it ends quite abruptly with a crotchet, corresponding to a quaver of the original. The finality of the effect is absolute. And with this clear proof that Bach achieved such results with deliberate intention, we may perhaps begin to see the folly of supposing that we can treat him as a formalist.

4. SANCTUS

SIX-PART CHORUS. *Sanctus*

Bach is here conducting the angelic hosts. The strings represent the swinging of censers: the various antiphonal sections of the choir sing to each other like the two seraphim so often represented in the finest sixteenth-century motets for Trinity Sunday on the text that comprises that pious fraud about the Three Witnesses. The threefold 'Trisagion' is well displayed in the theme.

The basses move in giant strides under the mighty sustained
chords and rolling themes of the other voices. The architecture is
not founded on a ritornello, but is more like that of a great arpeggio
prelude, or such a movement as the Organ Toccata in F.

Suddenly the chorus breaks into a new movement in shorter bars.

CHORUS. *Pleni sunt coeli*

This chorus is a fugue with a countersubject that is capable, together with the subject, of being doubled in 3rds.

Ex. 44.

Already near the beginning Bach saves time by bringing on
two voices at once. Such combinations give rise to great variety
of tone-colour according as the themes interlock, or the 3rds
become 6ths, or move wide apart. Here, for example, is a position
with a trumpet in 3rds removed by three octaves from the bass,
while some inner voices move in close 3rds.

Ex. 45.

Another resource is a stretto of the main theme at one bar's
distance. An autograph sketch of the theme in crotchets instead
of quavers shows that the tempo should be majestic.

DOUBLE CHORUS. *Hosanna in excelsis*

The Hosanna follows immediately. It is an eight-part chorus in
double choirs, with the orchestra as a third choir. Bach had just
written it as the opening chorus of an Accession-day Cantata for
His Majesty Augustus of Saxony, who paid him no less than 50
thalers for the whole cantata. Beyond omitting the opening
symphony Bach found few details to alter in turning this into a
Hosanna. The scheme, with voices and instruments entering in
antiphonal song and dance in all manner of groupings, is better
suited to the heavenly hosts than to the poor mortals to whom
Bach was beholden for fifty thalers and a court title. The opening

displays the antiphonal groupings well. It also contains Bach's
only two notes of *genuine* unaccompanied chorus!

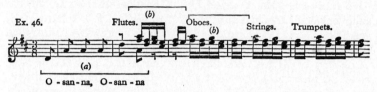

Ex. 46.

Another important theme is treated more or less fugally, and runs
thus—

Ex. 47.

Meanwhile the trumpet-like hosannas continue, in trumpets and
voices; making at one point the following rhetorical climax—

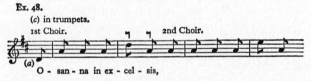

Ex. 48.

One of the rare *pianos* which Bach allows to interrupt his
jubilation greatly enhances the joyousness of the whole by providing an effect of distant echo. Much as I admire the Hosanna, and
perfect as I find it in its place, I can by no means agree with those
critics who see in it the climax of the whole Mass. That position
I would assign to the Sanctus, if such questions were not vexatious.
The Hosanna I regard rather as a deliberate step towards the
anticlimax which is inevitable in every orchestral Mass, and which
therefore must be made artistically intelligible. Moreover, Bach
himself wishes to proceed to the Benedictus, and he therefore
retains the final ritornello of the Hosanna though he had deprived
it of the introductory one. Before the Benedictus, then, this
ritornello should be retained. After the Benedictus the Hosanna
is to be repeated. This, perhaps, is a liturgical rather than a
musical necessity. But if the Hosanna is repeated, then its effect
need not again be weakened by this final ritornello.

ARIA for Tenor. *Benedictus*

Schweitzer finds the declamation of the Benedictus rather
artificial, and suspects it of being another adaptation from a lost
original. I have heard the voice-part sung too beautifully to leave

any trace of artificiality in its declamation. There is no clue as to
what the accompanying instrument should be. No one seems to
have questioned the decision of the Bachgesellschaft editor that
such beautiful music must be for the violin. But I have grave
suspicions of violin music that never goes below the compass of
the flute, and I do not see any unmistakable violin figure in it,
while any of Bach's slow flute solos in minor keys will present
constant resemblance to its turns of phrase. Here is its theme,
which begins violinistically enough, but is not even there unlike
flute music, while the violin character soon disappears. Modern
prejudice is sceptical of the flute as an emotional instrument; but
this music expresses far more on the flute than on the violin.

Ex. 49.

V. AGNUS DEI

ARIA for Alto. *Agnus Dei*

Of the Agnus Dei in relation to its origin I have already spoken.
Here is its main theme with indications in small notes where the
cantata version differs—

Ex. 50.

And here is the new theme with which the voice begins—

Ex. 51.

Bach shows no consciousness that the Agnus Dei is properly a
threefold petition, twice with *miserere nobis*, and the third time
with *Dona nobis pacem*.

CHORUS. *Dona nobis pacem = Gratias agimus tibi*, &c.

Listen to this for its own sake, and you will find it a worthy and
peaceful close to Bach's Mass in honour of the Divine Glory.

MAGNIFICAT

1. *Chorus.* Magnificat anima mea Dominum.
2. *Aria* (Soprano II). Et exsultavit spiritus meus in Deo salutari meo.
3. *Aria* (Soprano I). Quia respexit humilitatem ancillae suae: ecce enim ex hoc beatam me dicent—
4. *Chorus.*—omnes generationes.
5. *Aria* (Bass). Quia fecit mihi magna qui potens est: et sanctum nomen ejus.
6. *Duet* (Alto and Tenor). Et misericordia ejus a progenie in progenies timentibus eum.
7. *Chorus.* Fecit potentiam in brachio suo: dispersit superbos mente cordis sui.
8. *Aria* (Tenor). Deposuit potentes de sede, et exaltavit humiles.
9. *Aria* (Alto). Esurientes implevit bonis: et divites dimisit inanes.
10. *Trio* or *Semi-chorus* (Soprano I, II, and Alto). Suscepit Israel puerum suum, recordatus misericordiae suae.
11. *Chorus.* Sicut locutus est ad patres nostros: Abraham et semini ejus in saecula.
12. *Chorus.* Gloria Patri, et Filio, et Spiritui Sancto: sicut erat in principio, et nunc, et semper, et in saecula saeculorum. Amen.

Bach's *Magnificat* is one of his most comprehensively representative works. From it almost any point in Bach's treatment of words, of musical forms, and of instruments can be brilliantly illustrated. Opinions may differ as to whether it is a representative setting of the Song of the Virgin Mary, or whether that question is important to Bach-lovers. One of the greatest of these, my beloved master Hubert Parry, complained almost angrily that there is nothing feminine in it. On the other hand, a not less impassioned Bach-lover, Widor, quotes the aria *Quia respexit* as a perfect example of the exquisite femininity of the oboe d'amore, inspired by Bach's treatment of the words. And perhaps Bach's defence would be that in setting each verse as a complete sound-picture, he cannot be limited by the consciousness that the words were first pronounced by a woman.

Certainly a feminine treatment of 'He hath shewed strength with His arm' would be disastrous on a large scale. Parry, setting the *Magnificat* as a single design, can retain throughout these words the note of the Virgin adoring the remote power as well as the intimate mercy. In other words, Parry can dramatize the whole text in such a way as to relegate the illustration of its details to a subordinate place.

It is therefore beside the mark to complain that Bach forgets that it was a woman who first sang the words that he illustrates according to their substance. Where the substance and subject are feminine, as in *Quia respexit humilitatem ancillae suae*, he is feminine enough; and it is no mere coincidence that the first words of the whole work are given to the sopranos and altos. Nor is it without conscious purpose that the aria, *Et exsultavit*, as well as the *Quia respexit*, is for a soprano voice. And nobody can mistake the purpose of the stupendous chorus, *Omnes generationes*. The more we emphasize the weight of that chorus, the more deeply do we feel moved at the thought of the innocent singer whom all generations call blessed. With this chorus Bach passes, by a stroke of something akin to dramatic genius, beyond the range of dramatization; and, as if to emphasize this, he sets the next words ('for He that is mighty hath magnified me'—*fecit mihi magna*: 'hath done great things for me') as an aria for a bass voice. One reason for this is that he happened to have five solo singers who each required an aria: another reason is that the aspect of the text that he is illustrating is that of '*qui potens est*'.

It will now be convenient to describe the work theme by theme. As Bach's *Magnificat* is an original work, with no antecedents set to other texts, we shall find Bach's musical symbolism here in its quaintest and most powerful forms. Bach took it for granted, and did not attach to it anything like the importance it is apt to assume in the minds of readers who learn of its rediscovery to-day. Good music was to him a thing that could be used to any good new purpose, regardless of what its details may have symbolized in their first setting. When Hercules had to choose between Pleasure and Virtue, the presumption was that the pleasures of a demigod would not be less refined than those of the Duke for whom Bach was writing a birthday cantata; and so the song of Pleasure enticing Hercules away from the strenuous pursuit of Virtue could serve for the cradle-song of the Virgin in the *Christmas Oratorio*. Sometimes Bach thinks fit to add new symbols, but he seldom troubles to remove old ones merely because they no longer happen to illustrate the words. His symbolism therefore does not relieve us of the task of interpreting his forms as pure music: on the contrary, it is apt to mislead critics who are not strong in their grasp of musical form.

1. *Chorus*. (My soul doth magnify the Lord.)

In the *Magnificat* we see very clearly a treatment of words on a method often found in Bach's choruses. First there is a main theme by which the words are stretched out in coloratura. Then, before our up-to-date critics have time to point out that coloratura is unrealistic, another theme appears in the natural rhythm of the words, and pervades the rest of the design.

Overleaf is given the unquestionably feminine coloratura with which the sopranos and altos begin—

Ex. 1.

Mag - - - - - ni - fi - cat

And here is the natural rhythm of the first word:

Ex. 2.

Mag - ni - fi - cat

But there is a third and equally important theme which does not immediately explain itself.

Ex. 3.

Mag - - - - ni - fi - cat

If it had no other purpose, it would justify its existence at the present day as a drastic refutation of the heresy that Bach's long phrases are to be sung or blown without change of breath. This heresy is the ruin of just the best and most enterprising class of chorus-singers. And it is quite unnecessary. When I first met that exquisite artist the late Louis Fleury, he astonished me by playing the greatest of Bach's flute sonatas with a phrasing as free as that of the finest violinists. When I asked him how he managed never to chop up the phrases he answered 'by taking breath very often'. The more often breath is taken the quicker it can be snatched. I never could detect when Fleury took breath. And, long before such a consummation is attained, the listener will find that a slight hiatus after each accented beat (not before) almost immediately ceases to attract attention. On the other hand, nothing can remedy the loss of tone towards the end of a phrase that is too long for the breath. So, if you object to Bach's way of singing 'ma-ha-ha-ha-ha-ha-ha-ha-ha-ha-gnificat', kindly extend your objection to all coloratura-singing whatever, and to all things in eighteenth-century music that would not occur spontaneously to a musician whose range extended only from *Elijah* to *Götterdämmerung*.

The further purport of Ex. 3 will not appear until much later. Meanwhile, let us consider the form of this opening chorus. Like most of those florid choruses of Bach that are not fugues (and like some that are) it is a concerto in which the chorus-voices play the part of the solo-instrument. (Bach once turned a movement of the first Brandenburg Concerto into a chorus, the whole vocal mass corresponding to the solo violin.) Accordingly the themes are all grouped into a rounded orchestral paragraph of thirty bars. The voices repeat the first half of this in their own style, up to the middle close in the dominant. For the second part they substitute a new development, which covers a wider range of key, but is hardly longer than the original second part. When the voices have come to a close in the tonic, the orchestra repeats the last sixteen bars of its paragraph.

Bach's ways of ending a movement form an important subject in musical aesthetics. A final orchestral ritornello is used by him for the express purpose of destroying finality by giving a formal anticlimax to a chorus that would otherwise eclipse what is to follow. Thus in the B minor Mass it is a great mistake to omit the cool ritornello which Bach has so carefully put at the end of the *Et resurrexit*. In spite of its enormous expansion by the treatment of every clause as a separate movement, the Nicene Creed is for Bach, as for all orthodox Christians, a single thing. Finality comes, not after the Resurrection, not even after the Last Judgement, but when the Amen has been sung to the expectation of the life of the world to come. And Bach's most solemn finality is always simply punctual; sometimes to the verge of abruptness, but never otherwise than at the exact end of a melodic phrase. Supplementary chords filling an architectural space apart from formal melody are necessary in a later symphonic and dramatic music which will sound either epigrammatic or archaic if it is deprived of them; but they are inconceivable in Bach's art. If a chorus ends without an orchestral ritornello the voices will still end in the very terms of the ritornello. The only question is whether Bach will see cause, as in this opening chorus, to let the orchestra recapitulate the last paragraph. Apart from this, Bach's last chords, vocal or instrumental, are always written with deliberate purpose as to their length. We find quite short final chords with rests to finish the bar, and a pause clearly placed over the rest instead of over the chord. We find chords that complete or fill the last bar without pause, or with a pause over the double-bar instead of over the chord. Lastly, we find the familiar Handelian pause on a long final chord; but rarely except in fugal choruses where the orchestra is merely supporting the voices. The grand Handelian adagio cadence I cannot remember to have found in any of Bach's choral works, though something like it occurs at the end of his toccatas, and once, very impressively at the end of the first movement of the C major Double Concerto. Ah!—but was I not forgetting '*mente cordis sui*' in this very work? Well, that is rather another story. The rhetoric may be Handelian; indeed, what good rhetoric is not? But here instead of the quintessential expectedness of Handel's adagio cadence, we have something very unexpected indeed. We do not even know what key the whole movement is in until the last moment.

The first chorus has ended with its orchestral ritornello, to which we will *not* add the emergency-brake ritardando which is often supposed to be the only correct way to produce Bach's full closes.

The last chord is short, and Bach puts his pause on a subsequent rest.

2. *Aria.* (And my spirit hath rejoiced in God my Saviour.)

The aria *Et exsultavit* is terse, like all the movements in this highly concentrated work. The orchestra sums it up in the first twelve bars.

Ex. 4.

There is an early version of Bach's *Magnificat* in which some other church songs were inserted, some in German, some in Latin. After this aria came a figured chorale, *Vom Himmel hoch da komm ich her*, one of the very few movements in which Bach, writing ostensibly for unaccompanied chorus, does not show that he is really relying all the time on a sixteen-foot organ bass. The interpolated numbers are well worth performing; but this can be done without making them interrupt the *Magnificat*, which Bach evidently preferred to keep in its integrity.

3. *Aria.* (For He hath regarded the lowliness of his handmaiden: for behold from henceforth . . . shall call me blessed—)

4. *Chorus.* (—all generations.)

Widor's favourite illustration of the modest femininity of the oboe d'amore sums up the first part of the aria *Quia respexit*.

Ex. 5.
Adagio.

It does not sum up the whole; for there is a new tone in the voice-part at *ecce enim ex hoc beatam me dicent*; though the oboe d'amore still accompanies this with the old material. The voice does not quite reach the end of the sentence. This is taken out of the singer's mouth by all the generations that are calling the Virgin blessed while the millennia unroll.

Ex. 6.

om-nes, om-nes gen-e - ra-ti-o - - - nes

I see no ground, either in tradition or in the musical sense, for
the prevalent custom of taking this as a quick movement, or even
as one appreciably faster than the aria of which it finishes the words.
Be this as it may, nothing need prevent the listener from enjoying
the rhetorical points by which Bach keeps the impression of inexhaustible multitude always augmenting. First the theme is given
in normal tonic and dominant positions, until, in the first four bars,
all the five chorus-parts have had it. Then the voices take it in
steps rising up the scale at half-bar distances. Ignoring changes
of octave as the theme alternates between male and female voices,
the steps are: F sharp: G sharp: A, B, C sharp: D, E, F sharp:
with a close in A major. Then the voices enter at intervals of
fourths and fifths so contrived as to drift through several keys.
When the dominant of the key of the movement is reached, we
soon become aware that another scale of rising entries is in progress.
This time it has ten steps: G sharp: A, B, C sharp: D, E, F sharp:
G sharp: A, B sharp, leading to a close in the dominant. Then the
voices concentrate their entries on to the one note of the dominant
and gather into a pause thereon. After this all the voices, except
the bass, deliver the rhythm of the theme in full harmony, the bass
entering with the theme itself half a bar later; upon which an
answer in the sopranos brings this tale of generations to an end
which symbolizes things not ended here and now.

5. *Aria.* (For He that is mighty hath magnified me: and holy
is His name.)

Inspired, as has already been said, by the words *qui potens est*,
Bach sets this as an aria for a bass voice. The accompaniment is for
continuo alone, and we do not even possess a figured bass to tell
us what harmony Bach intends for the superstructure. The common sense of the matter begins with the plain fact that when Bach
writes an aria with a merely continuo-bass accompaniment, that
bass will, wherever it stands alone without the voice, constitute
a main theme in itself. Yet, not only do many commentators
express the utmost bewilderment at the 'incompleteness' of Bach's
finest continuo-arias, but, conversely, an editor of one of the later
Bachgesellschaft volumes has gravely printed an aria in which the
bass is obviously a mere bass without the smallest pretensions to
a sense of its own; and has let this pass without any hint that
something is missing. In the *Magnificat* nothing is missing except

the figures, and this lacuna is not unusual in eighteenth-century manuscripts.

This aria is not only a continuo-aria, but it is almost entirely confined to a ground bass which is diversified here and there by little interludes that enable it to change its key. The unwritten superstructure should be smooth; and there are places where it is difficult to find a good construction, in the absence of any help from figures. But it cannot be too simple in its effect; and the bare bass is at all events a main theme which is as fit to stand alone as any other specimen of Bach's glorious 'one-part counterpoint'.

Ex. 7.

In the earlier version a lively figured Chorale, *Freut euch und iubilirt*, follows here.

6. *Duet.* (And His mercy is on them that fear Him, throughout all generations.)

An orchestra of muted strings, with flutes in unison with the violins, gives the gist of this movement in the first four bars.

Ex. 8.

The voices bring a new figure at the words *timentibus eum*; and at the end Bach actually gives a slow vibrato—

to the tenor on the word *timentibus*.

7. *Chorus.* (He hath shewed strength with His arm: He hath scattered the proud in the imagination of His heart) [*sic*: 'mente cordis sui', and not in agreement with '*superbos*'.]

Starting on the subdominant side of G major, this chorus gradually reaches the dominant side of D and passes beyond it, until it is brought to a surprising end, reaching its final D major from a distance. A coloratura theme uproots the mountains (figure (*a*)), and brandishes a mighty fist (*b*)—

Fe-cit po-ten - - - - - - - - - - - - - - - - -

- - - - ti-am in bra - chi-o su-o

while other voices and antiphonal groups in the orchestra give the
natural rhythm of the words—

Ex. 10.

Fe-cit po-ten - ti-am

and the foundations quake unceasingly.

Ex. 11.

The coloratura theme rises in fugue through all the five voices,
and is then taken up by one of Bach's shrill agile trumpets. Meanwhile the chorus is mentioning a particular exercise of the Divine
might. '*Dispersit, dispersit, dispersit . . .*' What, or whom? Nothing
of importance. The chorus, accustomed to repeat important words
until fugues have run their course, merely mentions the *superbos* in
one derisive shout. The earthquake is over, and the sun scatters
the clouds. When the heart of God imagines the proud dispersed,
they are dispersed beyond our reckoning. (Bach, following the
reading *sui*, is in agreement with the practice of all the liturgical
composers. The Greek Testament is unmistakably in agreement
with our Prayer Book as well as our Authorized Version, in reading
'their hearts'. But this reading would hardly have given Bach the
opportunity for so grand a change at this point.) In the early version a short Latin *Gloria in excelsis* follows here.

8. *Aria.* (He hath put down the mighty from their seat: and
hath exalted the humble and meek.)

The opening ritornello gives a general idea of the mood of this
aria—

Ex. 12.

but the detailed symbolism appears when the voice enters; the
violins (the whole body in unison) illustrating *deposuit* thus—

Ex. 13.

while the tenor, as in Handel's 'Every valley', illustrates *exaltavit*
by long rising coloraturas.

9. *Aria*. (He hath filled the hungry with good things: and the
rich He hath sent empty away.)

Symbolism is at its quaintest in this delightful aria, which ends
with a downright practical joke when the flutes omit the resolution
of their penultimate notes. The writers of the printed continuo-
fillings are desperately afraid of this child-like trait, and they all
try to make the continuo contradict it. But may we not ask in all
reverence whether this childlike humour does not actually belong
to the words? The dethronement of the mighty is a serious matter,
which the humble will regard with awe in the midst of their own
exaltation. But it is no such tragedy for the rich to be sent empty
away while the hungry are filled with good things. There would
be something dangerously like malice if there were no humour in
the zest with which the Psalmist says that the Lord has prepared
a table 'for me in the presence of mine enemies'. Anyhow, Bach
does not seem to suppose that the rich have any worse fate than to
be sent empty away in respect of their having asked for more than
they already possess. This aria expresses the delight of the hungry
in the good things. To the rich it only says, 'This is not for you!'

Ex. 14.

In the early version a Latin duet, *Virga Jesse*, is intended to
follow here, but is left unfinished. A complete German version
of it is found in one of the Cantatas.

10. *Trio* or *Semi-chorus*. (He remembering His mercy hath
holpen His servant Israel.)

There is no evidence to show whether this is a trio or a chorus.
Bach's solo singers were members of the choir, so that he did not
need to specify such details in unpublished works that were always
performed under his own direction. I greatly prefer a choral performance of this highly imaginative movement. While the feminine
voices weave a flowing texture in close polyphony above a bass of
high violoncellos, the oboes (tutti in unison) play an old Canto

Fermo used for German settings of the *Magnificat* ('*Meine Seel'*
erhebt den Herrn')—

EX. 15.

[Mei - ne   Seel'   er - hebt   den   Her • ren: &c.

Mozart uses this in his Requiem at the words beginning *Te decet
hymnus*.

11. *Chorus.* (As He promised to our forefathers, Abraham and
his seed for ever.)

Ex. 16.

Si - cut lo - cu - - tus est ad pa - tres nos - tros,

A not uncommon mistake in criticism is that of treating a
classical composer as if he were a candidate for a musical degree.
If a student writes a fugue in which the subject is invariably so
harmonized as to make a full close, and the answer invariably
enters on a unison with the last note of the subject, it is very
unlikely that the examiners, whether internal or external, will suppose that the student knows much about fugues. For no other
reason than this so great a Bach-lover as Spitta thought that the
G sharp minor Fugue in the first book of the 48 must be an early
work, though it is one of the maturest and most beautiful things in
the whole collection. Two important facts about full closes are
involved here. First, beginners have to begin by mastering full
closes because they can do nothing else. Secondly, full closes, if
at short and regular distances, will chop up the style and destroy
the sense of movement. Very well then; the full closes in this
Sicut locutus chop up the style and destroy the sense of movement.
To which Bach is able to add 'Quod erat faciendum'. Each movement in this *Magnificat* has been wonderfully terse; and each has
been independent of the rest in all but the common ground of
harmonious contrast. And now all these independent pieces are to
be rounded off as parts of a single whole, and rounded off in an
astonishingly short, almost abrupt, though perfectly final way.
As we listen to the stiff little periods of this simple fugue we feel
a new sense of leisure, and we enjoy its sonorous euphony, which

would satisfy even an examiner. Moreover this stodgy style does take up a certain amount of time, which passes very pleasantly. Only the organ and the basses support the chorus. At the end there is an effective climax, with a chain of suspensions in the treble, and the music draws a longer breath before finally closing with another regular period.

12. *Chorus.* (Glory be to the Father, and to the Son, and to the Holy Ghost: as it was in the beginning, is now, and ever shall be, world without end, Amen.)

After that rigid little fugue, anything in a more free rhythm would sound big. And the opening of the Gloria sounds gigantic. First, on the dominant of D there is a mighty shout of the word *Gloria* in its natural rhythm, in which the whole orchestra takes part. Then, over a deep organ pedal-note, the voices arise swarming in coloratura. With each clause the process is repeated and developed. Like Browning's Spanish monk, Bach frustrates the Arian in three sips, putting the words together in this form: *Gloria Patri; Gloria Filio; Gloria et Spiritui Sancto.*

All this makes a magnificent introduction—to what? It takes time, but it covers only introductory ground. There is only one thing big enough to follow it, and well enough prepared by its antecedents to be heard without fatigue; and that is the whole *Magnificat!* Fortunately the beginning may stand for the whole. Bach finishes in two-thirds of a minute; and now at last we learn the meaning of Ex. 3. The text is built up as in the previous verse; *sicut erat in principio; in principio et nunc; nunc et semper et in saecula; et in saecula saeculorum. Amen.* The coloratura of Ex. 1 makes a grand climax in the bass on the word '*saeculorum*'; and the precise meaning of Ex. 3 is 'as it was in the beginning'.

Ex. 17.

Si-cut er - at in prin - ci - pi - o

BEETHOVEN

CHORAL FANTASIA, OP. 80

1 *Adagio.* (Pianoforte Solo.) C minor.
2 FINALE: *Allegro* (Introductory dialogue with orchestra).
3 *Meno allegro.* C major (Statement of theme, with group of variations and coda).
4 *Molto allegro.* C minor (Variation followed by development).
5 *Adagio.* A major (Slow variation with coda), *leading to*
6 *Alla Marcia: assai vivace.* F major (Variation followed by development).

7 *Allegro*. C minor (the first introductory dialogue resumed).
8 *Allegretto moderato quasi Andante con moto*. C major (Vocal statement
   of the theme to a poem by Kuffner).
9 *Presto* (Coda).

There are certain works of Beethoven that seem foreign to his
style; yet they are historically among the landmarks in his art.
They are the works in which he is really breaking fresh ground.
The great works which fully reveal his conquests come later, and
show no more violence than these almost quaintly conciliatory
forerunners which legitimate his claims. The Choral Fantasia is
the herald, many years in advance, of the Choral Symphony. It
is in a light vein which admits of little cadenzas in a style Beethoven
had elsewhere long ago regarded as inadmissible, except perhaps
when he was extemporizing. It has also a touch of the insolent
bravado of an 'academic' masterpiece: and if we ask how the
result can be anything but insufferable, we shall soon find where
Beethoven's spirit parts company with 'academicism'. It is just
because the mood is naïvely gay and the form conspicuously
new that the result is so delightful as to put to shame the long
faces which solemn Beethoven-lovers sometimes pull over such
lapses. The insolence of 'academicism' is always standing on
its dignity, and its forms are neither new nor old, but purely
diplomatic.

A glance at the list of movements given above will make the
plan of Beethoven's work clear. The introductory pianoforte solo
is the finest written record we have (except one cadenza to the
early C major Concerto) of what Beethoven's manner must have
been in one of his many styles of extempore playing. It was not
written down until long after the disastrous first performance of
the work.[1]

The orchestra enters with the tread of conspirators; then there
are horn-calls, with oboe echoes, in a rhythmic figure that foreshadows figure (*a*) of the theme, which the pianoforte states in full.

Ex. 1.

[1] December 22, 1808, in a hall where the heating apparatus failed and
the orchestra broke down in the A major adagio. The Fantasia came at
the end of a programme in which the Fifth and Sixth Symphonies, the
Fourth Concerto, an aria, and about half of the C major Mass were performed, all for the first time! Beethoven also extemporized another
fantasia (possibly op. 77) as well as the introduction to this work. The
concert can hardly have taken less than 3½ hours.

Few things in Beethoven's art are more curious than the family likeness of this soft-limbed, childlike tune (an earlier song of Beethoven's) to that consummation of manhood in melody, the choral theme of the Ninth Symphony. The comparison, as the present statement and group of variations get more and more playful, is so quaint as to inspire affection for the Fantasia rather than contempt. Why should one not feel kindly to the child who is father to such a man? The plan of the work obviously follows the lines of an ode to St. Cecilia: the characters of various instruments and groups (the flute, oboe, clarinet, and bassoon, and solo string-quartet) are exhibited in turn, and then various styles of music are passed in review on a larger scale. But first the full orchestra bursts out with the theme, and appends to it a codetta—

which has the same function as the similar codetta at just the same point in the Ninth Symphony. The pianoforte takes it up and soars aloft into a cheerful cadenza from which it bursts into a violent temper with the variation in C minor (molto allegro 2/2). To this it appends a cadence-phrase on the harmonic lines of the codetta, and continues it in a gradual modulation to a very distant key, where it begins another variation of the theme. Three bars (5, 6, 7) of this are promptly taken up by the violins in a gently ruminating passage in three-bar rhythm, which suddenly flares up in A minor and eventually leads to the adagio variation in A major 6/8 (in dialogue with clarinets), gentle, pleading, and ornate. Here, too, the codetta is used to bring about the slow dramatic change to the March, in F major.

The March-variation is again followed by a codetta phrase; and then comes a passage of great poetic power, in which the pianoforte moves in a dream of solemn concords, while pizzicato strings in subdued agitation feel for the first notes of the theme (figure (a)). Suddenly there is a crash: the orchestral introduction is resumed, and leads to the return of the original theme, a little slower. Solo voices bring it in, with the following poem, which the chorus takes up at the third stanza. The codetta follows ('receive the gifts of Art divine') and leads to triumphant final developments.

> Soft and sweet thro' ether winging
> Sound the harmonies of life;
> Their immortal flowers springing
> Where the soul is free from strife.

Peace and joy are sweetly blended,
Like the waves' alternate play;
What for mastery contended
Learns to yield and to obey.

When on Music's mighty pinion
Souls of men to heaven rise,
Then doth vanish earth's dominion,
Man is native to the skies.

Calm without and joy within us
Is the bliss for which we long,
If of Art the magic win us,
Joy and calm are turned to song.

With its tide of joy unbroken
Music's flood our life surrounds;
What a master mind hath spoken
Through eternity resounds.

Oh! receive, ye joy-invited,
All the gifts of Art divine:
When to love is power united
Music makes the Gods benign.

MISSA SOLEMNIS, FOR CHORUS AND ORCHESTRA (OP. 123)

I

Kyrie eleison [Ex. 1, 2].
Christe eleison [Ex. 3].
Kyrie eleison [Ex. 1, 2].

English Prayer-book version.
Lord, have mercy upon us.
Christ, have mercy upon us.
Lord, have mercy upon us.

II

Gloria in excelsis Deo [Ex. 4].
Et in terra pax hominibus bonae voluntatis.

Laudamus te [Ex. 4], benedicimus te, adoramus te, glorificamus te; gratias agimus tibi propter magnam gloriam tuam [Ex. 5]; Domine Deus [Ex. 4], Rex coelestis, Deus pater omnipotens.

Domine fili unigenite [Ex. 4 *transformed*] Jesu Christe; Domine Deus agnus Dei, filius Patris;

Glory be to God on high, and in earth peace, good will towards men.[1] We praise thee, we bless thee, we worship thee, we glorify thee, we give thanks to thee for thy great glory, O Lord God, heavenly King, God the Father Almighty.

O Lord, the only-begotten Son Jesu Christ; O Lord God, Lamb of God, Son of the Father, that takest away the sins of the world, have mercy upon us. Thou that

[1] The Latin reading means, of course, 'peace to men of good will'.

Qui tollis peccata mundi, miserere nobis [Ex. 6]. Qui tollis peccata mundi suscipe deprecationem nostram. Qui sedes ad dexteram Patris, miserere nobis;

Quoniam tu solus sanctus [Ex. 7], tu solus Dominus, tu solus altissimus Jesu Christe, cum sancto spiritu in gloria Dei Patris. Amen [Ex. 8, 9].

takest away the sins of the world, have mercy upon us. Thou that takest away the sins of the world, receive our prayer. Thou that sittest at the right hand of God the Father, have mercy upon us.

For thou only art holy; thou only art the Lord; thou only, O Christ, with the Holy Ghost, art most high in the glory of God the Father. Amen.

III

Credo [Ex. 10] in unum Deum, Patrem omnipotentem, factorem coeli et terrae, visibilium omnium et invisibilium;

Et in unum Dominum Jesum Christum, filium Dei unigenitum, et ex patre natum ante omnia saecula, Deum de Deo, lumen de lumine, Deum verum de Deo vero, genitum, non factum, consubstantialem Patris per quem omnia facta sunt;

Qui propter nos homines et propter nostram salutem descendit de coelis,

Et incarnatus est de Spiritu Sancto ex Maria Virgine [Ex. 11], et homo factus est [Ex. 12];

Crucifixus etiam pro nobis [Ex. 13], sub Pontio Pilato passus [Ex. 14] et sepultus est;

Et resurrexit tertia die secundum Scripturas;

Et ascendit in coelum; sedet ad dexteram Patris [Ex. 15], et iterum venturus est cum gloria judicare vivos et mortuos, cujus regni non erit finis;

Et in Sanctum Spiritum [Ex. 10] Dominum et vivificatatem, qui ex patre filioque procedit, qui cum patre et filio simul adoratur et conglorificatur, qui locutus est per Prophetas, Et in unam sanctam

I believe in one God the Father Almighty, Maker of heaven and earth, And of all things visible and invisible:

And in one Lord Jesus Christ, the only-begotten Son of God, Begotten of his Father before all worlds, God of God, Light of Light, Very God of very God, Begotten, not made, Being of one substance with the Father, By whom all things were made: Who for us men, and for our salvation came down from heaven, And was incarnate by the Holy Ghost of the Virgin Mary, And was made man, And was crucified also for us under Pontius Pilate. He suffered and was buried,[1] And the third day he rose again according to the Scriptures, And ascended into heaven, And sitteth on the right hand of the Father. And he shall come again with glory to judge both the quick and the dead: Whose kingdom shall have no end.

And I believe in the Holy Ghost, The Lord and Giver of life, Who proceedeth from the Father and the Son, Who with the Father and the Son together is worshipped and glorified, Who spake by the Prophets. And I believe one Catholick and Aposto-

---

[1] The punctuation of the Latin text gives 'He suffered under Pontius Pilate, and was buried'. This is very clearly brought out by Beethoven.

catholicam et apostolicam ecclesi- | lick Church. I acknowledge one
am, Confiteor unum baptisma in | Baptism for the remission of sins.
remissionem peccatorum, et ex- | And I look for the Resurrection
specto resurrectionem mortuorum, | of the dead, And the life of the
Et vitam venturi saeculi. Amen | world to come. Amen.
[Ex. 16, 17, 18, 19].

IV

Sanctus, sanctus, sanctus, Do- | Holy, holy, holy, Lord God of
minus Deus Sabaoth [Ex. 20]. | hosts, heaven and earth are full of
Pleni sunt coeli et terra gloria tua; | thy glory. Hosanna in the highest.
Osanna in excelsis [Ex. 21, 22]. | Blessed is he that cometh in the
Benedictus qui venit in nomine | name of the Lord.
Domini [Ex. 23, 24, 25, 26, 27]. | Hosanna in the highest.
Osanna in excelsis [Ex. 25].

V

Agnus Dei qui tollis peccata | O Lamb of God, who takest
mundi, miserere nobis [Ex. 28]. | away the sins of the world, have
Agnus Dei qui tollis peccata | mercy upon us.
mundi, | O Lamb of God, who takest
Dona nobis pacem [Ex. 29, 30, | away the sins of the world, give us
31, 32, 33]. | peace.

The Mass in D occupied Beethoven from the years 1819 to 1823.
It was written with the intention of having it ready in time for the
installation of Beethoven's beloved friend and patron, the Archduke
Rudolph, at Cologne, as Archbishop of Olmütz, but it was not
finished until two years too late for that occasion. Nevertheless, it
is unique in the history of music as being a Mass actually designed
for a certain liturgy of exceptional pomp and magnificence, and
written at a time when music with the aid of the symphonic
orchestra was compelled to take whatever text it had to illustrate in
a much more dramatic sense than any liturgical music requires.
Thus it is only the exceptional pomp of the installation of a Royal
Archduke as Archbishop that has rendered the large scale of the
music possible or conceivable for an actual service. This distinguishes Beethoven's Mass from such works as the Mass in B
Minor of Bach, which is practically an oratorio on a text which
happens to be that of the Catholic Mass. It is therefore a mistake
to regard Beethoven as composing his text in any agnostic spirit
of art for art's sake. He achieves art which maintains itself as purely
artistic, by really inspiring himself with the definite needs of the
occasion; and whether we agree with his treatment of the text or
not, we are compelled, the more we study it, to realize that Beethoven's insight into its meaning is, from a certain point of view,
profound. The point of view is not that of Palestrina, nor indeed
of any one, whether Protestant or Roman, who is in touch with

ecclesiastical traditions. But nothing could be more misleading than to say with Rubinstein that Beethoven treats the text in a disputatious or criticizing mood.

Another subject on which we must clear our minds from pre-judice is Beethoven's choral writing. Its difficulties are appalling, and even Bach seems easy in comparison. Yet it is not unlike Bach in its rewards for those choirs that grapple with it. Every-body can see that Beethoven puts a terrible strain upon the voices. This is evident when they are singing prolonged high notes, and still more so when they are trying to articulate many syllables on these high notes. We do not notice the equally serious diffi-culties arising from Beethoven's reckless use of low notes; because the passages which lie too low simply fail to be heard. However, these defects, for such they are, must not be imputed to a lack of choral imagination. Beethoven does many things which he and lesser musicians ought not to have done, and so his choral style is not a 'good model'. But he leaves nothing undone which he ought to have done. There is no genuine choral possibility unde-veloped by Beethoven in the Mass in D. His high notes may be too high, but he has not failed to imagine their resonance. He does not inadvertently write high; he merely over-estimates the capacity of voices to sing so high with comfort. Again, though the low passages certainly are not well heard on the voices, they are very well supported in the orchestra. A case can be made out for saying that Beethoven gives his voices relief by these low passages. That, I fear, was not his motive. The same charac-teristic happens constantly in the choral writing of Bach, and is there mainly accounted for by much the same methods of sup-porting those passages by the orchestra. The only other respect in which Beethoven's choral writing is abnormal, is that he seems to think that voices can determine rhythms with the same kind of percussion as instruments. One of the leading features of Beethoven's polyphony is the use of rhythmic figures that could be recognized if merely drummed upon a table. Voices do not express those rhythmic figures nearly so well as instruments, especially when they are to be declaimed on one note to a word like 'kyrie', where the middle consonant is a liquid, and two of the syllables are successive vowels. The singer is at the mercy of his words in these matters, and requires to be taught a some-what artificial staccato before the rhythms will come out as Beethoven intended them. Lastly, it must be confessed that when Beethoven is writing a contrapuntal scheme or combination of themes, he has no facility in handling his accessory parts. Any chorus that tries to sing a big choral work of Bach will find that, immensely difficult as much of the music is, there is hardly any passage which does not remain in the memory. Even the parts that are merely filling in, and not contributing actual themes to the design, have some inherent sense. This is very rarely the case with any of Beethoven's accessory counterpoints. It is possible for the pianoforte player to memorize a Beethoven fugue, because he has the whole design in his two hands. But it is difficult to see how any choral singer can get one of Beethoven's inner parts into his head except where he comes upon one of the main themes.

These reservations then cover a wide ground; but the positive fact nevertheless remains, that Beethoven's choral writing contains everything that a chorus can do. It neglects no opportunities. Not even Bach or Handel can show a greater sense of space and of sonority. There is no earlier choral writing that comes so near to recovering some of the lost secrets of the style of Palestrina. There is no choral and no orchestral writing, earlier or later, that shows a more thrilling sense of the individual colour of every chord, every position, and every doubled third or discord. I well remember, a good many years ago, Sir George Henschel, happening to glance at the score of the D major Mass, open at its first page, putting his finger upon the first chord and saying, 'Isn't it extraordinary how you can recognize any single common chord scored by Beethoven?'

Let us now turn to the themes and structure of the composition as a whole. The form of the Mass in D is as perfect as the form of any symphony, or, in other words, of any purely abstract music. This is not in spite of but because of the fact that it is in every detail suggested by the text. The forms of purely instrumental music are not suggested by any text or any external programme, but they are acquired by a profound experience and a profound conviction of the meaning of music. They are developed by the material of the music, and when many works arrive at the same form, they arrive at that form through development from within, exactly as do living creatures. The form of this Mass will not therefore be the form of a symphony, nor will it be the form of any other Mass. It could not have been written except by a man to whom the prayer for peace with which every Mass concludes was, as Beethoven calls it, a 'prayer for outward as well as inward peace'. It could not have been written except by a composer to whom instrumental and orchestral music had attained a dramatic power fiercer and more concentrated than any that finds expression on the stage; and it could not have been written for a smaller occasion than that which we know to have called it forth. The way to grasp the form of this Mass is therefore to treat it exactly as we would treat a Motet by Palestrina. That is to say, we take each clause of the text and find out to what themes that clause is set. Where we find these themes recur, we shall find either that the composer has returned to the words associated with them, or that he has some more than merely conventional reason for reminding us of those words. It is through analysis on these lines that we are enabled to come to certain general conclusions as to how Beethoven treats his text; and I will begin with these general conclusions.

In the first place we find that, unlike many contemporary composers who were quite familiar, perhaps more familiar, with the service of the Mass, Beethoven has taken great pains to inquire into the meaning of the text. He did actually consult people who knew something about it, not having much confidence in his own recollections of the small Latin he learned as a boy; and he arrived at perfectly definite notions as to what doctrinal aspects of the text he would bring out. First then, he brings out an overwhelming and overwhelmed sense of the Divine glory, with which he invariably and immediately contrasts the nothingness of man. The very first notes of the Kyrie, as stated in the orchestral introduction, assert the two conceptions, with the great massive chords and rhythm on the word *Kyrie*, followed by the pleading of the solo wind instruments, afterwards to become solo voices.

Then the prayer rises, passing from one harmony and one position of the key to another on the word *eleison*. This word has a new theme, adorned by a more florid version in the wind instruments.

At the appeal *Christe eleison* comes the expression of the idea that Christ is the mediator for our prayers. The movement becomes more agitated, and the pair of themes with which the solo voices build up their polyphonic texture—

develops in one of Beethoven's characteristic fugue passages in which the sound recedes into vast distances and then grows with almost threatening power, only to recede suddenly again. The *Christe eleison* dies away on an incomplete minor chord which, by Beethoven's favourite method of modulation, becomes part of the original major tonic chord of the Kyrie. The rest of the design is a recapitulation, altering the order of the keys and ending in the tonic with one of Beethoven's most beautiful quiet codas. Throughout the Kyrie the choral writing must be granted to be quite normal, and nobody would ever have suggested a moment's doubt, on the evidence of this piece alone, as to Beethoven's being a choral writer with imaginative power at least equal to that of Bach or Handel.

With the Gloria we may expect the difficulties to begin. The first clause, *Gloria in excelsis Deo*, is a blaze of triumph in which the whole orchestra and the voices work out this theme—

Ex. 4.

Glo - ri - a   in ex - cel - sis   De - - - o

accompanied by the strings in a long passage which is like the ringing of all the bells in Christendom. As is natural, the words *et in terra pax* bring a dramatic contrast—the first such feature we have as yet encountered in the Mass. The moment of this contrast is impressive, and, like most of the impressive things in this Mass, extreme; but nothing could more thoroughly justify such extremities than the pious beauty and calm of the harmonies which follow. The blaze of glory, with the opening theme, is resumed with *Laudamus te*. The words *benedicimus te*, *adoramus te*, and *glorificamus te* are declaimed to short fresh points, for the simple reason that their rhythm does not fit the original theme; and there is the characteristic sudden hush at the words *adoramus te*. Here then, as everywhere, we see Beethoven enraptured at the thought of the Divine Glory, but immediately prostrated by the sudden consciousness of the nothingness of man. With the text *Gratias agimus tibi propter magnam gloriam tuam*, the notion of 'thanksgiving' suggests to Beethoven a happy and quiet mood; and there is a radical change of key to B flat with a new theme in a somewhat slower tempo.

Ex. 5.

Gra - - ti - as   a - - gi - mus   ti - bi   prop - ter

mag - nam   glo - ri - am   tu - am

Then at the *Domine Deus* the original Gloria theme returns (in the instruments, not in the voices, because here again new themes are required by the rhythm of the text); and the words *Pater omnipotens* call forth the full power of the orchestra, the first entry of the trombones, the first use of the full organ with pedals, and one of the mightiest modulations Beethoven ever wrote. Then with *Domine fili unigenite* comes the thought of the God-head becoming human. This thought is not yet defined. The definition is reserved for the Credo; but the actual theme of the Gloria is transformed into pleading and touching tones, in order to suggest the contrast that is already in Beethoven's mind between the inaccessible Divine glory and the incarnation. But as the *Domine Deus* is resumed, to culminate in the address *filius Patris*, the blaze of glory mounts again to a climax. As in all orthodox and liturgical settings of the Mass, the words *filius Patris* mark the end of a section. The choral harmony at the extreme top of the voices dies away in the sustained and spacious manner so characteristic of Beethoven's last works. Clarinets are discovered leading down from a high note to the slow movement to which Beethoven sets the prayer *Qui tollis peccata mundi*. This is worked out in a manner that brings out clearly the idea of a threefold prayer, the main theme being given out by the wind instruments and re-stated by the voices thrice, each time with a different continuation in different keys, F, D, and B flat.

Here is the first vocal statement:

Ex. 6.

As the text changes, so does the prayer increase in intensity. The most dramatic expression of the contrast between the Divine glory and the nothingness of humanity is reached in the great cry *Qui sedes ad dexteram Patris*, followed as it is by the most awe-struck prostration, before the voices, now in the dark and distant key of D flat, resume their pleading *miserere nobis*. The pleading rises now to its climax,[1] this time a climax of human prayer, and

[1] Beethoven goes so far as to add an interjection 'ah, miserere nobis!' (corrected in later editions to 'o'). This is for him a measure hardly to be distinguished from such points as the astonished stammering of the word

at last dies away in the same spacious manner as the visions of
Divine Glory. With a sound like distant thunder, a new movement
(allegro maestoso) begins with the text *Quoniam tu solus sanctus.*

Ex. 7.

The word *sanctus* is almost whispered in the midst of the solemn
shouts of praise, and this allegro maestoso, which maintains a
clearly introductory character, expands with great pomp, indulging
in solemn flourishes of trumpets. At last, with characteristic
swelling and receding and swelling out again, the chorus leads
into the final fugue *In gloria Dei Patris. Amen.* This begins on
normal lines with a subject of what we would call Handelian
majesty if we had not learned to call it Beethovenish.

Ex. 8.

The fugue takes its leisure in covering its ground, and is evidently
going to be on a gigantic scale. Unlike most of Beethoven's fugues,
it has started with full volume of tone. What it has in reserve is,
not any increase of power, but a strange event that occurs when
we feel that we have just got well into the swing of its development. Suddenly the chorus recedes into distance. The solo voices
enter, while the choral tenors and basses declaim to a solemn
canto fermo the words *Cum sancto spiritu.* The question in the
listener's mind is, What new developments are going to happen?
Certainly something great is in prospect. But the practical question
is how the fugue can be carried out on this scale at all. A more
guileless composer would have tried to work it out normally, and
would not have got through it in twenty minutes. What happens
with Beethoven is that within the compass of six bars he contrives

'et' in many passages of the Credo. These procedures are very unliturgical;
but so is the notion of using Beethoven's symphonic orchestra in church.
The liturgy is too reticent for oh's and ah's, if it is to receive a purely
choral setting of its text. But reticence is relative to the whole (unless
we are to confuse it with comfortable inefficiency); and the reticence of
voices in a dramatically orchestral ensemble suffers little from an interjection necessitated by the broad rhythm of a beautiful new melody introduced
after the final climax of the prayer.

to give a sense that this passage has gone round the universe.
While the tenors and basses are twice quietly declaiming *Cum
sancto spiritu*, as if they were singing two phrases of a slow recitative, the solo voices are just as quietly climbing in an adumbration of a stretto. Meanwhile the harmonies are rising through
a series of six modulations, each a tone higher than the last. The
result is that the listener, although the sequence of harmonies is
quite simple, entirely loses his sense of key. He knows only that
he is being whirled through a vast distance, but loses all consciousness of time. The whole of this process is shown in the
following illustration:

The chorus then re-enters for one line and a half of stretto; and the
result is that within thirty bars the whole middle and peroration of

the fugue are accomplished. Majesty and breadth are given to the short choral stretto which finishes this astonishing passage, by the fact that the subject is treated in 'augmentation' (i.e. in notes twice as slow as before). Then follows a coda in nearly double the tempo, in which Beethoven is no longer preoccupied with the old-world architectures of the fugue style, but is able to expand in symphonic forms. The solo voices enter, while the chorus in awe-struck whispers, repeats *Cum sancto spiritu* as in a prayer; until suddenly the chorus bursts out in full speed with *in gloria Dei Patris*, and brings the scheme to an end with tonic and dominant passages somewhat in the style of Handel's Hallelujahs. The whole edifice is crowned with a return to the text *Gloria in excelsis Deo* in the final *presto*; and the actual last chord is the word *Gloria* thrown into the air by the chorus after the orchestra has finished.

In the Credo Beethoven has the longest text to illustrate, and this means, as it meant to the sixteenth-century composer, that he is compelled to develop the tersest and most concentrated resources of his style. He at once begins by asserting a key that is dark in contrast with the Gloria, though the first chord is a semitone higher than that last heard. The opening chords define the key of B flat through the chord of E flat, and the basses declaim the word *Credo* to a mighty musical motto, the pregnancy of which carries Beethoven through all the most difficult and musically thankless parts of his text.

Ex. 10.

Cre - do, cre - do.

But there is no difficulty for Beethoven in building up a sublime structure for the opening clauses. Such ideas as 'Maker of all things, visible and invisible', inspire him to moments of awed prostration, from which the praises of 'God of God, Light of Light', arise with renewed vigour. There is no contrast between the clause *Credo in unum Deum* and that of the belief in Christ. The topic here is the Godhead of Christ in inaccessible glory. The change of tone, and the change to a darker key, comes where we ought to expect it, at *Qui propter nos homines et propter nostram salutem descendit de coelis*. The word *descendit* is set with naïve symbolism, as it has always been in every setting of the Mass since polyphony began. And now comes the great mystery. Here Beethoven suddenly changes his tempo and goes for the first time in this Mass unmistakably into modal harmony. Such harmony had not been heard since the time of Palestrina, except in a

modernized form in certain works of Bach which Beethoven did
not know, and in academic exercises by persons who themselves
regarded such modes as archaic. Beethoven was enormously in
advance of his time in recognizing that they are nothing of the sort;
and until we begin to share his culture in this matter, we have no
more qualifications for appreciating the aesthetics of choral music
than an eighteenth-century dandy, fresh from his Grand Tour,
would have had for appreciating the Elgin Marbles. The Incarnatus is set to mysterious and devout strains in purest Dorian
tonality (pure, that is, from Palestrina's point of view). We may
notice here, what will have already aroused attention in the setting
of earlier clauses, that the word *Et* is treated by Beethoven
extremely dramatically. It bursts forth from the lips of the singers,
both choral and solo, almost with a stammer; being nearly always
followed by quite a long pause, and then repeated before the sentence
is continued.

Ex. 11.

In the original edition, and in some modern editions, this theme
is announced by the solo tenor; but it is possible that Beethoven's
intention was to announce it by the choral tenors, and for the solo
quartet to take it up in the following harmonized passage. The
result is certainly both more mysterious and more beautiful. As the
solo quartet develops its harmony, supported by throbbing chords
from soft wind instruments, a flute is heard mysteriously warbling
in the heights. There is no reasonable doubt that the picture in
Beethoven's mind is that of the Holy Ghost hovering in the likeness of a dove. Perhaps one of the most touching notes in the whole
Mass is the sunshine and warmth of the change into D major in
triple time, when the tenor, with his excited repeated *Et*, comes
to the consummation *et homo factus est*.

Ex. 12.

The joy lasts for a short time before it is broken in by the terrible
sorrow and mystery of the Crucifixus.

Ex. 13.

The profoundly impressive voice parts of the solo quartet, supported by solemn sustained notes in the chorus, are heightened by the orchestra that has its own more elastic means of expression. Thus it may be claimed that the main theme of the Crucifixus is on the violins as an expression of the word *passus*.

Ex. 14.

We expect some dramatic contrast when we come to the Resurrexit. Beethoven's Crucifixus has ended in a darkness and a modulation not unlike the end of the Crucifixus of Bach's B minor Mass, a movement which we know Beethoven had studied. Bach's Resurrexit is one of his most glorious and highly developed choruses, and starts with a splendid formal melody. Beethoven's contrast is not less startling, but much more unexpected. He does not develop this text at all. He simply has an excited outburst of unaccompanied chorus led by the tenors with their feverish detached *et*; and the sentence is given in four bars of pure Mixolydian harmony, pure, that is to say, as Palestrina would conceive it, with the B flattened in order that it may bear an effective triad. This is the only unaccompanied choral passage in any Mass of the period. The descriptive music comes with all the greater *naïveté* with *et ascendit*. Beethoven has been ridiculed for illustrating the word *ascendit* by an ascending scale. But it was really less trouble to do what every composer up to Beethoven's time had done automatically, than to go and look for some more out-of-the-way illustration, or to avoid illustrating. We may dispute whether the terms 'high' and 'low' have the same meaning in music as they have in space. But we cannot deny that to sing high notes on the voice is to raise one's voice, or at all events to make an effort undoubtedly suggestive of raising something; and it cannot be said that there is anything inherently absurd in Beethoven's using a rising scale for symbolizing one of the central miracles of Christianity. In any case, the theme of the text *et ascendit* is not a cardinal theme in the piece, but a mere local descriptive touch. The real theme of the whole of this movement is again in the orchestra, the voices having nothing to do but to declaim each

sentence of the text in their simplest natural rhythm, while the
strings are busy with this theme—

Ex. 15.

which they carry through a wide range of well contrasted keys.
And so we come to the statement, *et iterum venturus est cum
gloria*. How is this tremendous text to be illustrated? Berlioz in
his *Requiem*, under the provocation of a text which deals in three
impressive lines of verse with the trumpet that 'scatters a wondrous
sound through the regions of death', tries to illustrate the Last
Trump by four brass bands placed at the four corners of the
concert-room. No doubt he achieves some impressiveness by this
material outlay. Beethoven ventures to allude to the Judgement
Day by an unexpected note upon a solitary trombone. The point
is not that it can make a great noise, but that the harmony is
unexpected and unsupported. Beethoven took an infinity of pains
over this passage, of which there are many sketches. The whole of
his effort is devoted simply to getting subtlety into his rhythm and
distinction into his modulations. The conception is as spiritual
and as immaterial as if he was writing for a string quartet. The
words *vivos et mortuos* suggest again one of those startling
contrasts, with a sudden pianissimo, with which Beethoven contrives to punctuate his designs and at the same time to keep in
touch with the text. This contrast would perhaps not have occurred
to anybody else at that particular place, but it would be a mistake
to suppose that it does not serve its purely musical purpose as well
as its characteristically naïve illustration of the text.

And now, after the words *cujus regni non erit finis*, we come
to the most difficult part of the composer's task, a long series
of doctrines which do not lend themselves to illustration. *Et in
spiritum sanctum* might very well have served as the text of
an independently inspired movement of the utmost mystery and
devotion, but the note required there has already been sounded in
the Incarnatus. What Beethoven here has to do is to provide
a bridge from the mention of the Day of Judgement to the final
clause about 'the life of the world to come'; and this very passage,
which with so many composers is a source of weakness in the
composition, becomes for Beethoven the key-stone of his design.
He contrives to give relief from the purely dramatic aspects of his
text by achieving here a not less conspicuous beauty of form.
The whole of the next six clauses are dealt with in a recapitulation of the opening movement of the Credo, and all difficulty

in illustrating their individual meaning is evaded, as it ought
to be evaded in a musical setting. Unless you are writing purely
formal music, and unless you can, like Bach, make an aria upon
any text whatever, and rely upon intrinsic beauty of design without illustrating it at all, it is impossible to do anything but cover
the whole design with a general theme. One of the things that
Beethoven hereby brings out is the grammar of the whole text. We
may not be able to hear the individual words of the clauses, but
we do hear now, and are reminded thoroughly, that the whole
text from beginning to end is one sentence, the object of the verb
credo. Thus by purely musical means a master of musical form
can hold a sentence together across an unlimited interval of time.
Bach in his *Magnificat* takes advantage of the fact that in Latin
the subject will come at the end of the sentence, instead of at the
beginning; and so he is able to unroll the tale of *Omnes generationes* to sublime lengths. And Parry is able to hold together
fifteen lines of Milton's *At a Solemn Music* with a musical punctuation exactly analogous to that of Milton's enormous verse-paragraph.
These examples are not more wonderful than Beethoven's achievement here. The whole procession of doctrinal clauses marches to
its climax, to the tune of the word *credo*, with its conclusion in
et expecto resurrectionem mortuorum; and so leads into the final
fugue *et vitam venturi saeculi*. This starts with an orchestral
introduction in which Beethoven strikes one of his irresistible
tender notes, anticipating the main rhythmic figure, 3/2 𝅗𝅥|𝅘𝅥 𝅘𝅥 .
Here is the calm opening pair of themes of the double fugue *et
vitam venturi saeculi*, with the second subject to the word *Amen*.

Ex. 16.

The orchestration maintains a note of devout peace. There are no
violins; the voices are supported by exceptionally low flutes and
clarinets, and no higher octave is sounded. The pair of themes
becomes inverted as the fugue develops.

Ex. 17.

In spite of the calm tone of the whole, Beethoven is ruthless in
ascribing to the sopranos the power to sing the theme at the top of
their voices, articulating the syllables on the high B flat; and this is
one of the few places where a note is forced before Beethoven
really intends to make a climax. But by the time the fugue has
reached what is evidently its middle development, he rises to a
genuine climax and seems to be closing in his main key, when
suddenly the violins burst in with a new modulation. The time
quickens, the orchestra whispers a preliminary announcement of
the theme 'diminished' (i.e. stated in notes of twice the pace), with
results rhythmically new, besides a hint of a third subject.

Suddenly the chorus bursts out with perhaps the most difficult
choral passage ever written.

This 'diminished' fugue soon reaches a tremendous climax on the
dominant, and the two versions of the main subject are combined
(i.e. the treble of Ex. 16 is sung simultaneously with the lower voice
of Ex. 19).

Now comes a much misunderstood feature of classical choral
music. When a chorus finds itself singing a long series of final
chords, the singers of the highest notes naturally imagine themselves to be the main object of attention. But when we look at such
passages in, say, Handel's autographs, we shall find disconcerting
signs that the only thing Handel wrote first, in blocking out, was
the bass, that he usually filled in all those top parts afterwards, and
that he does not care what they sing, so long as they sing the right
notes for the harmony. Yet I have seen the parts of the Beethoven
Mass edited by a famous choral conductor in Germany, who
altered the orchestral parts in order to support the voices better,

and who took particular pains to get the trumpets to support the
sopranos in their climax. Now, as a matter of fact, the trumpets
are wanted by Beethoven for a very different purpose, and the
sopranos are a mere accessory. What is meant to dominate the
whole peroration of this fugue is the figure of the first bar of Ex. 19
on the brass instruments, and we cannot spare the trumpets for
any other purpose.

This peroration rises once more to its climax, which is just the
same as the climax before the original fugue broke off; but it
is now in quite a slow tempo. The grand cadence dies away with
Beethoven's favourite choral effect of suddenly receding into the
depths of the universe. And then the heavens open.

Ex. 20.

We now come to the central part of the Mass. Here Beethoven,
for the first time since Palestrina, reconciles the needs of an actual
liturgy with the needs of the highest order of music. To the
sixteenth-century composer a voluminous text was a restriction
upon the scale of his work, rather than a stimulus to his invention. The medium of unaccompanied choral music is not dramatic; it is purely rhetorical; and though the chorus can give
dramatic outcries, it is quite incapable, without instrumental
accompaniment, of providing any background for them. The
sixteenth-century composer therefore treats the Gloria and Credo
of his Mass in a much simpler style than the rest. He sets the words
in a not elaborately polyphonic way, and hardly repeats a clause
more than once. It is just in the Sanctus and Benedictus, where
the words are few and where the moment in the liturgy is supreme,
that the sixteenth-century composer is able to unfold a broad
musical design, and he accordingly uses his opportunity.

We have seen how Beethoven's eminently dramatic genius
responded naturally to the possibilities of a chorus supported by
an orchestra that had for more than a generation been accustomed
to express itself dramatically; and how in the Gloria and Credo
the multiplicity of words gives Beethoven occasion to produce
some of his most gigantic symphonic designs. I say 'symphonic'
in full view of the fact that the forms thus produced are in no way
a priori, but are dictated at every point by the course of the words.

But now Beethoven, who had no models for these special choral-symphonic designs, transcends them all, and comes, like Palestrina, into his full heritage where symbols and forms transcend all words. The forms he now develops are easily identifiable with certain types of sonata and concerto form; and until we have better notions of musical forms than we shall find in the text-books, this may mislead us. The great creative artists have an idea of form which is so free that it becomes a matter of unconsciousness to them whether the form they have in hand has been classified or not; the right thing will enter in the right place, and no naïve listener will be able to tell from its manner whether it happens to be a subversive paradox or the most familiar convention of its epoch. In art there is no fundamental distinction between form and matter; but every work of art is created under practical conditions which the artist regards as his data. These conditions are given and cannot be altered. The tendency will be to call these data the 'form', and everything else in the work the 'treatment'. In the last resort a correct analysis will break down the distinction between form and treatment. The portrait-painter, if he has retained his interest in his art as a thing in itself, regards his sitters as among the data from which he makes works of art. The relatives of the sitter regard all the artists' technique as among the data to which they may ascribe his failure to realize their idea of the sitter. In the last resort we may suppose that everybody is satisfied; in other words, that form and matter become one and inseparable. The musical student who has been trained to think that the sonata forms are rigid, and that to do without them is to be 'free', naturally thinks that in the Gloria and Credo Beethoven is handling 'free' forms. There is no text-book which tells him that you start a Gloria in a certain key, that you make this or that section of it 'the recapitulation' of this or that other section, and that you assign a certain portion of the text for 'the development'. And so it will appear that Beethoven is 'free' in his Gloria and Credo, and 'strict' when in the Benedictus he writes one of his most profound symphonic slow movements in a form readily recognizable as a type of concerto-aria or concertante-sonata movement. But Beethoven was always free; and never more perfectly free than in this Benedictus, one of the most simply beautiful and easiest of all his slow movements. Nor is he less free in the *Dona nobis pacem*, one of the most difficult and elaborate designs he ever achieved.

And so from this point onwards in the Mass Beethoven is free to produce forms much more like the symphonic music he had been producing all his life. For that reason, and because he had to write for a special ceremony which was sure to be of abnormal length, we have the unique phenomenon of a Mass really written for a liturgy, but of such proportions that, in spite of full indul-

gence in the resources of a dramatic orchestra, the weight of
the music is concentrated where the liturgy requires it to be most
impressive. Now if Beethoven had ever seen the Sanctus of
Bach's B minor Mass (which we do not know to be the case),
it would be very significant that he did not allow himself to be
influenced by it. Bach was not writing for the Roman liturgy.
He was merely setting the text, and he was at liberty to make the
sound of the seraphim blowing their loud uplifted angel trumpets,
to let his rhythms represent the swinging of censers before the
starry throne, and generally to portray in sounds a vision of Divine
glory. But that is quite inappropriate to a liturgical Sanctus during
which everybody present is absorbed in the most awe-inspired act
of worship. With no nearer classical models than the negative
asceticism of Cherubini, Beethoven instantly achieves the right
contrast here. His distant vision of the life of the world to come
has vanished into the heavens; and we are on earth, kneeling before
the altar.

Ex. 21.

This quotation gives the voice-parts, but the voices do not enter
until the orchestra has completed an introduction on the theme
represented in the lower stave. After the close of the Credo in B flat,
it would be impossible to select three opening notes which more
mysteriously and radically change the key and arouse solemn
expectation. After that first awe-struck moment, the harmony
unfolds itself on broad and clear lines, until solemn chords on
the trombones, closing into the entry of the voices, bring the
balance of key round to that of the main design. The Sanctus is
sung by the solo quartet, and is a short intensely devout movement,
ending with a note of the kind of fear that would be cast out by
perfect love. The next clause (*pleni sunt coeli et terra gloria tua*)
is a brilliant fugato (Ex. 22) accompanied by the organ and full
orchestra, even the trombones entering towards the end. In
all editions, and presumably in the autograph, the voice parts
are assigned to the solo quartet, and this is also the case with
the Osanna. Nobody has been able to explain how Beethoven
came to let these two movements be printed on the solo staves

Ex. 22.

The accompaniment makes the supposition of solo singing so impossible, that one would be surprised to hear that in any performance it had ever been attempted without the full chorus. The Osanna is another short fugue—

Ex. 23.

hardly more than an exposition of the four voices; and it comes rapidly to a climax and finishes abruptly with a very unexpected cadence.

So far, we see no sign that Beethoven has any intention of expanding. These three movements are no longer than the corresponding settings in a short Mass by Mozart. They are, of course, intensely dramatic, and expressive of the fiery excitement that pervades the whole Mass; but it is evidently no part of their purpose to make a broad design in themselves. The three short movements are designed to throw into the greatest possible relief the breadth of what is to follow.

Now comes the elevation of the Host, accompanied by a piece of solemn instrumental music called by Beethoven *Praeludium*. The lower strings and the flutes translate into living tones the devout harmonies of quiet organ music over the miraculous depth of one of those 32-foot pedal notes which only the organ itself can produce. Over this immense darkness there suddenly breaks a ray of light. The entry of a solo violin, supported by two flutes, is one of those completely simple strokes of genius which, once accomplished, seem to have been in the world since time began, and which can never be repeated. Certainly there has been no composition for the Church or for any form of religious music, in which the idea of accomplishing a miracle, the descent of something divine, has been more simply and convincingly expressed. As the solo violin comes down, the basses of the chorus are heard softly intoning the words *Benedictus qui venit in nomine Domini.*

Ex. 24.

Ben - e - dic - tus   qui   ve - nit   in no - mi - ne Do - mi - ni,

The violin settles down into a broad melody, the phrases and interludes of which are going evidently to be the main themes of a kind of aria-concerto of violin, voices, and orchestra. The interludes of the wind instruments lay the foundations for the new Osanna.

Ex. 25.

Ben - e - dic - - tus   qui   ve - nit,   qui

Ben - e - dic - - tus qui

ve - nit in no - mi - ne Do - mi - ni   &c.

ve - nit,   qui   ve - nit   in no - mi - ne

Ex. 26.

Cantabile.

O - san - na,

The brass instruments accompany the violin in solemn chords which, as far as rhythm and musical idea are concerned, are repeating the word *Benedictus*. (These chords, among the most solemn inspirations in Beethoven's works or in any church music, were those which Sir Michael Costa angrily struck out of the score, because they impressed his gigmanity as resembling, on paper, the chords of dance music.) The melody, which the violin delivers to that solemn accompaniment, becomes a remarkably expressive canon when the solo voices take it up. (In Ex. 25 it is given in that form.) A contrapuntal device does not lose expressive power by being quotable in text-books. It so happens that canons in the upper second or in the lower seventh have a special accent of pleading, because the second voice repeats the phrases of the first a step higher in the scale; so that, unless the composer mishandles his resources, the answer can hardly fail to out-vie the original subject in its intensity. We shall find that the canon in the upper second or in the lower seventh has always had this effect wherever it has been used (e.g. the *Recordare* of Mozart's *Requiem*). Beethoven, immediately after finishing the Mass, used this very same device in one of the variations in his C sharp minor Quartet. The second of the phrases which the violin announced—

Ex. 27.

develops into a regular second subject in the dominant. When the design comes to its close in the dominant, the words *in nomine Domini* break out from the chorus as if to make a formal cadence; but the harmony diverges, and happening to light upon a subdominant chord, surprises us by leading to a new episodic theme.

Ex. 28.

This episode does duty for development, and turns round into C major. The choral writing is of bold simplicity, consisting of a mere bass sung by all the chorus in octaves while the solo violin is bringing out the first theme in C major. From this point onwards, the chorus plays the same role that was so wonderfully played by the brass instruments at the beginning of the movement before the voices had entered. The solo voices bring the music back to the main key and resume the theme which we have learned to regard as the second subject (Ex. 27). Now we have a regular sonata-like recapitulation in the tonic, leading to the same close as we had at the end of the exposition, and the same pause on the subdominant. And so the coda begins with the new theme (Ex. 28) and works it out with great breadth, until at last the chorus takes up the unassuming instrumental interlude for the wind instruments that separated the phrases of the violin melody (Ex. 26). The chorus turns this instrumental interlude into a short fugue on the text *Osanna in excelsis*, which rises to a powerful climax, culminating in a pause. Then the violin resumes the second subject (Ex. 27), which the chorus accompanies with extraordinarily impressive octaves in monotone, till the tenors and other voices break through once more with the Osanna; and so in a few more bars the Benedictus dies away in quiet glory.

The Agnus Dei, in the key of B minor (which for some obscure reason Beethoven regarded as extremely dark), begins with a cry *de profundis*. Its broad melody is harmonized in sombre colour, and given to a deep bass voice.

Ex. 29.

The low tenors and basses of the chorus answer it; and, in a structure realizing the ancient conception of the Agnus Dei as a threefold prayer, we have this theme exposed in three stages, rising among the voices until it fills the chorus. This design is laid out very broadly, and is completely rounded off. Having eventually died away in the key of B minor in which it began, it turns in a new direction with a quiet modulation like an approaching dawn. Then the *Dona nobis pacem*, entitled by Beethoven 'Prayer for inward and outward peace', enters softly with an introductory theme—

Ex. 30.

leading to a calm pair of subjects in double fugue—

Ex. 31.

which is exposed systematically in all the four voices, culminating in one of the most striking and haunting phrases in the whole Mass.

Ex. 32.

This gives rise to a short, dignified fugato, which modulates in symphonic style to the dominant. Now we have one of those second groups, typical of Beethoven's finales at all periods of his work, and especially characteristic of his last period. The type consists of a number of short themes, depending on sharp contrasts of colour and rhythm. First there is the following simple anti-phonal piece of vocal euphony—

Ex. 33.

accompanied by the instruments in delicate staccato scales.

It is answered by a paragraph of variously contrasted phrases, ending in a burst of triumph, that asserts with great confidence the chords of the key in a formal cadential manner. Suddenly the triumph dies away, and there are sounds as of distant war. The voices, both solo and chorus, renew with expressions of terror the prayer, *Agnus Dei, qui tollis peccata mundi,* and the threatening sounds draw nearer. Quotation is unnecessary: no listener can miss the meaning of those drums and trumpets.

But the danger passes away, and the peaceful current of the *Dona nobis pacem* is resumed in a variety of modulations, till we come to a quite regular recapitulation of our second group (Ex. 32 and its sequels) in the tonic. This ends, as before, in triumph. But now the triumph breaks away in a very strange instrumental fugued passage, in which one of the subjects is evidently derived from the double-fugue theme.

Ex. 34.

It is permissible to interpret this as the change from prosperity to arrogance followed by its Nemesis. At all events there is no doubt that the chorus has ended in triumph, and that this first outbreak of independent energy in the orchestra is not in itself agitated, but rather exultant. But this fugue passage becomes alarmingly rough and wild, and it is scattered in a strangely excited and headlong way over the various groups in the orchestra.

Suddenly the trumpets and drums return with terrible power. The prayer of the chorus is mightier, and peace returns with a deeper mystery. The end is one of Beethoven's most touching and subtle codas. All the themes of peace are there, resounding close at hand and dying away in heights and depths. There is the calm principal theme of the second group (Ex. 33); above all there is the haunting climax of the first group (Ex. 32), which is the actual last word of the chorus. It is twice answered by faint echoes of the war—broken rhythms on the drum, entirely unaccompanied, in their distant key. The chorus ends in peace, and the orchestra abruptly closes the mighty work with chords of innocent triumph.

BRAHMS

'REQUIEM', OP. 45

The great choral work which brings all the resources of Brahms's art to maturity is a Requiem only in the most general colloquial sense, and has no connexion with any liturgical office. The full original title is *Ein Deutsches Requiem, nach Worten der heiligen Schrift*: a German Requiem with scriptural text. It was composed in memory of the fallen in the war of 1870[1]; and, in glaring contrast to the *Triumphlied* which followed it, has no hint of earthly warfare in its contents. Brahms's knowledge of the Bible was exhaustive. On the other hand, it is extremely unlikely that he knew anything about the liturgy of the Church of England, and quite certain that he had no other liturgy, Protestant or Roman, in mind, when he selected words that so frequently remind English listeners of the Church of England Order for the Burial of the Dead. One thing we may be sure of, that his mind was always alert to the context of every sentence he chose; and that, while it would be fantastic to

[1] Wild nonsense: it was performed in its entirety in 1868, except for No. V.—D.F.T.

draw inferences from his omission and inclusion of this doctrine and that, we can hardly exaggerate the completeness and intensity of his poetic insight into the words he has chosen, and the depth of the musical symbolism of his setting. Some of the finer detail is lost by translation. The best available English will not always bring the rhetorical point where the music puts it; and some of the repetitions of English words, where Brahms had no such stammering in his setting of the German, should make us consider whether the certain foolish mannerisms in nineteenth-century English church-music may not have originated in the assumption that the inspiration of the foreign composer extends to the translation of his text. Brahms is not responsible for saying, 'For the trumpet, the trumpet shall sound'; nor, on the other hand, does he give two notes of melody to one syllable without some rhetorical point. Where such irritating things happen with an English version, we must realize that Brahms would have composed the English text differently. Some of the finest passages are barely intelligible as rhetoric with the English text; and it is a sad fact if nobody cares. A Master of Balliol once said that 'the British schoolboy generally believes in his heart that no nonsense is too enormous to be a possible translation of a classical author'; and so there will always be people, and even composers, who combine a correct appreciation of Brahms's treatment of the words 'sorrow and sighing' with a failure to see anything queer about his terrific emphasis on 'shall flee, shall flee FROM THEM, FROM THEM!' But the German words are '*wird weg* müssen', an idiom which is both Lutheran and colloquial at the present day. We may not render it 'shall hence must'; but we can sing it and hear it with much greater conviction when we know that that is the shape of the phrase.

In my musical quotations I shall give the German text only; but the analysis will be an almost tabular arrangement of the themes as they occur in the course of the words. I take the words from the Authorized Version and the Prayer Book, omitting further reference to the makeshifts of their adaptation to the music.

No. I

An orchestra without violins plays, in the solemn veiled tones of violas and violoncellos, a ritornello which adumbrates several important themes, as my quotation indicates by citing the words hereafter set to this music.

Ex. 1.

The chorus, after adapting the first bars of the ritornello to the words 'Selig sind', gives out the whole Beatitude,

Blessed are they that mourn, for they shall be comforted (Matt. v. 4),

to the following theme—

Ex. 2.

which is then continued in dialogue with the orchestra, so as to make a large musical paragraph, at the echoing close of which the figure marked (c) becomes prominent. The last orchestral close plunges into the dark warm key of D flat, where a new theme appears with a new text.

Ex. 3.

They that sow in tears: shall reap in joy (Ps. cxxvi. 5).

The contrast between the two clauses is grandly expressed. At the close the orchestral basses descend in utter darkness to the note of the opening. The whole prelude, with very slight change, is now recapitulated as a setting of the first clause of Ps. cxxvi. 7:

He that now goeth on his way weeping, and beareth forth good seed—

This now leads to D flat with Ex. 3, wherewith (the orchestra slightly varying the beginning of the theme) the whole clause is set:

—shall doubtless come again with joy, and bring his sheaves with him.

This is now followed in D flat by the preamble 'Selig sind', which modulates back to F major. The Beatitude is now resumed, a short version of the theme (Ex. 2) being given to soft wind instruments in a high octave, while the altos and tenors sing its bass. This solemn device is followed by a full recapitulation of the whole section, including the dialogue between voices and orchestra, the parts of which are at first interchanged. A coda introduces a new treatment of figure (b).

The voice parts seem here to be a mere neat counterpoint, but, like many apparently accidental things in art and nature, their new figure bears a mountain of meaning afterwards revealed.

No. II

The orchestra plays a solemn march in a triple time, which implies some grave dance-measure, since plain marching is possible only in duple rhythms. The impression of a dance is confirmed by a second theme which, rising up plaintively in the dominant major, resembles a Viennese *Ländler* clearly enough to have given great offence to some critics even among Brahms's contemporary supporters. Now a Viennese *Ländler* is, at its best, a very pretty thing. So is a Dresden Shepherdess, and so are the human dancers of *Ländlers* and models of Dresden Shepherdesses. And can you realize the pathos and tragedy of death if you confine your attention to its most sublime victims? There are two main types of failure in the Grand Style: one is the sentimental confusion between the Sublime and the Pretty; the other is the ambition to achieve the Sublime in relation to nothing else. And the second error is the graver, for everybody thinks himself warned against sentimentality, while the ambition to achieve the Sublime is universally believed to be a fine strenuous motive.

Whatever issues of taste may be involved, there are no oversights in Brahms's Requiem. His march theme proves to be a counterpoint to a solemn iambic hymning of the text (1 Peter i. 24):

For all flesh is as grass, and all the glory of man as the flower of grass.

Here is the combination—

And with the rest of the verse Brahms gives us the crowning touch of pity for the withering of flowers that in life made no claim to be among the more pompous glories of man.

Ex. 6.

Das   Gras   ist ver - dor - ret

The grass withereth, and the flower thereof falleth away.

In a second strain the orchestra prepares a mighty crescendo on a dominant pedal, which brings back the whole chant with full unison chorus, closing with Ex. 6 in the tonic.

Then, like a trio to the march, a quiet middle section in lighter rhythm deals with a new text. Here again it is possible to misjudge the melody by assuming that a comparative lightness is an absolute defect. When a master who knows the foundation of hope advises one in deep grief to be patient, his tone at once achieves its aim whilst it jars by its lightness.

Ex. 7.

So   seid nun ge - dul - dig,   lie - ben Brü - der,

Be patient therefore, brethren, unto the coming of the Lord (James v. 7).

If, after repeating this, Brahms had nothing broader to give, then there would be a lapse of style; but there is no such danger. As the rest of the text expands, so does the music, without making the mistake of becoming heated, though it is most poetically descriptive.

Behold, the husbandman waiteth for the precious fruit of the earth, and hath long patience for it, until he receive the early and latter rain.

The chorus dies away reiterating 'so seid geduldig', the echoes of which drop downward to the key of the march, which is repeated in full.

When it is over the full chorus bursts out solemnly in massive major chords with the conclusion, deferred till now, of St. Peter's quotation from Isaiah:

But the word of the Lord endureth for ever.

Through the massive chords the trumpets build up the figure (*a*) of the main theme of the ensuing chorus:

And the ransomed of the Lord shall return and come to Zion with songs—(and)

Ex. 8.

Brahms's text has a different punctuation from our Authorized Version, giving the remaining clause as a new sentence (completed by the bracketed words):

—everlasting joy [shall be] upon their heads (Isa. xxxv. 10).

This he sets in a mighty musical sentence in the dominant, which comes to a wonderful soft close. The middle section of the chorus begins with a new theme curiously combined with itself in 'augmentation' (like Handel's 'Let all the angels of God worship him').

Ex. 9.

They shall obtain joy and gladness, and sorrow, and sighing shall flee away.

The 'sorrow and sighing' plunge into keys infinitely remote; and the German idiom 'wird weg müssen' enables Brahms to shoo them away with his 'müssen' right round the harmonic sphere, while the omnipresent figure (a) of Ex. 8 summons the ransomed of the Lord from all points of the compass and all beats of the measure, until the whole theme expands itself in the tonic with enormous energy, concluding therein with the sentence about 'everlasting joy'.

This reverberates quietly in a great solemn coda on a tonic pedal, over which the omnipresent figure (a) builds itself up in orchestral columns and architraves, among which separate voices wander here and there until they gather themselves together in a cadence expressive of yearning hope.

No. III

So far we have listened to the parable of the seed which must die before it can live. Except for the opening Beatitude, the whole of the text has been in parables, and its application is not to ourselves,

but to those for whom we mourn. Now comes the direct and literal
message; and it concerns ourselves. There are similes in plenty till
the end of the work, but the teaching is no longer by parables.

A baritone solo teaches the chorus the following verses of the
thirty-ninth Psalm, the first of which I must translate literally
from Luther's Bible, which differs from our Authorized Version
and Prayer Book version to an extent that influences Brahms's
musical conception:

4. Lord, teach me that there must be an end of me: that my life has a
   term and I must hence.

6. Behold, thou hast made my days as it were a span long; and mine age
   is even as nothing in respect of thee.

Brahms represents the 'span' by a swift journey right round
the harmonic world, and the chorus repeats the journey in a
steeper ascent to a great climax, after which the baritone solo
recapitulates the first strain (Ex. 10), the chorus intervening at
the end. Then the orchestra crashes in with a burden derived
from Ex. 11 (b).

With tragic irony the next section begins in the tonic major. The
English text does not quite accurately correspond to the change of
tone, partly because the adapter has skipped half a verse, and
partly because, even if the right clause had been chosen, the German

version of our A.V., 'at his best state,' is 'die doch so sicher leben', which means 'who nevertheless live so sure of themselves'.

Ex. 12.

Ach, . . . wie gar nichts sind al - le Men - schen

Verily every man at his best state is altogether vanity.

In the next verse the music alludes to Ex. 10 in a fragmentary inconclusive style exactly expressing the sense of the words, which Brahms would never have set to the broad melodic pathos of Ex. 12.

Surely every man walketh in a vain show: surely they are disquieted in vain: he heapeth up [riches], and knoweth not who shall gather them.

Into this the chorus bursts with Ex. 12 in F major. Then the baritone solo resumes its allusion to Ex. 10 with the words best represented in the Prayer Book version:

And now, Lord, what is my hope?

This the chorus takes up in great excitement.

Ex. 13.

Nun Herr, wess soll ich mich trös - ten?

(a)

Nun Herr, wess soll ich mich trös - ten?

When the climax has died away on a sobbing chord, there arises from the depths a glorious choral cadenza in the major, to the words

My hope is in Thee.

This closes into a fugue the unique features of which, like every musical phenomenon in the work, are profoundly symbolical of the text.

The souls of the righteous are in the hand of God, and no torment shall come nigh unto them.

Ex. 14.

Der Ge - rech - ten See - len sind in Got - tes

Hand und kei-ne   Qual rüh - ret sie an

This is really a double fugue, not in the usual sense of a fugue on a pair of subjects, but in this way, that the chorus sings a complete fugue which the orchestra accompanies with another almost complete instrumental fugue. As the quotation shows, the vocal and the instrumental subjects imitate each other, but the two fugues are none the less remarkably independent in their completeness. Below them both is a thundering organ-point, holding the two simultaneous fugues from the first note to the last through their widest modulations and most crowded stretti (overlapping of subject with answer). Never has musical symbolism been more powerful and more unmistakable.

No. IV

In a key far away, yet easily connected with that of the last number, the orchestra announces a yearning phrase which, inverted, becomes a broad lyric melody.

Ex. 15.

(a)   (a) inverted.

Wie lieb - lich sind dei - ne Woh - nun - gen.

O how amiable are thy dwellings: thou Lord of hosts! (Ps. lxxxiv. 1).

A second theme is set to the same text, the tenors imitating the violins, and the basses *at the same pitch* imitating the tenors with a beautiful and rare contrast of tone.

Ex. 16.

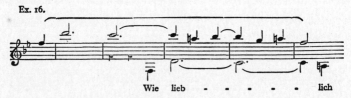

Wie   lieb - - - - - lich

A widely modulating middle section or development sets the next verse to appropriate phrases:

My soul hath a desire and longing to enter into the courts of the Lord: my heart and my flesh rejoice in the living God (Ps. lxxxiv. 2).

Brahms's modulations lead him back to the tonic for a recapitulation of Exx. 15 and 16. The latter is now a regular 8-bar tune in one plane, first on the orchestra, and then on the chorus. It now has a text of its own:

> Blessed are they that dwell in thy house (Ps. lxxxiv. 4),

the second part of which is set to a triumphant double fugue—

Ex. 17.

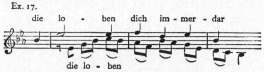

out of the climax of which a quiet coda on the words and music of Ex. 15 arises, and comes to a close with a wonderful device of vocal octaves. Once, when Joachim was deploring the growing tendency of composers to reduce choral writing to a lazy, degenerate mass of chords doubled in octaves, Brahms said in reference to this passage, 'Ah, I set them a bad example there!'

No. V.

Some time after the Requiem was completed and performed, Brahms lost his step-mother, to whom he was devoted. Her monument is here.[1]

The orchestra establishes the key of G major with the figure given in quavers in Ex. 18, whereupon a soprano solo enters with a broad and melodious declamation, all on the dominant, giving the first clauses of the text their true force as a mere concessive preamble to the promise introduced by the word 'but'.

> And ye now therefore have sorrow: but—

Ex. 18.

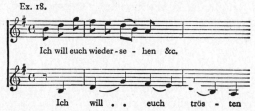

I will see you again, and your heart shall rejoice, and your joy no man taketh from you (John xvi).

For convenience I quote, in Ex. 18, the combination of themes as it occurs in the recapitulation when both are in the tonic; but the

---

[1] More nonsense: the step-mother died some time after this movement was added. The death of Brahms's mother in 1865 was the most probable inspiring cause of the whole Requiem.—D.F.T.

wonderful 'augmentation' which the chorus utters like a voice from
the grave, is first heard as a 'second subject' in the dominant. Its
text is:

> As one whom his mother comforteth, so will I comfort you
>
> (Isa. lxvi. 13)—

and that is the text of the chorus throughout, including the new
theme which it contributes to the widely modulating middle
section and the coda.

Ex. 19.

Ich will euch trös - ten

During this middle section the soprano sings:

Look upon me. A little while I have had tribulation and labour, and
have found great comfort.

No. VI

In harmonies and melody, which, without going beyond the
limits of a modal freedom of key, shift vaguely as the words imply,
the chorus announces the following theme—

Ex. 20.

Denn wir ha - ben hie kei - - - ne blei - ben - de Statt

For here we have no continuing city, but we seek one to come (Heb. xiii).

The key of C minor, around which the harmony hovers, is instantly
relegated to extreme distance by the baritone solo, whose message
the chorus repeats in an awakening dream.

Ex. 21.

Sie - he, ich sa - ge euch ein Ge - heim - - - - niss.

(a)

Wir wer - den nicht alle ent-schla - - - - - - - fen

(The resemblance of its preamble to the main figure of Ex. 8 is
accidental: a theme cannot purposely refer across five intervening

movements to a declamatory formula without collateral evidence
in the context.)

Behold, I shew you a mystery: We shall not all sleep, but we shall all
be changed, in a moment, in the twinkling of an eye, at the last trump.
(1 Cor. xv. 51, 52.)

Brahms, like Beethoven, attempts no realistic trumpet-sounds,
though he uses the brass grandly. It is the voices, with their triplet
flourish and their grand modulation (unquoted here) from C minor
to E minor, who make poor Berlioz's four brass bands at their four
points of the compass as harmless as that once famous pianoforte
piece *The Battle of Prague.*

Ex. 22.

Denn   es   wird   die Po - sau - ne schal - - - - len

For the trumpet shall sound, and the dead shall be raised incor-
ruptible, and we shall be changed.

The baritone resumes (with its recitative preamble adapted to
triple time):

Then shall be brought to pass the saying that is written—

The chorus recapitulates Ex. 22 to the new text:

Death is swallowed up in victory—

and then drives Death into a corner by a series of rising modula-
lations—

Death, where is thy sting? Grave, where is thy victory?

At last the revelation bursts forth. Its import lies not so much in the
text of the grand subject as in those of the countersubjects, which
bring 'the ransomed of the Lord' and 'the souls of the righteous'
under the Fatherhood of 'all created things'.

Ex. 23.

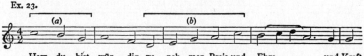

Herr, du bist wür - dig zu neh - men Preis und Ehre . . . und Kraft

Thou art worthy, O Lord, to receive glory and honour and power:
for thou hast created all things, and for thy pleasure they are and were
created (Rev. iv. 11).

Although Brahms naturally sets this as a fugal exposition, it is no
part of his intention to write a fugue. His plan is that of a series
of spacious episodes in which often a single vocal part floats

through the orchestra in a manner characteristic of Handel, but
almost totally neglected by other composers. Thus every clause of
the text becomes clearly emphasized, and then the voices gather
together on the main theme, first piling up figure (*a*) in close stretto,
and then making Jacob's-ladder sequences on figure (*b*).

The stretti on (*a*) are systematically ranged in order of rhetorical
force, the first notes of each entry successively making a climbing
series, now in thirds (as G, B, D, F; it makes no difference whether
these be rising thirds or falling sixths as a lower or an upper voice
leads), now in fourths (with reckless modulating, as C, F, B flat,
E flat), and lastly in rising steps (G, A, B, C, D, E, F). The
Jacob's-ladder device culminates in two stupendous examples on
the following model—

after each of which the clause 'for thou hast created all things' is set
to an almost lyric expression of the loving Fatherhood of the
Creator.

No. VII

The great theme which opens the final chorus is scored in a way
which shows that Brahms is thinking of its context. The sopranos
reverberate through a surging accompaniment that reaches from the
depths to the heights of the orchestra, and their theme is answered by
the basses. 'I heard a voice from heaven, saying unto me, Write'—

Blessed are the dead which die in the Lord from henceforth.
(Rev. xiv. 13.)

The basses having answered in the dominant, the whole chorus
expands the text in a massive paragraph in that key, coming to a

quiet close. Upon this the orchestra utters a terse cadence theme
ending in a rising scale.

Ex. 26.

A solemn rhythmic dialogue, almost in monotone, between low
voices and brass tells us:

Yea, saith the Spirit, that they may rest from their labours—

and this text is taken up in a gentle cantabile in the bright key of
A major—

Ex. 27.

dass . . . sie . . ru - hen von ih - rer Ar ‑ beit

the new theme concluding the text in the dominant:

and their works do follow them.

Then the solemn rhythmic dialogue with the brass modulates to a
remote key, from which the return to A is achieved quietly by a
swift stroke of genius, the tenors leading the theme and its conclusion being brought into the tonic of A.

Suddenly the tonic of F breaks through, and the first section
(Blessed are the dead) is recapitulated, the main theme (Ex. 25) by
the tenors, and the full choral paragraph in the tonic.

The orchestra gives the terse cadence theme (Ex. 26), but the
chorus joins in its final scale, which leads astonishingly and
abruptly up to E flat, the key a tone below our tonic. This is a
relation used by great composers only where it may appropriately
convey a sense of something seen through a veil, whether of
memory or of distance. And so in E flat we hear, to the next text
('Blessed are the dead'), the theme of the first chorus (Ex. 2) as it
appeared in the coda when altos sang its bass below high soft wind
instruments.

With an effort the harmony is wrested back to F, and the scale
rises again to a remoter chord from which we reach D flat, the key
of the middle section of the first chorus. From this key the chords
that were used to effect its original return to the tonic are naturally
available, and so now the whole work closes (to the present text) in

the full daylight of its key, F major, with the original close of the first chorus. But who would have thought that the gentle accessory vocal detail of Ex. 4 was to be the main figure in the theme of the mighty voice from Heaven?

RHAPSODIE FOR ALTO VOICE, MALE CHORUS, AND ORCHESTRA, OP. 53

(*Literal translation*)

But who goes there apart?
In the brake his pathway is lost,
Close behind clash
The branches together,
The grass rises again,
The desert engulfs him.

Who can comfort his anguish,
Who, if balsam be deathly?
If the hate of men
From the fulness of love be drained?
He that was scorned, turned to a scorner,

Lonely now devours
All he hath of worth
In a barren self-seeking.

But if from thy psaltery,
All-loving Father, one strain
But come to his hearing,
Oh, enlighten his heart!
Lift up his o'er-clouded eyes
Where are the thousand fountains
Hard by the thirsty one
In the desert.

Goethe's *Harzreise im Winter* is an ode in which the poet uses the winter scenery of the Harz Forest as a background for the figures of huntsmen and foresters happy in the brotherhood of their crafts, contrasted with the solitary misanthrope whose embittered soul has poisoned all that human loving-kindness can do for him. A God has appointed to each man his path; the happy man runs his course swiftly to its joyous end; but he whose heart misery has contracted, struggles in vain against the iron bonds which only the bitter shears of fate shall sever at last. It is easy to follow the carriage which Good Fortune drives, as the leisurely cavalcade on the new-levelled road follows the Prince's entry in state.

At this point Brahms begins his interpretation of the poem, selecting with a musician's insight the three middle stanzas which, without rising to the Pindaric ecstasy of the climax, contain in a completeness of their own the poet's heartfelt prayer to the Father of Love to restore the soul of the lonely hater of men. With shudders the orchestra presents an introductory picture of the slow steps of the recluse, the springing back of the bushes through which he breaks, the slow rise of the tall grass he has trodden, and the solitude that engulfs him. Then the alto gives words to the description, following the tracks through wider modulations, and thus rounding off this introduction with great musical breadth and simplicity.

The next stanza, which tells the history of the misanthrope's soul, is treated with equal breadth and simplicity in a sustained lyric melody.

Ex. 1.

The cross-rhythm (3 × 2 against 2 × 3) is very characteristic of Brahms, and I cannot illustrate the continuity of musical history better than by the strokes which I add at the normal rhythmic divisions, on a plan which proves to be convenient in displaying to modern singers the cross-rhythms of Palestrina.

By repeating the first four lines after the other four, so as to get a da capo after a middle section, Brahms does no violence to the poetic sense, though he thereby gains a perfect and purely musical form. He even brings out the highest refinement of poetic interpretation by his choice of another key (the dominant major) for its close, which thus approaches the prayer of the third stanza with a growing dawn of hope.

The psaltery of the All-loving Father is materially suggested by the harp-like pizzicato accompaniment of the violoncellos; and the tone which shall reach the ear of the self-tortured misanthrope swells gently upward in men's voices beneath the glorious melody of the alto.

Ex. 2.

This melody alternates with another, in which a modulation, near and yet infinitely far, brings out the full pathos of the prayer to open his clouded sight to the thousand springs that surround him athirst in the wilderness.

Ex. 3.

With perfect musical form Brahms combines the minute illustrative accuracy of the vocal music of the sixteenth century. Modern criticism is apt to disbelieve this, for want of realizing that true musical forms are means of expression not less direct and characteristic than details of harmony, instrumentation, and declamation.

'SONG OF DESTINY' ('SCHICKSALSLIED'), FOR
CHORUS AND ORCHESTRA, OP. 54

Friedrich Hölderlin's poem is set by Brahms in a form which has
been thought to go beyond the mandate of its text in a fundamental
matter. I think that on mature reflection we shall find that the
setting does no such thing, but that we are apt to forget or ignore
the privilege of music to treat the time-direction in a way of its
own, retracing the past and grasping the future without regard to
the way in which human life is confined to one order of events.
Brahms, the last great master of sonata forms, could not be expected to ignore that privilege; and Wagner committed himself to
no assertion of personal immortality when he made Isolde die beside
the corpse of Tristan to the music of their love-duet, nor when he
made Siegfried die to the music of Brünnhilde's awakening.

A literal translation of Hölderlin's poem can bring out the meaning more closely than can be managed in a singable version. The
otherwise excellent version of Troutbeck may be sung, with a change
in one detail where that eminently musical translator lost faith in
Brahms's rhythm and, counting the bar-periods wrongly, assumed
that the German text was wrongly accented, whereas it is perfectly
correct. Instead of Troutbeck's ' At last do we pass away ' I read
' In doubt and darkness . . . we fall '.

An orchestral introduction expresses the most wistful longing—

Ex. 1.

A solemn rhythm in the drums pervades most of this paragraph.

The close anticipates the first theme of the chorus, which is
announced by the altos and repeated in full harmony—

Ex. 2.

Ihr wan-delt dro - ben im Licht auf wei-chem Bo-den, se - li - ge Ge - ni - en

Ye walk on high in light, upon soft ground, ye spirits blest! (*selige
Genien*).

Gleaming breezes divine lightly stir you as the artist stirs the sacred
harp-strings with her fingers.

The *glänzende Götterlüfte* are represented by a new figure that modulates in subtle chords divided among antiphonal groups of voices, wood-wind, and brass; while the *heilige Saiten* are represented by Ex. 3.

The next stanza freely recapitulates the music of the first, to words of the following purport:

(Ex. 2) Free from Fate, as a sleeping babe at the breast, the heavenly ones draw their breath: chastely guarded in its modest bud, their spirit blooms for ever; (Ex. 3) and their hallowed eyes gaze in calm eternal clearness.

The orchestra resumes the close of its introduction. Suddenly there is a new chord, ambiguous and ominous. Upon this the orchestra flares out in wild agitation, and the chorus re-enters, bewailing the helpless state of man in his darkness and doubt—

Doch uns ist ge-ge - ben auf kein-er Stät - - te zu ruh'n.

But to us it is given to find rest nowhere: suffering mankind dies away and falls blindly from hour to hour, like water hurled from rock to rock, year in, year out, down into the unknown.

Brahms develops this theme and these words in a huge movement which goes again and again through its cycle of despairing thoughts, finding no way out except by sheer exhaustion. Yet, like the representation of Absence in Beethoven's Sonata *Les Adieux*, the movement is not inordinately long, and its form is perfectly clear. The simile of water hurled from rock to rock is graphically represented by the cross-rhythm—

Ex. 5.

Wie Was - ser von Klip - pe zu Klip - pe ge - wor - fen,

and when this point is reached again in recapitulation, the key is unexpectedly remote. In the final stages of exhaustion the rhythm of Ex. 4 becomes—

Ex. 6.

and the orchestra has dying flickers of energy, with a pathetic augmentation of its figure of accompaniment—

Ex. 7.

When no thought is left except that of the dark unknown, the longing for light arises again. In ruthless beauty the orchestral prelude returns, in C major. At first the drums are silent; and nothing darkens the '*stiller, ewiger Klarheit*' of the melody with which the flute soars up. Towards the end the drums are heard, but their rhythm is not so solid as at first. We may not know that because this vision rouses our longing it is an answer to our doubts and fears. It must suffice us that music is capable of such visions.

DEBUSSY

'THE BLESSED DAMOZEL'

Debussy's setting of *The Blessed Damozel* was sent by him to the Section des Beaux-Arts from Rome after he had obtained the Prix de Rome in 1884. It shocked professors by its unorthodoxy; and the biographers have ever since pointed out how history repeated itself after similar events in the early career of Berlioz. There is really no close parallel, for Berlioz was a difficult subject whose mastery in certain directions contrasted with such clumsiness in other directions as would bewilder the judgement of the best of critics in the best of circumstances; his *Mort de Cléopatre* (which caused all the trouble) is a work which nobody cares to revive, except for a single passage which Berlioz himself incorporated in a riper work, itself unproducible nowadays. Sir Henry Hadow has pointed out that the harmonic progression which most shocked the judges can be found in Mozart's pianoforte works; so that, while on the one hand it was not so much the work itself as the subsequent fame of Berlioz that stultified the judges of his day, there is little or no question of its containing anything nearly as revolutionary as they seem to have thought it. In short Berlioz's rejected work was not a masterpiece and was not epoch-making, though it was admittedly the best sent in for the competition. Debussy appears to have had no difficulty in obtaining the Prix de Rome for his cantata *L'Enfant Prodigue*. *La Damoiselle Élue* shocked the Institute because it was throughout based consistently on principles for which they were unaccustomed to legislate. There is no question whatever that it is a masterpiece; there is also no question that it could never have fallen in with the requirements of a body of examiners proceeding on known principles. With our experience of Debussy's later works we are able to recognize in it a wide range of resources in common with older music. Debussy had not as yet reduced his harmonic and melodic schemes to an alternation between whole-tone and pentatonic scales; nor had he consistently excluded all chord-progressions that depend on polyphonic principles. But he already freely used progressions that explicitly deny the polyphonic principles; that is to say, progressions in which a chord simply moves up and down the scale as a primitive sensation instead of behaving as if each of its component notes were part of an independent line. In other words it was possible for an exceptionally stupid critic to point out that he wrote consecutive fifths, as it was possible for Artemus Ward to point out that Chaucer, though a man of 'considerble literry parts, could not spel'. But I do not think this was the attitude of Debussy's judges, nor do I see any parallel between his case and Berlioz's. *The Blessed Damozel* is a masterpiece, but it was possible to rule that its music is no more eligible for prize competition purposes than the poem would be eligible for the Newdigate. What really damned the Parisian adjudicators of Debussy and Berlioz was what always betrays itself in such cases, the clumsy admission that the condemned work was really the best sent in.

The hardships of this work of genius did not cease with its recognition as not only the early work of a master but a master-piece in itself. What Debussy set to music was a faithful and singable translation into French of the poem in its original form. The editor of the score with English text has tried to fit the music to Rossetti's deplorable later attempt to reproduce his poem from memory, whereas not only the sense of the French translation but its rhythm correspond fairly accurately both to Debussy's music and to Rossetti's original version of 1850; but throughout the printed copies the English words have been set under Debussy's notes in a very crude fashion with many clumsy repetitions, and there is dire necessity for a completely new edition of the vocal score with English words.

The orchestra begins with the figure of plain triads—

Ex. 1

which afterwards becomes associated with the fifth of the selected stanzas ('The sun was gone now', &c.), reappearing at the end of the work, and serving generally to indicate the vast calm of space in which this vision of Heaven is seen. Soon there follows a calm devout theme, not unlike those in *Parsifal* expressive of faith.

We meet with this in stanza 3 (. . . 'lovers, . . . Spoke evermore among themselves Their heart-remembered names'); stanza 6 ('Are not two prayers a perfect strength?'); stanza 11 ('angels meeting us shall sing To their citherns and citoles'); and finally in the last stanza but one ('Her eyes pray'd, and she smil'd').

These two themes expand broadly in the manner of a great introduction. Still profoundly calm, but at a slightly quickened pace, a new theme appears to which all the introduction has been leading.

It may be taken as representing the Blessed Damozel herself; and it underlies all the stanzas that describe her: stanzas 2 and 4, and (in combination with Ex. 1) stanza 5 ('And now She spoke through the still weather'); also stanza 10 ('Our love, Not once abashed or weak') and stanza 12 ('Only to live as once on earth With Love'); and lastly in the final two stanzas ('She gazed and listened . . . And laid her face between her hands'). The chorus for the most part goes straight through the words in very simple declamation with exquisitely coloured harmonies. When the Blessed Damozel herself speaks, she begins with a phrase—'I wish that he were come to me'—

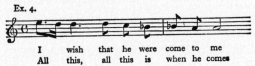

which, in itself merely an appropriately musical declamation, first reveals its depth fully when we hear it again, to her last words 'All this is when he comes'. One other theme may be quoted, that which belongs to the words 'There will I ask of Christ the Lord Thus much for him and me', and to 'That living mystic tree Within whose secret growth the Dove Is sometimes felt to be', since it is remembered with such moving effect *pianissimo* at the very end of the work.

Ex. 5.

For the rest, it will be found that the work can be easily followed by reading the selected stanzas of the original poem as given here with the marginal references to the musical examples. Every detail in the orchestra illustrates the words which Debussy had before him. In spite of all that can be done short of preparing a new English edition of the music, there are still some annoying misfits and one or two ineradicable repetitions of words in the setting. For these Debussy is in no wise to blame. His French declamation is supremely natural, and he has no repetitions whatever; but there are unfortunately far more syllables in the French text than in Rossetti's.

THE BLESSED DAMOZEL

The blessed damozel leaned out
   From the gold bar of Heaven;
Her eyes were deeper than the depth
   Of waters stilled at even;
She had three lilies in her hand,
   And the stars in her hair were seven.

(Exx. 1, 3)   Her robe, ungirt from clasp to hem,
   No wrought flowers did adorn,
But a white rose of Mary's gift,
   For service meetly worn;
Her hair that lay along her back
   Was yellow like ripe corn.

. . . .

Around her, lovers, newly met
   'Mid deathless love's acclaims,
(Ex. 2)   Spoke evermore among themselves
   Their heart-remembered names;
And the souls mounting up to God
   Went by her like thin flames.

And still she bowed herself and stooped
   Out of the circling charm;
(Ex. 3)   Until her bosom must have made
   The bar she leaned on warm,
And the lilies lay as if asleep
   Along her bended arm.

. . . .

(Ex. 1)   The sun was gone now; the curled moon
                     Was like a little feather
                 Fluttering far down the gulf; and now
(Exx. 1, 3)   She spoke through the still weather.
                 Her voice was like the voice the stars
                     Had when they sang together.

                         .   .   .   .   .   .

(Ex. 4)   'I wish that he were come to me,
                     For he will come,' she said.
                 'Have I not prayed in Heaven?—on earth,
                     Lord, Lord, has he not pray'd?
(Ex. 2)   Are not two prayers a perfect strength?
                     And shall I feel afraid?

                 'When round his head the aureole clings,
                     And he is clothed in white,
                 I'll take his hand and go with him
                     To the deep wells of light;
                 As unto a stream we will step down,
                     And bathe there in God's sight.

                         .   .   .   .   .   .

                 'We two will lie i' the shadow of
                     That living mystic tree
                 Within whose secret growth the Dove
(Ex. 5)   Is sometimes felt to be,
                 While every leaf that His plumes touch
                     Saith His Name audibly.

                         .   .   .   .   .   .

                 'We two', she said, 'will seek the groves
                     Where the lady Mary is,
                 With her five handmaidens, whose names
                     Are five sweet symphonies,
                 Cecily, Gertrude, Magdalen,
                     Margaret and Rosalys.

                         .   .   .   .   .   .

                 'He shall fear, haply, and be dumb:
                     Then will I lay my cheek
                 To his, and tell about our love,
(Ex. 3)   Not once abashed or weak:
                 And the dear Mother will approve
                     My pride, and let me speak.

                 'Herself shall bring us, hand in hand,
                     To Him round whom all souls
                 Kneel, the clear-ranged unnumbered heads
                     Bowed with their aureoles:
(Ex. 2)   And angels meeting us shall sing
                     To their citterns and citoles.

(Ex. 5) 'There will I ask of Christ the Lord
   Thus much for him and me:—
   Only to live as once on earth
(Ex. 3) With Love,—only to be,
   As then awhile, for ever now
    Together, I and he.'

(Ex. 3) She gazed and listened and then said,
   Less sad of speech than mild,—
(Ex. 4) 'All this is when he comes.' She ceased.
   The light thrilled towards her, fill'd
   With angels in strong level flight.
    Her eyes pray'd, and she smil'd.

   (I saw her smile.) But soon their path
(Ex. 3) Was vague in distant spheres;
   And then she cast her arms along
    The golden barriers,
   And laid her face between her hands,
    And wept. (I heard her tears.)
(Exx. 5, 1)

HANDEL

'ISRAEL IN EGYPT'

A Selection

Some effrontery is needed to present my selection from *Israel in Egypt* as comprising the 'authentic portions' of that monumental work. What is published as *Israel in Egypt* exists throughout in Handel's autograph, and was produced by him on the 4th of April 1739. It contained too many choruses and not enough arias for the public taste, and was, in fact, a work of a kind that had never been heard in London before. Subsequent performances were few, and at them a half-hearted attempt was made to lighten the work by inserting a few more arias adapted from Handel's operas, a procedure quite exceptional in his oratorios. Largely as Handel's works support themselves by taking in each other's washing, his operas and oratorios have practically no dealings with each other. The operas gave no scope for choruses, and the Italian singers did not sing English. The borrowed opera arias did not help matters much, and performances of *Israel in Egypt* remained rare in Handel's lifetime, and did not become commoner until the public learned that choral music was greater than solo arias.

As a whole, then, *Israel in Egypt* suffered less alteration than most of Handel's oratorios during his lifetime; yet it has since been found to be perhaps one of the most composite and heterogeneous works of art in the history of music; and the discovery of its patchwork construction has caused a real distress, ranging, according to one's temper, from cynical contempt to moral indignation, and producing pathetic efforts to explain away a situation shocking when presented crudely to the sensibility of the naïve music-lover.

I propose to deal with each detail of the situation as it arises. This is a much shorter method than that of discussing the general principles first; since most of these general principles can then appear as *obiter dicta*, whereas their more systematic discussion can only give an audience the impression of rising temperature in a hall full of earnest persons, holders of pious opinions, and iconoclasts, all set at loggerheads by technical experts. Two general principles only will I mention as of paramount importance: first, that in the eighteenth century an oratorio, even more than an opera, was only in the rarest instances a single composition, and was always an entertainment filling several hours. The author was neither anonymous like the master-builder of a medieval cathedral, nor multiple like the authors and composers of a modern revue, who are proverbially supposed to outnumber the stage crowd. But, as the provider of some four hours' musical entertainment he had the right to insert acknowledged favourite arias, to invite contributions from pupils, and, in course of time, to neglect the formula of acknowledgement. Two volumes of Mozart's arias, including trios and quartets, were written by him as insertions in operas by forgotten composers; and passages from Handel's works more important than any which Handel borrowed have become incorporated into the structure of some of Mozart's greatest choral music, not because Mozart is a plagiarist, conscious or unconscious, but because such choral music is like architecture in being often constructed of extensive procedures and elements that are common property.

The other general principle which must be laid down is that Handel, like Bach and other great masters, differs from his predecessors and contemporaries in that he is a composer, as most of them are not. This is a very important principle, which is less understood in English musical orthodoxy than almost any other fact in art. The fourth volume of the *Oxford History of Music* is entitled 'The Age of Bach and Handel'. It contains great wealth of information about the contemporaries of those composers, and shows, more by accident than design, a kind of historical sense inasmuch as it fails to make Bach and Handel more prominent otherwise than by bulk than they were to their contemporaries. This leaves the naïve reader at a loss to understand why two composers so indistinguishable from the common run should nowadays be selected for the title of their age. But the author of the volume shows, without admitting it, that he himself is equally at a loss on this matter. He sums up the fullest pontifical ineptitude of British nineteenth-century musical criticism in the following paragraph:

'In Theodora's first song, the slow crotchets on which she sings the word "Angels" have nothing to do with the more rapid phrase to "ever bright and fair".... The continuation of a subject from the germ contained in its opening notes was never a very strong point with Handel, and in "Sweet rose and lily" we have an opportunity of comparing his methods in this respect with those of his quondam rival Bononcini, who hit upon nearly the same melodic idea in his best-known song "Per la gloria".

(a) HANDEL;

Sweet rose and li - ly, flow - 'ry form, Take me your faith-ful . . guard.

(b) BONONCINI transcribed to same key and time.

Per la glo - ria d'a - do-rar - vi, voglio a - mar-vi o lu - ci ca - ro.

It will strike every reader that the melodic germ of the subject, which is the figure in the second bar of each, is left by Handel quite undeveloped, while Bononcini carries it on in a delightful addition of two bars, and alludes to it again in the last bar but one, giving the whole strain a more obviously flowing character.'

Let us try some literary criticism on these methods.

Milton begins *L'Allegro* thus:

> Hence loathèd Melancholy
> Of Cerberus and blackest midnight born
> In Stygian Cave forlorn
> 'Mongst horrid shapes, and shrieks, and sights unholy!

Compare this disjointed sense and irregular rhythm, held together only by the imperfect rhyme of 'Melancholy' and 'unholy', with the symmetry of Shakespeare at the end of *A Midsummer-Night's Dream*:

> Hence away;
> Make no stay;
> Meet me all by break of day.

It will strike every reader that the intellectual germ of both passages, which is the word 'hence', is left by Milton quite undeveloped, while Shakespeare carries it throughout the whole passage, with a delightful and logical inversion in the word 'meet'. (It is unnecessary to point out that Shakespeare wrote 'trip' instead of 'hence'; for the Oxford historian remarks in a footnote that 'it is unnecessary to point out that the key and time-values in Bononcini's song have been changed in order to facilitate comparison'.)

It was unfortunate for the doyen of English musical critics, as well as for criticism itself, that, for those who like that kind of thing, music can be enjoyed in the series of mere tastes of 'sugar piled upon honey' which was all that Charles Lamb made of the art in his *Essay on Ears*. This one comparison of Bononcini and Handel sheds far more light on our British standardized ignorance of composition than upon Handel's ultimate victory over his rival. The composer of a witty symmetrical tune like *Per la gloria* may or may not be able to carry it out on a larger scale than is revealed by its self-contained symmetry. The composer who gets as far as the first twelve bars of *Sweet rose and lily* must be intending to go much farther, and shows every sign of being able to do so.

This quality of composition is not the only condition of greatness in music or art; and it is compatible with childish immaturity and with insolent rubbish. A composition ascribed to Handel cannot be proved spurious on the ground that it is rubbish, nor can it be proved spurious because, whether otherwise good or bad, it is extremely careless in style; but, if a thing ascribed to Handel or extant in his writing has not at all events 'the gift of the gab', then you may be quite certain that he did not himself compose it at any period of infancy, youth or age. The six oboe duets which he wrote at the age of twelve differ from his later work chiefly in two facts: that there is much more in them line for line, and that there is much less evidence that they might not go on for ever.

At all periods of Handel's life his musical form is too improvisatorial to be amenable to any specially musical rules. He must be judged as a rhetorician, exactly as we would judge of a master of prose or a speaker. His work at the age of twelve has occasional defects, mostly in the nature of redundancies or tautologies, which do not occur in his mature works. When he was confronted with these juvenile sonatas at the height of his fame in London, he was quite unsentimentally amused, and laughed, saying: 'I wrote like the devil in those days, and chiefly for the oboe, which was my favourite instrument.' A sympathetic reader or hearer of these oboe sonatas might almost have expected Handel to show some signs of regret that his later compositions did not always maintain his early enthusiasm; but, on the contrary, Handel was capable of tempting a friend, while promenading in Vauxhall Gardens, to comment on the stuff that was being played by the band, and of replying: 'You are quite right, sir; it is very poor stuff, and I thought so myself when I wrote it.' But whether Handel was writing cynically poor stuff or recording his most sublime inspirations, he never wrote a page that halted. He did not always write at a tearing pace; and, though his average time for the first half of a three-act oratorio was a week of continuous writing, he would sometimes revise a single aria several times, or make a great many alterations in drafting a single version of it. Sometimes the results of such labour were what we regard as inspired, like the intensely pathetic 'Waft her, angels, to the skies' in *Jephtha*. Sometimes it is impossible to guess why Handel was so scrupulous, as in the case of the aria *Thou art gone up on high* in the *Messiah*, to which the most pious editors append the footnote: '*This air is generally omitted*'. The reasons for the omission are obvious. What is mysterious is, not only that there are six extant versions of the aria, but that there is no means of telling why any of them should be considered better than the others. As a whole the score of *The Messiah* was written in twenty-one days. Some of the six versions of its dullest aria were probably transpositions for the benefit of various singers at various performances; but I doubt whether any general principle will emerge from the study of Handel's revisions of his own work, such as can be shown in every detail of Beethoven's sketches. What is quite certain is that Handel could neither copy nor invent a paragraph of music without making it fluent. To this subject I must return each time that we come upon adaptations of earlier or foreign works in the course of *Israel in Egypt*. Let us now begin the point-to-point analysis of the selection which I produce as containing the 'authentic essence' of this mighty work within the compass of a little more than an hour.

As published, *Israel in Egypt* has no overture, but begins abruptly with a narrative recitative introducing the story of the plagues of Egypt and the exodus as told in Psalms lxxviii, cv, and cvi. Chrysander has restored Handel's own titles to the main sections of his work. The first part is called *Exodus*, and the second part *Moses's Song*. We are spared the duty of keeping our tempers and restraining our guffaws at the well-meaning absurdities of Handel's librettists, because in *Israel in Egypt*, as in *The Messiah*, Handel's words are entirely Biblical; and in the case of *Israel* there is no record that he did not select them himself. *Moses's Song*, which is considerably the larger part of the work, was written first, and occupied Handel from the 1st to the 11th of October 1738. The first part, or *Exodus*, was then written between the 15th and 28th of the same month. The reason why it begins so abruptly was that Handel prefaced it by his already-written Funeral Anthem for Queen Caroline, *The Ways of Zion do Mourn*, which he adapted under the title of *The Lamentation of the Israelites over the Death of Joseph*. This more than thoroughly explains the present opening of *Israel*; but the gain in a further volume of Handel's greatest choral music is outweighed by the fact that the Funeral Anthem is not well contrasted with what is to follow, and keeps us for half an hour with only Handel's new title to tell us that it has anything to do with either Israel or Egypt. After much thought, I have come to the conclusion that an ideal and very short way to introduce the oratorio and indicate the situation Handel has in mind is to use the Dead March in *Saul* as an overture.

After this plain indication of mourning, we see the point of the first sentence of the opening recitative.

I. RECITATIVE

Now there arose a new king over Egypt, which knew not Joseph; and he set over Israel task-masters to afflict them with burdens; and they made them serve with rigour.

Then follows an 8-part chorus in Handel's noblest style.

II. CHORUS

Ex. 1. And the children of Israel sighed by reason of the bondage:
Ex. 2. And their cry came up unto God.
    They oppress'd them with burdens, and made them serve with rigour.

An alto solo delivers the first clause in one of Handel's finest examples of perfect melody and perfect illustration, the orchestra contributing to the realization of the word 'sighed'.

Then the orchestra develops an energetic theme, over which the sopranos and altos of an 8-part chorus sing a solemn *canto fermo* suggestive of modal harmony. The meaning of the energetic theme appears when the chorus takes it up, and the combination is shown in Ex. 2.

Thus Handel has stated his whole material with his maturest simplicity and breadth. This chorus would repay such an analysis as I have attempted to give of Beethoven's *Weihe des Hauses* Overture; but the analysis would be quite as difficult to write as to read. Meanwhile, it is easier to listen and enjoy the chorus, which is true Handel of the highest order. Apart from time-limits, that is one reason against adopting Handel's plan of using the great Funeral Anthem as a first part to *Israel in Egypt*. This chorus must be allowed to make its full impression without being forestalled by half an hour's music of the same quality and tone. A detailed analysis of it would soon show its difference from the second-hand parts of *Israel in Egypt*, if these also were thoroughly analysed; but as I am not producing the second-hand stuff, we can spare ourselves the trouble. We must not lump together as second-hand all the stuff where Handel borrows themes, or even whole passages, from other works. Originality lies in the whole. Nobody would be surprised if the *canto fermo* in Ex. 2 should prove to be liturgical: indeed, I should be surprised if it were not. Nor have I the slightest interest in the possibility that the other two themes of this chorus have been found elsewhere. They are, rather, such as it might be difficult to avoid in the musical language of the seventeenth and eighteenth centuries. All that matters is their perfect fitness for their text, and the grandeur of the form into which they are built. The chorus is in eight parts, but, although written for convenience as a double chorus, is hardly, if at all, antiphonal.

III. RECITATIVE

Ex. 3. Then sent He Moses, His servant, and Aaron, whom He had chosen: these shew'd His signs among them, and wonders in the land of Ham.

He turned their waters into blood.

Handel's recitatives are written with the same secretarial efficiency as his other work. I hear rumours that the profounder Italian scholars can detect that his Italian recitatives are not quite the genuine article as supplied by the direct apostolic successors of the Neapolitan School. The evidence is doubtless as cogent as the evidence that Handel was not an Englishman. Recitative is a technical term meaning solo vocal music in which the composer's only purpose is to 'stylise' in musical notes the natural rise and fall and rhythm of spoken words, excluding all symmetries and ornamentations that might distract attention from this purpose. As this art was first developed in Italy, its recognized classical formulas naturally suit the Italian language. And we have no better reason to expect them to suit other languages than to translate *Qu'est-ce-que c'est que ça?* by *What is this that this is that that?* Nevertheless, already in the eighteenth century it was orthodox to comment upon Purcell's sturdy independence of foreign culture, that 'he did not adopt the art of recitative as recently developed in Italy'. Why should he? Purcell's declamation is English; and the only way in which his recitative deviates from what is universal in the Italian art is that he cannot resist the temptation to break into illustrative coloratura. In the same, but in a simpler, way Handel transcends the realism of recitative, and marks his intention of doing so by a renewed time-signature and key-signature, in what has always been rightly admired as one of his greatest strokes of musical rhetoric.

Ex. 3.

He turn-ed their wa-ters in-to blood.

As a rule, tenors do not like to expose the weakness of their low notes; but no tenor has ever failed to enjoy convincing the listener of the gruesomeness of his low D on the word 'blood'.

IV. CHORUS

Ex. 4. They loathed to drink of the river:
        He turned their waters into blood.

Ex. 4.

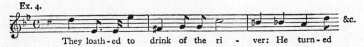

They loath-ed to   drink of the ri - ver: He turn-ed

This is an excellent Handelian fugue, slightly above Handel's usual standard of solidity, and expressive of the words by reason of two points: its chromatic harmony, and the fact that its theme takes the extreme form of what is otherwise a matter of common property. The theme must have come into existence as soon as a solid minor scale had ousted the ecclesiastical modes. Its essential feature is the diminished seventh on the syllables 'to drink'. In its mildest form the first interval is a third, as in *And with his stripes we are healed*, and in Bach's A minor Fugue in the second book of the Forty-eight. The intermediate form begins with a fifth, as in the fugue of Haydn's F minor Quartet Op. 20, No. 4. I cannot off-hand say how many instances might be found of Handel's major seventh, but it is obviously selected here for expressive purposes, and chorus singers will perhaps pardon my remarking that, unless they are very experienced, they 'loathe' being caught by it unawares; which, of course, with experience they never are.

V. ARIA

It is highly undesirable nowadays that performances of *Israel in Egypt* should appeal, intentionally or otherwise, to one's sense of humour. I have no doubt that Handel enjoyed allowing his string-band to hop in a pretty pattern through the shocking tale of the frogs that infested even the king's chambers, and possibly (since the pattern prevails throughout the aria) had some causal connexion with the blotches and blains that broke forth on man and beast. Except for this pattern and its relation to the text, the aria might just as well be sung to some edifying moral; and it is certainly the more agonizingly funny the more beautifully it is sung. Only once have I heard it given with an accurate sense of the situation. That versatile artist, Marie Brema, instead of using the full fog-horn powers of the British contralto, presented it with the tremulous horror of a *Hofdame* clinging to the faint hope that the mess might be cleared up before Pharaoh could discover it.

VI. CHORUS

Ex. 5. HE spake the word: And there came all manner of flies and lice in all their quarters.

HE spake: and the locusts came without number and devour'd the fruits of the land.

We now come to what is really important in Handel's borrowings. Handel has represented for all time the rhythm and the solemn implications of the statement: 'HE spake the word.' With trombones and with echoes from antiphonal groups of orchestra and chorus, nothing can be simpler or more exclusive of other possibilities. As for the flies, the violins represent them with furious efficiency, and are joined by the basses in heavier flight when the locusts come without number. The whole conception shows Handel at his utmost efficiency, and is too grand to be comic. This being so, one of the greatest mysteries in the history of music is the fact that Handel took the trouble to copy the whole of an instrumental *sinfonia* from a Serenata by Stradella (1645–82), comprising twenty-six bars of the whole of forty-one of which this number consists. It saved him no trouble. Stradella was an interesting historical figure, the facts of whose real life were early in the eighteenth century completely obliterated beneath a romantic story which is now far better known than any of his music. The pathos of his style is said to have been such that the assassins who were commissioned to slay him for having eloped with the mistress of a Venetian nobleman desisted from their purpose on hearing his aria *Pietà signore* sung in church, and warned the lovers of their danger. The aria is supposed to have come down to us in unquestionably beautiful terms that certainly never took shape until early in the nineteenth century. In power of composition Stradella's genuine work shows a definite advance on what had been achieved by the middle of the seventeenth century, and the twenty-six bars which

Handel transferred to the present chorus show neither strength
nor weakness of form, but do contain at the outset quite interesting
modulations—

Ex. 5.

to which Handel gives proper weight by having established his
key in eight previous bars. These eight bars and a final ritornello
account for the difference between Stradella's twenty-six bars and
Handel's forty-one. For the rest, we may fairly say that Stradella
wrote this chorus first, with the exceptions that HE, the choral
writing, and the flies are omitted.

VII. CHORUS

Exx. 6–7. He gave them hailstones for rain;
Exx. 8a–8b. fire, mingled with the hail, ran along upon the ground.

We never know where we are with Handel. It is an absolute law
that his recitatives must lead correctly or effectively to what follows; and there are plenty of cases where the key-sequence of
complete movements is artistic. But there are plenty of cases where
it is quite crass. The great Funeral Anthem is firmly in and around
G minor, except for one number in the pointlessly incongruous key
of A minor; and *Israel in Egypt* has two examples of the same crass
indifference side by side with Handel's deepest harmonic thoughts.
The sequence of keys in ball-room dances is not more casual than
the C major of the famous Hailstone Chorus after the B flat of the
Chorus of Flies. But this is less mysterious than the fact that
Handel should have again troubled to draw upon the Stradella
Serenata for this famous chorus. Space obviously fails to go into
the intricacies of the case. By far the most able extant collection of
arguments on the matter is to be found in *Handel and his Orbit*,
by P. Robinson, who stoutly maintains that the main works in
question, the Stradella Serenata, the Erba *Magnificat*, and the Urio
Te Deum, are early works of Handel's own. Arguments based upon
minutiae of style are absolutely hopeless with Handel. The folios
and quartos of Shakespeare are not more careless than Handel's
autographs; and wherever Handel encountered any feature that
pleased him in any composer's style, he promptly imitated it, so
that you can almost date his settling in England by his adoption of
some pleasant archaisms in the style of Purcell. But, as I must still
insist, the one thing that I cannot find in any of Handel's earliest

works is an inability or indisposition to compose. 'Interminable cantatas of no great merit' is what his quarrelsome friend Mattheson imputed to his nonage; but never until the fourth volume of the *Oxford History of Music* has any critic committed the ineptitude of mistaking the alternate abruptness and expansiveness of a Handelian exposition for shortness of breath. The first ten bars of the following extract are common to Stradella's Serenata and Handel's Hailstone Chorus, except that Handel begins with a bass note on the organ, and that his key is C instead of D. But at the twelfth bar Stradella stops and begins again on the dominant.

Ex. 6.

I am not clear what his overture represents. The initial rhythm may mean whatever 'Pip-pip' means, or it may mean knocking at a door. Far be it from me to be inattentive to its fitness for its own comic purpose; but, to borrow the admirable phrase sometimes heard in committees, what Opens a Serious Door is that neither here nor in the other two movements of his overture does Stradella even feebly begin to compose in any real sense of the term, whereas Handel's hailstones are beginning to fall thicker at the eleventh bar, and are soon coming down in spate, while he draws upon the last extant number of Stradella's Serenata to bring his twenty-one bars of introduction to a climax.

Ex. 7.

In Ex. 7 Stradella is illustrating the wrath of a presumably elderly gentleman whose lady has tricked him. The shaking of his fists has become the whiplash of Handel's hailstones; and one of his vocal expressions has become the bass of Handel's most definite vocal theme.

I flatly refuse to believe that the Serenata ascribed to Stradella is an early work of Handel's. It has a certain number of pretty ideas which attracted Handel, and a large number of equally pretty ideas that were common currency. It has also, what is more material to the Chorus of the Flies and the Hailstone Chorus than any number of thematic borrowings, the idea of antiphonal groups of instruments, which Handel has gigantically supplemented by antiphonal groups of chorus.

This raises the general question of the purpose of eight-part writing. In the first chorus, *And the children of Israel sighed*, the only use of antiphony is to enable the word 'sighed' to be detached as a separate harmonic mass from the surrounding fugato; but in the Chorus of Flies and the Hailstone Chorus antiphony is of the essence of the contract. Handel had already written ostensibly eight-part choruses in 1733 in the oratorios of *Deborah* and *Athalia*. Only in one case, in *Deborah*, when the faithful Israelites are in altercation with the Baal-worshippers, are the voices grouped in opposite masses for obvious dramatic reasons. In *Israel* the reasons are purely musical. Genuine eight-part writing is a rich fabric and laborious to calculate and write. Its technical difficulty has always been overrated, even in the most classical times; and no academic tradition is more infantile than that which still occasionally survives in academic regulations ordaining five-part counterpoint for Bachelors of Music and eight-part for Doctors. I seriously question whether any ten bars of Handel's eight-part writing would satisfy an old-fashioned British examiner for a Mus.Doc. degree; and, in fact, though his eight-part choruses, whether antiphonal or not, require eight staves to set out the notes as Handel distributes them, they contain a very small percentage of real eight-part writing, and would lose much of their cumulative effect if they contained more. Bach's eight-part writing is, like every aspect of his forms, much more true to the terms of its contract than Handel's, though an old-fashioned British examiner would again have to learn Bach's aesthetic system from the rudiments upwards before he was qualified to examine it. With *Israel in Egypt* Handel evidently acquired an appetite for eight-part writing, and an insight into its true aesthetic principles. The richness of eight parts, independent as such, very soon palls; but 'he opposition of complete masses of harmony is of elemental power. And when the masses overlap, the eight-part harmony is a by-product, enjoyable both for its own richness and for the way in which it happens. But increase of power comes not from the multiplying of the parts, but from their occasional or gradual fusion towards ordinary four-part writing, and further, down to the thunderous unisons for which Handel is famous, and fatally imitable by composers who have developed the modern orchestra to an organization which no chorus less than a football crowd can dominate. Ten years after *Israel in Egypt*, Handel designed *Solomon* expressly for the purpose of reviewing most of the subjects of Solomon's wisdom, sacred and profane, in a series of descriptive choruses, mainly antiphonal. It is interesting that only once should the motive of his antiphonal writing have been dramatic, and that in *Deborah*, the earliest case of all. The total bulk of Bach's eight-part choral writing is hardly greater than that of Handel's. About half of it is contained in the *Matthew Passion*, where the antiphony is mainly dramatic and is implied by the text. The rest is comprised in four of the so-called 'unaccompanied' motets, two of the church cantatas, and the Hosanna of the B minor Mass. As may be expected of Bach, the eight-part writing is perfectly systematic; and so is the scheme by which Bach makes his double choruses gradually coalesce into four-part harmony. He thus appears to miss the opportunity for the local nuances Handel commands by doubling any voice as he chooses; but the limitation is only apparent, for Bach's orchestra is often a systematically independent chorus in itself, as in the multi-choral Psalms of Schütz a century earlier, where the instruments, sometimes described merely as *vox instrumentalis* and always provided with the words, exactly like the voices, are grouped in a separate *capella* or two. If you have leisure to think of such things while you listen to a hailstorm as suggestive as Handel's, I can only wish you joy of your scholarship; and, as for Stradella, he extinguishes himself at the eleventh bar.

VIII. CHORUS

He sent a thick darkness over all the land, even darkness, which might be felt.

Handel's greatest power and depth are here manifest in every particular. And I do not see how any quotation, short of the whole chorus, can illustrate them. The chief difficulty in realizing his intentions nowadays comes from the fact that the modern orchestra provides a first and second bassoon to play the notes written for these instruments by Handel, but does not provide the twenty bassoons which seemed to him a reasonable number to balance his twenty oboes and his string-band of ordinary modern size. However, as the writer of the fourth volume of the *Oxford History of Music* remarks, our ancestors had no sense of proportion, any more than the composer of *Sweet rose and lily* had a sense of composition.

This raises the question of 'additional accompaniments', a matter far more difficult in the case of the improvisatorial Handel than in that of Bach, whose schematic accuracy compels us at all events to play exactly what he wrote, however we may be compelled to redistribute it. The trouble with additional accompaniments began, as all the world knows, with Mozart, who certainly in the case of *The Messiah* was often distressingly out of touch with Handel's subject, but whose exquisite work on *Acis and Galatea* and the smaller *Ode for St. Cecilia's Day* results in a delicious compound style nowhere as incongruous as the elements which Handel has admitted into *Israel in Egypt*, and everywhere finished and imaginative where Handel is perfunctory to the extent of simply not condescending to write his music down at all so long as he was himself able to gag at the organ or harpsichord. Pious opinions have been the origin of dangerous heresies no less often, if not oftener, than they have attained the rank of orthodox doctrines. And of all pious opinions in music perhaps the most woolly-headed was the dictum of Rockstro in the first edition of *Grove's Dictionary* that all accompaniments added merely for the sake of noise are wholly indefensible. Here the word 'noise' is a crassly question-begging epithet for which the legitimate meaning is 'volume of sound', the offensive term being chosen to represent a sound which the writer does not like. The truth is that with the modern orchestra additions to increase the volume of sound are the only ones that can restore

Handel's balance of tone, and that the whole mischief of corruption that has obliterated Handel's style for a hundred and fifty years consists in the self-indulgence of composers and conductors who find the bare walls of Handel's edifices an admirable surface to scribble upon and to bedaub with the contents of more or less expensive paint-boxes. With ten or twelve oboes and ten or twelve bassoons to play the parts that Handel writes for them, we might recover something tolerably like Handel's orchestral colouring. Strange to say, modern developments of the orchestra have not helped us appreciably far towards this consummation. But we need not be very fastidious about the precise quality of tone that we may get by putting into unison all the wind instruments we have. Handel himself is evidently sometimes as vague as Schütz with his *vox instrumentalis*. In the whole of *Israel in Egypt* flutes are indicated in one passage in unison with the violins. Taken literally in terms of the modern orchestra, this would be represented by solemnly engaging two gentlemen (or ladies) to sit for two hours in the orchestra for the purpose of doubling the violins in some twenty bars. We cannot suppose that this was Handel's intention. Probably most of his oboists could play the flute, and probably half of them were detailed to do so for any appropriate passages; while, no doubt, numbers of players were available whose main instrument was the flute. These would be encouraged to play for the very purpose so sternly reprobated by Rockstro. Handel set great store by the importation, or even the special manufacture, of a contrafagotto for use in his works. He never wrote a part for it; but he certainly used it to reinforce his basses whenever he could get it.

As to the quality of tone produced by twenty oboes, nothing like it has been heard in modern music, not even in Mahler's Eighth Symphony, a work which is known as the 'Symphony of a Thousand', because an orchestra and chorus of seven hundred and fifty is its minimum necessity and a thousand is what it needs for comfort. But what does appear from the disciplined and experienced handling of such vast combinations is that the resulting tone-colours are neither so varied nor so vivid as those of music on a smaller scale. We may be certain that the general unison of all the wind instruments of the modern orchestra that can play at the same pitch will produce a tone fairly capable of replacing that unknown quantity, the tone of a dozen Handelian oboes. It is mere pedantry to say that the associations and sound of clarinets, or even of saxophones, are so foreign to Handelian aesthetics that their mixture with oboe tone is an outrage. So long as the players play in tune and the really Handelian opposition between brass and wood-wind and the rest of the orchestra is not obliterated, it does not matter

two hoots of a saxophone what sort of soprano or alto wind instrument we use to impart to our orchestra something like the reedi-
ness which must almost have overwhelmed Handel's violins. I
have not the slightest doubt that two clarinets, two cors anglais,
and four muted horns, in unison with Handel's two bassoon parts,
will approximate closely enough to his representation of darkness
for all genuine aesthetic purposes; and I am equally certain that he
would have thrown his wig at me if I had tried to fob him off with
two bassoons alone.

The chorus becomes something like a choral recitative as the
voices give up full harmony and grope their isolated ways through
vastly remote keys; and when I speak of vastly remote keys I do
not refer to that feeble-minded criterion which esteems all strokes
of genius as 'remarkable for the time at which they were written'.
The fact that our loud-speaker can give us an orchestral concert
from the Antipodes before the sounds of the orchestra have
travelled from the platform to the back of the hall, does not annul
the record of a Channel swimmer. Handel's modulations are related, not to the time at which he wrote, but to the structure of his
musical language. In the Chorus of Darkness they are as extensive
as the modulations in Bach's Chromatic Fantasia, inasmuch as they
traverse most of harmonic space. On the other hand, they differ
profoundly from the Chromatic Fantasia, and from Handel's own
Passion recitatives in *The Messiah*, because they are not enharmonic
—that is to say, each step is known as far as it goes, but there is no
general aim and the end of the groping is incalculably remote.
(Handel's declamation is subtle to the extent of making distinctions
between 'over all the land' and 'o'er all the land'; 'e'en darkness'
and 'even darkness'. These should not be corrected. On the other
hand, he puts an intolerable strain on the indefinite article when he
makes it come, not only on an accented beat, '*A* thick darkness',
but on the highest note of the four. So long as the notes are level,
it would be pedantic to make any change; but in this last case I feel
justified in reading 'Darkness sent He', especially as Handel continues by shortening the words into 'A darkness'.)

IX. CHORUS

Ex. 9. He smote all the first-born of Egypt, the chief of all their strength.

Daylight follows with drastic effect, which Handel enjoys as fiercely
as the Psalmist. His twenty oboes and twenty bassoons double the
voices, while the trombones and the violins put a very literal interpretation on the word 'smote'. Towards the end of this double
fugue, the chorus does its own smiting with great zest, before
bringing the fugue tersely to an admirable climax. Not less

admirable is the anticlimax of the seven bars of final orchestral ritornello.

X. CHORUS

Ex. 10. But as for His people,
Ex. 11. He led them forth like sheep.
Ex. 13. He brought them out with silver and gold: there was not one feeble person among their tribes.

One of the most perfect transitions, both in mood and harmony, in all music is that effected by the first chords of this wonderful chorus. After the close in A minor, the impact of the dominant of G major perfectly represents the blessed change of mood from the malicious joy at the smiting of the enemy to the deep gratitude for God's care of his people.

These simple-seeming opening bars might have been written by anybody, but could never have been placed where they are by any but a very great composer; and, as far as intrinsic beauty can be conveyed in a theme of four bars and accumulated in echoes and sequences for another thirty or forty, Handel continues to give us his very own at its very best.

Ex. 11.

He led,   He led them   forth   like   sheep, ...

Flutes and Violins.

. . . .   He

The orchestral colouring, even with a poor couple of oboes and couple of bassoons, is beautiful according to the most exacting modern orchestral criteria; and the theme is surely one of the most beautiful that Handel ever *wrote*. Therefore it now behoves us to follow the pious advice given to the young man who asked for authoritative counsel how to deal with the arguments that assailed his orthodoxy: 'Look them boldly in the face and pass them by.' This wonderful theme fills several more or less lively pages of the Stradella Serenata, where its text, *Io pur seguirò*, inspires its canonic imitations. Stradella's treatment of it becomes faster and faster, until it reaches a presto; upon which the gentleman furiously answers: *Seguir non voglio più* in the terms afterwards used by Handel in the Hailstone Chorus, as shown in Exx. 7, 8a, and 8b. I am as ready as any one to respect Stradella on his own merits as an interesting historical figure, or even as something more; but the rightful owner of an idea is the person who understands it, and Stradella is the rightful owner of the comic chase-me-Charlie affair that he makes of this theme. His own continuation of it at once relegates it to its native seventeenth-century limbo of shreds, patches, and frustrations.

Ex. 12.

It is also quite sufficient to dispose of any theory that the Serenata can have been an early work of Handel's own. But the potential beauty of those first four bars explains all the rest. After turning Stradella's theme into a sublime vocal pastoral symphony, Handel repeats his introduction (Ex. 10), and continues with a setting of the words 'He brought them out with silver and gold' in a solid and appropriately broad fugue, which lasts for some sixty-four bars.

Ex. 13.

He then summarily recapitulates his three sentences with their three themes, and ends in overwhelming triumph with neither themes nor polyphony, to the text: 'There was not one, not one feeble person among their tribes.' (The repetition of 'not one' is a glorious stroke of rhetoric and rhythm.) It is a popular opinion that Handel has an unmistakable style. The many difficulties in this proposition begin with the questions of what is a style, and how much of Handel's works are by Handel. But this chorus could have been designed, invented, composed, and compiled by no one but Handel. It is a pity that the word 'poet' has no verb in English, so that we cannot translate Beethoven's admirable epigram: 'Gedichtet, oder wie man sagt, componirt.' The least understood and most Handelian feature of this chorus is the two extra bars in which the orchestra quietly remarks—

Ex. 14.

Orthodox theologians and gastronomes tell us that, though it were impious to doubt that the Almighty could have created a better fruit than the strawberry, the fact remains that he never did.

XI. CHORUS

Egypt was glad when they departed, for the fear of them fell upon
them.

In a complete performance of *Israel in Egypt* it would be a mistake
to omit the note-for-note transcription of an organ canzona by
Kaspar Kerll (1627–93) which Handel adapts to the text: *Egypt was
glad when they departed, for the fear of them fell upon them.* Hawkins, who, with all his unclubbability, sometimes knew a good thing
when he saw it, gives the whole of Kerll's organ piece in his
History of Music, without showing the slightest consciousness that
Handel had used it. Mr. Robinson in *Handel and his Orbit* argues
that the piece was the kind of thing that was highly esteemed by
the promoters of the Concerts of Antient Music; and that, like
Handel's other plagiarisms of whole pieces, its inclusion in such a
four-hours' entertainment as an oratorio or an opera would be a
compliment to the taste of his more learned patrons, and would
require no acknowledgement. Certainly Handel was bitterly aware
that his enemies were on the prowl for any opportunity of discredit-
ing him; and certainly in the matter of plagiarisms his behaviour
shows, not so much that he had no fear of detection, as that he had
no reason to fear its consequences. The counterpoint of Kerll's
double fugue in contrary motion is much more solid than any that
is habitual with Handel. Kerll's canzona falls into two parts, which
are repeated. The second part introduces the second theme,
which Handel sets to the words: 'For the fear of them fell upon
them.' Handel has taken considerable pains with the orchestration,
although its sole function is to support the voices, which sing Kerll's
canzona note for note. The first part is supported by the wind, the
organ, and the basses. With the second part the strings and trombones enter, the strings doubling the voices in the higher octave,
and thus attaining a powerful climax. The pitch is a tone higher
than the original, so that Handel's version presents the appearance
of a modernized Phrygian mode, which corresponds closely to the
facts of its harmonic style. The whole thing perfectly expresses the
glum relief of the Egyptians, and neither Bach nor Handel could
have put anything better in its place. But it so happens that the
next chorus, and the next topic, can follow 'But as for his people'
just as effectively.

XII

We now come to the second and larger of the early sources of
Israel in Egypt. Mr. Robinson is very anxious to prove that, Erba
and Urio being the names of places at which Handel probably
stayed during his Italian visit, the composers, the Rev. Don

Dionigi Erba and Padre Francesco Urio, may not have written them at all, and that ascriptions on Italian manuscripts often confuse the words *dal* and *del*. *Dal* simply means 'at the house (or place) of', while *del* means 'composed by'. Our view of the case will be obscured by the slightest anxiety to vindicate Handel's moral and artistic integrity, or even to consider them as involved in the question. Those who feel any such uneasiness ought to take courage from the fact that the fiercest champion of the author-hood of Stradella, Urio, Erba, and other *Händelquellen*, is Chrysander, who not only devoted his life to editing the works and writing the biography of Handel, but revered him so far on the further side of idolatry as to believe that music had done little but decline since Handel's death. Chrysander gives a reduced facsimile of two pages from Handel's autograph copy of the Erba *Magnificat*. Both of these show that when he made this manuscript he was not composing, but copying from a set of parts: a fact obvious at a glance to any one who knows how composers write and how they copy as distinguished from professional copyists. Chrysander does not tell us how he further deduces that the parts from which Handel copies must have been not only incomplete, but printed. The Erba *Magnificat*, says Chrysander, shows every sign of an Italian hand; and, moreover, one of the last decades of the seventeenth century. I do not myself feel confident that many pages of Handel do not show signs of an Italian hand, and even traces of the last decades of the seventeenth century; but poor Rockstro opined on pp. 221 ff. of his *Life of Handel* that this *Magnificat* might still be regarded as Handel's composition, for which Chrysander relegates him to the category of 'unauthorized persons who rummage now and then in Handel's manuscripts and get their opinions printed before they have acquired the capacity to form a judgement'. So we had better be careful.

The Erba *Magnificat* is alleged to have inspired Handel's setting of the following words:

He rebuked the Red Sea, and it was dried up.

The setting of this has a considerable resemblance to the first four bars of the Erba setting of the text *Quia respexit humilitatem ancillae suae*. The resemblance is not nearly good enough to make the case interesting, and it would never have been noticed but for its occurrence in a work otherwise as full of quotations as *Hamlet*. The passage is so drastically simple that even a slight inaccuracy or addition to the quotation is as ruinous to the case as the evidence in favour of the court-martialled officer who wished to be wakened and called early, which would have exonerated him from the charge of riotous behaviour had not his faithful servant on further question-

ing added that he said he was to be the Queen of the May. To my
great loss I have never heard, and now never shall hear, a Handel
Festival at the Crystal Palace. Those great occasions were doubtless great mistakes; and very little has been said in their defence by
authoritative musicians. No music has ever been composed for
performance on so huge a scale. Even Berlioz directs that, if his
Requiem is to be performed by a really enormous chorus, only half
or a quarter of the chorus should be used normally, and the whole
mass reserved for the climaxes. The full mass is eight hundred
voices, with an orchestra in proportion. Our British ideas of the
balance between chorus and orchestra have always been inadequate
as regards the orchestra; but, in any case, Berlioz never imagined
that his *Requiem* would be performed by a quarter of the four
thousand singers and players of the Handel Festival of 1923, nor
has any composer made the slightest attempt to calculate for more
than the thousand performers that can comfortably produce
Mahler's Eighth Symphony. Even Berlioz's ideal scheme of what
Paris, with time and money, could achieve with an orchestra comprising, among other details, 32 pianofortes and 32 harps, amounts
to only 465 players and 360 singers. It is on record by an intelligent
critic that little contrast of tone or colour could be appreciated by
a well-placed listener to the vast forces of the Handel Festival; but
that an impressive exception was the effect of a contrast between
loud high chords and soft low chords in the case of *He rebuked the
Red Sea.* Here the *piano* at the words 'and it was dried up' came
out in clear contrast. In any performance the contrast ought to be
impressive, for two reasons: first, that these chords are the only
unaccompanied vocal chords in the whole work; second, that
they plunge into the dark key of E flat after the loud C major. The
whole conception is Handel's, and the traces of it in Erba omit
everything essential, and are suggested only by their surroundings.

XIII. CHORUS

Ex. 15. He led them through the deep as through a wilderness.

No two persons have the same sense of humour, and I have
been told that this chorus is one of Handel's funniest. To me the
only possible comic aspect must lie in difficulties of performance;

difficulties which ought to vanish in rehearsal, because it is a perfectly reasonable piece of choral writing, and, as far as I can understand music at all, a very impressive specimen of Handel's style at
its highest inventiveness. The fugue subject and its counterpoints
obviously illustrate the words; and the eye can easily perceive the
catch-as-catch-can appearance of the stretti to which the subjects
lend themselves. In rehearsal it may be legitimate or stimulating
to enjoy what fun is occasioned by the natural failure of sight-
singers to take exactly the right plunge on the word 'deep', but the
difficulties of rehearsals ought not to appear in performance.
Burney, commenting on what he believed to be the earliest specimen of recorded music, observed that, though it was not of such
excellence as to make us greatly regret the loss of things like it, the
disposition of those who were pleased with it may have been a great
blessing to them. I cannot emulate Burney's urbanity in my feelings towards those who find anything funny in Handel's setting of
He led them through the deep.

XIV. CHORUS

But the waters overwhelmed their enemies, there was not one of
them left.

Like all triumphs over enemies, this chorus is enjoyable in a less
solemn way. To all healthy-minded children, even in the days of
The Fairchild Family, the story of the plagues of Egypt has been so
enjoyable as hardly to fall within sabbatical limits. I, for my own
part, long misunderstood the exhortation at the beginning of our
Morning Prayer as telling us that the Scripture moveth us in 'Sunday' places; which places I naturally took to mean those which
should regulate our conduct, while other places, such as the story
of the Plagues and the Tower of Babel, were, with all due reverence, permissible sources of pleasure on week-days. The appearance of the orchestral accompaniment on paper is such that no
amount of zest on the part of chorus or orchestra will prevent profane persons and young children from remarking on the obvious
resemblance between this chorus and the act of splashing about in
a bath; but there is no reason why a young bath-spanker whose
favourite Bible lesson is the Plagues should not grow up into a
pious and heroic bishop or moderator. This would be much better
than that the child's natural pleasure in the vindictiveness of the
Psalmist should be unalloyed with the spirit of Handel and Haydn,
neither of whom could keep their cheerfulness within the bounds
of decorum when they thought of their Creator. No quotations
are needed: the chorus has no themes, but it declaims well and
leaves no doubt that 'there was not one of them left'. Handel
evidently expects the kettle-drums to enjoy themselves, and would

probably have been delighted to have two pairs, with two players. When he is in his best form the timing of his climaxes and contrasts is as magnificent as the ideas themselves. He now gives a great burst of slow eight-part harmony to the words:—

xv and xvi

And Israel saw that great work that the Lord did upon th' Egyptians; and the people feared the Lord.

He continues with a sober fugue to the words:

And believed the Lord and his servant Moses.

The subject of this fugue comes from the Stradella Serenata, much as the words 'And it came to pass' come from anywhere you please in the Bible. In a performance of the whole of *Israel in Egypt* this makes an adequate quiet end to Handel's first part; but the problem of selecting and arranging in an artistic order the great things, and none but the great, compels me to diverge at this point. Nothing important is lost by ignoring Handel's division between the narrative of the Exodus and the Song of Moses: certainly nothing so disastrous as Handel's own plan of preceding the first part by half an hour's funeral music to account for the statement that the reigning Pharaoh knew not Joseph. If we want a sublime contrast to the exultant shouts that 'there was not one of them left', we can obtain it, not only with decorum, but with the profoundest Handelian awe, in the short mysterious chorus, No. XXIV, *The depths have covered them, they sank into the bottom as a stone.* Handel has placed this chorus well on in the Song of Moses, between the famous duet, 'The Lord is a man of war', and not a very well declaimed rubadub to the words: 'Thy right hand, oh Lord, is *be*come glorious: thy right hand hath dashed in pieces the enemy', a chorus which contains nothing that Handel does not twice give with much greater force before and afterwards. In any case, Handel has placed *The depths have covered them* where it merely shows up the poverty of its surroundings and has no dramatic effect. I submit that where I propose to place it the dramatic effect is thoroughly Handelian, and the musical and harmonic values highly characteristic. It closes on the dominant of a foreign key, which leads quite naturally to the magnificent bright modulations with which Handel's orchestra introduces the Song of Moses.

XVII. CHORUS

Moses, and the children of Israel sung this song unto the Lord, and spake, saying:

I have called attention to Stradella's use of what the old theorists would have called an extraneous bright major mediant chord

(Ex. 5) and have suggested that, as with many passages in the Urio *Te Deum* and other bones from Handel's cache, this kind of bright modulation was what attracted him to various scrappy archaic composers. This introduction to the Song of Moses has not been traced to other sources, but consists essentially of such modulations. You will not find them in Bach, who is either orthodox or miraculous. They are not mysterious, they are bright flashes of colour, and the best-known early composer in whom you will find them is Domenico Scarlatti. The conception of this introduction is musically almost the archetype of Handelian grandeur, and its grandest literary aspect is the identifying of the act of singing with the words 'And spake, saying'.

XVIII

Then they spake and sang two interlocking fugues, not quite the same thing as a double fugue.

Exx. 16, 17, 18. I will sing unto the Lord, for he hath triumphed gloriously, the horse and his rider hath he thrown into the sea.

The first fugue is on one of the world's simplest and oldest canto fermos—

Ex. 16.

which is delivered in alternation, but not combination, with the subject of the second fugue.

Ex. 17.

The business of the second fugue is obviously to display some coloratura singing. That of the first fugue is to go into double fugue with the galloping horse and his rider who are thrown into the sea.

Ex. 18.

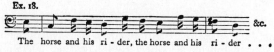

Both subjects of this double fugue can be sung in thirds, and could be so sung with pedantic accuracy if Handel had not the wisdom to diverge to more effective notes as occasion offered. The learned way of describing such counterpoint in added thirds is to point out that it is double counterpoint in the octave, tenth, and twelfth, and that ninety-six permutations of it are possible: the presumption being that the composer worked out each one of the ninety-six by trial and error. In the same way, as is well known, the Forth Bridge was designed from one rivet to the next. This chorus is a fine specimen of Handel's triumphal rhetoric, and is also a reasonably solid piece of counterpoint; but the pious habit of regarding it as a learned effort is as naïve as the theology which imputes to the Almighty the extraordinary power of throwing, not only a horse, but his rider as well, into the sea.

At this point the wholesale borrowings from Erba begin. I do not know why a duet for two sopranos should be pathetic when its text is 'The Lord is my strength and my song, He is become my salvation'; nor do I know why Erba, whoever he may be, should have made an earlier and duller version of it to the second verse of the *Magnificat*, '*Et exultavit spiritus meus, in Deo salutari meo*'. Handel has made a longer, a better, and a more pathetic composition of it: why, I cannot think. Erba continues with the burst of eight-part chorus which has been, as I think mistakenly, alleged to have inspired Handel to *HE rebuked the Red Sea*. Erba follows with the unimportant idea of *Thy right hand, O Lord, is become glorious*, set perfunctorily and patchily to the words: *Ecce enim ex hoc beatam me dicut omnes generationes*. Handel then proceeds to transcribe the eight-part opening of Erba's *Magnificat* to the words: 'HE is my God, and I will prepare Him an habitation.' Erba's eight-part writing is muddy, though correct according to archaic standards. Why did Handel trouble to transcribe it? He is obliged to add two bars to the words: 'My father's God.' These look less orthodox, for they make the voices skip awkwardly, but they would burst through Erba's fog like the sun through clouds; and it is not as if Erba's fog had any great aesthetic qualities.

Then follows an archaic fugue, not unlike Erba, to the words: 'And I will exalt Him': a double fugue, though there is only one text. This fugue is more solid than usual with Handel. But that is not the only reason why I cannot believe that it is an original composition of his; nor can I even rouse myself to much curiosity as to its origin.

XXII

Some of us can remember Barnumesque announcements that in such and such a performance of *Israel in Egypt*, not only in the Crystal Palace, but in the Albert Hall, 'the duet, *The Lord is a man of war*, will be sung by four hundred tenors and basses'. Under my direction it will not be sung even by the two basses for which Handel wrote it. The themes come from the Stradella Serenata, and from any other places where such clichés may be found. Otherwise the composition is deplorably genuine. Handel can keep the shouting and the piping and the fiddling going for 252 bars. Here I certainly would apply Burney's urbane dictum that the disposition of those who are pleased with it may be a great blessing to them. The seat of the scornful is a bad eminence; and its occupants are liable to blaspheme masterpieces like *He led them through the deep*. But people who have not outgrown the music of *The Lord is a man of war* are in as bad a case as Christians who have not outgrown the theology of its text. And I have grave doubts whether such naïve Handel-worshippers can appreciate the merits of the next chorus, *The depths have covered them*: merits which I hope will be obvious to every listener when that chorus is placed where I have transferred it.

Handel follows the chorus, *Thy right hand, O Lord*, with another fugue from the Erba *Magnificat*, *Thou sentest forth thy wrath, which consumed them as stubble*. The original text was: *Fecit potentiam in bracchio suo: dispersit superbos mente cordis sui*. If there is any appropriateness in this borrowing, it may be held to lie in the word 'superbos', which when treated *staccato* can be transcribed as an orchestral and choral representation of the words 'as stubble'. This is hardly a sufficient reason for executing eighty-four bars of mediocre seventeenth-century fugue, and it is still less reason for transcribing it at all.

The great problem in performing the genuine essence of *Israel in Egypt* is, not merely to get rid of Erba, but to arrange a coherent whole of what remains of the Song of Moses.

Another long duet, *Thou in thy mercy hast led forth thy people*, &c. (116 bars of larghetto), has been inflated by Handel from Erba's *Esurientes implevit bonis*. We need not trouble about that, though some of us may feel that the solo singers, already starved by Handel, are being brutally treated in my selection. However, now comes the occasion for amends. My problem is to find a way towards No. XXVII (*And with the blast of thy nostrils*), one of Handel's most picturesque choruses, which I cannot dream of omitting. Our way has now been blocked ever since the horse and his rider were thrown into the sea. But what could follow that triumph more appropriately than the famous and spirited tenor aria, No. XXVIII?

XXVIII. TENOR ARIA

The enemy said: I will pursue, I will overtake, I will divide the spoil: my lust shall be satisfied upon them: I will draw my sword: my hand shall destroy them.

The declamation of this aria is not as faulty as it looks. It seems to begin with a strong accent on '*The*', and this is not to be explained away by Handel's double-sized bar in triple-time cadences. But, besides the cadential ambiguity of ancient triple time (1, 2, 3, 4, 5, 6 versus 1, 2, 3, 4, 5, 6), there is a strong tendency, not yet extinct, though little recognized, for quick triple time to suggest the grouping 1, 2, 3, 1, 2, 3, rather than 1, 2, 3. Indeed, it is possible to maintain the view that this displaced accent, or amphibrachic lilt, is normal to the triple time of Palestrina and earlier music. Be this as it may, *The enemy said* is one of Handel's most spirited and Handelian bursts of jingoism, and deserves to be enjoyed with the utmost zest by singers and listeners.

XXIX

Handel follows it by one of the most picturesque and distinguished of his arias, wonderfully orchestrated and very difficult to perform. The organ, 'celli, bassoons, and violas keep up a perpetual flow, as a ground-bass. Two oboes, presumably soli, weave a tissue of various counterpoints and rhythms. Above and through this a soprano declaims the text, partly in sustained declamation, partly in coloratura.

Thou didst blow with the wind: the sea cover'd them, they sank as lead in the mighty waters.

XXX

Now comes another burst of eight-part harmony, declaiming the following words:

Who is like unto Thee, O Lord, among the Gods? who is like Thee, glorious in holiness, fearful in praises, doing wonders! Thou stretchest out thy right hand.

Handel modulates grandly, with an enharmonic change at the word 'holiness'. He follows these grand chords with the worst of all his borrowings: the most inappropriate in text, the clumsiest in music, and the least improved in transcribing.

Ex. 19.

The   earth   swal - - - - - - - - - - - low'd them.
Si - cut   e - rat   in   prin - ci - pi - o   et   nunc et   sem - per.

And here ends the deplorable mystery of Erba. Fortunately, it is possible and permissible to change the minor chord of 'right hand' into a major chord. This will enable us to pass to one of the most picturesque choruses in the whole work.

XXVII

Exx. 20, 21. And with the blast of thy nostrils the waters were gathered together, the floods stood upright as an heap, the depths were congealed in the heart of the sea.

The theme of *The waters were gathered together* comes from Erba's setting of the words *Deposuit potentes*; and Ex. 21 is, as the fifteen-year-old Jane Austen might have said, 'gracefully purloined' from *Et exaltavit humiles.*

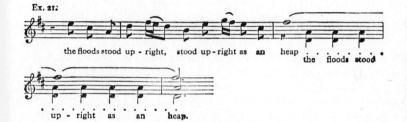

XXXIII

We can now pass on to the greatest of all Handel's choruses. The choice of such an epithet is not only obviously unwise, but contrary to every one of my principles of criticism. But I make it deliberately, for I think that it can provoke nothing less desirable than the attention of every listener, whether he be an idolater, an iconoclast, or a sensible person. And, after all, every great work of art is a microcosm, and, therefore, for the time being, the greatest thing in the world, inasmuch as it is the world so long as your attention is within it. To my amazement I have found that in selections from *Israel in Egypt* this chorus is generally omitted. It was even omitted in my experience at a Leeds Festival at which Joachim played and Stanford conducted. *Israel in Egypt* itself contains no mystery more surprising than that which has imposed upon it the decree that the people shall *not* hear a chorus in which all the noblest aspects of Handel's genius are concentrated and contrasted with a power unsurpassed and, I believe, unequalled, even in *The Messiah*.

Exx. 22, 23. The people shall hear (*p*) and be afraid:
  (*f*) sorrow shall take hold on them:
  (*ff*) all th' inhabitants of Canaan (*p*) shall melt away (*f*) by
    the greatness of thy arm.

(*p*) They shall be as still as a stone,
  till thy people pass over, O Lord,
  till thy people pass over,
  which thou hast purchased.

Throughout more than half the chorus the orchestra accompanies in dotted-quaver rhythm, ♩ ♪♩ ♪♩ ♩ ♪♩ ♪♩, broken only at the first appearance of the theme: 'shall melt away'.

Ex. 22.

Chrysander traces this theme to the Stradella Serenata. I can just see the resemblance of five notes, since he points it out. The 'development of this small harmonic progression from Stradella's duet in so gigantic a chorus' does, indeed, as Chrysander remarks, surpass all expectation. It is almost as astonishing as the power of the electro-magnet with which Chrysander has extracted this needle from a haystack. The remarkable feature of the progression is not traceable in Stradella, but is so remarkable that Mendelssohn shows himself afraid of it in the excellent and much misunderstood organ-part which he wrote for the edition of the English Handel Society. It consists in the fact that, while the accent in the voices falls upon tonic harmony, the organ chords off the beat are dominant, as shown by the figuring of the bass, and are resolved only by the voices. Both Mendelssohn and Chrysander are afraid of this, and represent the chords by the bass only, in spite of the explicit sharp third provided for each note in the figuring of both organ and cembalo. The chords should, of course, be staccato; and Handel's intention is a picturesque illustration of the words. Handel's marks of expression are unusually clear. He has a sudden piano on repeating the words, 'and be afraid'; he bursts into forte at 'sorrow shall take hold on them', and his whole development of the text 'shall melt away' is piano. In fact, the scheme can be represented as I have given it in setting forth the words here, on the plan of a too copiously marked hymn-book. The modulations are unusually wide, ranging as far as C sharp minor, at the approach to which key mistakes have arisen in many editions from misreading Handel's notation of a double sharp.

The second part of the chorus follows naturally upon the outburst at 'By the greatness of thy arm'.

Ex. 23.

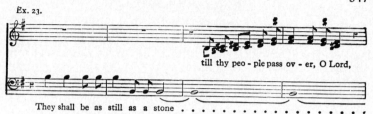

till thy peo - ple pass ov - er, O Lord,

They shall be as still as a stone . . . .

The bass lies still as a stone except when it rises a semitone, more or less as we are told that the coast of Norway rises eleven feet in a hundred years; and the people pass over for ever and ever, like the generations in Bach's *Magnificat*, the only passage in choral music which I can compare, *longo intervallo*, to this most moving of all Handel's climaxes. As with all the great schematic things in art, there are details not provided by the scheme; and of these the subtlest is the moment where one of the scales becomes gratuitously major, as I have foreshadowed by the sharp placed above the G in my quotation. Berlioz once sent a letter to a friend consisting simply of the melody of '*O malheureuse Iphigénie*' from Gluck's *Iphigénie en Tauride* followed by four notes of exclamation. I wish I might simply transcribe the whole of 'The people shall hear', and use Berlioz's commentary.

Yet it is not often artistic to end a work with its finest number. This chorus is best appreciated when followed, as Handel follows it, refreshingly in contrast and worthily in substance. From this point there is no more need to shorten the rest of the work, least of all to omit repetitions which grandly appeal to our sense of form.

XXXV. ALTO ARIA

Thou shalt bring them in, and plant them in the mountain of thine inheritance, in the place, O Lord, which thou hast made for thee to dwell in, in the sanctuary, O Lord, which thy hands have established.

XXXIV. CHORUS

The Lord shall reign for ever and ever.

Recitative

For the horse of Pharaoh went in with his chariots and with his horse-men into the sea, and the Lord brought again the waters of the sea upon them: but the children of Israel went on dry land in the midst of the sea.

Chorus

The Lord shall reign for ever and ever.

Recitative

And Miriam the prophetess, the sister of Aaron, took a timbrel in her hand, and all the women went out after her with timbrels and with dances, and Miriam answered them:

Soprano solo

Sing ye to the Lord, for he hath triumphed gloriously!

Tutti

The Lord shall reign for ever and ever.

Soprano solo

The horse and his rider hath he thrown into the sea.

Tutti

The Lord shall reign for ever and ever: I will sing unto the Lord, for he hath triumphed gloriously, the horse and his rider hath he thrown into the sea.

In the tonic major of 'The people shall hear', an alto aria has expatiated on Zion and the Promised Land in a style and rhythm such as we know from other evidence to have been among the things Handel most enjoyed creating. It has no reason to be as pathetic as 'He was despised'. Nor is there behind it the tension of 'Comfort ye, my people'; but it has the same Handelian tenderness, and its direction, *largo e mezzopiano*, describes it well. It would be a crime to shorten the final group of choral outbursts and recitatives. The words 'The Lord shall reign for ever and ever' are set like a majestic *canto fermo*; and the solo of Miriam the prophetess is left unaccompanied. One of the brighter humours of our Handel Festivals was the observation that in the gigantic reverberations of the four thousand performers Handel's sublimest clash at the throwing of the horse and his rider was adequately represented by a single pair of cymbals. No doubt it was; but the inspiration was not Handel's, nor Urio's, nor Stradella's, nor Erba's, nor of any person before Sir Michael Costa. It is perhaps arguable that Handel might have tried at least to represent the timbrel which Miriam took in her hand, and the other timbrels of the women who went out after her. But we may as well be content to relegate the precise meaning of 'timbrels' to archaeologists, and enjoy the less trivial realism of Miriam's unaccompanied voice with its power to evoke the whole mass of chorus and orchestra. Upon which Handel ends the Song of Moses with a recapitulation of its opening chorus from Ex. 17 to the end.

HAYDN

'THE CREATION'

The time is ripe for a better understanding of Haydn's *Creation* than can be inculcated by fashion. The reasons why it was out of fashion at the end of the nineteenth century are both obvious and obsolete; but they are much the same as the reasons which may now bring it into fashion again. When fashions are in revolt against the sublime and the romantic, Haydn may become fashionable, like Mozart, for the wrong reasons: that is to say, he is only too likely to become patronized by people who see in him exactly what the Philistine of the 'eighties saw who wrote in the first edition of *Grove's Dictionary* that Haydn, in his *Creation*, 'represents Chaos by means of an exceedingly unchaotic fugue'. It is better to risk losing such patronage than to lose what Haydn's contemporaries appreciated in him; the elements of the sublime and the romantic. Haydn's representation of Chaos is not a fugue; but the Chaos he intends to represent is no mere state of disorder and confusion. He has a remarkably consistent notion of it, which harmonizes well enough with the Biblical account of the Creation; not less well with the classical notions of Chaos, whether in Hesiod or Ovid; but most closely with the Nebular Hypothesis of Kant and Laplace, which almost certainly attracted Haydn's attention. Kant's speculations on the subject had been already published in 1755, and Laplace's discussion of it was published in a readable and popular form in 1796, two years before Haydn's *Creation*. Haydn, who did a certain amount of dining-out in *fin-de-siècle* London, was as likely to have heard of the Nebular Hypothesis as a modern diner-out is likely to hear of Einstein and Relativity. Moreover, he visited Herschel at Slough, saw his famous forty-foot telescope and his less famous but more successful other telescopes, and doubtless had much conversation with Herschel in German on both music and astronomy, Herschel having been a musician before he made astronomy his main occupation. Moreover, on May 3rd, 1788, Herschel published in the *Star and Evening Advertiser* a poetic 'Address to the Star' welcoming Haydn to England in glowing astronomical terms. Be this as it may, the evolution of Cosmos from Chaos might be taken as the 'programme' of a large proportion of Haydn's symphonic introductions for many years before he achieved its grandest illustration with recognized and confessed purpose.

The text of the *Creation* is founded, at several removes, on *Paradise Lost*, and more especially on the account given to Adam by the 'affable archangel' in Book VII. Haydn is much more likely to

have heard of the Nebular Hypothesis than to have read Milton.
His librettist, the Baron Van Swieten, did not give him Milton's
phrase 'loud misrule of Chaos', and this is just as well, for the work
has nothing to do with the fiery ocean into which the rebel angels
fell, and Haydn's symphonic nebular hypothesis is much more
musical, as well as more universal. Being an artist, Haydn represent Chaos in a thinkable aspect; that is to say, he chooses a
moment at which the evolution of Cosmos begins. Here is your
infinite empty space.

Ex. 1.

Strictly speaking, this mighty unison is the most chaotic part of
the introduction. A significant chord would obviously be as futile
a symbol of Chaos as an armchair; and a violent and unexplained
discord would, even in modern music, be a mere phenomenon of
human petulance. Classical tonality is Haydn's musical Cosmos,
and modern atonality represents, as the modern composer is beginning to find out, a much narrower range of possibilities. So Haydn,
like Herschel, proceeds to explore the musical universe with higher
and higher powers of his telescope. And, while Herschel arrives
at remarkably sound conclusions as to the motion of the solar
system in space, Haydn is establishing his musical Cosmos in and
about C minor—

Ex. 2.

with ambiguities and boldnesses which show that he is fully aware
of the paradox inherent in any thinkable notion of Chaos. You
may think that Cosmos has already evolved to a prosaic order of
tonality when Haydn's third and fourth bars can clearly assert so
commonplace a phenomenon as the dominant. But four bars will
no more make a Chaos than they will make a Cosmos; and you
will get a much more vividly chaotic impression from statements
arousing expectations which are contradicted than from statements
which arouse no expectations at all. If the writer who described
Haydn's Chaos as an 'unchaotic fugue' had condescended to look
at its first four bars, he would probably have guessed that they

would lead straight back to the opening unison and then be repeated with a new harmonic outcome. Such, for instance, is Haydn's procedure in his ninth London Symphony in B flat, and such, on a much larger scale, is Beethoven's in his Fourth Symphony. But Haydn's fifth bar shows that the explorer of his musical Chaos will meet with the common experience of scientific explorers, the discovery that his theory was too small for the facts. The fifth bar does, indeed, match the first in being an outburst from the full orchestra; but instead of a unison it gives us the vague chord attained in the second bar; and the second bar of Wagner's *Tristan und Isolde* does not strike a more ambiguous note than that at the beginning of Haydn's sixth bar. This comparison is worth following out. Wagner's ambiguous chord proves to be typical of a special harmonic style consistently developed through an entire work. Haydn's remains isolated; and though his Chaos contains many similar effects, they remain independent of each other, explained away on the spot, and undeveloped into systematic features. In other words, they are admirably chaotic; they are not nonsensical, for their resolution is quite orthodox, though they occur as shocks for which their antecedents did not prepare us. Thus, like all the features of imperishable works of art, they are details which it is quite impertinent to praise as 'remarkable for the time at which they were written'. Such patronage is tolerable only with works that are otherwise not remarkable now. The details of the imperishable works remain always astonishing, because only a man of genius can present them in constantly true relation to a consistent style. Only a supreme artist could maintain such a style as that of Haydn's representation of Chaos.

The difficulties of achieving a sublime style for such a purpose were much greater for Haydn than they would have been for Bach, since Bach's musical language, even in its most rococo ornateness, is naturally ready to express the sublime, and the most characteristic features of its larger art-forms are cumulative; whereas the language of Haydn and Mozart is not only essentially dramatic, but mainly comedic, and in their art-forms greatness is always expressed in terms of symmetry. Fortunately, Haydn habitually achieves his symmetry in a paradoxical way. From one moment to the next he is always unexpected, and it is only at the end that we discover how perfect are his proportions. With Mozart the expectation of symmetry is present all the time, and its realization is delayed no longer than serves the purposes of wit rather than humour. Both composers are so great that in the last resort we shall find Mozart as free as Haydn and Haydn as perfect in form as Mozart; but the fact remains that Haydn's forms display their freedom before their symmetry, while Mozart's immediately display their symmetry, and reveal their freedom only to intimate knowledge. Wise critics do not prophesy what Mozart could not have done if he had lived. But it is evident that, as far as his and Haydn's methods differ, Haydn's are the more ready to produce a representation of Chaos that should give the listener pleasure by arousing the expectation and delaying the emergence of Cosmos.

In a slow tempo the dominant in the fourth bar has, as we have already seen, led us to one revelation that the universe is not going to show its symmetry to a first glance. The Wagnerian shock in the sixth bar explains itself away, and the music drifts towards E flat, the proper tonal region for its first modulation, but defined very slowly and vaguely. Observe that it would be far less chaotic to have modulated in an unorthodox direction, as if Chaos had after all been something from which any nonsense might emerge. Haydn's Chaos gravitates, and E flat is the direction in which his C minor would naturally gravitate. But his time-scale is larger than we could expect, and when the musical astronomer is reaching a decisive dominant of E flat in his nineteenth bar—

Ex. 3.

he does not 'restore the *status quo*', but violently contradicts the E flat theory by a perfectly clear D flat, of all keys the most subversive of E flat, though by no means inconsistent with C minor. In this disconcerting key an actual theme emerges.

Ex. 4.

In three sequential steps it leads us to a point from which after all the key of E flat can be, and is, triumphantly established. And for a while the theme, diminished to human proportions, can disport itself on a tonic and dominant with all the zest of a popular exponent of a scientific theory. One might even accept the brilliant clarinet accompaniment—

Ex. 5.

as symbolizing the adornment of popular exposition. I do not
willingly introduce so frivolous a note into a review either of the
universe or of Haydn's representation of it. But popular science
is the only kind of science I can understand, and the profoundest
science can do no more than enjoy with Haydnesque zest each
discovery that enlarges our apprehension of Cosmos. The more
effectively it does so, the more will it show the absurdity of regarding Chaos as a desert or morass from which science can reclaim
any measurable area. Chaos will come again, not in poor Othello's
sense, but in the sense that the universe will always remain a
mystery rather than a mechanism. Nothing can be truer to art and
to nature than the steps by which Haydn returns from his triumph
in E flat to his original chaotic C minor. During each step, the
thematic figure (*a*) appears in various regions of the orchestra,
including a solo double-bass. Commentators have compared other
features in the orchestration to meteors, distant thunder, raindrops,
and the like. Be this as it may, the music makes a quite definite
return to the opening, representing the initial C not by a sustained
note, but by something like a peal of thunder. A fairly definite
effect of recapitulation is given by the presence of figure (*a*) on a
dominant pedal in C minor, culminating in an allusion to the close
which led to Ex. 4. It is as if it represented some actual knowledge
permanently gained.

The vision of Chaos ends in darkness with a sequence of the
suspensions of Ex. 2, but their drift is now steadily downwards
to a final close, and the figure (*a*) persists above them with wistful
questions, which, to music-lovers whose minds are tangential, are
prophetic of *Tristan und Isolde*.

The vision of Chaos is over, and Haydn makes no further allusion to it as soon as he begins to set the Biblical account of the
Creation and Van Swieten's adaptation of Milton. Van Swieten,

by the way, is alleged to have translated his text from the English of one Lidley, a name unknown even to the Post Office Directory. But I do not know what difficulty there is in regarding the mysterious Lidley as a misprint for Linley, the name of a family of well-known musicians, one of whom was a managerial musical factotum at Drury Lane from 1774 till his death in 1795. If, as is rumoured, the libretto had been offered to Handel and refused by him, the elder Linley must have been young but not impossibly young when it was drafted, for he was only 26 when Handel died in 1759. One of his sons was Thomas Linley, the remarkable boy violinist, with whom another prodigious boy, Mozart by name, struck up a great friendship in London; and the eldest of his three beautiful daughters was Mrs. Richard Brinsley Sheridan. The original edition of Haydn's score is thought to be the first that was published in Germany with an English as well as a German text, and there is reason to believe that Haydn himself attended to the difficult changes of detail needed to fit the Biblical words to the Authorized Version as well as to the German Bible. To persons who have more faith than I in long-distance thematic references, faint traces of figure (a) may be found in the interludes before and after the clause 'and the earth was without form and void'. My own opinion is that at the first words of the Bible Haydn has piously closed his mind to any thoughts it may have harboured of Nebular Hypotheses and the things he may have seen through Herschel's telescopes, and is now concentrated wholly upon the Bible and van-Swieten-Linley-Milton (I am sure that Lidley is only Linley with a cold in his head).

The handling of recitative shows unmistakably how far a composer is the slave of convention. Recitative formulas were evolved in Italy, and produced there in an enormous number of works which established the universal language of classical music. But the purport of recitative is to produce in musical form the natural inflexions of speech. Great composers like Purcell and Bach grapple with the problem in their own language, so that Purcell's recitative is English and Bach's is German. Second-rate composers may or may not have known the Italian language, but they used the Italian recitative formulas whatever language they happened to be setting. This does not do much harm, for Italian speech-rhythms do not inflict any irremediable hardship on other languages. There is a total defect of endings on an accented monosyllable, but the composer can always slur the necessary appoggiatura or omit it. With purely instrumental music, it is quite right that a recitative formula, if used at all, should be Italian. It must in any case be an allusion with a purport either sublime, like a Biblical quotation, or mock-heroic; and such allusions are either classical or unintelligible. By 1798 recitative was definitely an ancient language, except in comic Italian opera. Bach had not yet been discovered, or rediscovered; and Mozart had left only one important specimen of German recitative in the great scene between Tamino and the priest in *Die Zauberflöte*, his other great recitatives, such as 'Don Ottavio, son morta!' being Italian. For German opera preferred spoken dialogue, and all Mozart's other operas, except *Die Entführung*, are Italian. Haydn's achievement in the recitatives of *The Creation* is much more remarkable than it appears to be. Where the Bible is concerned, he is undoubtedly attending to two languages, neither of which can derive any benefit from Italian tradition. The subject is not dramatic, and, even in the description of the birds and beasts, is not meant to be comic. Hence, the virtues of Haydn's declamation are chiefly negative and can be discovered only by finding out the innumerable possibilities of going wrong. By these I do not mean slight faults of accentuation. The critics whose notions of declamation are confined to Wagner and Wolf are apt to betray a mere bell-metronome notion of rhythm and a far from poetic notion of prosody. Haydn never mastered English as thoroughly as did Handel. And, except when dealing with the words of the Authorized Version, to which he certainly gave his attention, he was not even dealing with an Englishman's English, for, as Messrs. Fox Strangways and Steuart Wilson point out, it is evident that the old English text of *The Creation* is a re-translation by a German from the German, not without refreshing details in the style of *English as She is Spoke*.

At the same time I respectfully and regretfully differ from the view of Haydn's recitative taken by the authors of the new translation. Their version of the choruses and arias is beyond cavil; but, like the distinguished authors of the new English versions of Bach's Passions, they seem to think that classical recitative formulas must be preserved note for note as if they were lyric or formal music; and that in that interest it does not matter how many notes go to a syllable, so long as they are the notes written by the composer. Now this is more superstitious than insisting on the syllabic Divine Inspiration of the translators of the Authorized Version; and it has not the excuse of the inconvenience of changing words that have acquired familiar and sacred associations. Nothing is more fatal to classical recitative than the putting of slurred notes to one syllable where the composer wrote a note to each syllable. To quote an example not from *The Creation*, a musical expression like—

Son   of Man

is a monstrosity that no singer or composer ought to dream of tolerating. On the other hand, it seldom matters a fraction of a hoot whether a long note in recitative is divided into two or any number of notes that extra syllables may require; and the difference between such forms as—

is in most cases quite negligible. Another object of superstitious reverence is the accent on the first of the bar, for the preservation of which most modern translators will submit words and notes to the thumbscrew and the rack. Classical recitative is not Wagnerian declamation; it is musical speech-rhythm; it is not only vague as to whether the first of the bar has an accent, but habitually contradicts its own notation in almost every bar, and especially at the cadences. For instance, there is no need to alter Haydn's German accent on the last syllable of 'firmament' in recitative: the singer need not stress it, though it may come typographically on the first of the bar.

If you want to preserve Haydn's or Bach's exact notes in their recitatives you must sing them in German. Bach and Handel were ready enough to sacrifice originally good declamation in transcribing formal music to new texts; but they never transcribed a recitative to a new text. It was infinitely less trouble to compose a new recitative. And recitative that does not fall into the speech-rhythm of the language in which it is sung is neither speech nor language nor music. I shall doubtless be severely dealt with for altering the notes of Haydn's music; but, unlike the old Scotch lady who enjoyed learned sermons but 'wudna hae the presoomption to understand them', I presume to understand Haydn's recitatives. I claim to take no liberties; once alterations are admitted, notes may be altered in a wrong way as well as in a right way; but the modern proposition that recitative-formulas must not be altered at all in translations is no more scholarly than translating 'qu'est-ce que c'est que ça' by 'what is this that this is that that'.

This point being disposed of, let us continue our analysis. I will not pause to ventilate in detail my grievances against the critical *Gesammtausgabe* of Haydn's complete works, which, since the death of my beloved old friend Mandyczewski, has decided wrongly about the musical text of *The Creation* on at least five points on which I happen to know that Mandyczewski had decided rightly. The first of these is the fine and characteristic idea (perfectly unmistakable in the original edition of the score—which is our earliest source, the autograph being lost) that Gabriel sings with the chorus-basses at the words 'And the Spirit of God moved upon the face of the waters'.

From this point, that is to say, from the beginning of the vocal music, I shall give the words, not always as they will be sung, but according to the new Oxford text, with explanations of the points where I see reason to take my own line or even to return to the *disjecta membra* of the Linley-van-Swieten-English-as-She-is-Spoke confection.

Linley and the Baron van Swieten have between them devised an excellent arrangement for the distribution of the text. The words of the Bible are divided between three archangels, Raphael, Uriel, and Gabriel, and a chorus which, throughout the whole work, may be considered as that of the heavenly hosts. The list and description of created things is not distributed at haphazard among the three archangels: Uriel is distinctly the angel of the sun and of daylight; his is the tenor voice, and his is the description of Man. Raphael sings of the earth and the sea, of the beginning of all things. and (according to the unmistakable direction of the original edition of the score) of the Spirit of God moving upon the face of the waters. His also is the description of the beasts, the great whales, and 'every living creature that moveth'; and it is he who reports God's blessing, 'Be fruitful and multiply', in a measured passage which is one of the sublimest incidents in Haydn's recitatives. Gabriel, the soprano, leads the heavenly hosts and describes the vegetable kingdom and the world of bird life.

Lastly, Adam and Eve (Soprano and Bass) appear and fulfil the purpose announced by Raphael while as yet 'the end was not achieved; there wanted yet the master-work that should acknowledge all this good'. Or, as the first answer in the Shorter Catechism has it,

> Q. What is the chief end of Man?
> A. To glorify God and to enjoy Him for ever.

Asbestos is not in common use as material for writing or printing, and so I cannot express my opinion of the cuts sanctioned by tradition in performances of Haydn's *Creation*. That some cutting is advisable I do not deny; and if *The Creation* were the kind of work which (like many great things by Schubert) puts its finest material into its digressions, the task of cutting it would be difficult and painful. But Haydn is a supreme master of close-knit form; and it so happens that the subject of this oratorio is quite clearly and positively the Creation, up to and including Man's capacity to glorify God; and it is equally clearly not Paradise Lost, nor the conjugal felicity of Adam and Eve ('Graceful consort! Spouse adored', &c.). Hence, the beautiful terzet (No. 28) that interrupts

the chorus at the end of Part II ('Achieved at last the glorious work')
is untimely and intrusive when it introduces the thought, 'But if
Thou turn away Thy face, with sudden terror are we struck: Thou
tak'st our breath away; we turn again to dust.' The first exposition
of the chorus and the whole of the terzet can therefore be cut out,
with loss of some beautiful music, but with positive gain to the
form of the whole. Only you must not begin No. 29, the resumption
of the chorus, as it stands, but must remember that, instead of its
allusive 2-bar opening, it needs to begin with the first seven bars
of No. 27. Cuts inside a number are wholly Philistine, and nowhere
more so than when they consist in skipping repetitions. We are
not dealing with the cabalettas of Rossinian operas, but with symphonic forms on Beethoven's plane of thought. Some of our
Bright Young Men (and even some Dull Old Men) are now beginning to cut the tuttis of Beethoven's Violin Concerto. I have fortunately not yet been present when this has been done; and, if it
ever should happen in my presence, no consideration for the knees
of my neighbours shall prevent me from instantly leaving the con-
cert-hall with anybody and everybody else who thinks as I do
about music.

Again, it is highly undesirable to spoil the Genesis-Milton-van-
Swieten-Haydn scheme of Six Days of Creation, with the Heavenly
Host singing in triumph after each. The fierceness of the Gothic
Revival is abated, and we need no longer purge our cathedrals of
every vestige of Grinling Gibbons. In musical affairs we feel
towards Bach and Handel as we feel towards Gothic architecture;
and our instinct is to confuse Haydn's irrepressibly cheerful worship of God (for which he himself hoped God would not be angry)
with the naughtiest features of the masses Mozart wrote, in a hurry
and a temper, for an Archbishop of Salzburg for whom nobody,
Catholic or Protestant, has ever had a good word to say. But
musical history is not as simple as our text-books would have it.
Bach's spirit may be what we understand by Gothic, but the nearest
architectural analogy to his musical language is rococo. As for
Handel, if he had been an architect he would have been Palladian;
and those people who sympathize with Burne-Jones's dislike of
St. Paul's Cathedral have a musical consciousness of quite a different order from their other aesthetic sensibilities if they can enjoy
Handel at all. This is quite possible; the wind bloweth where it
listeth; and Bach's rococo language is not spiritually akin to an
Austrian church decorated with wedding-cake cherubs. But the
gulf between Haydn and Handel in choral writing is nothing like
as great as we are apt to imagine; nor, except where Handel reaches
his highest level, is the advantage of sublimity always—or, I will
even say, often—with Handel. Moreover, to my unscrupulous

mind, Haydn's naughtiest brilliance, as in the solo coloraturas of
'The Lord is great, and great His might', is as glorious as Bach's,
though its symphonic foundations confine it to a much simpler
harmonic range.

Exaggerated ideas of the length of *The Creation* have, I believe,
been fostered by two disastrous misprints; the substitution of 4/4
instead of ₵ as time-signatures for 'The Heavens are telling' and
the aria 'On spreading wings'. (I do not myself see much amiss
with the old and faintly Miltonic 'mighty pens'.) The 4/4 signa-
ture, with Haydn's 'moderato' as tempo-mark, clips the eagle's
mighty pens to the capacity of the barn-door fowl, and accounts
for the tradition of omitting repetitions in the resulting tedium.
But, in a reasonable tempo, what sane person ever wished to prevent
a song-bird from repeating itself, since the time of the early English
saint who miraculously stopped a cock from crowing?

The case of 'The Heavens are telling' is far more disastrous. Like
most music-lovers of my age, I incurred in childhood the danger
not only of believing that where 'there is neither speech nor language' Haydn supplied the defect after this fashion—

but of the still more dangerous blasphemy of supposing that this
must be Good Music.

Besides the elimination of the terzet No. 28, with its redundant
introductory exposition of the chorus No. 27, my only other cut
in *The Creation* is the drastic one of ending with the greatest
design Haydn ever executed, and the sublimest number since the
Representation of Chaos, the duet of Adam and Eve with chorus of
angels, No. 30. Everything after that is not only an anticlimax but
involves the intrusion of the loss of Paradise ('Oh happy pair, and
happy still might be if not misled', &c., &c.). It is unfortunately
possible that Haydn might be shocked at the idea of ending without
another Palladian-Handelian double fugue; he probably thought

that such movements were intrinsically grander than those of the symphonic order in which he was supreme. But I prefer to imagine that he would, after some doubts, be glad to have due recognition of his real supremacy and would come to see that another Palladian double fugue in B flat, however grand, could add nothing but anti-climax to the symphonic and choral finality of the great Adagio and Allegretto which merge the praises of Adam and Eve in those of the Heavenly Hosts and establish the key of C major as the inevitable outcome of the C minor round which the first Chaos gravitated. Thus ended, the work is considerably shorter than Bach's B minor Mass,[1] and it falls into two parts; the two numbers (the E major representation of Morning, and the great duet and chorus) from Haydn's Third Part being only a few minutes longer than the two movements excised from his Second Part. The change from the B flat of 'Achieved at last the glorious work' to the indefinitely remote E major of the representation of Morning is a bold step to take without interposing an interval. But it is a Haydnesque step, and it differs from precisely the same juxta-position (D flat to G major) in the middle of Beethoven's Quartet in B flat, Op. 130, only in the Haydnesque particular that it remains a paradox whereas Beethoven's audacities of tonality are always rationalized.

Here, then, is the text of *The Creation* as I propose to perform it. I interpolate a few more comments where occasion arises. Haydn's (and Herschel's) Chaos we have already discussed.

THE FIRST DAY

Raphael sings:

RAPHAEL. In the beginning God created the heaven and the earth. And the earth was without form and void: and darkness was upon the face of the deep.

RAPHAEL *and Chorus.*

And the Spirit of God moved upon the face of the waters.
And God said, Let there be light: and there was light.

With effortless power the light bursts forth in music of a clear C major; the chorus on not at all a high note for any of the voices, but in simply a good average position for sonority, while the orchestra rises in vibrations that are slow enough to produce a maximum volume of tone.

Haydn's last appearance in public was at a performance of *The Creation* in Vienna. The old man was brought into the audi-

[1] The performance for which this essay was written began moderately punctually at 8 o'clock, and, with a ten-minute interval after Part I, was finished several minutes before 10.

torium in a chair. At the outburst 'and there was light' he pointed a trembling hand upwards and was heard by those near him to say, 'It came from thence'. He was evidently much moved, and could not stay after the first part.

URIEL. And God saw the light, that it was good: and God divided the light from the darkness (Gen. i. 1-4).

In the general history of music one of the greatest of Haydn's achievements was his exhaustive exploration of remote key-relationships. He did not, like J. S. Bach, live in a harmonic world of close key-relations liable to miraculous invasions from unknown regions; nor did he, like Philipp Emanuel Bach, explain away his remoter modulations by discursive rhetoric. But he also did not achieve, or attempt to achieve, Beethoven's processes, by which the whole scheme of remoter key-relations became as definite as Newtonian astronomy. Haydn's paradoxes in tonality are always true, and he is so sure of them that it would be impertinent to call them experimental. But he does not explain them; and if they explain themselves they do so only as things explain themselves to the child who 'understands quite well, if only you wouldn't explain'. Without any explanatory modulation the C major gives way to A major, as (with due explanation) in the first movement of Beethoven's C major Quintet, Op. 29, or as in the G major-E major schemes of his Trios, Op. 1, No. 2, and Op. 9, No. 1; or, again, as in the B flat-G major schemes of his Trio, Op. 97, and his Sonata, Op. 106. Some of Haydn's greatest symphonies, quartets, and trios show the same or similar key-relations, with the same brilliance of contrast. (By the way, the disastrous substitution of 4/4 for ₵ occurs here also.)

> URIEL. Now vanish before the first command
> The gloomy laws of ancient night,
> And light doth rule the world.
> Let chaos end, and order must prevail.

But suddenly our A major is brought into contrast with the C minor of Chaos.

> So Hell's black spirits seek the realms below,
> Down they sink to deepest abyss where light cannot come.

> CHORUS.
> In cursing snarling terror they fall beyond our sight.

The symphonic balance of keys is restored in favour of A major; and here is Haydn's notion of the new created world. I understand that once upon a time people found this trivial; but Beethoven has not indulged in the cruel sport of prig-sticking in vain, and I am proud to ally myself with the company of persons who are as completely and shamelessly bowled over by it as by anything in Bach's B minor Mass.

Ex. 7.

The first of days ap - pears;   the first of days ap - pears and

or - der reigns   at God's com - mand.

At each recurrence this is differently harmonized. Hence I quote only the melody, which is the quintessence of Haydn in his most dangerous innocence.

THE SECOND DAY

Secco-Recitative.

RAPHAEL. And God made the firmament, and divided the waters which were under the firmament from the waters which were above the firmament: and it was so. (Gen. i. 7.)

Descriptive Recitative.

Now all the powers of the sky are released,
The winds blow the clouds like chaff in the air.
And dreaded lightning burns in the sky,
And thunder answers the leaping flame.
Now vapour from the flood ascends to form the cooling rain,
The harsh and stinging hail, and softest flakes of snow.

The classical rule for the musical illustration of words is that, unless, as at the words 'And there was Light', the music is itself the action at the moment, the illustration should come first and the words afterwards.

The observance of this rule has two advantages. First it compels the composer to make his illustration intelligible as pure music. Secondly, the intelligible music being thus secured, the critic who chooses to say of the illustration 'Not a bit like it' can always be met with the retort 'Who said it was? I am a musician and am enjoying myself in that capacity'. This retort is hardly possible if the music has followed the words with the evident purpose of illustrating them. With the classical method there is always a reasonable chance that the illustration may be apt enough to make the listener greet the words with the delighted recognition 'So *that's* what the music means'; and whether this happens or not, the listener will at all events have heard some good music without annoyance or distraction.

The high soprano of the archangel Gabriel is now heard for the first time, and is joined by all the heavenly hosts.

GABRIEL *and Chorus.*

The angels rank on rank arrayed
Behold amazed the marvels done,
And sing in silver trumpet voice
The praise of God and of the second day.

In plausibility the case for canonizing Haydn ranks midway between the cases for canonizing Pepys and Dr. Johnson. But the critic who can frown at the glorious cheerfulness of this choric song has not the remotest conception of real saintliness; he is in the state of Bunyan's Talkative whose notion of the first workings of Grace is that it begins by producing 'a great outcry against sin';[1] and he can know nothing of Christian's or Bunyan's feelings when his burden fell off, or of Haydn's when, as he tells us, 'Never was I so pious as when composing *The Creation*; I knelt down every day and prayed God to strengthen me for my work'.

THE THIRD DAY

Secco-Recitative.

RAPHAEL. And God said, Let the waters under the heaven be gathered together unto one place, and let the dry land appear: and it was so.
And God called the dry land Earth: and the gathering together of the waters called he Seas: and God saw that it was good. (Gen. i. 9–10.)

Aria (the first part in D minor).

See how the rolling waters
In boisterous play uplift their heads.
Mountains emerge from the plains,
Their heads with drifting clouds are crowned
And from their heights to depths look down.
Through open plains of fair extent
In winding courses rivers flow.

With characteristic freedom of form Haydn now finishes his aria with a second part in D major that has only a faint trace of thematic relation to the rest.

Softest music murmuring
Through silent vales glides on the brook.

Some small part of Haydn's inspiration may be derived from the most beautiful tone-picture in Gluck's *Armide*, Rinaldo's enraptured descriptions of Armida's garden: 'Plus je vois ces lieux, et plus je les admire.' This, in its turn, is said to be hardly finer that

[1] *O brave Talkative!* (Bunyan's marginal comment).

Lully's setting of the same passage in his *Armide* of ninety years earlier. But Haydn's inspiration is also in large measure his own, or the answer to his prayers; and it became the source of many things in the style of Schubert, besides many solemn calms in Beethoven. (By the way, Haydn gives no authority for a slower tempo here; he leaves to a later poet the suggestion to 'Bear me straight, meandering ocean, Where the stagnant torrents flow'.)

Secco-Recitative.

GABRIEL. And God said, Let the earth bring forth grass, the herb yielding seed, and the fruit tree yielding fruit after his kind, whose seed is in itself, upon the earth: and it was so. (Gen. i. 11.)

ARIA (hitherto known as 'With verdure clad'). The new Oxford text aims not only at singability but at introducing some genuine Miltonic epithets where the resemblance of the Linley-van-Swieten-English-as-She-is-Spoke complex can be traced back to Milton. I am not sure that the result is always worth the trouble; the Miltonic epithets sound un-Miltonic and often puzzling when transferred from blank verse to the ambling rhymes of the oratorio librettist; and I have encouraged our present artists to return, now and then, to use and wont in this matter.

> The fields are dressed in living green
> That soothes the heart and charms the eye,
> While flowers of every hue,
> Bedeck the meads in trim array.
> With perfume sweet the air is filled
> And plants to heal abound.
> The pampered boughs with ripening fruit are full
> And leafy trees invite with deepest shade.
> On mountain side majestic forests grow.

I am told by one of the truest of Haydn-lovers that this aria does not stand the strain of 7,459 consecutive performances at Competition Festivals. Never having tried any such experiment, I am defenceless in still finding it as beautiful as anything else in Haydn, Schubert, Brahms, or any other master of lyric melody. Clearly there is need for a Society for the Prevention of Cruelty to Classics and Adjudicators. (Reverence dictates that we should put the Classics first.) Another brutal sport which I am ashamed to indulge is Mendelssohn-baiting. But here the occasion is too tempting; Mendelssohn is really asking us to show how neatly his unconscious misquotation displays the difference between a strong and a flaccid style. Among his *Lieder ohne Worte* the 'Duetto' is a very clever piece, though not one of the best; but the third and fourth bars of its melody (bars 4 and 5 of the piece) are a clinically perfect type of the weakness of his melodic constitution, which seldom has enough stamina to get through its second clause without giving at the ankles.

Ex. 8.

HAYDN. 'With verdure clad', bars 5-8.

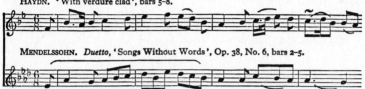

MENDELSSOHN. *Duetto*, 'Songs Without Words', Op. 38, No. 6, bars 2-5.

Another of Haydn's brilliant key-contrasts now follows; B flat yielding abruptly to D major. The recitative does not *lead* from B flat to the D major of the chorus; it asserts the D major at once.

Secco-Recitative.

URIEL. And the heavenly host proclaimed the third day, praising God and saying:

Chorus.

> Awake the harp, awake the lute,
> Let all the world your song re-echo,
> In praise of our God, the Creator of all,
> Who hath invested with splendour
> The earth and the sky and the sea.

This chorus, the first of what I call the Palladian architectural-musical features of Haydn's *Creation*, is admirably terse and of a brilliance and power that does not suffer by comparison with Handel at his best. My beloved counterpoint-master, James Higgs, had a keen nose for such game as Haydn's device of 'prolonging the first note backwards', as when the fugue-theme—

Ex. 9a.

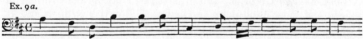

Who hath in - ves - ted with splen - dour the earth and the sky.

produces the full majestic effect of an 'augmentation' with no more loss of time than a single bar, by means of entries like this—

Ex. 9b.

and this

Ex. 9c.

(A complete augmentation would make the theme spread over four bars and a half.)

THE FOURTH DAY

Secco-Recitative.

URIEL. And God said, Let there be lights in the firmament of heaven
to divide the day from the night, and to give light upon the earth,
and let them be for signs and for seasons and for days and for years.
He made the stars also. (Gen. i. 14–16.)

Descriptive Recitative.

The sun is up, and from his chamber comes to run his course,
A bridegroom in his youth, a giant in his strength,
    Through highest heaven.
    With softer beams and milder light
    Sails on the silver moon through silent night.
The infinite space of open sky is filled with stars beyond all human
count,
    And the Sons of God proclaimed the fourth day,
    And all the morning stars
    Together sang his praise.

Of all the comparisons the most odious in its unfairness is that
between *The Creation* and *The Seasons*. I live in hope of an opportunity of reverently and enthusiastically producing *The Seasons*
some day, or preferably some two days, so that few cuts may be
necessary and better justice be done to the work than was done to
it by Haydn himself, who undertook it under protest, and said
much harsher things about it than have been said by anybody since,
condemning its whole scheme as Philistine, and declaring that the
undertaking of it had killed him. Some part of this complaint is
justified. The most alarming and pathetic sign of failing power is
that the 'Palladian' choruses are, on the average, twice the size
of those in *The Creation*, and thus and in other ways betray an
anxiety lest they should be inadequate. But the work is full of
glorious things; and perhaps the most cruel item of all that it cost
Haydn is that it compelled him to do another picture of a sunrise,
the words of which are assigned to the Farmer's Daughter, Hanne
(*anglice*, Jane), and to which the appropriate comment is the English text of the subsequent chorus, 'Hail, O Sun, be hailed!'

The sunrise in *The Creation* is as perfect and as simple as the
Parthenon; and if its method is obvious, that of the moonrise is a
paradox of astonishing accuracy and boldness. What composer of
less than the greatest order would have thought of beginning his
moonlight in the deep bass and representing its culmination by the
string band alone on its lower strings?

If any part of *The Seasons* must be regretted, it is that in which
the libretto imposes, as it were, upon the architect of the Parthenon the responsibility for the Edinburgh Folly of Calton Hill

The creation of the material world is now finished, and the First Part of Haydn's work ends with the well-known chorus so often misrepresented because of a long-standing typographical blunder as to its tempo.

Trio and Chorus (GABRIEL, RAPHAEL, *and* URIEL).

The Heavens are telling the glory of God,
The firmament itself shews forth his handiwork.
For day unto day doth utter his speech
And night unto night her knowledge doth shew.
Their sound goes out through all the lands,
Neither speech nor language, yet their voice is ever heard.

(Adapted from Ps. 19.)

Ex. 10.

Of the main theme the figure (*b*) becomes that of the fugal climax, while (*a*) becomes the starting-point of the dangerously simple passages for the trio of archangels. The danger of these passages lies in what I believe to be Haydn's discovery of the charm of simple cadential chords held with indefinite pauses by solo voices. Doubtless there is some learned historical sense in which this is not Haydn's discovery; for a prevalent view of the history of art is that its chief aim is to show that the most famous strokes of genius have been anticipated by from six months to two centuries, either in some dead and misunderstood convention, or in some work preserved in the British Museum in a copy which has hitherto remained unique because nobody has been stupid enough to think of transcribing anything so dull. I cannot cultivate a historic erudition that eliminates the rare accident of genius from works of art; and I shall continue to ascribe the strokes of genius in *The Creation* to Haydn without inquiring whether earlier composers may have produced semblances of them without the genius. Moreover, I shall go further, and continue to recognize Haydn's strokes of genius in their echoes *as strokes of genius* by later composers. Mendelssohn's *Duetto* (cited in Ex. 8) suffers from its resemblance to 'With verdure clad', because it misses the point. The climax of the coda in the first movement of Beethoven's Second Symphony does not suffer from comparison with the end of 'The Heavens are telling', because Beethoven no more misses Haydn's point than Virgil misses the point when he translates

Homer; and Virgil's achievement in erecting a mass of Homeric
and other lore into a monument to the glories of Rome is not essentially greater than Beethoven's in making a normal symphony capable of digesting a choral climax. And by this I do not mean the
problem of the Ninth Symphony with its actual chorus, but the
simpler and subtler questions of tonality and time-scale within
the limits of absolute music.

Ex. 11 *a*.
HAYDN.

Beethoven's harmonic range is wider, and while the second chord
here marked with an asterisk corresponds exactly with that marked
in Ex. 11*a*, it is the remoter marked chord (a 6/4 in E flat minor
or D sharp minor) that, together with the rising bass, is inspired
by Haydn.

Ex. 11 *b*.
BEETHOVEN, Second Symphony.

Quite a long book might be written about the influence of
Haydn's *Creation* on later music. The innocent solo-trio pauses
have been a danger to later musicians and critics because nothing
is easier than to live on the income of their natural effect. The prig
who is proud of his artistic conscience is in the long run (which,
however, the poor fellow never gets) less detestable than the
more fashionable prig who is proud of having none. It is mere snob-
bishness to say that Haydn's juicy vocal pauses are mere Sullivan;
the difference between Haydn and Sullivan is that Haydn's
self-indulgence in this matter is a small and severely disciplined

element of relaxation in some of the hardest work ever achieved by mortal man—whereas Sullivan—

il res - to nol di - co.

PART II

With the Fifth Day of Creation Animal Life appears. Haydn has the acumen to refrain from any attempt to stress a miracle not less stupendous than that of Light; he treats the whole scheme as one, and begins the second part of his work with a recitative that starts on a chord in middle position as if to continue a narrative that has been punctuated rather than interrupted.

THE FIFTH DAY

GABRIEL. And God said, Let the waters bring forth abundantly the moving creature that hath life, and fowl that may fly above the earth in the open firmament of heaven. (Gen. i. 20.)

Aria (F major).

On spreading wings majestic soars the eagle aloft
And cleaves the air in swiftest flight to the blazing sun.
His welcome bids to morn the merry lark,
Enraptured coo and bill and tender doves,
From every bush and grove resound
The nightingale's delightful notes.
No grief affected yet her breast
Nor yet to mournful tale were turned
Her soft enchanting lays.

The aria, redeemed from the disastrous consequences of a 4/4 instead of Haydn's alla-breve time-signature, illustrates its text with more discretion than some critics seem to realize. The right tempo gives something of the power of the eagle's flight. Ravel can attain the actual pitch of the lark's trill with violin harmonics which Haydn's ear and taste would fail to discriminate from a gas-escape. I do not for a moment suggest that Haydn would be justified in condemning either Ravel or the real lark, though both habitually emit sounds that would be merely destructive to Haydn's music. But Haydn is certainly right, for his own purposes, in generalizing the lark's morning welcome as a 'merry' tune on the clarinet. The nightingale is in another position; its note, as we know it, is well within the best cantabile range of the wind instruments of Beethoven's Pastoral Symphony, and Beethoven's nightingale is realistic as well as musical. But before you receive Haydn's nightingale with the Producer's proverbial criticism 'Not a bit like it', please note that the text expressly forbids Haydn to let his

nightingale say 'jug-jug' or 'Tereu! Tereu!' Thus Haydn has to
invent a bird of the same name, but peculiar to Eden; and his
invention no more failed him than it would have failed Lewis
Carroll. And perfect music unites with perfect realism in the bill-
ing and cooing of Haydn's doves. Tennyson's 'moan of doves in
immemorial elms' is not finer onomatopoeia than Haydn's combination of bassoons and violins in their fourth string.

Descriptive Recitative and Arioso (D minor).

RAPHAEL. And God created great whales and every living creature
that moveth, and God blessed them, saying,

> Be fruitful all and multiply, and fill the seas.
> Yea, multiply ye fowl upon the earth,
> And in your God and Lord rejoice.
>   (Adapted from Gen. i. 21–2.)

The arioso ('Be fruitful') is scored for divided violas and violoncellos with independent double-basses. It ought to be a *locus classicus* for such scoring, but perhaps the writers of text-books are
afraid to quote a passage more than usually full of the kind of
Haydnesque or Gluckesque inaccuracies which leave us in irre-
solvable doubt whether we are dealing with strokes of genius or
blunders. Still, there is no excuse for the modern editing of the
double-bass part which, because of a few outlying low notes such
as occur in every classical bass-part before Wagner, puts almost
the whole part an octave higher, and so confines God's blessing
to creatures who could be safely invited to fill the Round Pond in
Kensington Gardens.

Secco-Recitative.

RAPHAEL. And the angels struck their immortal harps and sang together
the wonders of the fifth day.

Terzet (A major).

GABRIEL. The hills in order stand new clad in grassy green,
> In thanks they lift their heads.
> Their pebbled freshets sing with everflowing gift
> Of water clean and bright.

URIEL. The birds in wheeling flight are playing in the air
> And sing their hymn of praise,
> And in their ordered ranks their wings reflect the sun
> In rainbow coloured light.

RAPHAEL. Now fish in glistening shoals abound,
> And play in schools a thousand strong,
> While monstrous from the deep, mighty Leviathan
> Upheaves his bulk immense.

All Three. How manifold thy works, O God! Who may their number
tell?

Haydn's glorious freedom of form is well displayed in the various phases of this tone-picture as delivered by the three archangels in turn. The three unite in a new theme which inspired Mendelssohn to the burden 'O blessed are they' in 'I waited for the Lord'; a fact disastrously evident on an occasion within my memory when his *Lobgesang* (without its three symphonic movements) was used as a substitute for the Third Part of *The Creation*.

The Terzet leads to the most brilliant of all Haydn's choruses. I refuse to concede any courtesy to the scruples of people who are shocked at the coloraturas of Gabriel and Uriel, which thrill me as much as anything in Bach or Handel, though they are confined to the cadential harmonies of an operatic cabaletta. Gothic revivals may have swept away Grinling Gibbons and the village crafts-man from our cathedrals with one hand while they built Albert Memorials with the other; but the monuments of music remain in print, and the 'restoring' of them need not be destructive.

Chorus (with the three Archangels).

The Lord is great and great His might,
His glory lasts for ever.

THE SIXTH DAY

Secco-Recitative.

RAPHAEL. And God said, Let the earth bring forth the living creature after his kind, cattle, and creeping thing, and beast of the earth after his kind. (Gen. i. 24.)

Now comes the most dangerous, disputed, and in some ways the most delightful passage in the whole work. Beethoven deserves forgiveness for angrily laughing at it. He was occupied in the gigantic task of raising the language of music from the level of comedy of manners to something equally beyond the Gothic sublimities of Bach and the Michael-Angelesque sublimities of Handel. His range was Shakespearean, and his sense of humour was at once the foundation of his sense of tragedy and his defence against egoistic pessimism. An artist's business is to get on with his own work, and we have no right to annoy him with requests to take a large-minded critical view of tendencies the vogue of which thwarts him. On the other hand, nobody but the artist so thwarted has any right to take less than a large-minded critical view, except people whose responsibilities are confined to knowing what they like, or (what comes to much the same thing) liking what they know.

I give the text of Haydn's menagerie as it has been ingeniously revised in the new Oxford edition. But in actual practice I find that in some details the old text, or some other alteration of it, is necessary. Nor can I wholly agree with the conclusion of my old friends the Oxford editors that 'Much of the amusement past generations have had from the text of *The Creation* has been enjoyed under a misapprehension. There was no intention to amuse, but rather to edify.' In the first place, Haydn's mind notoriously failed to draw a sharp line between amusement and edification. There is abundant evidence that he was often scolded for this failure; and his assertion, quoted above, that he had never been so pious as when writing *The Creation*, shows every sign of being a defence against some such scolding; just as Bunyan, who endured fiendish tortures of remorse for his deadly sins of church-bell ringing and tip-cat, flared up at once at any suggestion that he ever led an immoral life. Again, it is not implied by the Puritan Milton that in the Earthly Paradise itself amusement was inadmissible without edification; at all events Milton does not tell us what serious lessons Adam and Eve were to learn from 'the unwieldy elephant' who—

> To make them mirth, used all his might, and wreathed
> His lithe proboscis.

Haydn is no unwieldy elephant, but why should he be forbidden to use at least some of his might to make us mirth in the Garden of Eden?

The Oxford edition represents Haydn's animals as follows. I will not trouble the reader with my poor makeshifts where its literary merit seems to me to have been achieved at the expense of the music, but will merely indicate the difficulties in question.

Descriptive Recitative.

RAPHAEL. Straight opening her fertile womb
The earth obeyed the word, and lo,
Creatures innumerous teemed at a birth
All fully grown.
The tawny lion pawing to get free,
And, breaking from his bonds, the tiger leaps out;
The antlered stag protrudes his branching head,
With flying mane and spurning hoof
Impatient neighs the fiery steed.
The cattle graze, some rare and solitary,
Some in herds are seen.
And o'er the ground like fleecy plants
Arose the gentle sheep.
At once came forth whatever creeps the ground,
Insect or worm.
In sinuous trace, they their long dimension draw.

This text restores the picture given by Milton and many an old illustrated Bible; according to which the animals are seen in the act of struggling out of the ground. Unfortunately this picture was not presented to Haydn either by Linley-Lidley or the Baron van Swieten; and I find it a fatal objection to the use here of the Miltonic 'pawing to get free' that if Haydn had been presented with any such idea he could not have failed to illustrate it unmistakably in his music. The same objection applies to the 'bonds' of the tiger and the 'protruding' head of the stag. What Haydn does illustrate is animals already freely active. The action of the lion is very Haydnesque, but it has the misfortune to have been obliterated by an ancient piece of editorial stupidity which infuriates me all the more by reappearing in an aggravated form in the new critical *Gesammtausgabe*, ostensibly under the name of my beloved and lamented friend, Mandyczewski, who, as I happen to know, emphatically agreed with me on this very detail at least thirty years ago. Haydn's recitative begins with a *forte* of all the strings, plus bassoons.

Ex. 12*a*.

After the words 'All fully grown' this phrase is resumed *piano*, with the following result—

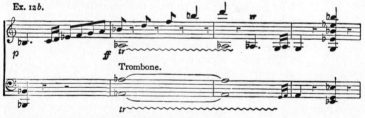

Ex. 12*b*.

The otherwise excellent Peters full score, published some sixty years ago, substituted a *forte* for the *piano*. The new critical edition seems to have been revised (I presume since Mandyczewski's death, or overruling his opinion) by some one who has had the intelligence to notice that the violins have no support from the basses, and who accordingly thinks *forte* insufficient and substitutes *fortissimo*. Swinburne would certainly have ascribed to 'the intelligence of a beetle' the capacity to see that the weakness of the unsupported first violins confirms the *piano* mark as correct. Haydn's lion is not 'pawing to get free'; all Haydn knows is that 'Vor Freude

brüllend steht der Löwe da', and I cannot see much objection to
the English text which he had before him; 'Cheerful roaring stands
the tawny lion'. What Haydn represents is this: the Editor not
having yet coiled himself round the Tree of Knowledge, some more
harmless and necessary animal, such as a goose, is walking past
the lion's ambush, whereupon that tawny animal, not being a beast
of prey until after the Fall of Man, plays his obvious and Haydnesque practical joke and says 'Bo!'

The listener will do well to remember the classical rule that the
illustration comes first and the words afterwards throughout the
recitative. To me the whole series is as delightful as the medieval
cries of the animals on Christmas Day; the cock with his 'Christus
natus est', the duck with 'Quando, quando?' the raven with 'In hac
nocte', the cow with 'Ubi, ubi?' and the sheep with 'In Bethle-
hem'. I am compelled to restore the line 'In long dimensions creeps
with sinuous trace the worm'. It is not much more absurd than
Milton's elephant; and the previous introduction of the worm into
Haydn's illustration of the 'host of insects unnumbered as the sands'
is a fatal mistake. In fact I cannot imagine how the Oxford editors
allowed themselves to obliterate the whole meaning of Haydn's
tremolo.

Aria (D major).

RAPHAEL. Now heaven in all her glory shone,
    Earth in her pomp consummate smiled,
    The vault of air by fowl is flown,
    The water swum by frequent fish,
    Behemoth's self doth walk the ground.
    But yet the end was not achieved.
    There wanted yet the master work
    That should acknowledge all this good,
    Adore and worship God supreme.

This is an entirely majestic composition, though Behemoth's
self (a more particularized item than Haydn's 'heavy beasts' or
'schwerer Last der Tieren') breaks through in the person of the
contrafagotto almost as subversively as cheerfulness broke into the
philosophy of Dr. Johnson's friend Edwards.

Still, there is nothing here that need minimize the grandeur of
the prophecy that Man was yet to be created in order to glorify
God and enjoy Him for ever.

Secco-Recitative.

URIEL. So God created man in his own image, in the image of God
created he him: male and female created he them. (Gen. i. 27.)
  He breathed into his nostrils the breath of life, and man became a
living soul. (Gen. ii. 2.)

Aria (C major).

In native worth and honour clad,
With beauty, courage, strength adorned,
His eyes to heaven turned upwards, stands a Man,
The lord and king of nature all.
His forehead broad and arching high,
Proclaims that knowledge dwells with him;
And through his eyes transparent
Shines the soul, the breath and image of his God.
While at his side his partner stands,
Made from his flesh for him,
A woman fair and full of grace.
Her glance of smiling innocence
As fair as blushing spring
Invites him to find there love and joy serene.

Here we have not only the quintessence of Haydn but the perfection of *bel canto*. We have also Haydn's freedom of form, shown in his instant readiness to follow the lines suggested by his text. The themes descriptive of Eve are only vaguely connected with those descriptive of Adam; the aria is allowed to fall into two subtly contrasted portions and there is no thought of complicating matters by a da capo. Another comparison with a later composition may be excused for its unfairness because of its aptness in showing the difference between a stroke of genius and an ambitious effort. Schubert at the height of his power has no cause to fear comparison with the greatest things in any art; but Schubert, after writing an ambitious exercise in his second-best style, would perhaps not be angry with us for using that exercise to measure the power of his beloved Haydn. The song *Die Allmacht* is an ambitious effort. Its very title, to say nothing of its text, would forbid us to blame Schubert for the contrast between its emphatic ponderosity and the heavenly lightness of Haydn's aria; but the two compositions have at least one thought in common, the thought that the Almighty's power is best felt in the heart of Man; or, as our Oxford text of Haydn's aria has it, 'through his eyes transparent Shines the soul, the breath and image of his God'. Now this climax Schubert represents with a beautiful purple patch in A flat major, the tonic being, as with Haydn, C major. The purple patch occurs twice, and the repetition is quite welcome and orthodox in form. Haydn, on the other hand, first modulates to the ordinary dominant, and it is at the moment of apparently repeating this modulation that he diverts it to the remoter key of A flat. This is, in its quiet way, as overwhelming as the outburst at 'and there was Light'.

When Vienna was bombarded in 1809, Haydn had long been

bedridden; but when the first shot fell near to his house he called out
to his servants, 'Children, don't be frightened; no harm can happen
to you while Haydn is by'. His last visitor was a French officer who
touched him greatly by his singing of 'In native worth'. Soon afterwards, at one o'clock in the morning of May 31st, Haydn died.

Secco-Recitative.

RAPHAEL. And God saw everything that he had made, and, behold it
was very good. (Gen. i. 31.)

And the Sons of God saw all the days of creation ended, and
shouted for joy.

The introductory statement of the angelic chorus is fine in itself,
and contains a short fugato not used afterwards, besides a short
postlude that significantly anticipates the double fugue to be
developed later. The terzet of the three archangels is a beautiful
slow movement (Poco adagio) which it is a pity to lose. But, as
I have already pointed out, it introduces thoughts that are not
clearly relevant either to the Six Days of Creation or to the Seventh
Day, on which God rested but certainly did not turn away His face
or strike us with sudden terror, take our breath away, and reduce
us again to dust. And I do not find, in actual practice, that, when
introduced by the right first seven bars, the last chorus of Haydn's
Second Part loses more than it gains by standing alone. It may
speak for itself, double fugue and all, without musical quotation.
A very detailed analysis would be needed to explain the subtle elements of its grandeur, which is rendered the more astonishing by
the fact that its cadential formulas are neither Bachian nor Handelian but purely symphonic, or, if you will, operatic, without the
slightest excuse for a ritardando. Technically the most surprising
thing in its orchestration is its almost completely modern treatment
of the brass. The classical treatment of trombones is nowadays
often misunderstood because of a failure to recognize that in the
organ-galleries of vaulted churches they assimilate themselves closely
with voices and have by no means the penetrating power that most
writers on orchestration ascribe to them. But Haydn shows that he
wrote *The Creation* for the concert-room rather than the church;
and his brass ensemble, including such Beethovenish clashes as—

Ex. 13. Trombones.

is at once safer and bolder than anything we are accustomed to
expect from Mozart, Beethoven, Schubert, or even Weber. By the
way, Haydn does not seem to know the modern or late-Victorian
rule that 'you must never use the bass trombone without the others'.
His rule appears to be that you may do so by all means, but need
neither presuppose that he will play like a pig nor compel him to
play thus by writing so low as to give him constant rapid changes
of his slide from the first position to the seventh. On the other
hand, Haydn entrusts to him, or to the conductor, the dangerous
task of simplifying the passages where a manifestly insane agility is
the result of the directions (Trombone III col Contrafagotto) ×
(Contrafagotto col Basso) × (Basso col Violoncello).

Chorus.

Achieved at last the glorious work,
The praise of God shall be our song.

Double Fugue.

Glory be to God eternal. He reigns on high for evermore. Hallelujah.

Let us disregard the suggestion of an interval between Part II
and Part III; and let us give its proper Beethovenish effect to
Haydn's extreme contrast between B flat and E major (equivalent
to Beethoven's contrast between the D flat Andante and G major
Tedesca of his Quartet in B flat, Op. 130). Morning arises on God's
Seventh Day of Rest.

Introduction and Descriptive Recitative.

URIEL. Now rosy-fingered, fresh awaked by music's sound,
The dawn lights up the sky.
And quiring angel companies sing purest harmony
To earth below.
See now the happy pair, how hand in hand they go,
Their shining faces show the unspoken thanks they feel.
Soon with expressive voice they sing the praise of God.
Then let our voices ring, united with their song.

Haydn's delicious three flutes are, except in one passage, supported
by strings with chords (sometimes, but not always, pizzicato) of
which the bass doubles the third flute three octaves below. The
sight of this in the score must set every musician's teeth on edge;
and I can find no theory to explain the astonishing fact that the
actual effect is not only excellent but that any correction of it
merely makes the flutes sound out of tune. Trust Haydn's ear;
he is one of the untidiest of artists; but, as he said to Prince Esterhazy, 'That, your Highness, is *my* business'.

Now comes the greatest thing in *The Creation* since the Chaos
and the Light. I will not distract the listener's attention by further

expressions of vexation at editors and cutters, except to express my gratification that my Oxford friends have refused to fall into the booby-trap into which a misprint in the original edition led the editors of the *Gesammtausgabe*. (Here again I cannot imagine how Mandyczewski's judgement came to be overruled.) The first long note of the oboe was misprinted as a minim in the middle of the bar. The editor of the Peters score, though he fell into the booby-trap of the cheerful tawny lion, here had the gumption to see that, as semibreves in the old score were always printed in the middle of the bar, it was much more likely that the minim was a misprint for a semibreve than that an initial rest had been omitted. A semibreve produces the *messa di voce* characteristic of all vocal or sustained openings of this kind; whereas an entry at the half-bar is a mere grammatical possibility with no discoverable meaning. But it has been faithfully put into the band-parts.

Analysis of this grand pair of movements would be futile unless it were an exhaustive précis. I merely indicate the key-sequence in the Allegretto, the wanderings of which are as spacious as the review of the heavens and earth by Adam and Eve, who anticipate the Song of the Three Children in Nebuchadnezzar's burning fiery furnace ('O all ye works of the Lord').

Adagio (C major).

ADAM *and* EVE.

Thy bounteous care, O Lord and God,
Fills heaven and earth with good.
This world so great, so wonderful,
Thy mighty Hand has made.

Chorus of Angels:
(pianissimo)

We know the mighty power of God.
We praise His name for evermore.

Allegretto (F major).

ADAM.

Of stars the brightest,
Shine thou on, fair harbinger of day.
Shine on, thou too, O sun on high,
Thou universal flame.

Chorus:
(forte)
EVE.

Proclaim in music of the spheres
The mighty God and praise His name.
And thou, the solace of our nights,
And ye, O starry host,
In all your galaxies declare His praise
While constellations sing.

ADAM.
(B flat major)
(Drift towards
A flat)

And ye, O elements,
By whose work new shapes and forms are made,
Ye, O clouds and lightnings,
Whom the winds assemble and disperse,

With Chorus:

We bid you magnify the Lord:
Great is His name and great His might.

EVE.   O singing streams, acclaim your fount,
(A flat)   Bow down your heads, O trees,
                    And show your fragrance, plants and herbs,
                    For all sweet smells are His.

ADAM.   Ye who on mountain heights do dwell,
(Drift through   And ye of lowly ground,
E flat minor   Ye who in flight cleave upper air,
and beyond)   And ye who swim below.

With Chorus: All creatures magnify the Lord,
(Dominant of G) Praise Him all ye works of His.

ADAM *and* EVE. Ye shady wood, ye hills and dales,
(G major; destroying Be witness of our thanks:
the initial effect of Re-echoing from morn till night
F major and firmly Our grateful hymns of praise.
establishing C major)

Final Section in C major.

Chorus: (piano)   Hail, bounteous Lord! Creator, hail!
                    For by Thy word the world was made.
(forte, in fugato)   Both heaven and earth Thy power adore,
                    We praise Thee now and evermore.

But the best way to raise the reader's expectation to the height of
Haydn's great argument is to quote Milton's version of this song,
which is dimly but unmistakably traceable throughout the Linlev-
Lidley-van-Swieten-Fox-Strangways-Steuart-Wilson evolution.

These are thy glorious works Parent of good,
Almighty, thine this universal frame,
Thus wondrous fair; thyself how wondrous then!
Unspeakable, who sitt'st above these Heavens
To us invisible or dimly seen
In these thy lowest works, yet these declare
Thy goodness beyond thought, and Power Divine:
Speak ye who best can tell, ye Sons of light,
Angels, for ye behold him, and with songs
And choral symphonies, Day without Night,
Circle his Throne rejoicing; ye in Heav'n.
On Earth join all ye Creatures to extol
Him first, him last, him midst, and without end.
Fairest of Stars, last in the train of Night,
If better thou belong not to the dawn,
Sure pledge of day, that crown'st the smiling Morn
With thy bright Circlet, praise him in thy Sphere,
While day arises, that sweet hour of Prime:
Thou Sun, of this great world both eye and soul,
Acknowledge him thy Greater, sound his praise
In thy eternal course, both when thou climb'st,
And when high noon hast gain'd and when thou fall'st.

Moon, that now meet'st the orient Sun, now fly'st,
With the fix'd Stars, fix'd in their Orb that flies,
And ye five other wandering Fires that move
In mystic Dance not without Song, resound
His praise, who out of Darkness call'd up Light.
Air, and ye Elements the eldest birth
Of Nature's Womb, that in quaternion run
Perpetual Circle, multiform; and mix
And nourish all things, let your ceaseless change
Vary to our great Maker still new praise.
Ye Mists and Exhalations, that now rise
From Hill or steaming Lake, dusky or grey,
Till the Sun paint your fleecy skirts with Gold,
In honour to the World's great Author rise;
Whether to deck with Clouds the uncolour'd sky,
Or wet the thirsty Earth with falling showers,
Rising or falling still advance his praise.
His praise ye Winds, that from four Quarters blow,
Breathe soft or loud; and wave your tops, ye Pines,
With every Plant, in sign of Worship wave.
Fountains and ye, that warble, as ye flow,
Melodious murmurs, warbling tune his praise.
Join voices all ye living Souls: ye Birds,
That singing up to Heaven Gate ascend,
Bear on your wings and in your notes his praise.
Ye that in Waters glide, and ye that walk
The Earth, and stately tread, or lowly creep;
Witness if I be silent, Morn or Even,
To Hill, or Valley, Fountain, or fresh shade
Made vocal by my Song, and taught his praise.
Hail universal Lord, be bounteous still
To give us only good; and if the night
Have gathered aught of evil or conceal'd,
Disperse it, as now light dispels the dark.

The last three lines are, of course, relevant only to the subject of
Paradise Lost', referring, as they do, to the disquieting dream sent
as a warning to Eve. But it would be a pity to cut Milton's paean
short of its appointed end.

On the other hand, the more I study *The Creation*, the better I
am satisfied to end it here. The love-duet between Adam and Eve
I dearly want to hear, and without cuts; but on some other occasion.
And another Palladian chorus would need to be even finer than the
end of Haydn's Part II if it were to command our attention after
what I believe to be the greatest movement, or pair of movements,
that he ever wrote, whether vocal or instrumental. Haydn's actual
last chorus 'Praise the Lord all ye his creatures' is good, but does
not, like the last chorus of *The Seasons*, achieve another opening

of the gates of Heaven. The sublimest note is undoubtedly that of Haydn's innocent symphonic style when the human voices of Adam and Eve in the Garden of Eden lead the choirs of angels.

'THE SEASONS'

Haydn's *Seasons* (*Die Jahreszeiten*) has suffered from the hard things he was the first to say about it. He began it in 1799, immediately after he had finished *The Creation*, but yielded with reluctance to the persuasions of his librettist, the Baron van Swieten, saying in the first place that he was old and his powers were failing, and in the second place, in terms diplomatically modified for van Swieten, but more direct to other friends, that the whole scheme of musical illustrations to common objects of the countryside was Philistine. Afterwards, when the success of the work was hardly, if at all, less than that of *The Creation*, he resented being praised for his imitations of the croakings of frogs and the bleatings of sheep, saying 'dieser französische Quark ist mir aufgedrungen' (this Frenchified trash was forced upon me). He also often complained that '*The Seasons* gave me my finishing stroke'. We have exaggerated ideas as to the length of Haydn's career and even as to the volume of his work. Verdi was 80 when he wrote *Falstaff*; but Haydn was 77 when he died in 1809, and after *The Seasons* was performed in 1801, he wrote only some vocal quartets, a fragment of a string quartet, and some accompaniments for Scottish, Welsh, and Irish airs for an Edinburgh publisher.

During the composition of *The Creation* Haydn had already feared that he might have a stroke, and his pessimism about *The Seasons* no doubt had its physical causes. It is the more unfortunate for the reputation of a great work that his self-criticism should amount exactly to what any fool can say beforehand. It is much more true that the obvious defects are the most negligible aspects of Haydn's qualities. The *französischer Quark* was forced upon him largely in consequence of the success of what it is now becoming priggish to condemn in the word-painting and animal-painting of *The Creation*. It is an automatic function of his sense of humour, which, as is now proverbially known, was never so irrepressible as when he rejoiced in the goodness of God.

I have refrained from announcing *The Seasons* as an oratorio, because only a small part of the work has any pretensions to be sacred music at all. And I dislike the alternative title 'cantata' because, except in the case of Bach, it has become associated with a kind of village harvest festival music: an association which is the more unfortunate because it derives some details of its style from Haydn's *Seasons*. The best way to rid oneself of prejudices is to take advantage of the fact that hardly anybody nowadays has ever heard a performance of *The Seasons* in its integrity, and to treat such a performance as that of a new discovery of a work *sui generis*.

Thomson has suffered almost as much as Haydn from the Baron van Swieten's acknowledgement of indebtedness. I have read Thomson's *Seasons* in the critical edition of Dr. Otto Zippel, 'a reproduction of the original texts, with all the various readings of the later editions, historically arranged', and have failed to find in it more resemblance to Haydn's text than *Paradise Lost* shows to the text of *The Creation*. As in my analysis of *The Creation* I quoted Milton in preference to the obligatory Mongrelian of the English libretto, so here I shall quote Thomson wherever I can substitute him for a lingo that has not yet had the advantage of drastic re-writing by musical editors in the Oxford University Press.

As a matter of fact, the Baron van Swieten is guilty of the grossest slander in coupling his name with Thomson's at all. The indebtedness of *The Creation* to Milton is by no means as obvious as its indebtedness to the Bible, and Milton could almost as well afford to be indebted to the Bible as he could afford to be faintly recognizable here and there in the Mongrelian language of the committee of translators and adaptors of Haydn's libretto. But poor Thomson cannot afford to be misrepresented. To the incurious his name recalls the exclamation from his *Tragedy of Sophonisba*: 'O Sophonisba, Sophonisba O'; because of the critic's retort 'O Jimmy Thomson, Jimmy Thomson O'! In Thomson's (but not in Haydn's) *Spring* you will find a much more famous line, 'To teach the young idea how to shoot'; but this does not provoke critics to call attention to its authorship. More famous still is 'Rule Britannia', which even Tennyson and Palgrave allowed to appear in *The Golden Treasury* with the feeble indicative 'Britannia rules the waves' instead of the authentic imperative 'Britannia rule the waves'. To either version Carlyle's pencilled comment was 'Cockadoodle doo!' A revival of Haydn's *Seasons* will incidentally revive a few other lines from the opening of Thomson's *Spring* in a chorus which has never lost its popularity; and this is unfortunate, because it will create in most listeners, as it created in me, the expectation that the rest of Haydn's libretto is equally indebted to Thomson. It would be really scandalous to perpetuate such a libel on the *magnum opus* of an English poet who, as Dr. Johnson said, 'has as much of the poet about him as most writers. Everything appeared to him through the medium of his favourite pursuit. He could not have viewed those two candles burning but with a poetical eye.' Haydn's most depised *Tonmalerei* has precisely this Thomsonian quality. I don't know how you would express two burning candles musically, but Haydn could no more help hearing the bleating of sheep and the croaking of frogs than the goodness of God with a musical ear. As to the libretto, not only has every vestige of poetry vanished from it, but Thomson's attitude towards at least two of the principal things he describes has been flatly contradicted and replaced by vulgar conceptions which we need not even recognize as specially English. Great Britain is not a wine-growing country, unless you count whisky, but one of the finest things Haydn ever wrote is the chorus in praise of wine at the end of *Autumn*. Beer is not mentioned, though Thomson has his vivid word for the 'brown October'; and, while Haydn's dancing to pipe and tabor and some kind of bagpipes is entirely delightful, we must not ascribe to Thomson the leading words of the chorus, 'Revel, riot'. This, however, is not because Thomson has a more sympathetic view of alehouse festivities. On the contrary, here is part of his account of what happens when

> ... the dry divan
> Close in firm circle; and set, ardent, in
> For serious drinking. Nor evasion sly,
> Nor sober shift is to the puking wretch
> Indulg'd askew; but earnest, brimming bowls
> Lave every soul, the table floating round,
> And pavement, faithless to the fuddled foot.

The real Thomson is gloriously quotable; but if van Swieten had allowed Haydn to get a glimpse of him, there would have been less wonder that Haydn thought the scheme unmusical. My own belief is that his quarrel with van Swieten would have become serious, and that he would have developed an interest in a real English poet of kindred spirit. We should have lost a great choral work which Haydn himself underrated; and I am not sure that the few more symphonies and string quartets that we might have gained would have overtaxed Haydn less than the composition of *The Seasons*. The more I study the technique of Haydn's middle and later works, the more I am impressed with his own conviction that he was neither a facile nor a quick writer, and that his mature handling of musical form needed immense reserves of energy used in procedures which were individual for each work. It is significant that that most pathetic of fragments, his last quartet, consists of the two middle movements, the andante and minuet, and that there are no traces of the first movement or the finale.

In *The Seasons* I do not find any abatement of power as compared with *The Creation*. Except in the last chorus, the whole subject is of a lower order, and its appropriate treatment represents Haydn at his best. There is more that can be cut out than in *The Creation*, but cuts within an individual number are quite as unpermissible. I used to think that the greater length of what I call the Palladian choruses was a sign of old age, representing a nervous fear lest their size should be inadequate, but on rehearsal I find them terse and their choral power as great as that of any choral music. The time is ripe for us to recognize in Haydn and Mozart choral writers of the calibre of Handel. The rediscovery of Bach, who, as Schweitzer very truly says, is Gothic, has blinded us to the merits of other styles of musical architecture; but the choral art of Mozart and Haydn has yet the power to rise out of all the squalor in which their patrons tried to keep it.

SPRING

With the orchestral introduction and first numbers of *Spring*, Thomson is not worse misrepresented than can be expected in the circumstances of an eighteenth-century musical libretto. Haydn begins with a glorious symphonic orchestral representation of winter weather.

Ex. 1.

I learn from the article on Haydn in the first edition of *Grove's Dictionary of Music and Musicians*, written in the 'seventies, that opinions are divided as to the relative merits of *The Creation* and *The Seasons*. The solemn goose-step tempo ($\rd = 138$) given for the vivace in the vocal scores is one of the traditional ineptitudes that make it a miracle that the work should ever have had any popularity at all, and the hired orchestral material nowadays available shows alarming signs that such traditions have been quite recently followed. Haydn, like Bach, is notoriously inconsistent in his use of the C and ₡ time-signatures; but this should not prevent even classical music from being played as music. Haydn is always splendid when his temper is blustering. His representation of winter gains both in realism and musical power from its concession to sonata form when Haydn modulates to the orthodox complementary key and gives us a brief glimpse of snowdrops.

Ex. 2.

The wintry storms return and develop. A symphonic return

is made to a full recapitulation and expansion of Ex. 1; and the stormy material is only further developed, with no trace of Ex. 2, until the voices of Simon and Lucas (*alias* the Baron van Swieten distantly translating from Thomson) explain that all this blustering is merely winter's Parthian shot. Where I can quote Thomson I shall spare the reader our efforts to adjust to music the traditional mistranslations of van Swieten's rhymed prose. Thomson says:

> And see where surly Winter passes off,
> Far to the North, and calls his ruffian Blasts;
> His Blasts obey, and quit the howling Hill,
> The shatter'd Forest, and the ravag'd Vale:
> While softer Gales succeed, at whose kind Touch,
> Dissolving Snows in sudden Torrents lost,
> The Mountains lift their green Heads to the Sky.

These seven lines go a little further than what Haydn had before him, but they give all the better idea of Haydn's music.

Now follows the best-known item in all Haydn's *Seasons*. Van Swieten has meticulously omitted every detail that could possibly catch a poetic eye or distract an incorrigibly illustrative composer; so the listener need not know the bittern's time, nor trouble about the wild notes of the plovers.

> Come, gentle Spring, Æthereal Mildness, come,
> And from the Bosom of yon dropping Cloud,
> While Music wakes around, veil'd in a Shower
> Of shadowing Roses, on our Plains descend.
>
> As yet the trembling Year is unconfirmed,
> And Winter oft at Eve resumes the Breeze,
> Chills the pale Moon, and bids his diving Sleets
> Deform the Day delightless; so that scarce
> The Bittern knows his Time, with Bill ingulpht
> To shake the sounding Marsh; or from the Shore
> The Plovers theirs, to scatter o'er the Heath,
> And sing their wild Notes to the listening Waste.

The Baron and the Translator then inform us through the mouth of that typical British farmer, Simon, that

Now in his course the sun has reach'd the winter-butting Ram.

This is ingenious; but perhaps Thomson's reference to the signs of the Zodiac is a little more clear, so let us see the matter through Thomson's poetic eye.

> At last from Aries rolls the bounteous Sun,
> And the bright Bull receives Him. Then no more
> Th'expansive Atmosphere is cramp'd with Cold,
> But full of Life, and vivifying Soul,
> Lifts the light Clouds sublime, and spreads them thin,
> Fleecy, and white, o'er All-surrounding Heaven.

Then comes the other of the two most famous numbers of Haydn's *Seasons*. Let us again listen to Haydn's music with the aid of Thomson's poetic eye.

> Joyous th'impatient Husbandman perceives
> Relenting Nature, and his lusty Steers
> Drives from their Stalls, to where the well-us'd Plow
> Lies in the Furrow loosen'd from the Frost.
> There, unrefusing to the harness'd yoke,
> They lend their Shoulder, and begin their Toil,
> Chear'd by the simple Song, and soaring Lark.
> Mean-while incumbent o'er the shining share
> The Master leans, removes th'obstructing Clay,
> Winds the whole Work, and side-long lays the Glebe.
>
> White thro' the neighbring Fields the Sower stalks,
> With measur'd Step, and liberal throws the Grain
> Into the faithful Bosom of the Earth,
> The Harrow follows harsh, and shuts the Scene.

In this splendid aria perhaps the most remarkable fact is that in representing the husbandman's 'wonted lay' by the famous tune borrowed from the 'Surprise' Symphony, Haydn has chosen a melody which for all its extreme rusticity can be neither whistled nor sung. (The Baron's 'flötend nach' is truer to the original than the Translator's 'wonted lay'). Try it, and however brilliant you may be at whistling you will be surprised at your inefficiency as a piccolo in this instance.

Ex. 3.

So Haydn gives the singer counterpoints.

Ex. 4.

In a short further recitative the British farmer is praised for having done all that can be expected of him, and the prayers of the poet and the composer now rise in one of Haydn's finest movements.

The slow movement of Haydn's Symphony in B flat No. 98, with its unmistakable reminiscence of that of the 'Jupiter'

Symphony, has always seemed to me a kind of requiem for Mozart. It also closely resembles the following trio and chorus:

Ex. 5.

Sei   nur   gnä - dig,   mil - der   Him-mel!

but the fugue with which it ends is hardly less than a direct allusion to the *'quam olim Abrahae'* of Mozart's Requiem.

Ex. 6.

Uns sprie-sset   Ue - ber-fluss und dei - ner   Güte

&c.

Ex. 7.

&c.

quam o - lim   A - bra-hae   pro - mis - is - ti

The fugue subject is, of course, an inevitable tag; but the figures of the orchestral accompaniment, though equally conventional, make a combination the resemblance of which is beyond coincidence. Also, the beautiful hush towards the end seems to ask for Mozart's blessing upon this work of Haydn's old age.

In the next recitative, Jane, the farmer's daughter, comments favourably upon the weather in terms which it were an irksome task to discover in Thomson. The ideas have, as a matter of fact, been entangled in the previous recitative and chorus. Perhaps the following quotation may cover the ground:

> Be gracious, Heaven! for now laborious Man
> Has done his Due. Ye fostering Breezes blow!
> Ye softening Dew, ye tender Showers descend!
> And temper all, thou influential Sun,
> Into the perfect Year!

Then follows a delightful trio with occasional outbreaks of chorus. For all I know, the Baron may have appreciated the surroundings of his country estate, but he does not commit himself to more than a townsman's vagueness in enumerating the common objects of the country. To quote the Translator, Jane remarks,

> 'Oh what num'rous charms unfolding shows the country now!
> Come, ye virgins, let us wander on th'enamell'd fields';

to which Lucas answers, substituting 'gay fellows' for 'ye virgins'. Further particulars are

> Lilies, roses and the flowers all;
> Groves, meadows and the landscape all;
> Land's surface, waters and the lucid air;

the frisking and capering of 'the lamkins'; the flouncing and tumbling of the fishes; the swarming and rambling of bees; and the fretting and fluttering of birds. (The listener need not listen for *these* words when I produce *The Seasons*, but I shall not trouble him with my makeshifts.) What Haydn's musical ear catches is the precise difference between the bleat of a lambkin and that of a sheep, and the glitter of sunlight upon the wings of bees. Incidentally, he breaks the otherwise inviolable classical rule that the musical illustrations should precede and not follow the words; but the dominating sentiment is that expressed in all Haydn's music by his own confession and here clearly aimed at as the conclusion to which this movement is to lead. The music pauses on the dominant of an unorthodox key, and then the praise of the Almighty is inaugurated with the full power of the orchestra. Here is Thomson's summing-up of the whole matter:

> What is this mighty Breath, ye Curious, say,
> Which, in a Language rather felt than heard,
> Instructs the Fowls of Heaven; and thro' their Breasts
> These Arts of Love diffuses? . . . What? but God!
> Inspiring God! who boundless Spirit all,
> And unremitting Energy, pervades,
> Subsists, adjusts, and agitates the Whole.

After a majestic formal introduction Haydn's vocal trio sings a lyric song of gratitude in a short poco adagio punctuated with doxologies from the chorus. Then the song of spring is concluded with a majestic fugue—

Ex. 8.

Eh - re, Lob und Preis sei dir

which is a masterpiece in its terseness and the variety of means by which contrast and climax are achieved. Great power emanates from the partial augmentation of the first two notes of the subject—a device already effective in the choruses of *The Creation*. These

two notes underlie the coda, in which symphonic formal elements
are allowed to relieve the polyphonic style.

Ex. 9.

&c.

It is perhaps not without practical grounds that *Spring* is the
best-known part of Haydn's *Seasons*. But I cannot go so far
as to admit that it has any marked superiority over the rest, except
in this, that it is the only part in which the text has any but the
most negligible traces of that genuine poet, Thomson. The
improvers of the first translator have tried to increase the percentage of Thomson; mostly with the obviously disastrous result
of misfitting the music of Haydn.

SUMMER

Haydn's *Summer* begins with a recitative describing the approach
of dawn. The Baron's mythical and un-Thomsonian creatures—
Lucas the young countryman, Simon the farmer, and his daughter
Jane—take it in turns to describe in flat German and inflated
English the approach of dawn, the retirement of the night-birds, and
the awakening of the shepherd by 'the crested harbinger of day'. The
last-named bird is brilliantly represented by one of Haydn's most
famous oboe solos. The only possible matter for doubt is whether
the oboe, rather than heralding the dawn, has not laid an egg.

Haydn's shepherd is not a little boy, nor are we told that his
garments are blue, but he blows his horn as characteristically as
Siegfried in an aria which, together with Jane's following recitative,
fortunately describes the sunrise efficiently enough to enable us
to omit the following chorus, which, though brilliant in its way,
suffers sadly by comparison with the magnificent and simple sunrise and moonrise in *The Creation*. As I have already said, cuts
within any of Haydn's movements are as criminal as cuts in
Beethoven, but *The Seasons* is unquestionably too long for complete performance in less than two evenings. And I confess to a
great sense of relief on finding that the recitatives will join together
without traceable scar if we omit one of the most difficult and at
the same time most conventional of Haydn's choruses. So let us
say with the first English translator: 'Hail, O Sun, be hailed, in
shouting praise resounds thy name through Nature all'; and let
us proceed to Haydn's description of noonday heat in a wonderful
recitative and cavatina, in which the tenor voice, muted strings,
an oboe, and a flute express Haydn's full power and breadth of
rhythm in a slow tempo.

Jane, the soprano, follows with a recitative describing welcome woodland shades and the refreshing coolness of a rivulet. The Baron has not allowed the composer any opportunity for Thomson's charming episode of the virtuous countryman chivalrously refraining from taking Actaeon's advantage of his Diana and seeing that no other profane eye shall approach the pool in which she is bathing. You can trust the Baron to present the composer with no pictures whatever; but the countryman's rustic pipe is allowed speech in one of the most beautiful of coloratura duets for oboe and soprano.

I approached the production and discussion of Haydn's *Seasons* in the conviction that my experience with *The Creation* had familiarized me with all the conceivable mistakes of our oratorial traditions. I was right, but what I had not foreseen is that these would be far outnumbered by the inconceivable ones that have been added to them. The original, or shall we say the aboriginal, English translation is often ridiculous, but in the following recitative, and in several other places, I have found it not impossibly ridiculous, and do not think the desire to restore Thomson a sufficient excuse for texts which make Haydn interpolate a five-bars' rest between a verb and its object; which speak of the rising sun where the music is describing the flight of hares; which mention lightning flashes that the music has no opportunity of noticing; and which twice cause Haydn's drum-rolls of distant thunder to come in the wrong place. Few things in descriptive music are more accurate than the recitative in which the three country folk describe the approach of a thunderstorm. To trace the Baron's indebtedness to Thomson is to look for needles in haystacks. Thomson has described the storms and earthquakes of every known earthly climate, and the Baron has merely generalized the result with as few particulars as possible, and has never dreamt of venturing upon Thomson's tragic detail of the English countryman who has seen his beloved struck by lightning. But, as Haydn's recovery to fine weather is distinctly European, if not English, we may take it that we are not dealing with the destruction of Pompeii, although we are told that the 'deep foundations of earth itself are moved'; and it is surprising to find even the later English translations making the chorus translate 'Weh' uns' by 'O God!' 'Woe's me' is quite adequate for the situation. Anything stronger rests upon the misapprehension of Mark Twain's German friend who said, 'The two languages are so alike: how pleasant that is; when we say "Ach Gott", you say "Goddam"'.

Ex. 10.   Weh   uns!

Er - schüt - tert wankt die Er - de bis in des Meeres Grund.

When the storm has died away a delightful allegretto describes the clearing of the evening sky. There is also a charming collection of Haydn's *französischer Quark*: the return of the cattle to their stalls with lowings admirably imitated by Haydn and completely missed by the improvers of the English translation; the call of the quail to her mate, a sound less known to the British than to the Germans, who proverbially represent the bird as saying *Lobet Gott*; and realistic, with Straussian dissonance, the chirp of the cricket;

Ex. 11.

the frogs in the pond, again represented by Haydn with a sweetness much more true to nature than our libellous word 'croak'; and, lastly, the toll of the curfew. Then the summer's day closes in peace with a description of the evening star and the country folk virtuously going home to bed at the command of the curfew. From the first edition onwards the translators have been misled by the word 'winkt' (*Von oben winkt der helle Stern*). *Winken* does not mean wink, but beckon or make a sign, and the 'clear star' is not the host of glittering stars, which in any case do not appear all at once in evenings with a long twilight; and a planet does not twinkle. *Von oben*, 'from above', is, of course, the Baron's mistake, for Venus can never be very high up in the sky either as evening or morning star. Be this as it may, Haydn's picture is correct, and we do not want it set to obvious mis-statements.

AUTUMN

I neither expect nor desire complete assent to the omissions I have to make in order to bring *The Seasons* within the compass of an evening's performance; and in defence of my drastic reduction of Haydn's *Autumn* I can plead only that I have omitted a large tract where I have always found my attention apt to wander, and where I am reminded chiefly of things which Haydn has treated more impressively elsewhere. Probably, if I had once begun rehearsing my omissions, nothing would have induced me to part with them, but nothing should prevent the audience from enjoying the whole of Haydn's *Winter*, which is to me as moving as anything in *The Creation*.

The *Autumn* begins with a movement expressive of sentiments proverbially unknown to the British farmer, viz. the husband-man's satisfaction at the abundant harvest. In real life we know that, even if all records for more useful crops had been broken, it must have been 'a main poor year for mushrooms!' I do not say that this is an excuse for my omitting the trio and chorus in praise of industry: 'From thee, O Industry, springs every good'. The text has faint traces of Thomson, and the music represents Haydn better than the chorus in praise of the sun. The country folk then proceed to gather nuts (in May?), in the course of which occupation Jane and Lucas sing a love duet which I am very sorry to omit. In the middle and towards the end it glows with real warmth, but in the first part the Baron has imposed upon Haydn and the lovers a needless preoccupation with the spuriousness of townsfolk and the superiority of real complexions over lipstick. No doubt Jane is quite right in saying: 'Ye vain and silly fops, keep of! (*sic*) keep of! here wily tricks and cheats are lost and glozing tales employ'd in vain; to them we listen not'; but Haydn, too, is not inclined to listen or to rouse his humour to more than a perfunctory playfulness; though I am sorry to miss the glow of the passages in which the lovers have forgotten their superiority to the townsfolk.

Having reluctantly skipped the harvest and the love-making, we will let Haydn's recitative tell us how 'Anon the sportsman's voice is heard', and we will listen to an aria describing with admirable music and realism the pointer in full pursuit until he makes his point and the huntsman fires his fatal shot. Haydn has timed the gunshot accurately with the words, which is more than can be said for the translators.

Then comes a hunting scene which seems to owe more to continental ideas of a *battue* than to any traditions of British sport. Still, that is no reason why the translators should represent the rounding-up and panic of hares by phrases about the orient sun and the assembling of huntsmen to the meet.

The following hunting chorus is a delightful movement showing Haydn's utmost freedom of form. But the merest justice to the reputation of Thomson compels us to protest against associating his name with its sentiments. His own feelings towards sport were substantially those of the Member for Burbleton, the Lady Topsy Haddock, *née* Trout; and his description of a stag at bay is of high pathos, of which the Baron allows Haydn no nearer hint than will illustrate a cheerful soprano episode in the subdominant, expressive of the British huntswoman's faith that the quarry enjoys the chase. The range of country covered by the huntsmen is well symbolized by Haydn in the fact that his chorus begins in D but eventually settles in E flat. As the Baron has given us no evidence that the country is British, or anywhere in particular, I see no reason for altering the French hunting cry *Hallali* used by Haydn, especially as Haydn associates with it the ancient French horn tunes used by Méhul in his overture to *La Chasse du Jeune Henri*, a very pretty

piece which was once popular and may as well become popular
again.

Ex. 12.

Great Britain does not claim to be a wine country, but neither
Haydn's music nor the translators have been able to avoid the
associations of the Rhine and the Moselle; nor is it possible to
adapt the ensuing glorious bacchanale to any particular place.
The translation of the original edition will not do. No choir-
master can ask a British chorus to sing: 'Now let our joy break
out, and heyday, heyday, hey, in loudest strains resound.' We are
told that 'the bulky tuns are filled'. From the music it would rather
appear that they were being emptied and that some other pinguid
bodies were being filled. I have already pointed out with quotations
that Thomson is not weakly optimistic about the festivities in a
British alehouse; but, while the listener may neglect our feeble
efforts to provide singable English for one of Haydn's greatest
movements, there is no reason why we should not enjoy the music.
The first section, in quick common time, modulates widely and
wildly, only to settle in a quite orthodox dominant. Then the dance
begins. Skirling pipes, rolling drums, scraping fiddles, and snarling
drones are duly catalogued and illustrated. The chorus is ejaculatory
and spasmodic, but the music is gloriously continuous in a way
which possibly inspired Mahler in one of his best movements, the
Scherzo of his Second Symphony. At last the orchestra becomes
learned and works out a quite solid fugue on the following subject:

Ex. 13.

It is some time before this theme penetrates the intellect of the
chorus; but at last the whole chorus, having been helped into the
home tonic, joins *en masse* to an extempore accompaniment of
triangle, and tambourine. Thus ends the *Autumn*, with a display
of Haydn's highest symphonic powers.

WINTER

Thomson's *Winter* appeared as a separate poem before the other
Seasons. I believe that it was always considered the finest part of

the work, and I find Haydn's setting of the Baron's alleged extracts from it an inviolable self-contained masterpiece.

'The overture paints the thick fogs at the beginning of winter' in a beautifully orchestrated Adagio; after which Simon explains the wintry details. What is now known more scientifically as a 'depression from Iceland' is illustrated by an admirably startling and shrill chord of A major, which Jane explains as 'rough winter stepping forward from Lapland's vaults'. She then sings a cavatina which is a wintry twin brother to that in which Lucas described the height of summer. Lucas now describes the frozen lake and the snowbound landscape. Then, in an admirable aria, he describes the traveller lost in a blizzard. Haydn's presto, not being alla breve, implies a tempo which is able to deal both with the wayfarer's efforts to press on and his sinking courage and the danger of abandoning effort. Suddenly he sees a cottage light. And all is well if editors and conductors will realize that, in spite of the anomalous time-signature, the ensuing allegro in E major is allabreve, and not slower, but faster, than the presto.

The traveller reaches the hospitable cottage and finds in a large warm room a gathering of country folk occupied in conversation, basketmaking, netmending, and spinning.

The spinning song is in D minor, and its rustic modulations to C major and E minor foreshadow in mere picturesqueness the most heartbreaking features of Schubert's *Gretchen am Spinnrade*.

When the spinning song is over, Jane entertains the company with a tale akin to the rhyme of 'Where are you going to, my pretty maid?'

In spite of his protests, the young Lord's intentions are presumably not honourable, and the company is slightly shocked and greatly puzzled by the Young Person's apparent readiness to listen to his suggestions. The more modern translators seem to be shocked also, for they make her display virtuous scruples, which would entirely spoil her plan of getting his lordship to look over the hedge to see if her brother is in sight. As soon as his lordship's back is turned she jumps upon his nag and rides away, leaving him all agape; a less drastic remedy than Randolph Caldecott's reading of 'Sir, she said', according to which the pretty milkmaid's companions took up the unfortunate man and set him on the back of a lively bull-calf. At all events, the chorus is quite satisfied with the capacity of the Young Person to take care of herself; and, as for his lordship, 'Ha, ha, ha, ha, and serve him right!'

Now comes the solemn end of Haydn's last great work. The text owes something to Thomson and more to the 15th Psalm. First, Simon, after describing the conquest of the year by winter, sings a solemn aria comparing the winter of the year to that of man's old age. *Où sont les neiges d'antan?* The Baron reduces Thomson's noble climax to platitudes; but Haydn's music more than reinstates the poet, who concludes:

> —And see!
> 'Tis come, the glorious Morn! the second Birth
> Of Heaven, and Earth! Awakening Nature hears
> The new-creating Word, and starts to Life,
> In every heighten'd Form, from Pain and Death
> For ever free.

The final trio and chorus is as moving as anything in *The Creation*. The squalors of any practicable vocal score give no idea of the heavenly boldness and radiance of the orchestral opening, which, owing to a timely birthday present from an aunt, I had the advantage as a boy of knowing from the full score before I knew that anything worse could be made of it. For which, as Bunyan would say, 'The trumpets sounded for her on the other side'.

Ex. 17.

After joining in dialogue with the trio in some lines suggested by the 15th Psalm ('Lord, who shall dwell in Thy tabernacle?'), the chorus settles down to a fugue.

Ex. 18.

Uns lei - te dei - ne Hand, O Gott! ver - leih uns Stärk' und Mut

To which Haydn answers *Amen*, in strict time, with one of the
most overwhelmingly energetic closes I have ever heard.

GUSTAV HOLST

'THE HYMN OF JESUS', OP. 37

The Hymn of Jesus is a poem found in the apocryphal Acts of St.
John. Holst has set an English version of it for two full choruses,
a semi-chorus of trebles and altos, and orchestra. The score is very
full, and the resources of its style range through all the centuries in
which music has been intelligible to western ears down to the present day. There is no essential novelty in the musical aesthetics of
Strauss, nor in the diametrically opposite musical aesthetics of
Ravel, which may not be found in this score, and found in its clearest
and simplest form. There is no musical truth known to Palestrina
that is not also to be found here, if our analysis is broad enough
and deep enough to reach the fundamental principles. There are
older truths still, truths of musical resonance that are older than
Palestrina's classical harmony. These lie deeper than that treatment
of complex chords as mere primitive sensations which we find in

Debussy and Ravel. It would therefore be entirely mistaken to ascribe to French influence the rising triads in the oft-repeated Amen in the semi-chorus. Generally speaking, the work gives no temptation for question as to its musical origins. I shall not easily forget the first impression I had on merely reading it. The whole of the music seemed to have projected itself into the words and vanished. Or, rather, the words seemed to shine in the light and depth of a vast atmosphere created by the music. But nobody, having once read the music, could say whether the poem by itself would have made the right impression at all. It is obviously inspired by the profoundest emotional sense of the Eucharist and all that that implies; and in its archaic symbolism it evidently demands to be rendered into the simplest English without regard for any prejudices against plain words. Accordingly the only way to describe it is to set out the words and mention here and there the mode and tempo of their musical treatment.

The work begins with an orchestral prelude. Trombones declaim freely (as if uttering the words) the plain-chant hymn *Pange lingua* (see Ex. 3 below).

The last note becomes a far-off chord which fades into other mutually remote chords on various groups of the orchestra. Again the *Pange lingua* is declaimed by a cor anglais, and this dies away into slow swinging chords on three flutes, below which long-drawn impassioned cries resound in falling modulations.

Ex. 1.
Lento.

The chords float down, and from the deepest organ pedals the first line of another hymn (*Vexilla Regis*, see Ex. 2) slowly leads to a note from which soft chords in slow 4/4 time mount like clouds of incense to vast heights, and swing on indefinitely while a distant choir of sopranos sings a stanza of the *Vexilla Regis*:

Ex. 2.

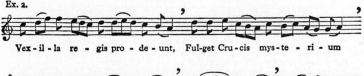

Vex - il - la re - gis pro - de - unt, Ful-get Cru - cis mys - te - ri - um

Quo car - ne car - nis Con - di - tor Sus - pen - sus est pa - ti - bu - lo

The King's banners come forth; shines the Cross's mystery,
Whereby in the flesh the Creator of all flesh is hung upon the gibbet.

This is answered by tenors and basses with the first stanza of
Pange lingua:

Rehearse, O tongue, the battle of glorious strife, and above the trophy
of the Cross tell out the noble triumph, how the World's Redeemer,
being sacrificed, hath vanquished.

The Amen is echoed by a few instruments in the orchestra; the
slow swinging chords die away; there is a silent pause, and then the
Hymn begins with the full double chorus, answered at each clause
by *Amen* from the distant semi-chorus.

THE HYMN OF JESUS

Double Chorus   .   .   Glory to Thee, Father!
Semi-Chorus (*distant*)   .   Amen.

Throughout the work the *Amen* is of the following type, of which I
give the three main versions:

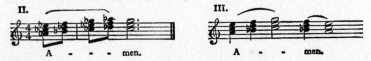

Double Chorus   .   .   .   Glory to Thee, Word!
Semi-Chorus .   .   .   Amen.

Double Chorus (softly) .	Glory to Thee, O Grace!
Semi-Chorus . . .	Amen.
Double Chorus (dispersedly, spoken) . . .	Glory to Thee, Holy Spirit!

(The spoken words reverberate like the Gift of Tongues through a distant
sound as of a mighty rushing wind)

Semi-Chorus . . .	Amen.
Double Chorus (singing, building up the harmony part by part, antiphonally) . .	Glory to Thy Glory, We praise Thee, O Father, We give thanks to Thee, O Shadowless Light! Amen.

This is the exordium to the Hymn, which now begins; telling of
mysteries which the anthropologist recognizes as older than Christianity,
and the Christian recognizes as before all worlds.

Andante 4/4

Chorus II . . .	Fain would I be saved:
Chorus I . . .	And fain would I save.
Semi-Chorus . . .	Amen.
Chorus II . . .	Fain would I be released;
Chorus I . . .	And fain would I release.
Semi-Chorus . . .	Amen.

Now the two choruses begin to overlap:

Chorus II . . .	Fain would I be pierced;
Chorus I . . .	And fain would I pierce.
Chorus II . . .	Fain would I be borne;
Chorus I . . .	Fain would I bear.
Chorus II . . .	Fain would I eat;
Chorus I . . .	Fain would I be eaten.
Chorus II . . .	Fain would I hearken;
Chorus I . . .	Fain would I be heard.
Chorus II . . .	Fain would I be cleansed:
Chorus I . . .	Fain would I cleanse.
Chorus I and II . .	I am Mind of All!
Semi-Chorus . . .	Amen.
Chorus I and II . .	Fain would I be known.

Allegro 5/4—two unequal beats in the bar:

Semi-Chorus . . .	Divine grace is dancing;
Chorus I . . .	Divine grace is dancing.
Chorus II . . .	Fain would I pipe for you,
Chorus I and II . .	Dance ye all.
Semi-Chorus . . .	Amen.

Chorus II . . . Fain would I lament:
Chorus I and II . . Mourn ye all.
Chorus I, II, and Semi-
    Chorus (*dispersedly*) . Amen.

Heav'n-ly   Spheres   make   mu - sic   for   us

Chorus I and II . . The Heavenly Spheres make music for us,
Semi-Chorus . . . Amen.
Chorus I and II . . The Holy Twelve dance with us;
                        All things join in the dance.

Short orchestral tutti:

Chorus I and II . . Ye who dance not, know not what we are
                        knowing;
Semi-Chorus . . . Amen.
Chorus I and II . . Fain would I flee;
                        And fain would I remain.
Semi-Chorus . . . Amen.
Chorus II . . . Fain would I be ordered;
Chorus I . . . And fain would I set in order.

The rhythm here begins to broaden; alternating 5/4 with 5/2:

Chorus II . . . Fain would I be infolded;
Chorus I . . . Fain would I infold.
Chorus II . . . I have no home;
Chorus I . . . In all I am dwelling.
Chorus II . . . I have no resting-place;
Chorus I . . . I have the earth.
Chorus II . . . I have no Temple;
Chorus I . . . And I have Heaven.

The rhythm has now become a slow and solemn 5/2:

To   you   who   gaze,   a   Lamp   am   I . . . .

These discords, frightful if played on two pianofortes, are aston-

ishingly natural and clear on the double chorus, their principle
being as obvious as Mozart's way of emerging from unison, thus:

Mozart. K.V. 575.

&c.

&c.

Chorus I and II	. .	To you who gaze, a Lamp am I:
Semi-Chorus .	. .	Amen.
Chorus I and II	. .	To you that know, a Mirror:
Semi-Chorus .	. .	Amen.
Chorus I and II	. .	To you who knock, a Door am I:
		To you who fare, the Way.
Semi-Chorus I and II	.	Amen.
Chorus I and II (to the first		
line of *Pange lingua*)	.	Give heed unto my dancing: (see Ex. 3)
		In Me who speak, behold yourselves:
Semi-Chorus .	. .	Amen.
Chorus I and II	. .	And beholding what I do, keep silence on
		my mysteries.

The first line of *Vexilla Regis* is faintly heard on the organ pedals; and
then the orchestra takes up the swaying chords of the introduction.

Chorus I and II	. .	Divine ye in dancing what I do;
		For yours is the passion of man that I go
		to endure.

Sound of distant trumpets with strange harmonies are heard, answered
by the *Vexilla Regis*, rapidly intoned in the thin high tenor of the bassoons. The sopranos of both choruses in unison take it up exultantly,
without words, to the martial sound of side-drums. It dies away suddenly into the cloudy chords which we heard in the three flutes, with
the long-drawn impassioned cry resounding below them, towards the
end of the prelude (see Ex. 1). The double chorus re-enters above an
enormously deep pedal note:

Chorus I and II	. .	Ye could not know at all;
		What thing ye endure,
		Had not the Father sent Me to you as a
		Word.

Ex. 1 is resumed as accompaniment to an impassioned new
theme which is developed to a tremendous climax.

Ex. 7.

Be-hold-ing what I suf - fer, ye know Me as the Suf - fer-er.

Chorus I and I!   . .   Beholding what I suffer, ye know Me as
                         the Sufferer.
                         And when ye had beheld it, ye were not
crescendo and   unmoved;
accelerando   But rather were ye whirled along,
                         Ye were kindled to be wise.
Chorus I and II   . .   Had ye known how to suffer,
                         Ye would know how to suffer no more.
Lento   Learn, and ye shall overcome.
                         Behold in Me a couch:
pianissimo   Rest on Me!

Soft common-chord of C in the Double Chorus, with the bell-tolling scales of Ex. 4, I, in the extreme bass and the Amen of Ex. 4, III, in the Semi-Chorus. And so the Burden fell from Christian's shoulders.

Semi-Chorus   . . .   Amen.
Chorus I and II   . .   When I am gone, ye shall know who I am;
                         For I am in no wise that which I seem.
                         When ye are come to Me, then shall ye
                           know:
                         What ye know not will I myself teach you.
Semi-Chorus   . . .   Fain would I move to the music of holy
                         Souls! (A slow and soft version of Ex.
                         5 in A flat.)
Chorus I and II   . .   Know in Me the Word of wisdom.

With closed lips at the end of the word 'wisdom' the double chorus holds the mysterious but not harsh dissonance of the notes of the whole-tone scale—

and, after a silent pause, ends with a shortened recapitulation of the exordium, substituting 'Holy Spirit' for 'Grace'.

Chorus I and II   . .   And with Me cry again
                         Glory to Thee, Father!
Semi-Chorus   . . .   Amen.
Chorus I and II   . .   Glory to Thee, Word!
Semi-Chorus   . . .   Amen.
Chorus I and II   .   Glory to Thee, Holy Spirit!
Semi-Chorus I and II   .   Amen.

PARRY

'AT A SOLEMN MUSIC', FOR CHORUS
AND ORCHESTRA

Parry's setting of Milton's Ode was produced in 1887, and though it is not his first important choral work it marks an epoch in British musical history. It represents classical choral writing at the height of maturity and natural resource. There was plenty of good English choral writing before it; the musical discipline of our old-fashioned University degree examinations has retained, though in a sadly debased form, many vestiges of sixteenth-century culture: and British musicianship was throughout the nineteenth century too much concentrated on the training of church choirs to remain ignorant of the practice as well as the theory of vocal harmony. We were, no doubt, in a sad and stagnant backwater of musical culture, but, as a modern poet has remarked,

> 'All is not false that's taught at public schools,'

and our knowledge of vocal writing has been a real enough thing as far as it went. It ought to be quite easy to see how immensely further Parry's work has taken it. We have only to consider the experienced writer of words for music, the musical journalist who purveyed oratorio-libretti to the Festival composer with one hand, while with the other he wrote hostile criticisms of the composers who preferred Milton and Robert Bridges; and we shall soon see what was needed to rescue British music from its contentment with that state of culture to which it pleased Mr. Chorley to call it. Let us begin by reading the first sentence of Milton's poem:

> Blest pair of Sirens, pledges of Heav'n's joy,
> Sphere-born harmonious Sisters, Voice and Verse,
> Wed your divine sounds, and mixt power employ
> Dead things with inbreath'd sense able to pierce,
> And to our high-rais'd phantasy present
> That undisturbed Song of pure concent,
> Aye sung before the sapphire-colour'd throne
> To Him that sits thereon,
> With Saintly shout and solemn Jubilee,
> Where the bright Seraphim in burning row
> Their loud uplifted Angel trumpets blow,

There; that is not the whole sentence for it ends only with a comma, but it is the first possible stopping-place after telling what Voice and Verse are to do. The style is not in the least long-winded; the clauses are thoroughly varied in length and none of them clumsy. But the composer who would set this to music must be able to produce a musical paragraph of the same structure. Not only that, but if his musical paragraph is merely declamatory it will be no paragraph at all, however just the emphasis. Many a talented and cultivated musician has taken the greatest pains to give the right emphasis to each and every word of a passage of prose or verse; and in so doing has arrived at something which sounds, in the first place, as if the singer was talking right across the beautiful instrumental accompaniment which contains all the real musical sense, and, in the second place, was delivering these words as instructions to a well-meaning but rather stupid servant. The greatness of Parry's life-work is shown here in the fact that his mass of pure eight-part harmony sweeps through this whole verse-paragraph in a perfectly natural flow of melody. There is no nonsense of the kind so familiar to conventional musicians, where words are repeated when there are too many notes for them in the tune, and notes are repeated where there are too many syllables for the tune in the words. The only clause which Parry repeats here is the line 'And to our high-rais'd phantasy present'; and this is no vain repetition, nor is it a rhetorical point to emphasize those words. It does not emphasize them; it does not even suggest that anybody is saying them twice over. The eight-part chorus is broken up into its main divisions, and we hear these words in one group of voices after another till they gather together again in 'That undisturbed Song of pure concent,' thus throwing into relief the meaning of the word 'concent'. Now let us proceed a stage further with this verse-paragraph:

> And the Cherubick host in thousand quires
> Touch their immortal Harps of golden wires,
> With those just Spirits that wear victorious Palms,
> Hymns devout and holy Psalms
> Singing everlastingly:

And so after broadening to a great climax in the bright foreign key in which this passage has been set, the orchestra bursts in with its introductory theme, which will be heard for the third and last time at the very end of the work.

Milton has not yet come to a full stop, and Parry, in holding the immense structure together by this return of the orchestral introduction, does not violate Milton's continuity, for the orchestra has not played more than eight bars when the chorus, without interrupting the symphony or diverting its course, re-enters with a counter-point of its own, singing in octaves for the first time. This use of plain octaves carries our musical consciousness back to the ages when the octave was the only 'perfect concord' accepted; and it is the exact translation of Milton's notion of 'undiscording voice' and 'perfect diapason'. Parry knew his musical history as Milton knew his classical scholarship, but it follows no more in his case than in Milton's that he worked this all out quasi-etymologically with no direct instinct to inspire him. We may not rashly put the composer on the same supreme plane as the poet; but it is not too much to say that the failure to appreciate Parry will generally be found to coincide with a failure to appreciate Milton. One negative thing is obviously instructive in Parry's treatment of his text; and most people would call it by the misleading name of 'reserve'. I well remember the indignation of a contemporary of mine, full of the resources of modern orchestration, when he found that Parry used no such measures as might be taken by forced notes on stopped horns to illustrate the 'harsh din' which 'broke the fair musick'. But Parry has given it perfectly adequate vocal expression for a chorus that is deploring the fact instead of describing it; nor did Parry see reason to interest himself in any orchestration beyond what is suited for supporting and relieving his chorus. Otherwise, no doubt, instead of letting the chorus sing in peace about the Cherubic host touching 'their immortal harps of golden wires', he might have directed our attention to all sorts of glissandos and harmonics on half a dozen mortal harps with cat-gut 'wires'; an obviously more important matter than the continuity of Milton's paragraph. A change of rhythm to triple time, a change of mode to the key of G minor, and a sufficiently but not extravagantly high chord on the words 'harsh din', are exactly to the point as Parry uses them. The words stand out as if there were no musical artificialities whatever to come between them and us. Parry's devices are adequate in exactly the same way as Milton's unexpected pauses in the long line 'Jarred against nature's chime, and with harsh din'. Let us finish the verse-paragraph from the point where the symphony was resumed:

> That we on Earth with undiscording voice
> May rightly answer that melodious noise;
> As once we did, till disproportion'd sin
> Jarred against nature's chime, and with harsh din
> Broke the fair musick that all creatures made
> To their great Lord, whose love their motion sway'd
> In perfect Diapason, whilst they stood
> In first obedience, and their state of good.

Here is Milton's first full stop! And here, too, in spite of (or rather because of) his beautifully clear form, is Parry's first real full stop; for the orchestra now enters with a new theme and thus carries the mind definitely away from any longer retrospect over what has been so firmly welded together. The new theme (it is only a single figure) rises and falls in wistful sequences. At last it dies away in the depths; and the sopranos re-enter with a melodious cantabile in a common time considerably quicker than that of the first part. This is answered by the tenors and soon brought into four-part harmony; whereupon, with a further quickening of time, a final theme bursts out and is developed in a stirring fugato rising from climax to climax until the orchestra crowns the last chords by the third and final allusion to its opening theme. The words consist of the four remaining lines of the Ode; they bear repetition because they are clearly the summary and object of the whole poem; and they need repetition because with them, and especially with the last line (the theme of the fugato), lies the possibility of making a musical climax that shall balance the rest of the music, as these four lines in themselves balance the huge verse-paragraph which has led to them:

> O may we soon again renew that Song,
> And keep in tune with Heav'n, till God ere long
> To his celestial consort us unite,
> To live with him, and sing in endless morn of light!

VERDI

REQUIEM IN MEMORY OF MANZONI

The genius of Verdi developed in ways that have provided many a pitfall for critics. For three-quarters of the nineteenth century Italian opera presented the phenomenon of a great tradition of singing, flourishing hectically on an orchestral tradition that had never been really alive and was not so much decadent as decayed.

You cannot allow dry-rot in the orchestra without eventually destroying vocal ideas also; and perhaps that is one reason why Italian opera, which flourished as comedy in the spacious days of the *Barbiere* (to say nothing of Mozart), needed, by the middle of the century, to keep itself alive on blood-and-thunder tragedy. For this tragic purpose it employed much the same orchestral habits and melodic idioms that it had drifted into for comic purposes. If a flute, a piccolo, two oboes, two clarinets, and all the violins faithfully double the melody of the heroic tenor, he will get the credit for the noise they are making. The necessary harmonic support may be furnished by the whole mass of brass instruments playing thick-set chords in dance-rhythms—for what other rhythms are there? In the country that still possesses the most wonderful voices, and is the historic ground of the Golden Age of Music that culminated in Palestrina, this dramatic and operatic technique seemed, in the mid-nineteenth century, to be common sense. In other countries, especially Germany, other methods had arisen, but such foreign fads were mere protestantisms and provincialities. Professor Basevi, writing on the 28th of April 1858 in *L'Armonia* at Florence, could, after referring respectfully to Mozart as *quell'animo tutto melanconico*, stoutly maintain that since Rossini's *Guillaume Tell* had been produced in 1832 '*non ha interamente progredito in Italia l'Opera in musica*'. This is hard upon Verdi, who had produced *Rigoletto* in 1851 and *Il Trovatore* and *La Traviata* in 1853, and who was about to produce *Un Ballo in Maschera* in 1859. But in some ways it was arguable; for the Parisians had roused Rossini up to making his orchestration remarkably interesting, whereas Verdi's orchestral habits changed slowly. And yet there are strokes of genius, both dramatic and orchestral, in *Rigoletto* that are utterly beyond Rossini's depth.

How is a composer going to rise to refinement, as well as to other aspects of greatness, from post-Rossinian antecedents? And how is criticism to deal, not only with the transitional stages, but with the survivals in the mature style of practices that obviously have a humble origin? One thing experience abundantly shows; that a conflict between artistic civilizations on two different planes always produces disagreeable effects, and will continue to do so long after we have forgotten the origins of the works which show it. To use the present psychological jargon, such works are bound to show an inferiority complex, and this produces a squalid style in which the elements belonging to the less highly-organized art are either feeble or blatantly self-assertive against the others. Such a style is painfully evident in Wagner even as late as *Lohengrin*; and it accounts for some of the difficulty which his reforming principles had in making their way. *Tannhäuser* and *Lohengrin* are Wagnerean operas that owed some measure of popularity to the anti-Wagnerean music that they contain.

Now the remarkable thing in Verdi's later development is that it shows no conflict of style. Verdi once said of himself: 'I am not a learned composer, but I am a very experienced one.' That is the word of power. Walter Bagehot once divided men into those who have an experiencing nature and those who have not. Macaulay, who had the *'inexperiencing* nature' in a high degree, could never have fallen between two civilizations, and could never have extricated himself if he had been born between them. Wagner did extricate himself. Verdi never fell. All his experience went into his music and enlarged it, crowding out what it superseded, without demanding transplantation and without injuring its foundations. Not one of his habits did Verdi change as his style developed. Those that would have been weaknesses in his later art were crowded out: the rest became like material instruments. Their limitations were to be used, without inquiry as to the existence elsewhere of other stylistic instruments without these limitations. How, for instance, is Verdi going to extricate himself from the bad Italian valve-trombone technique, when his art rises to levels beyond the dreams of Italian mid-nineteenth-century music? The foreigner answers glibly that Verdi ought to learn the noble technique of Wagner's trombones, and to space out their harmony on true acoustic principles. That is not Verdi's solution. To him the Italian method is common sense, and his inspiration cannot wait for the process of reconstructing the common sense of his art. He uses his trombones in the old Italian way. They make lumps of heavy and hot chord low down in the harmony, and now and then burst out in ferocious barkings and sputterings, with a technique of fantastic agility. The only difference that Verdi's later art shows is the all-important fact that he now knows exactly what these effects mean. The result is that so great a composer and shrewd an observer as Richard Strauss regards Verdi's later treatment of brass as 'quite individual, though without the right feeling for the soul and true character of trumpet and trombone tone'. Correctly deducing this from the nature of the 'vulgar-toned valve-trombones', Strauss does not stop to ask whether Verdi was not justified in suiting his style to the nature of his instruments. The interesting point is that Strauss should describe as a style quite peculiar to *Falstaff* and *Otello* a method which differs from that of earlier Italian works in no particular, except that it is applied with imagination.

The reasoning that applies to this special case will account for more important aspects of the style of Verdi's *Requiem*. All his life Verdi had been a composer for the theatre. The ideals of church music realized by Palestrina three hundred years before him were never more absent from the European musical consciousness than in 1873, and nowhere more forgotten or more tardily recovered than in Italy. To expect Verdi to produce anything like an ecclesiastical music would be humanly absurd. It ill becomes us to dogmatize as to the limits of divine patience; but we may be very sure that Verdi's *Requiem* stands before the throne at no disadvantage from its theatrical style. As human documents go, this work is of a flaming sincerity. The language of the theatre was Verdi's only musical idiom; and our musical culture, resting securely on its foundation on Bach and Beethoven, can derive nothing but good from realizing that to object to the theatricality of Verdi's *Requiem* is about as profane as to point out that Beethoven lacked the advantages of a university education. When Verdi's *Requiem* shocked all Hans von Bülow's classical susceptibilities, the defence came from the purest classical aristocrat of the later nineteenth century. Brahms had no mercy on music that fell between two civilizations, and some of his judgements of musical half-breeds are not quotable in the smoking-room without apology. But his comment on Bülow's *Schand-Artikel* was: 'Bülow has given himself away (*hat sich blamirt*): Verdi's *Requiem* is a work of genius.'

To the memory of his friend, the poet Manzoni, Verdi devoted his greatest inspirations, with the whole resources that he had accumulated in *Aïda*. Manzoni died in 1873: Verdi had already written the *Libera me* for a memorial service for Rossini, who died in 1868. Early in 1871 Mazzucato, writing from Milan, where he was professor of composition, reminded Verdi of this piece. Verdi replied that Mazzucato should be more careful of his praises; for the *Libera me* already contains passages belonging to the *Dies Irae*; and such praises are dangerously near to an incentive to composing the entire *Requiem*, which would be a dreadful consequence of Mazzucato's thoughtlessness. But have no fear. Verdi does not care for useless matters. There are so many, many, *and* many *Messe da morto*. It is useless to add another.

Two years later, the death of Manzoni, 'the only great Italian left after Rossini', caused Verdi to finish what he had begun. It was no addition to 'many, many, *and* many works'. It is as unlike any other Requiem as its text permits. There is no trace of Mozart; and its theatrical language only accentuates its utter remoteness from the spirit of Berlioz's *Requiem*. Even the distant trumpets in the *Tuba mirum* have an almost opposite purpose to that of Berlioz's four sets of brass and drums at the north, south, east, and west of the concert-room. Berlioz wishes to astonish: while Verdi merely wants some trumpet-notes off-stage to get the actual fact of distance, without any attempt at a realistic treatment of a supernatural event.

I am not aware that Verdi ever encountered the kind of prig who would try to alter his ideas of religion, or of music, or even of religious music. But it might have been at least theoretically possible to point out that Mozart's *Requiem* (itself a very theatrical work from Palestrina's point of view) moves the listener by an architectural and vocal beauty which is itself unshaken; whereas Verdi's constant effort is to make the voices and structure express consternation and the abandonment of grief. And can we not see the great simple old Italian saying, with no mock modesty, that the great method of Mozart is not for him; but that consternation and the abandonment of grief he can and will express? In the last resort, his humble method achieves the greater qualities also. Verdi's *Requiem* is full of strokes of genius; and they are, one and all, architectonic features. Schumann's friend, Thibaut, who, in discovering the purity of Palestrina's style, took umbrage at the theatricality of all music since 1600, made much of the fact that Mozart, in setting the words *Liber scriptus proferetur*, uses the same musical language as that of the child Barbarina hunting for a lost pin in *Figaro*. Of course the real point of Mozart's musical vocabulary is the reverse of Thibaut's way of thinking: Barbarina sings the most tragic music in *Figaro*, because a child doesn't know the difference between losing a pin and facing the Day of Judgement. There are other pitfalls in these criticisms of an artist's vocabulary: for the languages of the arts develop and decline like other languages; words becoming loftier as they drop out of familiar use, until perhaps the heroic language becomes mock-heroic or even slang. And so theatricality itself is but a relative term; and I am not sure that Palestrina has not been quoted with a theatrical gesture in modern times.

All choral music, except movements that are worked out extensively on a single text, is best analysed by quoting the words in full, with whatever musical illustrations are necessary.

The first number of the *Requiem* corresponds to the Kyrie of the Mass, and ends with that text:

I. REQUIEM AND KYRIE

Requiem aeternam dona eis   Grant them eternal rest, O Lord:
Domine:

Ex. 1.

et lux perpetua luceat eis.   and let everlasting light shine on them.

Ex. 2.

The theme and harmony are in the instruments; the voices accompany with broken declamation in monotone. The characteristic change from minor to tonic major, before the music can have accomplished any action, is an Italian idiom which Schubert caught from Rossini. It reverberates here both from Verdi's own traditions and from his love of Schubert, which is often evident in his work. The music closes unexpectedly into F major, where the unaccompanied chorus delivers the next clauses in a simple but sonorous and devout paragraph.

Ex. 3.

Te   de - cet   hym - nus

Te decet hymnus, Deus, ex Sion, et tibi reddetur votum in Jerusalem. Exaudi orationem meam: ad te omnis caro veniet.

To thee, O God, praise is meet in Sion, and unto thee shall the vow be performed in Jerusalem. Hearken unto my prayer: unto thee shall all flesh come. Ps. 65. (The Bible and Prayer Book versions differ from the Vulgate.)

The *Requiem* and *lux perpetua* passages are repeated. Then the solo voices enter with the Kyrie, which is worked out in the most moving passage in all Verdi's works; unquestionably one of the greater monuments of musical pathos.

Ex. 4.

Ky - ri - e   e - le - - - - - - - i - son

Kyrie eleison: Lord, have mercy upon us:
Christe eleison: Christ, have mercy upon us:
Kyrie eleison.   Lord, have mercy upon us.

II. DIES IRAE

The Dies Irae begins with the most naïve passage in the whole work, a passage which recurs on several later occasions, and which is always developed with great breadth. Eventually its powerful stride carries us beyond our first impression of its *naïveté*, and we recognize the great master of the Kyrie.

Ex. 5.

Dies irae, dies illa
Solvet saeclum in favilla
Teste David cum Sibylla.

The Day of Wrath, that day shall dissolve the world in ashes, as witnesseth David and the Sibyl.

The music dies away, without losing its swing, and the voices declaim in broken monotone the next terzina.

Quantus tremor est futurus
Quando judex est venturus
Cuncta stricte discussurus!

What trembling shall there be when the Judge shall come who shall thresh out all thoroughly!

Distant trumpets answer the trumpets of the orchestra in a crescendo which leads to the following text:

Tuba, mirum spargens sonum
Per sepulcra regionum,
Coget omnes ante thronum.

The trumpet, scattering a wondrous sound through the tombs of all lands, shall drive all unto the Throne.

Bass solo: slow declamation with long pauses, and broken rhythms in the lower registers of the orchestra.

Mors stupebit et natura
Cum resurget creatura
Judicanti responsura.

Death and Nature shall be astounded when the creature shall rise again to answer to the Judge.

Soprano solo: a long sustained slow movement, punctuated now and then by the chorus singing the words *Dies irae* in low monotone.

Liber scriptus proferetur
In quo totum continetur
Unde mundus judicetur.

A written book shall be brought forth in which shall be contained all for which the world shall be judged.

Judex ergo cum sedebit
Quidquid latet apparebit:
Nil inultum remanebit.

And therefore when the Judge shall sit, whatsoever is hidden shall be manifest; and naught shall remain unavenged.

Suddenly the orchestra flares up and the chorus bursts out with the latter portion of the Dies irae movement, just before its diminuendo. This now leads to a trio for soprano, mezzo-soprano, and tenor, in adagio 6/8 time, G minor (the key of the *Dies irae* as a whole). It is worked out as a long sustained pathetic movement, and is a *locus classicus* for its combination of voices and upper strings with a solo bassoon as an expressive flowing bass.

Quid sum miser tunc dicturus,	What shall I say in my misery?
Quem patronum rogaturus,	Whom shall I ask to be my advo-
Cum vix justus sit securus?	cate, when scarcely the righteous
	may be without fear?

At last the three voices ask their questions one by one alone. Then the basses of the chorus thunder out the beginning of the next movement, an adagio maestoso in C minor, of which I quote the third line, which the solo voices sing, and which is developed to one of the principal emotional climaxes in the work.

Ex. 6.

Sal - va me, fons pi - e - ta - tis

Rex tremendae majestatis	King of awful majesty, who
Qui salvandos salvas gratis;	freely savest the redeemed; save
Salva me, fons pietatis.	me, O fount of mercy.

Duet for soprano and mezzo-soprano.

In the same tempo (which is Verdi's fundamental tempo for Church music; common time with crotchets ranging between 72 and 88 to the minute) the *Recordare* deals with the next terzina in a broad lyric movement. The childlike rhythmic figure of the wind instruments recalls, perhaps not accidentally, the cries of *salva me* in the preceding movement.

Ex. 7.

Re - cor - da - re, Je - su pi - e

Recordare, Jesu pie,	Remember, merciful Jesu, that
Quod sum causa tuae viae	I am the cause of thy journey, lest
Ne me perdas illa die.	thou lose me in that day.

The next lines are those which Dr. Johnson sometimes tried to quote, but never without bursting into tears. The first line I take to allude to the woman of Samaria.

Quaerens me sedisti lassus;	Seeking me didst thou sit weary:
Redemisti crucem passus.	thou didst redeem me, suffering
Tantus labor non sit cassus.	the cross: let not such labour be
	frustrated.

Juste Judex ultionis	O just Judge of vengeance, give
Donum fac remissionis	the gift of remission before the day
Ante diem rationis.	of reckoning.

In an almost recitative-like passage the tenor interpolates the next terzina before proceeding to another lyric movement.

Ingemisco tanquam reus:	I groan as one guilty; my face
Culpa rubet vultus meus.	blushes at my sin. Spare, O God,
Supplicanti parce, Deus.	me, thy suppliant.

Then follows a movement in E flat with two themes, both intensely Italian, of which the second (accompanied by high tremolo violins) comes at the lines beginning *Inter oves*.

Qui Mariam absolvisti	Thou who didst absolve Mary,
Et latronem exaudisti,	and didst hear the thief's prayer,
Mihi quoque spem dedisti.	hast given hope to me also.

Preces meae non sunt dignae,	My prayers are not worthy, but
Sed tu, bonus, fac benigne,	do thou, good Lord, show mercy,
Ne perenni cremer igne.	lest I burn in everlasting fire.

Inter oves locum praesta	Give me place among thy sheep
Et ab haedis me sequestra,	and put me apart from the goats,
Statuens in parte dextra.	setting me on the right hand.

If proof were yet needed that Verdi's theatrical language is of untainted sincerity, good evidence might be found in the fact that the next terzina is still given to a solo voice, and that the stress is laid not on the obvious contrast between the first pair of lines and the third, but on the contrite prayer which follows.

Confutatis maledictis	When the damned are confounded and devoted to sharp flames, call thou me with the blessed.
Flammis acribus addictis,	
Voca me cum benedictis.	

An interesting document in the history of modern harmony is the following passage, which (like the treatment of *omnis terra veneretur* in Verdi's last work, the *Te Deum*) shows that to him the negation of classical part-writing expressed by the series of consecutive fifths is appropriate to the sentiment of utter self-abasement:

Oro supplex et acclinis,	I pray, kneeling in supplication,
Cor contritum quasi cinis,	a heart contrite as ashes, take thou
Gere curam mei finis.	mine end into thy care.

Finally the voice seems to be closing in E minor; but, by one of the greater architectonic strokes of this work, Verdi makes the chord resolve into G minor, and the chorus resumes the opening of the Dies irae, with the whole text of the first terzina (Ex. 5).

This dies away into the dark key of B flat minor, where the final movement carries out its solemn design. The melody of the Lacrimosa is naïve enough for *Il Trovatore*.

Ex. 9.

Lac - ri - mo - sa di - es il - la qua re - sur - get ex fa - vil - la

Lacrimosa dies illa	Lamentable is that day on which
Qua resurget ex favilla	guilty man shall arise from the
Judicandus homo reus.	ashes to be judged.

Those to whom Verdi's style is a stumbling-block may feel some relief that the first two bars of Ex. 9 were followed by other figures instead of immediately repeating themselves. But, as Bülow might have said before his noble recantation in 1892, *das fehlte noch*; and it does happen later, but not until a fine arch of counterpoint is stretched over it by the solo voices when the chorus proceeds to the last lines, which mark the end of the hymn by adding a fourth line to the previous terzina (*huic* is two syllables), and concluding with two short rhymeless lines and an Amen.

Huic ergo parce, Deus.	Spare then this one, O God,
Pie Jesu Domine:	merciful Lord Jesu: give them
Dona eis requiem. Amen.	peace. Amen.

The Amen is one of the subtlest and most impressive strokes of genius in all Verdi's work, being unexpectedly on a chord of G major; after which the orchestra ends with the chord of B flat major.

III. OFFERTORIO

The whole of this important section is set as a solo quartet. The main movement is an andante mosso in 6/8 time and the key of A flat major. A quiet introduction for the violoncellos and a few wind instruments gradually arrives at the main figure—

Ex. 10.

to which the soprano and tenor add, in broken phrases, the invocation. The bass then completes the sentence, using the theme of Ex. 10, and the movement develops in a flowing style, to the following words, the terrors of which are unable to prevail over the calm of faith expressed by the music.

Domine Jesu Christe, Rex gloriae, libera animas omnium fidelium defunctorum de poenis inferni et de profundo lacu; libera eas de ore leonis; ne absorbeat eas Tartarus, ne cadant in obscurum.

O Lord, Jesu Christ, King of glory, deliver the souls of all the departed faithful from the torments of hell and from the bottomless pit; deliver them from the mouth of the lion; lest Tartarus swallow them; lest they fall into the darkness.

Now the soprano enters. This is one of the great moments.

Sed signifer Sanctus Michael repraesentet eas in lucem sanctam—

But let Saint Michael the standard-bearer bring them forth into the holy light—

Then the music breaks into a quick almost alla-breve tempo, treating with simple lyric fervour a text that has almost always been set as a fugue. But nothing in Verdi's *Requiem* is an addition to the *tante tante e tante* Requiems written before it.

Quam olim Abrahae promisisti et semini ejus.

which thou didst once promise unto Abraham and his seed.

The climax leads suddenly to a quiet slow movement in a bright key.

Ex. 11.

Hos - ti - as   et pre - ces ti - bi, Do - mi - ne

Hostias et preces tibi, Domine, laudis offerimus. Tu suscipe pro animabus illis quarum hodie memoriam facimus. Fac eas, Domine, de morte transire ad vitam.

To thee, O Lord, we render our offerings and prayers with praises. Do thou receive them for those souls which we commemorate today. Make them, O Lord, pass from death unto life.

The *Quam olim Abrahae* is repeated in full as the completion of the sentence. This time it leads back to the original 6/8 movement, and the quartet, in octaves, with impressively sombre scoring, concludes with Ex. 10, to the words *libera animas*, &c.; adding *fac eas de morte transire ad vitam*.

IV.   SANCTUS

Sanctus, sanctus, sanctus Domine Deus Sabaoth. Pleni sunt coeli et terra gloria tua. Hosanna in excelsis. Benedictus qui venit in nomine Domini. Hosanna in excelsis.

Holy, holy, holy, Lord God of Sabaoth. Heaven and earth are full of thy glory. Hosanna in the highest. Blessed is he that cometh in the name of the Lord. Hosanna in the highest.

The most unexpected of all features in this extraordinary work is the Sanctus. For reasons probably liturgical and certainly beyond my information, the Sanctus of every Requiem known to me is very much shorter and slighter than the Sanctus which forms the central feature of an ordinary Mass. Verdi gives no exception to the rule, but he achieves a vivid contrast to the rest of the work. After some trumpet-calls the chorus, divided into two choirs, sings the whole Sanctus, Pleni, Benedictus, and Hosanna in one unbroken double fugue, which, like most post-classical Italian fugues, revolves in four-bar periods.

Ex. 12.

But the effect is not stiff, and if it is dance-like, the dance is that of the Sons of the Morning. Towards the end the words *pleni sunt coeli et terra* recede into distance with the Hosannas, becoming slow, quiet, and vast, while the orchestra dances on. Then suddenly the music blazes out again and comes to a brilliant end.

V

The Agnus Dei is another strange and unique conception. Two solo voices, unaccompanied, give out a melody of twice seven bars, grouped as 4 and 3. Here are the first seven bars:

Ex. 13.

This is repeated by the chorus in a lower octave, also unharmonized, but accompanied in unison by most of the orchestra. The solo pair repeat it harmonized in a minor variation; the chorus replies with a fully harmonized major variation. (I speak of variation in reference to the accompaniment: the vocal melody never alters, except in as far as it was put into the minor.) Then comes the passage, quoted in every book on instrumentation, where three flutes surround the two voices with a flow of counterpoint. The chorus repeats the last six bars with a new harmonization, and a short coda in echoing dialogue on the words *requiem sempiternam* ends the movement.

Liturgically the idea is that the prayer is uttered three times, and the last time with the addition of the word *sempiternam*, so that it should be set forth as follows:

Agnus Dei qui tollis peccata mundi: dona eis requiem.

Agnus Dei qui tollis peccata mundi; dona eis requiem.

Agnus Dei qui tollis peccata mundi; dona eis requiem sempiternam.

Lamb of God, that takest away the sins of the world: give them rest, ... give them eternal rest.

VI. LUX AETERNA

A trio for mezzo-soprano, tenor, and bass. Below a soft high tremolo starting in B flat major, but modulating mysteriously, the mezzo-soprano declaims the whole text. Then the bass interpolates the text *Requiem aeternam*, over a dark chord of B flat minor (roll on drums in fifths, and low trombone-chords). In G flat major the unaccompanied vocal trio again deals with the rest of the text. The dark B flat minor passage returns, with the addition of the upper voices, and at last the movement settles to a lyric melody in B flat major, exquisitely scored.

Ex. 14.

Lux aeterna luceat eis Domine cum Sanctis tuis in aeternum quia pius es. Requiem aeternam dona eis Domine, et lux aeterna, &c.

Let everlasting light shine on them, O Lord, with thy Saints for ever; for thou art merciful. Grant them, O Lord, eternal rest and let everlasting light, &c.

VII. LIBERA ME

When Verdi replied to Mazzucato in 1871 that the *Libera me* written for Rossini already contained a recapitulation (*riepilogo*) of the *Requiem aeternam* and *Dies Irae*, he showed that the order of composition did not interfere with the logic of his ideas. When the time came to write the whole work, everything led up to the incidents of the already finished *Libera me* as cause to effect. The design begins with an introduction in which the soprano solo and the chorus declaim the words sometimes on a mere reciting note, sometimes in dramatic recitative-like phrases.

Libera me, Domine, de morte aeterna in die illa tremenda quando coeli movendi sunt et terra; dum veneris judicare saeculum per ignem.

Deliver me, O Lord, from eternal death in that awful day when the heavens and the earth shall be moved: when thou shalt come to judge the world by fire.

Then the soprano settles down, though in broken phrases, to a formal movement, which the orchestra holds together with a flowing accompaniment.

Tremens factus sum et timeo, dum discussio venerit atque ventura ira, quando coeli movendi sunt et terra.	I am become trembling, and I fear the time when the trial shall approach and the wrath to come; when the heavens and the earth shall be moved.

The voice dies away. After a pause the *riepilogo* of the Dies Irae (Ex. 5) crashes in. The text, however, is not the same. For one thing, it is not metrical. (Was this, then, an older part of the liturgy, and the hymn written after it and suggested by it?)

Dies irae, dies illa calamitatis et miseriae, dies magna et amara valde.	A day of wrath, that day of calamity and woe, a great day and bitter indeed.

The diminuendo is more impressive than on any previous occasion, which shows how Verdi, in the heat of inspiration for the rest of the work, could hold in reserve what had already been written to come at the end. And now comes the most moving and most architectonic stroke in the whole work. The *riepilogo* of the *Requiem aeternam* (in B flat minor and major) gives to the unaccompanied chorus, led by the solo soprano, the music which at the outset of the work was given only by the orchestra, the voices having nothing but broken monotone. The effect, which Mazzucato thought unsurpassable in itself, seems now to depend on the whole weight and dimensions of the complete work. (See Exx. 1 and 2.)

Requiem aeternam dona eis, Domine, et lux perpetua lucat eis.	Grant them, O Lord, eternal rest, and may light everlasting shine upon them.

With a startled tremolo on the violins the soprano resumes the text *Libera me*, and the work concludes with a fugue.

Ex. 15.

Li - ber-a me, Do - mi - ne, de mor - te ae - ter - na . .

. . . in die il - la tre - men - da

Classical practice is not in favour of full closes in fugal expositions, but Verdi likes them well enough to mark them with the full orchestra. They are in keeping with the rest of his style; and a

fugue that would satisfy examiners might not so easily satisfy Verdi.
Yet this fugue is no poor example of resources, contrapuntal and
dramatic. The subject is inverted—

Ex. 16.

&c.

and, later on, augmented at the entry of the soprano solo, a passage
of high pathos; and the whole movement expands on lines of form
as near to Beethoven's as anything so completely Italian could be.
The quiet end is perfect in its poetry and solemnity.

'STABAT MATER', FOR CHORUS AND ORCHESTRA

Of the Four Sacred Pieces which constitute Verdi's last work, the
Stabat Mater is the most important and the most perfect. The *Te
Deum* is a little more voluminous, but does not achieve the consistency of style shown in the *Stabat Mater*, nor is it so unquestionably beautiful in conception, though it is very impressive. To
complain that either work is theatrical or unecclesiastical is as
relevant as the discovery that it is not only foreign but positively
un-English. Verdi at eighty was no more aware than Verdi at
thirty that music could be anything but theatrical. He was hardly
aware that it could be theatrical. In Italy an Englishman, and *a
fortiori* a Scot, may be known by his tendency to remark that 'it is
a fine day'. This puzzles the native, who gets his bad weather in
very effective doses when it does come, but whose fine days are
just 'days'. The strangest thing about the inveterately theatrical
Verdi is that he had a profound love of Palestrina; and the strangest thing about Verdi's *Stabat Mater* is that in spirit and also in
form it resembles Palestrina's *Stabat Mater* more than any other
setting of that poem, though the more you study it the more
its at first sight glaring difference from the Verdi of *Trovatore*
vanishes.

The spirit of the work is not a matter of language. The style of
the stage is not ecclesiastical. The Latin of St. Jacopo di Todi is
not classical. And there we may leave the stylistic criticism of
words and music. Questions of form and method are less jejune.
The poem falls into two parts, a meditation and a prayer. The
meditation is a series of the simplest possible mental pictures of the
Virgin Mother standing by the Cross; the prayer is for a share in
her sorrows, with the hope of Paradise after death. Tolstoy's three
staretsi hardly attained a more simple saintliness. But the
simplicity itself is mystical, though the substance is concrete and

emotional, with none of the close-packed parables and metaphors of the *Pange lingua*. Palestrina's setting is one of the simplest compositions in the world, as simple as Bach's Chromatic Fantasia, the purest cloud-scape in the world of harmony, without even a flight of birds to show the scale of its mighty perspective. The rhythm is that of the quantities of the words; there is no polyphony and no themes. Translate the tonality from free Dorian to modern minor and major with unlimited range of key; add a full Italian orchestra with Italian traditions of scoring, grandiose and whole-sale in method, yet refined by the experience of an octogenarian; and the analysis of Palestrina's *Stabat Mater* will fit Verdi's better than you might expect. Palestrina's Dorian mode keeps his strange harmonies together. Verdi's modulations are instinctively balanced around the G minor of his beginning and end. His last notes are those to which the three words 'Stabat Mater dolorosa' are set at the beginning; otherwise there is no theme to hold the work to-gether. His enormous talent for composition enabled him in his earlier works to give life to the crudest schemes of rhythm and phrasing; and now it enables him to make the lines of the poem roll on in their groups of three like a planet in its orbit. He does not overburden his declamation with grammatical analysis; for example, he is content to set 'Me sentire vim doloris' as a complete line without running on to the word 'fac', which is needed to com-plete the sense; but he does not, like Pergolese, make it impossible to understand by repeating the line again and again and then set-ting 'fac ut tecum lugeam' as an entirely separate proposition. In short, he is neither conventional nor pedantic: he knows how words actually are spoken and does not argue, like Dr. Johnson, that a negative commandment such as 'Thou shalt not steal' should stress the word 'not', in defiance of the plain fact that in common speech 'shalt not' has become 'shan't'.

INDEX

Those works to which a complete essay is devoted have their
titles printed in small capital letters.

accent, reversal of, 115, 150, 343;
hemiole ($\frac{3}{2}$ v. $\frac{6}{4}$), 33, 200, 210, 309
afterthoughts, 199 *passim*, 246–7
Albert Hall, the, 342
Allen, Sir Hugh, 151
architecture, and music, 358, 365, 384,
410
arrangements and conjectural restora-
tions, 12–14, 27–32, 35–7, 39, 42,
43–6, 239, 240, 242, 245, 247, 248,
252, 254, 256
art forms in Bach's choral music, 231
augmentation, examples of, 91, 202, 220,
239, 244, 251, 280, 299, 303, 365,
388
Austen, Jane (*Love and Friendship*
quoted), 345

Bach, Carl Philipp Emanuel, 361
Bach, J. S., 4, 7, 8, 10–15, 27–46, 88, 91,
103, 126, 154, 194, 210, 211, 227–67,
273, 276, 281, 284, 288, 329, 330,
332, 336, 341, 354, 355, 358, 359,
381, 384, 409, 421; and Handel, art-
forms of, 154; and Haydn, compared, 350, 356, 361, 362, 371, 384;
and stretto, 239, 244; as a contrapuntist, 28; 'Bachgesellschaft' editions, 239, 252, 256, 262, 267; compared with Palestrina and Mozart,
249; religious significance of his B
minor Mass, 229, 230
See also art forms; Balfour; eight-part
writing; Handel; joy-motives; quintessence
Works: *Concertos*: IN D MINOR FOR
CLAVIER AND STRINGS, 27–32; IN D
MINOR FOR TWO VIOLINS AND OR-
CHESTRA, 32–5; IN C MINOR FOR VIO-
LIN AND OBOE, 35–7; BRANDENBURG
IN G MAJOR, No. 3, 11, 37–40; BRAN-
DENBURG IN G MAJOR, No. 4, 40–2;
IN A MAJOR FOR OBOE D'AMORE, 43–5;
IN A MINOR FOR CLAVIER, FLUTE, AND
VIOLIN, 35, 45–6; Brandenburg No.
1, 13, 259; Brandenburg No. 2, 12;
Double in C major, 15, 35, 260; the
Italian, 41; MAGNIFICAT, 257–67,
347; MASS IN B MINOR, 227–56, 260,

272, 282, 288, 329, 360; Chromatic
Fantasia, 421; Fugue in A minor,
324; 'Matthew' Passion, 88, 329;
Sonata in B minor, 14
Bagehot, Walter, 408
balance of tone, Chopin and Klindworth
124; Handel, 331
Balfour, Lord, and Bach, 246
Basevi, Professor, 407
'Battle of Prague' (pianoforte piece by
Kotzwara), 305
Beethoven, 3–5, 7, 9, 14, 16, 18, 20, 23,
25–7, 47–86, 87, 89–92, 97, 101,
102, 103, 106, 107, 112, 134, 138,
154, 157, 160, 173, 176–80, 189, 191,
192, 206, 222–3, 230, 240, 247, 249–
51, 267–94, 311, 321, 323, 335, 351,
358, 361, 367–9, 371, 377, 389, 409,
420; as a contrapuntist, 273; as a
Latin scholar, 275; choral style of,
not a good model, 273; religious
significance of 'Missa Solemnis',
272–3; strain on voices in Op. 123,
273
See also Cherubini; Mendelssohn
Works: CHORAL FANTASIA, Op. 80,
267–70; *Concertos*: PIANOFORTE,
FIRST IN C MAJOR, Op. 15, WITH
BEETHOVEN'S CADENZA, 18, 47–52,
61; PIANOFORTE, THIRD IN C MINOR,
Op. 37, 16, 47, 48, 52–8, 61, 79, 90,
91, 125, 134, 173; PIANOFORTE,
FOURTH IN G MAJOR, Op. 58, 26, 48,
49, 54, 58–67, 79; PIANOFORTE, IN E
FLAT MAJOR, Op. 73, 26, 48, 54, 55,
67–70, 79, 83, 92; VIOLIN, IN D
MAJOR, Op. 61, 55, 70–9, 82, 86, 92,
101, 358; TRIPLE, FOR PIANOFORTE,
VIOLIN AND VIOLONCELLO, Op. 56,
54, 61, 79–86; 'MISSA SOLEMNIS', Op.
123, 230, 270–94. *Overtures*: 'Leonora' No. 1, Op. 138, 102; 'Corio-
lan', Op. 62, 125; *Symphonies*,
Second, in D major, Op. 36, 367–8;
Third, in E flat major (Sinfonia
Eroica), 4, 67, 69; Fourth, in B flat
major, Op. 60, 351; Fifth, in C
minor, Op. 67, 138; Sixth, in F
major ('Sinfonia Pastorale'), Op.

Beethoven (*cont.*):
68, 369; Ninth, in D minor, Op. 125, 86, 87, 102, 368; Concerto in B flat, Op. 19, 47, 61; 'Fidelio', Op. 72, 58; 'Kreutzer' sonata, Op. 47, 65; pianoforte piece, Op. 89, 84; *Pianoforte Sonatas*: Op. 31, no. 2, in D minor 179; 'Waldstein' Sonata, Op. 53, in C major, 48, 102; 'Les Adieux' ('Lebewohl') Sonata, Op. 81a, in E flat major, 222, 311; Op. 106, in B flat 362; Op. 111, in C minor (the last sonata) 59; *Quartets*: Op. 18, No. 4 in C minor 53; Op. 95, in F minor 179; Op. 130 in B flat 360, 377; Serenade Trio, Op. 8, 84; 'Sonata Appassionata', Op. 57, 76; *Trios*: Op. 1, No. 2, 361; Op. 9, No. 1, 361; Op. 97, in B flat, 361; Violin Sonata, Op. 30, No. 1, 53; Violin Sonata, Op. 30, No. 3, in A major, 59

Benedict, Julius, 221
Berlin, 48, 120
Berlioz, 69, 126, 215, 232, 283, 305, 338, 347, 409; and Debussy, 312–13; and the giraffe, 215.
    Works: Requiem, 283, 338, 401, 409; 'Mort de Cléopâtre', 312
Best, W. T., 150
birds, musical representation, of 369–70
    See also starling, Mozart's;
'Bo!', Haydn's lion says, 374
Bononcini (Buononcini), 319, 320
Brahms, 7, 8, 15, 18, 20, 22, 23, 55–7, 67, 68, 86–119, 121, 147, 156, 171, 176, 183, 189, 201, 206, 294–312; and Bülow on Verdi's Requiem, 409; as a contrapuntist, 91; on Dvořák's 'Cello concerto', 133; the religious significance of Requiem, 294, 295
    Works: *Concertos*: PIANOFORTE, NO. 1 IN D MAJOR, Op. 15, 22, 57, 86–92; PIANOFORTE, NO. 2 IN B FLAT MAJOR, Op. 83, 92–8; VIOLIN IN D MAJOR, Op. 77, 98–111; VIOLIN AND VIOLONCELLO, Op. 102, 111–19; 'DEUTSCHES REQUIEM', Op. 45, 294–308; 'RHAPSODIE' FOR ALTO VOICE, MALE CHORUS, AND ORCHESTRA, Op. 53, 308–9; 'SONG OF DESTINY' (SCHICKSALSLIED), FOR CHORUS AND ORCHESTRA, Op. 54, 310–12; *Symphonies*; No. 1 in C major, Op. 68, 56; No. 2 in D major, Op. 73, 98; No. 4 in E minor, Op.

98, 183; Sonata in G for violin, Op. 78, 15; 'Triumphlied', Op. 55, 18, 294
Brema, Marie, 325
Bridges, Robert, 232
British Grenadiers, *see* Beethoven
Browning, 201, 267
Bruch, Max, 98, 120–3, 206, 221
    Works, CONCERTO IN G MINOR FOR VIOLIN AND ORCHESTRA, 120–3, 206, 221; Concerto in D minor for two violins, 120; Kyrie and Sanctus, 120; 'Odysseus', 120; Scottish Fantasia, 120
Bruckner, 147, 206, 216
Brunetti, 193
Brussels, the Conservatoire of, 152
Bülow, Hans von, 98, 409, 415
    See also Brahms
Buononcini, *see* Bononcini
Bunyan, John, 360, 372
Burne-Jones, 358
Burney, Charles (his *History of Music*), 339, 343

Calverly, quoted, 364
Cambridge, 3 n.
Canon and imitation, 240, 244, 251, 290
Carlyle, 382
Carroll, Lewis, 370
Case, Professor, 399
Chaucer, and Artemus Ward on his spelling, 313
Cherubini, 80, 84, 288, 486; and Beethoven, 288
Chesterian, the, 180
Chopin, Frederic François, 54, 84, 123–7, 179, 184
    See also Schumann; balance of tone Polonaises, 84
    Works: CONCERTO IN F MINOR (PIANOFORTE AND ORCHESTRA), Op. 21, 54, 123–7; Concerto in E minor, Op. 11, 123, 126; Sonata in B flat minor, Op. 35, 123; Violoncello sonata, Op. 65, 123; Variations for Pianoforte, Op. 2, 123; chorale, ecclesiastical tones, 243, 244, 251, 266, 322 (Ex. 2), 397, 398
Chrysander, 321, 337, 346
CLASSICAL CONCERTO, THE, 3–27
Clement, 70, 71
Clementi, 7
combination of themes, 159–60, 250 (counterpoint in 11th and 13th), 254 (in 3rds), 341 (in 3rds)

composer, learned, *see* Verdi
concerto principle, the, 6–14; the sonata form, 14–25
Constance, 23
continuo, 341
Costa, Sir Michael, 124, 290, 348
Couperin, 210
critics, *see* experts
Crystal Palace, *see* Handel Festivals
Cyril Scott, *see* Scott, Cyril

Dannreuther, 179
Debussy, 128, 312–17, 397
   See also Berlioz
   Works: 'THE BLESSED DAMOZEL' ('La Demoiselle Elue'), 312–17; 'L'Enfant Prodigue', 312
Delius, 127–9
   Works: VIOLIN CONCERTO, 127–9; Double Concerto, 127
Dent, Professor E. J., 3
Deppe, Ludwig, 163
dictionaries of music, *see* Grove
dimension in music, 15
diminution: examples, 85 (Ex. 13), 89, 91, 96 (Ex. 8), 115 (Ex. 9), 285
Dohnanyi, 130–2
   Works: VARIATIONS ON A NURSERY SONG FOR ORCHESTRA WITH PIANOFORTE, Op. 23, 130–2
Dolmetsch, Arnold, 28
Dresden, 222, 229
Drury Lane, 354
Dvořák, 112, 133–7
   See also Brahms
   Works: VIOLONCELLO CONCERTO IN B MINOR, Op. 104, 112, 133–7

Edinburgh, 211
eight-part writing, Bach's and Handel's compared, 329
elephant, *see* Haydn
Elgar, Sir Edward, 137–46
   Works: VIOLIN CONCERTO IN B MINOR, Op. 61, 137–43, 298; VIOLONCELLO CONCERTO IN E MINOR, Op. 85, 143–6; Variations for orchestra, Op. 36 ('Enigma'), 137
Elssner, 124
England, 67, 201, 349, 393
English Handel Society, the, 346
enharmonic circles, 279
Erba, Dionigi, his 'Magnificat' and Handel, 326, 337, 338, 342–3, 348
Esterház, 152

Esterház, Prince, 377
Europe, 178
eurhythmics, 210
experts, *see* critics

Fay, Amy, 163
Finland, 206, 210
Fleury, Louis, 180, 259
Florence, 407
Forsyth, Cecil, 73, 185
Fox Strangeways, *see* Strangeways, Fox
Franck, César, 146–9
   Works: 'VARIATIONS SYMPHONIQUES', 146–9
fugue, 46, 91, 154–6, 235, 238, 243, 250, 254, 262, 266, 278, 284, 289, 301, 324, 333, 338, 340, 341, 365, 376, 387, 388, 393, 396, 417, 419; masked fugues, 264; round fugues, 231, 233, 237; fugues with ritornello, 231, 233, 243

Germany, 285, 407
Gevaert, 9, 152, 243
Gibbons, Grinling, 358, 371
giraffe, *see* Berlioz
Gluck, 8, 64, 183, 223, 347, 363
   Works: Iphigénie en Tauride, 347; 'Orfeo', 64, 183; 'Armide', 363
Goethe, 308
Golden Age, sixteenth century as the, 406, 407; and silver, 406
Great Britain, *see* England
Greene, 10
Grinling Gibbons (Gibbon), *see* Gibbons, Grinling
Grove, Sir George, 108, 131, 132
Grove's Dictionary, 330, 349, 384
Guines, the Duke of, 193, 194

Hadow, Sir Henry, 312
Handel, 7–9, 12, 150–1, 154, 194, 210, 232, 246, 274, 276, 280, 285, 299, 306, 317–48, 354, 356, 358, 371, 284; and Bach, 12, 194, 260, 265, 318, 329, 330, 356, 371; Handelian pause, 260; his death, 354; his musical form, 320; his triple time, 343, 344; in England, 326; on himself, 320
   See also balance of tone; Erba; Urio
   Works: 'ISRAEL IN EGYPT', 317–48; ORGAN CONCERTO, No. 7 (Op. 7, No. 1), 150–1; 'Athalia', 328; 'Deborah', 328, 329; 'Jephtha', 321; 'Messiah',

Handel (*cont.*):
321, 330, 332, 345; 'Every Valley', 265; 'Saul', 322, 326; 'Solomon', 329
Handel Festival, and the Crystal Palace, 338, 342, 348
Hanslick, 112
Haslinger, Tobias (Beethoven's publisher), 247
Hausmann, 133, 140
Hawkins, his history of music, 336
Haydn, Joseph, 7, 15, 56, 57, 152–4, 160, 177, 189, 194–5, 237, 251, 324, 339, 349–96; and Mozart, 351; his freedom of form, 371; 'not an elephant', 372.
  See also Herschel, paradox, quintessence
  Works: VIOLONCELLO CONCERTO IN D MAJOR, 152–4; 'The Creation', 349–81, 389–91, 395; compared with 'The Seasons', 383–4; 'THE SEASONS' (JAHRESZEITEN), 366, 380, 381–96; *Symphonies*: No. 94 in G major (the Surprise, Salomon No. 5), 386; No. 98 in B flat (Salomon No. 8), 386; in B flat (9th London), 351; Quartet in A minor, Op. 20, 324
Helmholtz, 232
Henschel, Sir George, 274
Herschel, Sir John, 349, 350, 354, 360; and Haydn 349
Hesiod, 349
Higgs, James, 365
Hipkins, A. J., 12, 98
histories of music (etc.), *see* Burney, Grove's, Hawkins, Oxford
Hölderlin, Friedrich, 310
Hollywood, 222
Holst, Gustav, 154–6, 396–402
  See also Mozart
  Works: FUGAL CONCERTO, Op. 40, No. 2, 154–6; 'THE HYMN OF JESUS', Op. 37, 396–42
Homer, 368
Huberman, 98
Hummel, 54, 127, 178

invisibility, how not to symbolize, 245
Italian opera, vocal tradition of, 406
Italy, 354

Jacobi, 203
Joachim, Josef, 54, 57, 71, 90, 103, 133, 171, 192, 303, 345
Johnson, Dr, 57, 193, 363, 382, 413, 421; his friend Edwards 374

'joy-motives', Bach's, 237

Kant, 349
Kensington, 201
Kerll, Kaspar, 336
  Works: Organ Canzona, 336
Kipling, Rudyard, 153
Klindworth, 124
  See also balance of tone
Kotzwara (Koczwara), Franz, *see* 'Battle of Prague'
Kortte, Dr, 12
Kraft, Anton, 152–4
  Works: VIOLONCELLO CONCERTO IN D MAJOR, 152–4
Kuhlau, 180

Lamb, Charles, 320
Laplace, 349
Lasso, Orlando di, 236
Leipzig, 86
Lidley, *see* Linley
Linley (Lidley), 354
Linley, Thomas, 354, 357, 373
Liszt, Franz, 63, 64, 68, 166, 223
London, 71, 99, 317, 320, 349, 354
Lully (Lulli), 364
  Works: 'Armide': 364
Luther, 300

Macaulay, 408
Mahler, 232, 331, 338, 393
  Works: Second Symphony, 393; Eighth Symphony, 331, 338
'Mahogany Age', *see* Golden Age
Maitland, Fuller, 10
Mandyczewski, 356, 373, 378
Mattheson, 327
Mazzucato, 409, 418, 419
Mehul, 392
  Works: 'La chasse du Jeune Henri', 392
Meiningen Orchestra, the, 99
Mendelssohn, 27, 55, 57, 90, 120, 156–60, 161, 180, 189, 196, 206, 221, 346, 364, 367, 371, 'Mendelssohn-baiting', 364
  Works: VIOLIN CONCERTO IN E MINOR, Op. 64, 156–60, 206; 'Elijah', 259; Duetto, Op. 38, No. 6, 367; 'Lobgesang', 371; Trio in C minor, 57
Meyerbeer, 222
Milan, 410
Milton, 32, 129, 182, 187, 245, 284, 319, 350, 353, 364, 372, 374, 379, 382
modes (ecclesiastical), examples: Dorian,

211; Lydian, 213; Ionian, 213; Aeolian, 213

Moschelles, 123

motet, Palestrina's meaning of, 274

Mozart, 3, 7, 14, 16–18, 20–7, 29, 38, 48, 49, 53, 54, 59, 63, 68, 71, 74, 83, 84, 91, 97, 112, 125, 154, 160–95, 211, 241, 249, 266, 289, 291, 312, 318, 330, 349, 351, 354, 355, 358, 377, 384, 387, 407, 410; and Holst, unison and discord, 401; and the pianoforte, 162; and rondo form, 24, 174; his use of polyphony, 22–3; neglect of, 3. *See also* Haydn

Works: ADAGIO IN E FOR VIOLIN WITH ORCHESTRA (Köch 261), 192–3; ANDANTE FOR FLUTE WITH ORCHESTRA (Köch 315), 184–5; *Concertos*: PIANOFORTE IN A MAJOR (Köch 414), 160–3; PIANOFORTE No. 15, in B flat major (Köch 450), 26, 163–6, 169; PIANOFORTE IN G MAJOR (Köch 453), 163, 166–9, 183; PIANOFORTE IN A MAJOR (Köch 488), 170–5; PIANOFORTE IN C MINOR (Köch 491), 55, 169, 170, 175–9; FLUTE IN G MAJOR (Köch 313), 180–1; FLUTE IN D MAJOR (Köch 314), 180, 181–4; CLARINET IN A MAJOR (Köch 622), 185–6; VIOLIN IN D MAJOR (Köch 218), 187–9; VIOLIN IN A MAJOR (Köch 219), 26, 187, 189–92; FLUTE AND HARP (Köch 299), 193–5; in D minor (Köch 466), 48, 177, 178; Pianoforte in C major (Köch 503), 16–24; in C major (Köch 467), 26; Violin in E flat, 163, 189; in E flat (Köch 271), 59; in F major (Köch 459), 161; in G 163: 184; in C major (Köch 415), 161; in F major (Köch 413), 161; (Köch 456), thematic example, 161; *Symphonies*: in C major, No. 36 (Köch 425), 164; in E flat (Köch 543), 170; in G minor (Köch 550), 170; in C major (Köch 551), 17, 168, 170, 386–7; 'Acis and Galatea', 330; Aria Buffa ('Voi siete un po'tondo'), 'Un bacio di mano' (Köch 541), 339; 'Die Entführung' (Köch 384), 183, 355; 'Die Zauberflöte' (Köch 620), 3 n., 168, 182, 184; 'Don Giovanni' (Köch 527), 167; 'Figaro', 160, 169, 410; 'Ode to St Cecilia's Day', 330; *Quartets*: D major (Köch 291), 183; Pianoforte

(Köch 478 and 493), 24–5, 174; Quintet for clarinet (Köch 581), 185; Requiem (Köch 626), 164, 266, 289, 291, 387, 410; Rondo (Köch 386), 169; Violin sonata in A major, 24 n., 174; Trio, Pianoforte, Viola and Clarinet (Köch 498), 185; (Köch 575), thematic example, 401; Mass (Köch 257), 'Credo Missa', 194

Museum, the British, 367

Neapolitan School, Handel and the, 323

Norway, 347

Nottebohm, 58, 148

Oakeley, 252

Ovid, 349

Oxford History of Music, 318, 327, 330

Palestrina, 236, 249, 272, 274, 280–2, 287, 344, 396, 407, 409; and triple time, 344; his cross rhythms, 309

Works: Palestrina, Mass *Sanctorum meritis*, an error for *Sacerdotes Domini*, 246; 'Stabat Mater', 420–1

Palgrave, 382

paradox and Haydn, 351, 360, 361

Paris, 86, 181, 189, 193, 338

Parratt, Sir Walter, 150

Parry, Sir Hubert, 257, 279, 403–6

Works: 'AT A SOLEMN MUSIC', 284, 403–6; Magnificat in F, 257

pedal, remarkable example, tonic, 301–2

Pepys, 363

Pergolese (Pergolesi), 421

Peters (scope of Haydn's Creation), 373, 378

Phrygian mode, 336

'pretty tinkle', *see* Mozart and the pianoforte

Purcell, 151, 247, 248, 326, 354; his independence 324

Works: 'Dido', 248

quintessence, of Bach, 243; of Haydn, 362

Raimondi, 29

Rasoumovsky, Count, 58

Ravel, 111, 211, 369, 396, 397

recitative, and language, 354, 355; classical, not Wagnerian declamation, 356

Reger, Max, 154

Works: Conzert im alten Stil, 154

Reicha, 83

resemblances, real and casual, 22, 50, 56, 152–3, 162, 165, 183, 319, 324, 325–8, 334, 335, 336–8, 340, 342, 343, 344, 365, 368, 386, 387
  See also top-knot exegesis
Ries, 179
Robinson (Handel and his Orbit), 326, 336
Rockstro, W. S., 330, 331, 337
Rome, 312, 368
Röntgen, Julius, 154
  Works: Triple concerto in B flat, 154
Rossetti, 313, 315
Rossini, 160, 182, 407, 409, 411, 418; Rossinian operas 358
  Works: Overture, 'Barbiere', 407; 'William Tell', 407
Rubinstein, Anton 158
  Works: Violin Sonata, 158
Ruskin, 219
Rust, Wilhelm, 43

Saint-Saëns, 141, 143, 195–7, 221
  Works: VIOLONCELLO CONCERTO IN A MAJOR, Op. 33, 195–7; Third Symphony, 196; Violin Concerto in B minor, 141, 196; Violoncello Sonata in C minor, 196
Saintsbury, Professor, 182
Salzburg, 189
Scarlatti, Alessandro, 7–12
Scarlatti, Domenico, 341
Schiller, 160
Schubert, 357, 375, 377, 394, 411
  Works: Symphony No. 8, in B minor, 'The Unfinished', 140; 'Die Allmacht', Op. 79, 375; 'Gretchen am Spinnrade', Op. 2, 394
Schumann, 8, 69, 70, 89, 123, 125, 144, 165, 198–205, 206, 410; on Chopin, 124
  See also scoring
  Works: INTRODUCTION AND ALLEGRO APPASSIONATO FOR PIANOFORTE AND ORCHESTRA, Op. 92, 204–5; PIANOFORTE CONCERTO IN A MINOR, Op. 54, 198–200; VIOLONCELLO CONCERTO IN A MINOR, Op. 129, 200–3; 'Carnaval', Op. 9, 70
Schumann, Clara, 63
Schütz, 244, 329, 331
Schweitzer, 230, 237, 240, 241, 244, 248, 250, 255, 384
scoring, Schumann's successful, 204
Scott, Cyril, 128

Seiffert, Dr Max, 33, 36, 150
Shakespeare, 23, 319, 326
Sheridan, Mrs Richard Brinsley, 354
Sibelius, 206–10
  Works: CONCERTO FOR VIOLIN, Op. 47, 206–10; Third Symphony, 210
Silver Age, *see* Golden Age
Slough, *see* Herschel and Haydn
Smyth, Dame Ethel, 249
  Works: Mass in D, 249
Spitta, 266
Spohr, 54, 84, 171
  Works: 'Gesangszene', Concerto, 221
S.P.C.C.A., *see* 'Mendelssohn-baiting'
Stanford, Sir Charles, 185, 345
starling, Mozart's, *see* Pianoforte Concerto in G major, 169
Stradella, 325–8, 334, 335, 337, 340, 346, 348; his Serenata and Handel, 325–8, 335, 340, 342, 346
  Works: 'Pietà Signore', 325
Strangeways, Fox, 187, 188, 355
Strauss, Richard, 3, 22, 53, 174, 408; his musical aesthetics 396
  Works: 'Also sprach Zarathustra', 22; 'Till Eulenspiegel', 174
Sullivan, Sir Arthur, compared with Haydn, 368–9
Swieten, Baron von, 350, 353, 357, 373, 381–3, 385, 387, 389–92, 394
Swinburne, 373

Telemann, 32
Tennyson, 370, 382
Terry, Dr Sanford, 230
Thibaut, Schumann's friend, on Palestrina, 410
Thomson, James, 382–95
Tolstoy, 420
top-knot exegesis, example, 319
triple time (and Sibelius), 210; *see also* Palestrina
Troutbeck, 310
trumpets, humorous imitation of, 187
Twain, Mark, 390

Urio, Padre Francesco, his Te Deum and Handel, 326, 337, 341, 348

Vaughan Williams, Ralph, 211–14
  Works: 'CONCERTO ACCADEMICO' IN D MINOR FOR VIOLIN, 211–14
Verdi, 381, 406–21; his fundamental tempo for church music, 413; his only musical idiom, 409

Works: REQUIEM IN MEMORY OF MAN-
ZONI, 406–20; 'STABAT MATER' FOR
CHORUS AND ORCHESTRA, 420–1;
'Aïda', 409; 'Falstaff', 408; 'Otello',
408; 'Rigoletto', 407; 'Te Deum',
420; 'Il Trovatore', 407, 415, 420;
'La traviata', 407
Vienna, 133, 230, 375
Violti, 171
Virgil, 367, 368
Vivaldi, 32
vocal polyphony, 230

Wagner, Richard, 38, 86, 127, 310, 351,
355, 370, 407
Works: 'Götterdämmerung', 259;
'Die Meistersinger', 97; 'Lohen-
grin', 407; 'Parsifal', 314; 'Tann-
häuser', 86, 207, 407; 'Tristan und
Isolde', 97, 351, 353
Wagnerian leit-motiv, 127, 138
Walton, William, 214–20
Works: VIOLA CONCERTO IN A MAJOR,
214–20
Weber, 221–3, 377; and Hollywood, 222
Works: CONZERTSTÜCK IN F MINOR FOR
PIANOFORTE WITH ORCHESTRA, Op.
79, 27, 221–3; 'Der Freischütz', 221
Widor, 240, 257, 261
Wieck, Clara, *see* Schumann, Clara
Wilson, Steuart, 355
Wordsworth, 173

Zippel, Dr Otto (his critical edition of
'The Seasons'), 382

OXFORD

MORE OXFORD PAPERBACKS

Details of a selection of other books follow. A complete list of Oxford Paperbacks, including The World's Classics, Twentieth-Century Classics, OPUS, Past Masters, Oxford Authors, Oxford Shakespeare, and Oxford Paperback Reference, is available in the UK from the General Publicity Department, Oxford University Press (JN), Walton Street, Oxford OX2 6DP.

In the USA, complete lists are available from the Paperbacks Marketing Manager, Oxford University Press, 200 Madison Avenue, New York, NY 10016.

Oxford Paperbacks are available from all good bookshops. In case of difficulty, customers in the UK can order direct from Oxford University Press Bookshop, 116 High Street, Oxford, Freepost, OX1 4BR, enclosing full payment. Please add 10 per cent of published price for postage and packing.

EDWARD ELGAR

A Creative Life

Jerrold Northrop Moore

In this major new biography, with access to much important and previously unavailable manuscript material, Mr Moore gives the fullest account ever written of the composer's life. He sees the formation of Elgar's musical style and the chronology of his compositions as an evolving autobiography of the spirit. The composer's preoccupation with certain themes and subjects is traced from his earliest music to the orchestral and choral works in which Elgar's greatness resides.

'the greatest book yet published on the subject' *Music and Musicians*

'a magnificent and enduring achievement' *Music and letters*

THE CONCISE OXFORD DICTIONARY OF MUSIC

Third Edition

Michael Kennedy

The third edition of this famous music dictionary has been thoroughly updated and revised. Biographies and technical terms alike—nearly everything has been written afresh. There is a vastly increased coverage of early music, and of music and musicians of the twentieth century. The articles on major composers now include comprehensive lists of works. As a result, this will prove the indispensable compact music dictionary for the 1980s.

Oxford Paperback Reference

PORTRAIT OF ELGAR
Third Edition
Michael Kennedy

The title—'Portrait' of Elgar—serves to emphasize that the book is neither an official biography nor an analytical survey of the music. Rather it is the author's attempt to paint, in words, the composer's portrait—a faithful and recognizable likeness, but at the same time a thoroughly individual interpretation of the subject. Indeed, Michael Kennedy's perceptive understanding of a complex personality has made this the classic study of Elgar, the man and the musician.

For this third edition, Michael Kennedy has added new material in the light of fresh discoveries about Elgar's life, especially his childhood.

ASPECTS OF WAGNER 2/e
Bryan Magee

'wholeheartedly recommendable' *The Times*

The man whom W. H. Auden called 'perhaps the greatest genius that ever lived' has inspired extremes of adulation and loathing. In this penetrating analysis, Bryan Magee outlines the range and depth of Wagner's achievement, and shows how his sensational and erotic music expresses the repressed and highly charged contents of the psyche. He also examines Wagner's detailed stage directions, and the prose works in which he formulated his ideas, and sheds interesting new light on his anti-semitism.

From reviews of the first edition . . .

'The revised edition of this brief but near-classic analysis of Wagner's work has not lost its most distinctive quality: unusually for a book of this kind, it demands to be read at one sitting.' *The Independent*

THE CONCISE OXFORD HISTORY OF MUSIC

Gerald Abraham

The Concise Oxford History of Music provides an account of the history of music as scholarly, as up to date, and as complete as is possible within the confines of a single volume. Gerald Abraham, one of the most highly respected contemporary writers on music, shares his knowledge of composers and compositions and his insight into the historical development of styles. The judgements are penetrating and the richness of content demands—and rewards—continuous attention.

Dr Abraham covers the whole history of music from its first recorded emergence in early civilizations to the death of Stravinsky. He also discusses non-Western music. He provides numerous music examples and the book is illustrated with plates throughout.

'provides all the answers clearly, sharply, authoritatively . . . the wonder here is that one man in his listening and researching can cover so much ground and illuminate it' Edward Greenfield, *Guardian*

I SAW THE WORLD END

A Study of Wagner's *Ring*

Deryck Cooke

Wagner's *Ring* is a great masterpiece, but because of its rich complexity it is difficult to think sensibly about its text and music, and a vast amount of nonsense has been written on the subject since its first performance over a hundred years ago. Deryck Cooke, author of *The Language of Music* and completer of Mahler's Tenth Symphony, displays his masterly common sense in this study of how and why *The Ring* took the shape it did. It is only a portion of the enormous book he had planned—his untimely death prevented his writing his analysis of the music; but even as it stands it will give fresh understanding and appreciation to every lover of Wagner's music.

AN INTRODUCTION TO ENGLISH FOLK SONG

Maud Karpeles

Our heritage of traditional folk song is remarkably rich, and most of us know all too little about it. What is folk music? How is it perpetuated? What are its dominant characteristics? And what is its role in modern life?

Maud Karpeles, for many years assistant to Cecil Sharp, the famous collector of folk songs, and herself one of the greater authorities on the subject, discusses these pertinent and absorbing questions. Among other things, she examines folk music from the points of view of musicology, literary criticism, and sociology, and provides a brief, informative account of the various forms of folk song, and of the people who collected and recorded them, illustrated with more than twenty of the loveliest songs.

THE CONCISE OXFORD DICTIONARY OF OPERA

Second Edition

Harold Rosenthal and John Warrack

Since its first publication *The Concise Oxford Dictionary of Opera* has established itself as an invaluable source of information on all aspects of opera. It contains entries on individual operas, composers, librettists, singers, conductors, technical terms, and other general subjects connected with opera and its history. This enlarged second edition includes many new articles on composers and performers, details of casts at first performances, and much additional information on the development of opera in different countries. Many of the existing entries have been rewritten and updated.

'You will ... discover here an enormous amount of information not available elsewhere.' *Daily Telegraph*

ARTHUR SULLIVAN

A Victorian Musician

Arthur Jacobs

Arthur Jacobs has seized on new documentary evidence, which includes relevations of Sullivan's sexual adventures, to paint a fascinating portrait of W. S. Gilbert's famous partner—the man, his music, and the Victorian musical world which he came to dominate.

'a wealth of anecdote, insight and incidental material . . . make the book fascinating reading as well as indispensable scholarship' *Classical Music Weekly*

TIPPETT

The Composer and his Music

Ian Kemp

The unique world of Tippett's musical and dramatic creation is critically surveyed in this authoritative study of Britain's major living composer. Professor Kemp scrutinizes the technical background to Tippett's art, paying attention to the musical and poetical origins of his idiosyncratic rhythmic language. The oratorio *A Child of Our Time,* the four operas, and *The Vision of Saint Augustine* are studied in detail as the most accomplished achievements of Tippett's creative output, and the stylistic and generative significance of these works is demonstrated in relation to his composition in other genres.

'a major work, a massive illuminating account, rich in detail' David Cairns, *Sunday Times*

'certainly the standard life-and-works' John Warrack, *Musical Times*

GUSTAV HOLST

Imogen Holst

'Gustav Holst was a great composer, a great teacher, and a great friend.' Ralph Vaughan Williams

Imogen Holst, the daughter of the composer, and herself a musician, composer, and critic, relates her father's life, quoting at length from his many letters to friends, and drawing from her personal memories of Holst's later years.

Holst struggled all his life against ill-health and bouts of depression, but his remarkable and good-humoured resilience enabled him to overcome his set-backs and to compose some of the greatest music ever written this century. In 1919 Holst's masterpiece *The Planets* was performed, and he was immediately recognized as one of our foremost composers. Imogen Holst describes the effect of this sudden fame on her father, and records his successful struggle to continue composing during the final years of his life.

OXFORD LIVES

R. V. W.
A Biography of Ralph Vaughn Williams
Ursula Vaughn Williams

'Mrs Vaughn Williams presents a crowded picture of the composer's ceaseless activity right into extreme old age, his persistent concern with new music and young musicians, his unabated instinct to compose and, at the end of his life, the new-found pleasure in travel and relaxation that was reflected in his last two symphonies.' *Daily Telegraph*

In addition to his great powers as a composer, Vaughn Williams was a man of strong character and unflagging energy, who lived a long, full life. He was at the centre of musical events in England for sixty years, a period which for sustained musical achievement is probably unequalled in the history of this country.

This intimate and detailed biography by his widow uses much material not available until recently.

Oxford Lives

NATIONAL MUSIC AND OTHER ESSAYS
Ralph Vaughan Williams

Ralph Vaughn Williams is one of the greatest English composers. He studied under Parry, Charles Wood, and Alan Gray, and later in Germany with Max Bruch and in France with Ravel, developing a strongly individual style that marked him out as one of the leaders of the twentieth-century revival of English music.

This collection contains all his writings that he thought worth preserving in book form. The themes and subjects discussed in these essays reflect his wide range of interests and cover topics such as nationalism in music, the evolution of folk-song, and the orgins of music, as well as pieces on individual composers such as Beethoven, Gustav Holst, Bach, Sibelius, Arnold Bax, and Elgar. Also included are more general reflections of the making of music, its purpose and effects, and the social foundation of music.

'He sees the familiar outlines with the freshness of discovery. Even his resistances quicken our own appreciation.' *Tablet*